MARKETING MANAGEMENT

Marketing Management

[For B.Com./M.Com., and other Management Courses of All Universities]

By
Ved Prakash

ANMOL PUBLICATIONS PVT. LTD.
NEW DELHI - 110 002 (INDIA)

ANMOL PUBLICATIONS PVT. LTD.
4374/4B, Ansari Road, Daryaganj
New Delhi - 110 002
Ph.: 23261597, 23278000
Visit us at: www.anmolpublications.com

Marketing Management

First Published, 2005

ISBN 81-261-2208-0

PRINTED IN INDIA

Published by J.L. Kumar for Anmol Publications Pvt. Ltd., New Delhi - 110 002 and Printed at Mehra Offset Press, Delhi.

Contents

Preface

Marketing Management as a paper is being taught at the graduate and post graduate level in B.Com., M.Com. and other Management courses syllabus in almost all the Indian Universities and Institutions. The various courses conducted by management institutions at the Central and State level too have been considered in respect of their syllabus, course contents and requirements. Thus the material presented here would be of interest as well as great use to the students of B.Com., M.Com. and other Management Courses. This book will provide complete knowledge of marketing issues, consumer research, marketing analysis and selection, marketing communication, rural and social marketing, marketing organisation and control, distribution channels, computer application, direct and online marketing etc.

The major topics dealt in this book are—Concept of Marketing; Developments in Marketing; Marketing and Consumer Research; Marketing Analysis and Selection; Promotion Decisions; Product Decisions; Pricing Decisions; Marketing Communication Decisions; Rural and Social Marketing; Marketing Organisation and Control; Merchandising; Distribution Channels and Physical Distribution Decisions; Advertisement Management; Computer Application in Marketing; Direct and Online Marketing; Export Marketing.

Ved Prakash

1

Concept of Marketing

The managerial awareness and desire reflected in the consumer orientation for an all-out commitment to the market consideration and to dovetail all marketing operations to the consumer needs has given birth to a new operational notion called the 'marketing concept'. This concept has been in vogue in the free economics for quite some time, and especially in the USA since 1950.

Even in the controlled economies like that of USSR, Hungary, Poland, Romania and Czechoslovakia this concept has found favour. It is evident by Khrushchev's speech at the plenary session of the CCCP, held in December. 1963 when he said that "a system should be introduced making factories and firms responsible directly to consumers for the quality of their goods, factories and firms should be made to work with an eye on the consumers via shops and not the shops alone."

The importance of this concept is being realised by Indian business houses also owing to the fast changing environmental context characterised by sectorial supply abundance, consumer resistance, and Government interest and participation in the marketing operations. As such, in many companies, attempts are under way to formally adopt this operational concept. A perusal of the following extracts from the speeches of some company chairman in India reflect the new-found need for its adoption.

According to Mr. R.K. Atal, Chairman the Vazir Sultan Tobacco Co. Ltd. "It is our commitment to the Marketing Concept... which lead us to believe that your company's existing and future brands will have an edge over competitors's and will provide growth in your company's market standing."

According to Mr. B.D. Garware, Chairman, Garware Paints Ltd: "The motto of the Company under Garware management is growth through customer service and satisfaction."

According to Mr. T. Thomas, Chairman Hindustan Lever Ltd: "What started in the last century as a sales organisation became a marketing company earlier in this century."

In this company of people, the most numerous and perhaps also the most powerful constituency is that of the consumers.

Although the description of the marketing concept has aroused some semantic controversies, it has retained a remarkable thematic similarity, emphasis variation notwithstanding. Felton views the marketing concept as "a corporate state of mind that insists on the integration and coordination of all marketing functions which, in turn, are welded with all other corporate functions, for the basic objective of producing maximum long-range corporate profits."

According to Kotler, "the marketing concept is a customer orientation backed by integrated marketing aimed at generating customer satisfaction as the key to satisfying organisation goals".

Although formulated for a specific research study, the definition by Mc Namara adequatley projects the meaning of marketing concept. According to him, "marketing concept is...a philosophy of business management, based upon a company-wide acceptance of the need for customer orientation, profit orientation, and recognition of the important role of marketing in communicating the needs of the market to all major corporate departments".

According to Lazo and Corbin, marketing concept is the "recognition on the part of management that all business decisions of a firm must be made in the light of customer needs and wants; hence, that all marketing activities must be under one supervision and that all activities of a firm must be coordinated at the top, in the light of market rquirements". However, in one of the most comprehensive descriptions of the marketing concept, King has defined it as "a managerial philosophy concerned with the mobilisation, utilisation, and control of total corporate effort for the purpose of helping consumers, solving selected problems in ways compatible with planned enhancement of the profit position of the firm".

The above description of the marketing cocnept brings out some managerial attitudes and concerns necessary for its implementation. These also describe as well as pinpoint the underlying meaning in the concept. These include:

1. Recognition of the need for marketing focus in coordinating company effort and in establishing corporate and departmental objectives consistent with the enhancement of the firm's profit position.
2. Recognition and appreciation of the role of marketing information system in sensing and monitoring information as regards market potential to serve as a base for goal and target setting.
3. Concern with the interest in the innovation of products and services so as to solve selected consumer problems.
4. Concern with the effect of new product and service introduction on firm's present and potential profit position.
5. Awareness of an concern with trans-departmnetal implications of an individual department's decisions and actions and their effect on the firm's equilibrium with its external environment, namely, consumers, competitors, Government, etc.
6. Awareness that consumers can only be helped to solve their selected problems through corporate efforts.
7. Awareness and appreciation of the crucial role of consumer in shaping decisions and of the profit as a basic foundation of the corporate existence, stability and growth.
8. Desire and preparedness for the creation, expansion, contraction, termination or in any way restructuring of any corporate function in order to mobilise, utilise and control corporate effort.

9. Awareness and appreciation of the role of formal, periodic, short and long-range, planning of company's goals, strategies and tactics resulting in an integrated system of marketing actions.

IMPLEMENTATION OF MARKETING CONCEPT

The managerial attitudes and concerns described above are undoubtedly essential so as to provide the requisite backdrop, but implementation of the marketing concept calls for some definite and tangible steps, some of which are described here.

Consumer Focus

The basic step that needs to be taken by a firm in order to implement the marketing concept is to focus all its attention on the consumer. It should attempt to ascertain consumer needs and desires before committing its resources to produce and distribute products and services. The consumer should be considered "sovereign", so to speak, whose preference shape the business decisions. "The principal task of the marketing function in a management concept is not so much to be skillful in making the customer do what suits the interest of the business as to be skillful in conceiving and then making the business do what suits the interest of the customer...The central meaning of the marketing concept to be decision structure of a business is that the major purpose of the venture is taken from the need to solve some problem in the outer environment—some betterment for the customer—and all subsidiary decision dealing with the acquisition and allocation of resources within the business are bent to that objective."

Lest all this merely remain empty talk, a cliche, the firm should address itself to the two relevant questions, *viz.* What businesss we are in ? and what market we are able to serve? The answer to the first question calls for, as far as possible, a precise definition of the consumer needs which the firm intends to fulfill by delivering products, services and other value satisfaction. The firm, therefore, has to define each opportunity in terms of some basic market needs to be satisfied, rather than a particular product(s) to be sold "Management must think of itself not as producing products but as providing customer creating value satisfactions". However, while attempting to answer this question, "the firm's cost of meeting all forms of new competition for the satisfaction of the same market need must be considered, since new products may involve such alien skills as different managerial abilities, production technology, and distribution structure".

The answer to the second question calls for an identification of the consumer profile and delineating market segments so that the firm's resources are best utilised to help consumers solve some of their selected problems in ways compatible with the planned enhancement of the profit position of the firm.

Traditional Definition

Marketing may be narrowly defined as an economic process by which goods and services are exchanged and the values determined in terms of money prices. The American Marketing Association has defined marketing as "the performance of business activities that direct the flow of goods and services through producers to consumers or users." That means marketing includes all those activities carried on the transfer of the goods from the manufacturers or producers to the consumers. It involves the exchange of goods and services for money. This way of defining marketing represents 'product orientation'. It concentrates on selling whatever has been produced or manufactured by a business concern without caring for the requirements or demands of the customers. This definition suited the earlier days of seller's market when there was shortage of goods.

The traditional definition of marketing is inappropriate in the present day business environment where there are a large number of substitutes and keen competition of the market. It presumes that the process of marketing begins after goods have been produced and ends with their sale. But in the present-day business marketing is done long before the goods are produced. The demands of the customers must be forecast before the product development and production take place. Marketing decisions must also be made regarding the market, pricing and promotion of the product. Marketing does not end with the final sale. The customer must be satisfied if a business enterprise expects his repeat orders. Because of these reasons the concept of marketing has undergone a change. Progressive firms of the world follow 'consumer orientation' in marketing because they recognise that consumers are often responsible for change in business policies. Consumers are the force which give direction to the business activities. Consumers' satisfaction should be the main aim of the business activities.

Modern Definition

According to Cundiff and Still, "Marketing is the business process by which products are matched with the markets and through which transfers of ownership are effected. Matching products with the marketing means determining the requirements of potential consumers and supplying the products which meet their requirements of prospective customers, it is more likely to be successful to achieve its objectives. The consumer-oriented marketing has given rise to a new philosophy in business known as 'marketing concept'. The marketing concept emphasises the determination of the requirements of potential customers and supplying products to satisfy their requirements. Modern marketing has, thus, become an integrated process of identification assessment and satisfaction of human wants.

William J. Stanton has given a systems definition of marketing. "Marketing is a total system of inter-acting business activities designed to plan, price, promote and distribute wants satisfying products and services should be market or customer-oriented. Customer's wants must be recognised and satisfied effectively. Secondly, marketing is a dynamic business process. It is an integrated process rather than a fragmented assortment of institutions and functions. It is not any one activity, it is a result of the inter-action of many activities. Thirdly, marketing activities start with the generation of a product idea and end only after the customer's wants are completely satisfied. Finally, it is also implied that marketing must maximise profitable sales over the long-run in order to be successful in business.

Under the systems approach to marketing, there is an intelligent coordination of the four 'P's of marketing mix, namely, product, price, place (channels of distribution), and promotion to build strong exchange relationship with the customers. In other words, the price should be made consistent with the product's quality, the channels of distribution made consistent with price, nature of product and nature of customer and the promotion made consistent with channels and product quality. The products should be developed according to the information provided by the marketing research.

Stanton further says that systems definition is a managerial definition of marketing and it views marketing solely as a business activity. There is also a need to recognise the social dimension of marketing which is far broader than may be apparent in the systems definition. "Societal perspective is more meaningful and truly descriptive of marketing today. Any inter-personal or inter-organisational relationship involving an exchange (a transaction) is marketing. That is, the essence of marketing is a transaction. Consequently, marketing occurs any time one social unit strives to exchange something of value with another social unit."

Distinction Between Marketing and Selling

The marketing concept is a course of business thinking, while marketing is a process or a course of business action. Naturally marketing is influenced by the course of business thinking (*i.e.* customer-orientation). Marketing concept focuses on customers for earning profits through customers satisfaction and follows integrated marketing. But formerly marketing focused on products to earn profits through sales volume and followed sales promotion techniques for this purpose. Thus marketing concept makes a sharp distinction between marketing and selling.

Markcting involves the design of the products acceptable to consumers and the conduct of those activities which facilitates the transfer of ownership between the seller and buyers. But selling is the performance of those activities which lead to obtaining orders from customers and supplying them the products. Thus, it involves activities connected with the sale of goods already produced. But in case of marketing the emphasis is on customer wants. Selling concentrates merely on increasing the sales volume whereas marketing first determines what the customer's wants are and then plans how profitably to make the delivery of product to satisfy those wants. Marketing emphasises buyers' needs whereas selling emphasises seller's needs. "Selling focuses on the needs of the seller, marketing on the needs of the buyer. 'Selling' is preoccupied with the seller's need to convert his product into cash, 'marketing' with the idea of satisfying the needs of the consumer by means of the product and the whole cluster of things associated with creating, delivering, and finally consuming it".

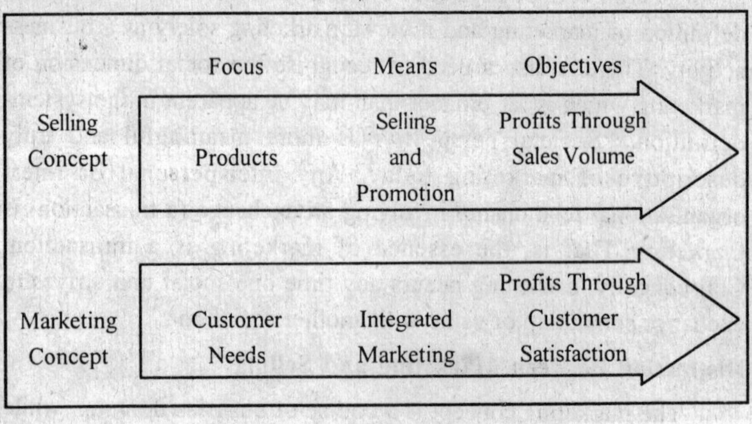

Fig. Selling Concept and Marketing Concept

Selling comes after the production has been undertaken, but marketing comes before the beginning of the production cycle and continues even after the sale has been effected because 'after sale service' may be necessary to satisfy the wants of the customers. Thus, marketing is a broader term and embraces selling which is only a part of promotion activities.

DISTINGUISH BETWEEN OLD AND MODERN CONCEPT OF MARKETING

Generally, marketing is understood to mean the sale and purchase of goods and services but it is narrow thinking to understand it so. The term 'marketing' is very wide. It does not mean only the sale and purchase of goods and services. It means entire process of satisfying the needs of consumers. It starts with discovery of needs and wants of the consumers, and it continues till these needs and wants are satisfied. To understand the meaning of marketing clearly, it becomes necessary that different concepts of marketing must be understood. For the convenience, the concepts of marketing may be divided into two parts : First, old concept of marketing or product-oriented concept, and second new concept of marketing or consumer-oriented concept. The details of these concepts are as follows:

Old Concept or Product-oriented Concept of Marketing

This is the classical concept of marketing. According to this concept, marketing is a part of production process. This concept is based on the assumption that the manufacturer must produce the goods and distribute them to the consumers. He need not bother about the choice of the needs of the consumers. Some important definitions of this concept are as under :

American Marketing Association 'Marketing is the performance of business activities that direct the follow of goods and services from the producer to consumer or user."

Tousley, Clark and Clark, "Marketing consists of those efforts which affect transfers in the ownership of goods and services and provides for their physical distribution."

This definition of marketing includes the factor of physical distribution also alongwith sale and purchase of goods and commodities. Thus, this definition is wider than the earlier definitions.

This concept of marketing stresses upon product only. It does not consider the choice, needs, wants, or behaviour of consumers. According to this concept, marketing is only the physical distribution of goods and services from producer to consumer. Therefore, this concept is known as product-oriented concept of marketing. This concept is not a practical concept now-a-days because it does not include many important activities which are necessary for the success of marketing. This concept assumes that marketing being only when the goods have been produced and it ends when the goods have been sold. This is incomplete, inadequate and impractical concept of the marketing because it is not at all possible for a producer to sell this product without considering the needs and wants of consumers.

Main characteristics of this concept of marketing are as follows:

1. It stresses upon production.
2. It assumes that marketing is only the physical distribution of goods and services from producer to consumer.
3. It does not provide for any allied activity of marketing such as, transportation, warehousing, insurance, financing, etc.
4. It assumes that marketing starts after the goods have been produced and it ends after the goods have been sold.
5. According to this concept, the ultimate object of marketing is to maximise the profits by maximising the sales.

New or Modern or Customer-oriented Concept of Marketing

Modern concept of marketing is a customer-oriented concept. This concept is based on the assumption that a business and industrial enterprise can achieve its object of maximising the profts only when it considers the needs and wants of its consumers and it tries for the satisfaction of these needs and, wants. Therefore, according to this concept, marketing starts with the discovery of needs and wants of consumers and ends with the satisfaction of these needs and wants. Important definitions of this concept are as under:

> *Prof. Paul Mazur*, "Marketing is the delivery of standard of living to the society."
>
> *Prof. Malcolm McNair*, "Marketing is the creation and delivery of standard of living to the society."
>
> *Cundiff and Still*, "Marketing is the business process by which products are matched with the market and through which the transfers of ownerships are effected."

On the basis of above definitions, it may be concluded that marketing is not only the physical distribution of goods and services but it relates to the whole process of satisfying the needs and wants of the society. It starts well before production and it ends well after production. It starts with the discovery of social needs and wants and the behaviour of consumer; then these needs and wants are converted into goods and services; then the demand is created for goods and services; then these goods and services are physically distributed to their real consumers and at the last, after-sale-services are provided so that the needs and wants of consumers may be satisfied in the best possible manner. Thus, marketing may very well be regarded as the creation and delivery of standard of living.

Thus, new concept of marketing emphasises upon the satisfaction of consumers. This concept believes that marketing begins and ends with the customers. It stresses that as business and industrial enterprise stands only for the customers. Satisfaction of consumer needs is the only way of success. This concept is based on earning the profits through the satisfaction of consumers. According to this concept producer must produce what his consumers need; price must be fixed what his consumers can afford; production must be in the quantity what his consumers require; and the goods must be distributed through the channels which are most suited to this consumers.

Important characteristics of this concept are as follows:

1. According to this concept, consumer is the key of the market and his needs and wants are the goals of the business activities.
2. Marketing is the entire process of understanding and satisfying the needs and wants of consumers.
3. Under this concept, first of all the needs and wants of consumers are discovered; then these needs and wants are converted into goods and services; then demand is created for these goods and services; then these goods and services are physically distributed from producer to consumer and after-sale-services and provides so that the needs to consumers may be satisfied in most effective manner.
4. This concept assumes that the object of earning the profit can be achieved only when the needs of society are satisfied.
5. According to this concept, marketing is the creation and delivery of standard of living to the society.

EVOLUTION OF MARKETING CONCEPT

An analysis of contemporary literature reveals vividly the conceptual variations in the use of the term marketing. They describe it as a 'function', 'an orientation', 'an approach or attitude', 'a philosophy of business' and 'a management science or technique'. A closer analysis would reveal that marketing, in fact, conveys all of these often more. An attempt is made here to trace the evolution of marketing from all the possible perspectives.

The traditional objectives of marketing had been to make the goods available at places where they were needed. This idea was later on changed by shifting the emphasis from 'exchange' to 'satisfaction of human wants'. As human needs and wants multiplied and technological progress supplemented such developments, the scope of marketing function had to be enlarged. Almost simultaneously new dimensions to marketing were incorporated due to changes in the organisational patterns of business and increase in their size of operation. The concept of marketing was subjected to changes not only from the aforesaid innovations but also from changes in concepts that were taking place within the sphere of marketing itself. In this process traditional ideas on marketing were replaced by modern concepts. These developments are easily recognisable along with the growth of civilisation; culturally, socially and economically. Each stage is explained in the following paragraphs:

(i) **Self-sufficient Stage.** After the stage of 'nomads' people started to settle on the banks of rivers. This had led to starting of economic activities, *viz.*, Agriculture. But each family then was a self-sufficient unit as far as production and consumption functions were concerned. They produced what they wanted to consume and practically no surplus was available to initiate the process of exchange. Hence, it may be stated that the concept of marketing was absent is this stage.

(ii) **Exchange-oriented Stage.** When 'nomads' chose to live permanently at river banks and continuously engaged in agricultural and allied operations, the problem of surplus production came. This necessitated exchange of surplus products with others. Gradually commerce and trade evolved emphasising the need for exchange. In order to smooth out exchanges 'Barter System' came into vogue, though the latent inconveniences of such a system were felt only a little later. It was gradually realised that the double coincidence of wants could be attained only if the products are brought to a central location so that exchange will take place smoothly. Thus 'Markets' came into existence.

This stage may, therefore, be considered as the corner-stone upon which evolution of marketing was founded. The shift from self-sufficiency to the exchange orientation may, therefore, be considered the first stage in the historical evolution of the term marketing.

Thus, the felt need for the development of central market was a logical step towards an efficient marketing. Through this system, exchange could be facilitated more smoothly and the gains of division of labour were thus related. Invention of money further facilitated to increase the momentum of exchange process and avoided inconveniences of barter system.

(iii) Production-oriented Stage (1869-1930) ("Make what you know how to make"). The next stage came with the dawn of the industrial Revolution. Everyone readily agreed when Adam Smith in his **Wealth of Nations** said, "Consumption is the sole end and purpose of all production, and the interest of the producer ought to be attempted to, only so far as it may be necessary for promoting that of the consumer." But under the mercantile system, the interest of the consumer was virtually sacrificed to that of the producer. It was believed that if the product is the quality and priced reasonably, nothing would prevent the producers from achieving satisfactory sales and profit. It was based on the premise that consumers were capable of selecting products from among the competing brands. This also led to a wrong belief that proper and timely communication to the buyer was not an inevitable adjunct in the process of selling. It appears that producers gave more emphasis to production (See Fig.) rather than consumption as the ultimate end and objective to trade and commerce. In essence, this stage is one where the role of marketing was rather ignored.

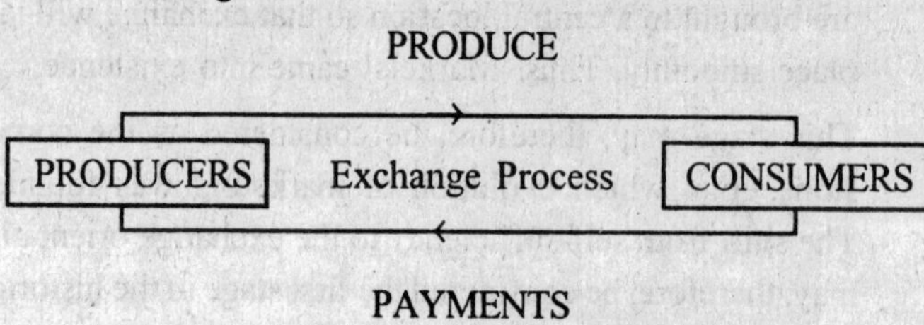

Fig. Production-oriented Stage

(iv) Sales-oriented Stage (1930-1950) ("Get rid of what you have"). The ripple effect of Industrial Revolution did not stop with the technological changes in industrial activities alone. It caused major social changes; there was a shift from agriculture to industry, increase in the living standards, development of transport and communication, growth of corporate form of organisation, etc. All these changes necessitated an organised marketing procedure. At this stage everyone started realising the purpose and importance of marketing. It assumed that consumers will normally not buy enough unless approached with a substantial selling and promotional effort. But no efforts were made to satisfy the particular needs of consumers. Under this concept the greater emphasis was on increasing the sales than on customer satisfaction. This was possible then, because the demand usually outstripped supply.

(v) Marketing-oriented Stage (1950-1960) ("Have what you can get rid of"). As the consumers, demand and the production capacity of the manufacturers came into an equilibrium, the producers were forced to re-think over the philosophy of marketing. Further, the evil effects of competition made the producers realise that the product could not be sold without an effective sales force. Customer's importance was further realised but only as a means of disposing of the goods produced. Essentially, this stage did not go a long way from production orientation, though for differentiation, it is termed as marketing-oriented stage. It was, however, accepted that the key task of the organisation is to determine the needs, wants and values of a target market and to adapt the organisation to deliver the desired satisfaction more effectively and efficiently than its competitors.

The distinctions between the selling and the marketing concepts were to be understood. Selling focuses on the needs of the seller, whereas marketing stresses on the needs of the buyer. Selling is pre-occupied with the seller's need to convert his product into cash; marketing with the idea of satisfying the needs of the customer by means of the product and the whole cluster of things associated with creating, delivering and finally consuming it.

(vi) Consumer-oriented Stage (1960s—present) ("Have what you can get rid of with responsibility"). The next stage that followed, however, witnessed a changed out-look of producers towards marketing. It became imperative to give equal consideration to production as well as consumption. competition became keen. Production was far in excess of demand. Rapid changes in consumer demand continually drove many organisations into turmoil. Investors started realising the greater risks involved in their investments if due consideration was not given to marketing. This led to a position where the factors of production had to be organised with as full *a priori* understanding as possible of the factors of consumption.

During this stage it was realised that measuring consumer needs or behaviour alone was not enough. 'Consumer satisfaction' should be the real and correct perspective on which marketing policies of an organisation should be built. This marketing concept is the modern philosophy of business that believes that 'satisfaction of the wants of the consumers' is the economic and social justification for the existence of the business. But it is said that a great number of companies really do not practise this concept though they claim it to be. Peter F. Drucker says that growth of 'consumerism' itself is a proof that companies do not adopt this concept in practice. According to him consumerism is the "sham of marketing". It is, therefore, doubtful whether the firm that does an excellent job of assessing, serving and satisfying consumer wants is necessarily acting in the best long-run interests of consumers and society.

(vii) Management-oriented Stage. This is the present stage of the evolution of the marketing concept. As consumer orientation became an accepted marketing philosophy, the entire business philosophy underwent a subtle change. Today, marketing consideration are most crucial in business planning and decision-making. The National Association of Manufacturers put this cogently, when it said, ".... In this exciting age of change, marketing is the beating heart of many operations. It must be considered a principal reason for corporate existence. The modern concept of marketing recongnises its role as a direct contributor to profits as well as sales volume... To endure in this highly competitive change-infested market, a company must first determine what it can sell, how much it can sell and what approaches must be used to entice the customer. Markets are ever-growing and rapidly changing. More and more money is needed to develop and support marketing programmes..."

Thus, the concept of marketing has underwent frequent changes in the past. In a very short span, its scope was redefined, remodelled and remoulded. These changes were in a way necessary as society too changed its value materially, technologically and culturally. It is true that changes have always been characterised as the essence of life. Marketing is no exception to this view.

In the above paragraphs it was shown how marketing evolved and developed into a full-fledged business philosophy. In the course of development, marketing underwent radical changes and its emphasis shifted from one concept to the other. This was mainly due to the change business outlook in the ever-changing environment. But "the marketing concept still suffers and limps along without the clarification and definition essential for understanding, perceptive adoption and substantial implementation.

These different concepts may be grouped under the following heads:

1. The Consumer-oriented School
2. The Balance Approach School
3. The Integrative School
4. The Reappraisal School
5. The Broadening School

The Consumer-oriented concept stresses that the economic justification and objective of the business enterprise is to satisfy human needs, wants and desires. Under this concept the consumer becomes the focal around which not only marketing but all business disciplines revolve. Supporters of this view hold that customer orientation is necessary in order to survive in a buyer's market. The imporance of customer orientation is reflected in the axiom, "The consumer is the king." According to this view, the needs, desires and buying responses of the consumers are considered as major determinants of a firm's success.

The Balanced Approach School, however, rejected the above interpretation on the ground that it limits the true meaning of the marketing concept. Instead, they interpreted the concept to be a balance of interests between the company's profit objectives and the needs and wants of its customers. Balanced approach is the only realistic way to bring about appropriate integration of marketing interests. There must be three interests: Markets, Customers and Products. The real meaning of an integrated marketing effort is the balancing of product and market orientation so as to "find markets for products of the one hand and products of markets on the other".

The Integrative School is aimed to broadening the meaning and includes three basic elements:

1. Company-wide acceptance of need for customer-orientation,
2. Company-wide recognition of profit-orientation, and
3. Recognition of an organisation structure for the performance of all marketing activities.

The Reappraisal School admits the necessity for trying the actions of business to the interests of consumers.

Integration of Marketing Functions

Broadening of marketing's functional base by itself does not ensure adequate operationalisation of the marketing concept, unless all these functions are closely synchronised to maximise influence of corporate exercises in the market place and on the consumer. This involves organisation of all marketing functions in such a manner that it results in their total intergation and co-ordination from the conception of a new product to its consumption by the ultimate user. It means that marketing is no longer a conglomeration of distinct and separate functions—there is a break down of the autonomous power of the functional executive, *i.e.*, sales, advertising, product planning. etc. and all others who communicate with the customer. "This" according to Cascino, "is the very essence of the modern marketing concept....When they (marketing functions) are integrated into a completely co-ordinated communication programme, the total impact is greatly compounded."

In order to bring about a compatible organisation, all the marketing functions, though retaining their individual identity, are brought together and integrated under a new department called the Marketing Department. The organisational implications of such an integration are as follows:

1. The marketing executive closely co-ordinates the activities of the different marketing functions right from the conception of production of product idea to the consumption of the finally developed and delivered product. The result of this intra-marketing co-ordination is the development of a marketing mix with built-in potential for the maximum impact in the market place. Besides, marketing division spear-heads co-ordination with other corporate functions, *e.g.*, production, finance, personnel, etc., so as to produce a well knit, effective and profitable corporate action directed towards achievement of the twin objectives of consumer satisfaction and targeted return on investment.
2. Each marketing function is managed by a separate executive (depending on the size and requirements of the individual company) who reports to the marketing executive and is accountable for the performance of his assigned functional responsibilities.
3. In terms of company organisation, the marketing executive occupies a position at par with the finance, production and personnel executives in the hierarchy. He communicates with them at the horizontal level and with the heads of the marketing functions at the vertical level.
4. The marketing executive is to be responsible for the performance of the marketing department which is now treated as an important profit centre in the company.
5. A new marketing department is carved out which is headed by a marketing Executive as distinct from the functional heads.

6. Under the organisational changes designed to implement the marketing concept, the function of personal selling becomes a part of the total marketing operation. The executive responsible for sales function reports to the marketing executive. While implementing the marketing concept, the difference between marketing and selling to quote Levitt, becomes more than "semantic". "Selling focuses on the needs of the seller, marketing on the needs of the buyer. Selling is preoccupied with the sellers' need to convert his product into cash; marketing with the idea of satisfying the needs of the customer by means of the product or service and by the whole cluster of customer getting value satisfactions associated with creating, delivering, and finally consuming it."

As such, "under the old concept the sales manager is primarily responsible for getting orders. His is the job of day-to-day selling, of hiring and training salesmen; order getting is his job, his life and responsibility. Under the new concept the sales manager is still responsible for these activities, but in addition, he has the responsibility of transmitting.

The Profit Focus

In order to implement the marketing concept, the consumer focus should be accompanied by the profit focus in all marketing decisions. Profit and rate of return on investment are conditions precedent (no objectives) for business existence, growth and stability. It is also necessary to ensure continuity of managerial efforts to solve select consumer problems. The marketing organisation is, therefore, made a 'profit responsibility centre and all its operations are planned and evaluated against its budgeted profit contribution. Sales volume, though important, is not by itself an indicator of marketing efficiency unless it has a profit contribution to make. For this purpose, periodic profit plans are formulated and each product and market segment is assigned volume and profit targets.

In India, profit focus may evoke some misinformed disapproval because it is thought to be inimical to the concept of the socialist pattern of society. However, in a mixed economy, profit focus is not eliminated either in the public or private sector companies. Even in the public sector companies, it is accepted as a necessary orientation to ensure existence so as to enable it to continuously serve the national development of objectives and help consumers solve some of their problems.

However, profits should not be mistaken for profiteering. Profits are the reward of managerial efforts directed towards creating and delivering value satisfactions to consumers in the form of products and services. Profiteering, on the other hand, is the result of purely trading speculative operations directed at manipulating supply of products and services often to the frustration of the consumer. Currently, companies manufacturing essential commodities in India are under a haze of consumer discontent owing to the short supply of these commodities and for alleged profiteering.

Profit is, therefore, a condition precedent to the implementation of the marketing concept, while profiteering is a contradiction of the concept.

Broadened Functional Base

The next step in implementing the marketing concept involves broadening the marketing functional base. It involves an attempt to include all those activities of business which impinge upon a company's efforts of delivering value satisfaction to its consumers. Traditionally, marketing was composed of those functions that directed the flow of goods and services from producer to consumer or user, and included the functions of selling, pricing, advertising and physical distribution. The marketing task started only after production had taken place which now needed to be disposed of reflecting production/sales orientation. Under the modern concept of marketing, however, the functional base of marketing is broadened by an extension backward towards marketing research and product planning and forward toward post-transaction research so as to sense and monitor consumer reactions about the level of value satisfaction obtained. The marketing functions, therefore, now include marketing research and product planning, besides selling, pricing, advertising and physical distribution.

The logic of broadening the functional base of marketing is to activise all market-related activities of the firm impinging on consumer satisfaction, profit attainment and enlargement of the market area. Consequently, marketing should include, as Togesen has remarked, "market research and analysis, market forecasting; market policy formulation, market planning including the determination of product design pricing, delivery and distribution sources—and the direction and control of advertising and sales promotion and sales solicitation". In India, serveral of these activities are either not undertaken by companies in general or if at all undertaken, fall within the province of production, finance or other executives.

Research Base of Decisions

Marketing research is recognised as a distinct functional area worthy of exclusive executive attention under the broadened functional base of marketing integrated under one department. But this serves the intended purpose only when marketing research is assigned as adequate role in the overall marketing exercise. Marketing research, and not intuition, should provide the base for all marketing decisions. "Research is any relatively systematic, formal, conscious procedure for evolving and testing hypotheses for making decisions. The words 'systematic', 'formal' and 'conscious' differentiate 'research' from "intuition". Marketing research identifies consumer needs, both liminal and subliminal, and market opportunities with profit potential. It provides information for target setting and programming the complete marketing effort. It furnishes feedback from the market in respect of consumer satisfaction, social reactions to firm's marketing operations and performance of the different components of the marketing-mix. The role-play of the marketing research function can be significantly improved by active membership of the marketing research executive on the various marketing and corporate committees in the organisation, encouragement to and use of scientific methods in dealing with information components, adequate budgetary allocation for research activities and desire of the top management to base their decisions on the research findings.

Innovation

According to Mc Kitterick, "Marketing concept insists upon constant innovation". In implementing concept, constant innovation is essential because the purpose of every business is to create a customer and, therefore, "any business enterprise has two and only these two basic functions: marketing and innovation." Innovation is "purposeful, organized, risk taking change introduced for the purpose of maximising economic opportunities". In terms of marketing it may mean, as Drucker has chosen to define, "provision of better and more economic goods and services", by introducing relevant changes in different components of the marketing-mix. It may take the form of lower price—the form with which many Indian economists, political leaders and public activists have been most concerned, it may be in the form of a new or better product, a new convenienec or the creation of new want, new use for the old product, improvement in design or even in the marketing technique. Based on consumer reactions, innovations may be delineated into three broad categories, *viz.*, adaptive, functional and fundamental. Adaptive innovation refers to the minor alteration of an existing product, for example changes in packages, colour, design, size and style. Functional innovations are those in which the product or service remains the same but the method of performing the functions is new, for example, automatic dish washers, domestic electric iron with heat regulators for different kinds of fabrics, jet planes, etc., Fundamental innovations represent complete break with the past both on the part of customer and the firm. They incorporate original ideas or concepts which perform new functions for the consumer, for example, television, computers, dehumidifiers, etc.

The innovation goals of a business under the marketing concept may be both short-and long-run depending upon the urgency of the market needs as also the perspective planning. Nevertheless, these goals may be as follows:

1. Innovations and improvements so as to keep up with the advances in knowledge and skill.

2. Product improvements required to attain the marketing objectives and to anticipate expected technological changes.
3. New processes and improvements in old processes required to satisfy, market goals—pricing, distribution, selling etc.
4. New products and services required because of technological changes consigning current product into obsolescence.
5. New products and services required to achieve the marketing objectives.

The realisation of these goals depends both on the quality of human resources at the helm of the business as well as on the capacity of management to stimulate creative potential amoung people working in the organisation. "Experience in a number of firms indicates that while innovation may rest basically on the creative and managerial powers of a relatively limited number of individuals innovation can be stimulated, produced and managed by systematic attention to the task".

One of the ways in which innovation, particularly product innovation, may be stimulated is by the establishment of a Research and Development Department in a company. When it operates in close co-ordination with the marketing research people, its potential to identify consumer needs and develop consumer-need-satisfying products is vastly increased. The R & D Department of Jyoti Ltd., Baroda, for example, has contributed largely to the growth of the company in the field of hydraulics, electrical engineering and power electronics, and is currently specialising in microphydel installations. The company's R & D operations are now directed into new fields like solar energy, fluidics, material science and laser technology.

The business firms purchasing the marketing concept achieve the following benefits:

(a) Marketing concept leads to follow an integrated and co-ordinated approach to marketing. By concentrating on consumers' wants, management can evaluate contribution made by the different parts of the firm in a better way.

(b) Marketing concept has philosophical and strategic implications as it allows the business firm to direct its activities towards the broader and long range objectives like sustained interaction with the customers, and stability and growth of the firm.

(c) Concern about market or consumers' needs rather than product reduces the changes of a business firm becoming a sick unit. It is obvious that the firm will produce those products which will satisfy the wants to the customers and they will be easily accepted by the customers.

MAIN FEATURES AND NATURE OF MARKETING

The main features and nature of modern marketing are as follows:

1. **Marketing is Consumer-oriented.** A business exists to satisfy human needs. Therefore, business must first find out what the consumers want and then produce goods according to the needs of the consumers. Only such products should be produced which best satisfy consumer needs and at a profit to the market. What is offered for sale should be determined by the buyer rather than by the seller. We must apply our creativeness more intelligently to people, and their wants and needs, rather than to products.

2. **Marketing Starts and Ends with the Consumer.** Often it is thought that marketing is concerned only with the flow of goods and services from the producer to the consumer. Under consumer oriented marketing, it is highly essential to know what the customers really want. This is possible only when information is collected from the consumers. In the older days the producer was in direct contact with the consumer. But after mass production system this limit was broken. Therefore, a formal mechanism is required to keep in touch with consumers. Marketing research and marketing information system have, therefore, emerged as a full fledged function of marketing.

3. **Modern Marketing Precedes and Succeeds Production.** A market transaction takes place when there is a successful matching of a buyer and a seller. The power of either party to influence a transaction is basically dependent upon the competitive strength. The seller has the bargaining power over the features of the product, its price comparability, etc. The buyer, on the other hand, acquires his bargaining power from the usefulness and acceptability of a product to him.

   For the earliest management, marketing was a peripheral problem in the same class as that of accounting. Firms tried to sell products that were successful in the past. They never made any effort to adapt themselves to the changing consumer needs. Some of them even underrated the critical importance of the customers and their behaviour.

   The above factors compelled the producers to accept "consumer orientation" as the marketing philosophy for their firms, if they ever wanted the bargaining power. This is exactly the most distinguishing feature of modern marketing. Today, all organisations accept that the marketing activities must start far ahead of production. It is not enough if the activities are begun after the prodcut is ready. The company appreciates and understands the consumer's strategic position as a determinant of the firm's survival and growth. In companies operating under the marketing concept entire marketing is designed to serve consumer needs. Thus, marketing, through its studies and research, "will determine for the engineer, designer and the manufacturing man, what the customer wants in a given product, what price he is willing to pay, and where and when it will be wanted. Marketing would have authority over product innovation and planning, production scheduling as well as over the sales, distribution and servicing of the product.

4. **Modern Marketing is the Guiding Element of Business.** It would be clear now that marketing has become a pervasive force capable of guiding and even controlling production. In fact, it is the market potential and not production resources that guide a business today.

   In the past, it was thought that marketing was only concerned with getting goods and services into the hands of ultimate consumers. But later it was realised that goods must reach customers at a maximum speed but with minimum cost. This involves the integration of a number of activities from the conception of a product idea to its profitable selling and ultimate consumption.

   In recent years marketing has assumed greater importance. This is mainly due to the rapidly increasing tempo of production of a wide range of goods and services. It is an undisputed fact that sustained economic growth depends, to a large extent on the performance of marketing activities, because it is only through marketing that the demand for goods and services is stimulated. This stimulation leads to the multiplication of products and ultimately leads to higher production. Marketing, therefore, is at the heart of all industrial activity. It is of vital importance for all businessmen to understand the role of marketing in the economic development of a country and in raising the standard of living of the people.

5. **Marketing is a Science As Well As An Art.** Marketing was born as the step child of economics. But it has moved into closer relationship with various social and behavioural sciences. Marketing is inter-disciplinary in nature, orientation and design. It has borrowed heavily from economics, law, psychology, anthropology, sociology, etc.

   To some marketing does not conform to the basic characteristics of a science. Most of them described it purely as an art. In the past, marketing was considered synonymous with selling, which is purely an art. But its recent developoments in theory and practice, however, have resulted in moving it towards the social sciences, especially psychology, sociology and anthropology. It is strongly felt that the non-experimental, over-rationalised nature of economics is not conducive to the development of a viable science of marketing.

In spite of this, the difference of opinion persists. This is mainly because of overlooking the simple differences between art and science. Art is the practical application of a set of rules or principles to practice. On the other hand, science is a system of facts and principles concerning any subject.

Marketing is an art in the sense that a considerable body of rules or principles on buying, seliing, financing, standardisation, market information, etc., have been put into practice to achieve success in the economic life of man. But later developments have changed the art base of marketing into a science base. This was necessary, for marketing is a study of behaviour in a particular setting. For example, it is the behaviour of individuals and institutions in the market-place. Human behaviour, of course, cannot be accurately measured. Since its rules or principles cannot be as accurate as those of science, such as, physics or chemistry, it has been contended that marketing is purely an art.

The coin has the other side too. Modern marketers heavily depend on the semi-social sciences (ethics, education, etc.) and the science with social implications (*e.g.*, biology, art) for assistance in determining market values and predicting the results of marketing activity. In addition, there exists a pressure to harness science and technology. As a result many social science disciplines are moving from the abstract and the theoretical to the pragmatic. Marketing is no exception to the rule. Moreover, many aspects of marketing are becoming increasingly technical.

This has created the need for complex tools of measurement and experimentation. Hence, it is not wrong to say that marketing is science-based.

Marketing at present is related to four groups of social science disciplines:

(a) Those that are directly linked with marketing as a result of their normal subject-matter, area and approach, *e.g.*, economic and political science.

(b) Disciplines that are related to societal issues and problems, *e.g.*, philosophy.

(c) Disciplines that are concerned with human behaviour, *e.g.*, sociology, psychology, etc.

(d) Disciplines concerned with tools and techniques *e.g.*, mathematics and statistics.

Thus, marketing is as complex phenomenon as human nature itself. The rules of both art as well as science are applied to marketing in order to obtain the best results.

6. **Exchange Process is the Essence of Marketing.** All marketing activities revolve around exchange process. Exchange implies transactions between buyer and seller. The seller hands over a product or service to the buyer who in turn gives money. There is also exchange of information between buyers and selllers.

7. **Marketing is Goal-oriented.** Like any other business activity, marketing seeks to achieve some useful results. The ultimate aim of marketing is to generate profits through the satisfaction of human wants. The following aims are sought to be achieved by studying marketing:

   (i) To develop an intelligent appreciation of modern marketing practices;

   (ii) To provide guiding policies regarding marketing procedures and their implementation;

(iii) To study marketing problems according to circumstances and to suggest solutions;

(iv) To analyse the shortcomings in the existing pattern of marketing;

(v) To enable successful distribution of agricultural products, our mineral wealth, and manufactured goods; and

(v) To enable managers to assess and decide a partcular course of action.

8. **Marketing is a Process.** It comprises a series of functions which are inter-related. It is a dynamic process because it keeps on adjusting to the changes in the environment of business. Marketing is also a social process in the sense that it is concerned with human needs. Marketing is a managerial process in so far as it involves the functions of planning and control. Marketing is an important functional area of management.

SCOPE OF MARKETING MANAGEMENT

On the basis of the above definitions it can safely be said that under marketing management a marketing programme is prepared on the basis of needs, wants, tastes and fashions of the customers. It involves decision making in regard to pricing of the products, publicity distribution and after-sales service. Thus marketing management is an action science consisting of principles for improving the effectiveness of exchange. It represents professionalization in the carrying out of exchange relationships. In recent times marketing management has become a self conscious craft. It is the analysis, planning, implementation and control of programmes designed to bring about designed exchanges for the purpose of personal or mutual gain. It relies heavily on the adaptation and coordination of product, price, promotion, and place for achieving effective response.

Assumption of Marketing Management

The major working assumption of marketing management is that desired exchanges do not automatically come about through any process of nature. Rather they require an expenditure to time, energy, skill and supervision. Designing, packaging, pricing and distributing require the use of managerial talents. Modern age is the age of cut throat competition and only those producers survive in this struggle who are able to compete successfully by envolving new techniques to reach the consumer. As consumer orientation became the accepted marketing philosophy, the entire business philosophy underwent a subtle change. Marketing management has become most crucial in business planning and decision-making. At present there is a growing recognition of the role of marketing management. Marketing today is a complex and complicated area for management. It has become a vital business philosophy, the value of which can not be ignored. Dynamic changes are taking place every moment and are likely to take place in future with the changes in attitudes and values of society.

OBJECTIVES OF MARKETING MANAGEMENT

The object of marketing as of all productive activities is to satisfy human wants. We do not consumers or take bread to give the farmer market for his produce but what he grows is the demand of the people and if not satisfied in the locality itself it is important from other centres of production.

According to Barker and Anshen, "the end of all the marketing activities is the satisfaction of human wants." The earning of profits is the incentive which induces businessmen to attempt to satisfy wants. Private business is organised to earn profits. A business may lose money for a time and continue to operate. Unless profits eventually appear that business must cease to exit. This principle guides the operations of every phase of marketing. The performance of a service which assists marketing activities, the handling of merchandise, the incurring of risk, merchandise flow direction, provision of storage, space, etc., all these are carried on because the men engaged in each one of them have invested money and are providing their services, their time, efforts and their brains in the hope of earning a profit.

In the long range view, the object of marketing is more than the securing of profit. It is the sucessfull distribution of the products of land, or its mineral wealth, and the products of factories. It is the raising of the standard of living by increasing the flow of goods and service to consumers. It is the ultimate satisfaction of human wants.

According to Hepner, the studying of marketing aims at:

A. Providing guiding policies regarding marketing proceeding and their implementations.

B. Developing a broader framework for thinking about marketing.

C. Developing an intelligent appreciation of modern market practices and the influences in marketing situations.

D. Intensifying one's feeling of participation in marketing.

E. Creating an open-minded, hopeful attitude towards efforts of those scholars in marketing who are trying to develop it into a science.

F. Indicating the sources from which further information can be obtained concerning marketing problems or situations.

G. Supplying the factual background and analytical judgment necessary for dealing with marketing problems.

H. Helping oneself to decide whether his career shall be in marketing.

ESSENTIALS OF MODERN MARKETING MANAGEMENT

1. **The Approach of Present Day** marketing is dynamic, progressive and active rather than passive.
2. **Markets of Today Represent Tendency Towards** the "equilibrium" of traditional economic doctrine *i.e.*, supply and demand are to be equated.
3. **The Present Concept of Modern Marketing** is to "create customers" rather than to "create products". The orientation is directed towards making markets rather making products.

4. **Marketing Today Portrays a Concept** of a total process that begins with product development and ends only with the goods that are in the possession of satisfied consumers.
5. **At One Time Consumers were Supplied With Product.** Present marketing management operates in the reverse fashion seeking to it that products are made as the consumers want them.
6. **Marketing System Increases Total Satisfaction** by enabling more people to enjoy the benefits of nature resources, technology and specialization than would be possible without the exchange goods and services.
7. **Modern Marketing has to do With the Building of Main Market.** Market building involves definite objectives, strategies, policies programmes: products and service must be developed, promoted, organised and executed and financing arranged.

IMPORTANCE OF MARKETING

Customer or consumer is the pivot around which the whole economic world clusters. Now-a-days, a manufacturer does not pay as much attention to the production as he pays to the consumer. It involves a fundamental change in the economic philosophy. At the early stage of economic development, the needs of a person were limited and he was capable enough in satisfying his needs on his own. Now the time has changed and circumstances too have changed. It is the time of large scale production with latest techniques which have resulted in the expansion of scope of market from a particular place to a state, from a state to the national level and from national level to the international level. Due to the increase in the scale of production and expansion of the market, the producer feels a need to take the help of different mediaries for distributing his goods and service to the real consumers. Alongwith it, product diversification and scattered location of consumers makes it compulsory for a manufacturer to adopt advertisement, sales promotion and salesmanship. As all these activities involve heavy expenditure, the cost of production is bound to increase day by day. The manufacturer wants to keep the selling price of his product comparable to that of his competitors so that he may maintain the demand for his product. Therefore, it becomes necessary that the cost of production must be controlled and the success of an enterprise in controlling the cost of production depends to a large extent upon successful operation of marketing activities and effective organisation of this department. Marketing has acquired an important place for the economic development of the whole country. It has also become a necessity for attaining the object of social welfare. As a result of it, marketing is considered to be the most important activity in a business enterprise while at the early stage of development, it was considered to be the last activity. The importance of marketing has been explained as under:

Importance of Marketing to the Society

Importance of marketing to the society can be explained as under:

(1) **Delivery of Standard of Living to the Society.** Main liability of marketing is to produce goods and services for the society according to their needs and tastes at reasonable price. Marketing discovers need and wants of the society, produces the goods and services according to these needs, creates demand for these goods and services, encourages customers to use them and, thus, improves the standard of living of the society. It is the reason why *Prof. Malcom McNair* has said, "Marketing is the creation and delivery of standard of living to the society." Marketing creates, maintains and increases the demands of new and existing products in the market. It is marketing through which the customers use new commodities day by day.

(2) **Decrease in Distribution Cost.** Second important liability of marketing is to control the cost of distribution. Decrease in cost of distribution directly affects the prices of products because the cost of distribution constitutes to be an important part of the total cost of the product. So the direct effect of decrease in cost of distribution is that the price of products come down and it can be purchased by

the customers or consumers which were unable in purchasing it so far because of high prices. Even if we assume that the price of product is not decreased by a manufacture even on the decrease in cost of distribution, it will increase the profit of the enterprise which will be divided among its shareholders and employees who are also consumers.

(3) **Increase in Employment Opportunities.** Employment opportunities are directly affected by the development of marketing. Successful operation of marketing activities requires the services of different enterprises and organisatons such as whole salers, Retailers, Transportation, Storage, Finance, Insurance and Advertisement. These services provide employment to a large number of persons. According to an estimate, about 40% of the labour force in developed countries like U.S.A., Japan, Canada, Germany, France, etc. is engaged in different activities of marketing such as marketing research, transport, communication, storage, warehousing, publicity and wholesale and retails trade. It is expected that in the underdevelped countries, like India, there is great scope of increasing employment opportunities by developing marketing activities.

(4) **Protection Against Business Slump.** Business Slump causes unemployment, slackness in the success of business and great loss to the economy. Marketing helps in protecting society against all these problems. Marketing includes the discovery of new markets for the goods, modifications and alterations in the quality of product, and development of alternative uses of a product. It reduces the cost of distribution and maintains the level of sales volume. All this protects the business and industrial enterprises against the problems of business slump.

(5) **Increase in National Income.** Successful operation of marketing activities creates, maintains and increases the

demand for goods and services in the society. It results in the increased level of proudction and it increases the scope and area of marketing. This increase, in turn, increases the national income which is beneficial to the society as a whole.

Importance of the Marketing to the Firm

Marketing is considered to be the most important activity of all the business activities. It has become a necessity for the successful operation of all other business activities.

Peter F. Drucker has rightly said, "Marketing is the business." All the business activities are directed on the basis of marketing decisions. The importance of the marketing to the firm can be explained as under:

(1) **Helpful in Business Planning and Decision Making.** It is very risky to take the decision in respect of production only on the basis of production capacity of an enterprise, especially in the light of increasing competition and changing circumstances. Therefore, it becomes necessary for a firm to decide what can be sold before deciding what can be produced. It is necessary to decide what quantity of a particular product can be sold in the market and what measures would be applied for getting loyality of customers to the product. Unless and until these key decisions are taken, it is not practical to take the decisions regarding production, purchase, finance, size of product, type of product and quantity of production. Marketing is very helpful in taking all such decisions.

(2) **Helpful in Communication between Society and Firm.** Marketing is an effective media of communication between society and firm. Various information regarding needs, attitudes, fashions, linkings and dislinkings, etc. are collected by marketing. Marketing provides valuable information to the top management of the firm regarding production policies of competitors, pricing policies of competitors, advertisement and sales promotion policy of competitors,

availability of different media of advertisement, etc., so that a suitable policy may be formulated by the top management. In addition to it, marketing provides extensive and deep information to the society regarding availability of new products, characteristics of these products, price of these products, utility of these products and the place of availability of these products, etc.

(3) **Increase in the Profits.** Main object of every firm is to earn the maximum profits by successful operation of its activities. Maximisation of profits can be possible only through the successful operation of the activities of the marketing department and not through the production or finance department. Though marketing department needs the help of other departments for discharging its duties successfully, ultimate liability of introducing a product into the market and of making it popular is of the marketing department. Marketing makes the goods and services available at reduced costs by decreasing the cost of production and distribution. It generates the demand for goods and services through various media of advertisement, sales promotion and salesmanship. All these efforts result in the increase of demand which increase the amount of sales and consequently the profits of the firm increase.

Importance of Marketing in Developed Economy

In all the developed countries of the world, marketing is considered to be the key of economic activities for industrial growth and expansion. Truely speaking, developed countries are in greater need of efficient marketing than underdeveloped countries because in a developed country, generally, the production is carried on at very large scale through the use of latest technology and equipments. In these countries, the production is much more than the demands. Therefore, production diversification takes place and a stiff competition is found in the market. It requires the marketing system to be much more effective so that the produced goods and services can be sold. In these countries, it is also not possible for the manufacturer to reduce the prices of their goods and services, because their prices are already very competitive. Therefore, these countries take the help of improved techniques of marketing and make very possible efforts to capture the market.

Importance of Marketing in Underdeveloped Economy

Marketing has a vital role to play in the development of an under-developed country. A rapid development of an underdeveloped country is possible only through the modern techniques of marketing. Importance of marketing goes on increasing in these countries with every increase in industrialisation and urbanisation because marketing is an important tool for production the goods and services at larger scale and for selling this production successfully in the market. Commenting upon the importance of marketing for developing countries, *William J. Emlen* said, "Production may be the door to the economic growth of underdeveloped countries but marketing is the key that turns the lock, *Bauer and Yemey* expressed their opinions in this regard as, "It is now strongly held that the process of economic growth is one of increasing the size of the market. Narrowness of market is characteristic of developed economy, which is in fact an impediment to economic growth."

Importance of Marketing in Indian Economy

Indian economy is a developing economy. During recent years, the functions of marketing in India undergone tremendous changes. It is being recognised as a profession based on a systematic part of knowledge. The development of new concept of marketing has brought some revolutionary changes in the thinking of marketing executives. Marketing, now, means the creation of demands and the creation of customers. It also means the satisfaction of needs of the society. It is regarded as the creation and delivery of standard of living to the society. These changes have increased the liabilities of marketing managers these days. This all has resulted in many important acheivements in India such as:

(i) Increase in employment opportunities;

(ii) Balanced growth of the country;

(iii) Increase in per capita income;

(iv) Increase in the sale of goods;

(v) Increase in profits;

(vi) Development of the means of communication;

(vii) Development of the means of transportation;

(viii) Development of the means of warehousing;

(ix) Development of new media of advertisement and sales promotion;

(x) Development of banking and insurance industries;

(xi) Development of packing industries;

(xii) Development of new means of finance;

(xiii) Expansion in the scope of art of marketing;

(xiv) Improvement in the standard of living;

(xv) Industrial progress;

(xvi) Maximum utilisation of available resources;

(xvii) Increase in exports; and

(xviii) Increase in the national income of the country.

MAJOR PROBLEMS OF MARKETING IN INDIA

So far India has lagged behind in developing marketing management techniques sufficiently. The main problems responsible for this lack of development in this direction are as follows:

1. **Need for Marketing Research.** Marketing decisions are a combination of judgment and information on facts. Marketing research helps in collecting the useful information. Today's executive has a difficult task in making decisions and appraisals. Marketing research by providing the relevant facts can help the executive much to raise the level of their work. Marketing research facilitates decision making. In India very little has been done in the field of marketing research. There is a great need of research in marketing management both for the development

of domestic as well as international trade. There are special considerations which must be borne in mind while preparing the marketing strategy for penetrating markets abroad. Even the sophisticated country like U.S.A. is faced with greater competition in international markets from other countries like Japan. In this complex task of finding and winning foreign markets marketing research is of great importance. Dunlop India Ltd., Calcutta has been able to export bycycle tyre to U.S.A. in the face of keen foreign competition on the basis of its marketing research. Therefore for good marketing management, there is great need for marketing research.

2. **Need of Marketing Personnel.** The lack of well trained, efficient and experienced personnel stands in the way of development of marketing management in India. Of late some institutions have been set up for imparting training in this important branch of knowledge and some universities have also included courses in teaching marketing management. But looking to the need of the country it requires larger number of such institutions to impart training and turn out larger number of well trained and competent personnel to handle the complex problems of marketing management in fast developing economy of India.

3. **Product Planning.** Another hurdle in the way of marketing management in India has been the absence of scientific product planning. Proper product planning is an act of marketing out and supervising the research screening, development and commercialization of new products, the modification of existing lines and the discontinuance of marginal or unprofitable items. In India very little attention is paid toward product planning. Development in marketing management and product planning go hand in hand. The consumers also fail to get the maximum satisfaction by their purchases when the products do not match their linkings. There are three aspects of product planning which

should always be kept in view developing, modifying or discontinuing products. Few products are development in some companies as they are afraid of taking risks.

4. **Marketing Costs.** Marketing research, promotional strategy advertising effort, packaging selling expenses are constantly mounting up. Sometimes their costs became forbidding and a great hurdle comes in the way of developing marketing management on scientific lines. With the growth of large scale industries in public sector and private sector after independence the need for development of marketing management is being specially felt in India. Efforts should be made to set up more and more institutions to impart training in the specialised fields of marketing research, product, planning and marketing management. Our industrialists should take more interest in improving equity of their products and reducing costs so that India can have an access to foreign markets and successfully face competition of the foreign producers. It will be possible for developing marketing management techniques.

MAJOR ISSUES RELEVANT TO MARKETING IN INDIA

Notwithstanding marketing's contributions to the economic development of a country, there are some issues relevant to marketing which are a typical of underdeveloped countries and India, in particualr. These issues deserve the marketers' attention and consideration. The major issues are as follows:

A. In an economy of scarcity, the problem is production and not consumption. One cannot distribute anything unless one possesses it. There are more mouth to feed than the economy can possibly produce.

B. For economic growth, production of capital goods is more important than consumption goods. The former breeds capital formation while the latter retards it.

C. Middlemen are superfluous and distribution—cost escalators. Distribution should be regulated.

D. National needs are more urgent and important than individual consumer needs. Demonstration—effect changes consumption-composition and damages growth.

E. Monopoly pricing and speculative profiteering are rampant.

F. Democratic way of life slows down development tempo but still it should be preserved.

Production of goods and services is undoubtedly a major national issue in almost all countries of the world. It is because it is a very potent instrument of economic growth as reflected in the national and per capital income. Developed countries have by and large an abundance of production whereas India and other under-developed countries have a scarcity of it. The latter are, therefore, naturally more concerned above augmenting supplies by producing more. The supply is short because natural resources are not fully utilised while the demand is more because there are more mouths to feed than possibly the country can produce. As such, the problem is not one of consumption of production but of production itself. It is not uncommon to see in India long queues of people at the State run and cooperative retail shops dealing with essential commodities. In India agricultural and industrial production has frequently fallen short of demand. As a result, there had often been rationing, quotas and some such restraining measures. Under these circumstances, people are prone to assign marketing and distribution a very low rank. It is, therefore, often said. "one cannot distribute anything unless one possesses it".

In India and other developing countries, the development strategy has been to increase the production of capital goods as compared to consumer goods so that the rate of capital formation is increased. The increased capital formation is considered a key to economic development. The meaning of capital formation is that "society does not apply the whole of its current activity to the needs and desires of immediate consumption, but directs a part of it to the making of capital goods, tools and instruments, machines and transport facilities, plant and equipment". By allocating its scarce resources to the production of capital goods and country attempts to increase its capital stock, national output and income.

In India, the corporate responsibility in respect of the development of product-mix and the use of advertising appropriate to the developmental needs is greater than in any other country of the developed areas. A corporate sense of proportion and discrimination is required in greater measure.

As regards the development of product-mix appropriate to the development needs, the arbiter ultimately shall be business and its marketing executives in a democratic India. However, these product decisions shall have to be taken by them within the national policy parameteres as laid down by the Government (Parliament, Planning Commission, and other relevant agencies). It is so because there can be no better, responsible and representative agency to formulate these policy parameters in a democratic Government. Consumer orientation can still persist in management styles but, if need be, consumer sovereignty will have to be adjusted with the devlopmental needs of the country. All business decisions have to conform to and reflect the national economic aspirations without which the process of environmental rejection will set in and create more problems for an organisation.

Contrary to general belief, under such conditions, advertising and other such communication media have a far more important and challenging role to play in India and other underdeveloped countries. Advertising is a component of the marketing-mix. It is an instrument which has the capacity to cut both ways. Truly, it can stimulate wants, but it can also help to contain, suppress, reduce and rechannelise them. It can, thereby, considerably reinforce the effectiveness of other fiscal and monetary policies aimed at achieving these objectives. As a part of the demarketing strategy implemented at the national level, it can increase the effectiveness of measures aimed it reducing the impact of demonstration—effect. For this, any advertising strategy will have to restructure consumer self-images to suit products images.

In developing countries monopoly pricing and profiteering are not uncommon. The former results out of the advantages position of the manufacturer on account of lack of competitors while the latter is an outcome of the overall scarcity of products and services needed to satisfy consumer wants. However, profiteering is different from profit making. According to Scott. Chairman, the Britannia Biscuit Co. Ltd. "there is a world of difference between earning a profit and profiteering, and the virtues of the former should not be confused with the vice of the later". He further, goes on to say that "profit earned in a competitive market is an indicator of operational efficiency and a necessary result of the enterprise....profit is the legitimate reward for the risk that an investor takes". Profiteering is synonymous with exploitation of consumers through higher prices on account of the imbalance in supply and demand.

In developing economies development receives the utmost attention in public policy formulations. As such, there is an understandable impatience with the slow tempo of development. Among factors to which this slowness is attributed, is the democratic way of life and value. As such, this way of life is always under threat and attempts are made to substitute it in the name of 'economic development'. The worst happens when the general public, too, start sharing this notion when they find that the fruits of development, in terms of product/service availability, are not available to them. It is indeed a catastrophe when people, the basis of democracy, themselves lose faith in the democratic way of life.

Therefore, in any developing country and particularly in India, for democracy to survive the fruits of economic development (products/services) should be evenly distributed without interruption. This call for an effective and efficient marketing system. Drucker, has, therefore, very cogently said, "if we want economic development in freedom and responsibility, we have to build it on the development of marketing." The freedom of choice, though regulated, is a condition of the democratic way of life and marketing honours this condition; the right to respectable sustenance and qualitative life style are the essentials of the democratic way of life and marketing strives to ensure them.

From the above it is obvious that in under-developed countries, there are some special which deserve discriminatory attention. Their study and understanding are of considerable relevance in appreciating markting's distinct role in these countries and in developing appropriate and different approaches in solving problems peculiar to them both at the macro and micro levels.

FUNCTIONS OF MARKETING

Marketing basically involves relating the needs and desires of people for products or services to the objectives of producers of the products and services to achieve transfers of ownership of products or enjoyment of services. A record company, for example, expects its marketing experts to provide information on consumer preferences as to music types and styles, and performers, the location of prospective buyers, and the relative strengths and weaknesses of competitors' products, tell prospective consumers about its products and where to buy them; make records and tapes available where consumers can buy them conveniently, and provide recommendations on prices that will sell the product and yield satisfactory profit. Marketing plays the same basic role for all producers of goods, whether they produce steel for industrial buyers, pencils for school-children, or fresh fruits and vegetables for household consumption.

Marketing, however, is not concerned solely with tangible goods. It also plays a similar role in the distribution of services. A life insurance company (which sells the protection service against potential losses) expects its marketing staff to provide information about potential buyers and the kinds of insurance service they need and want, provide channels through which these services are made available to prospective buyers, make potential buyers aware of the types and nature of services offered, and participate in the determination of prices that are both acceptable to buyers and profitable to the company. Whether the service is banking, dancing instruction, travel advice, or hair styling, marketing is responsible for the ultimate delivery of the service to buyers and for the inward flow of income to the organization.

Marketing is a vital function in both profit-seeking and not for-profit organizations. Marketing has traditionally been studied only from the viewpoint of profit-seeking institutions; only recently have the marketing-type problems of non-for-profit institutions been given more than scant attention. Perhaps because marketing is so essential to the production of income (and profit) in the profit-seeking organization, nonprofit types of institutions (such as community chests and charitable foundations) are reluctant to identify their own marketing activities marketing, lest their publics construe this as profit seeking. For example, the marketing, executive of a nonprofit institution may be called the director of public relations or the business manager. Nevertheless, the top management of a symphony orchestra needs very nearly the same kinds of help as does a profit-making record company with respect to identifying its market and its preference in music providing ways to make the music available to prospective patrons, informing them about and stimulating an interest in the music offered, and establishing a price that optimizes customer patronage and income. Similar marketing activities are essential, whether the nonprofit institution is a hospital, a university or school, or an art museum. Unfortunately, in the past, this reluctance to recognize marketing as a necessary and integral part of the nonprofit institution's total function has too often resulted in marketing inaptitude and operating inefficiency.

In order to achieve the objectives of marketing department, the marketing manager performs various functions which may be classified as follows:

(1) **Marketing Research.** The consumer oriented marketing is gaining popularity these days. It emphasises the determination of the requirements of potential customers and supplying goods and services to satisfy their requirements. If the objectives are to be achieved, there is great need for systematic marketing research. Marketing research means the careful and objective study of product design, markets, transfer activities such as physical distribution and warehousing and promotional activities

such as advertisement and personal selling. In short marketing research is the intelligence service of modern business.

(2) **Product Planning and Development.** A product is something which is offered by a business enterprise to customers to satisfy their needs. Product has great improtance in all other areas of marketing management. For instance, marketing research is mainly directed towards knowing the needs of the customers and increasing the sale of the product; and storage and transportation activities depend upon the nature of the product. Therefore, it is necessary to plan and develop products which meet the specifications of the customers. Products are the foundation of any marketing programme. The success of marketing department depends upon the nature of the product offered to the customers.

Customers purchase only those products which give them maximum utility or satisfaction. While purchasing the product, a customer perceives a bundle of satisfaction that he will obtain from it. If his perception does not come true, he will not place the repeat order and speak good of the product to others. In order to achieve continuous patronage of the customers, it is the duty of the marketing manager to determine the specifications of the product desired by various types of customers. The product should be what the users want it to be and not what the production manager thinks can, and should be produced.

Product planning and development involves a number of decisions, namely, what to manufacture or buy, how to have its packaging, how to fix its price and how to sell it. The design, quality, colours, size and other features of the product can be determined by conducting marketing research of the present and prospective customers. In case of manufacturing enterprise, the production department will be guided by the needs of the users to customers and it will procure those products which will satisfy the needs of the customers.

(3) **Buying and Assembling.** Buying and assembling of raw materials and goods are important functions of any business enterprise. Raw materials are purchased for further use by the manufacturing enterprise and goods are purchased for re-sale purposes by the trading enterprises. In both the cases the marketing department has to play an important role. It will participate actively in performing the purchase function of the enterprise. The raw materials or the finished products are purchased on the advice of the marketing department. The marketing department determines the requirements of customers and pass on the necessary information to the production and the purchase departments. It insists on the production and the purchase of goods of right quality in right quantity for meeting the requirements of the customers.

Analysis of customers' need is the pivot on which the decision to buy or make a product is based. In case of a trading concern, marketing, department is closely associated with the purchase of products. Systematic purchasing involves decision marketing in regard to need of determination in terms of quantity, quality and time, selection of the source of supply, settling the terms and conditions of purchase and other. The purchasing may be made by inspecting the goods in the seller's premises or by examining the sample of goods supplied by the seller. When purchase is made on the basis of the sample, it is assumed that the characteristics of the entire lot will be the same as those of the sample. The purchase may also be made by 'description' after going through the catalogue or price list and goods supplied by the seller. Sometimes goods of different grades are available. The purchase is also required to mention the grade of goods which he wants to buy. Purchase by description facilitates mail order buying.

The term 'assembling' is used in two sense. Firstly, raw materials may be purchased and assembled in order to manufacture or assemble a product Secondly, it implies gathering of products purchases from different manufactures at some central place for the purpose of re-selling them. Thus, assembling is different from purchasing. It simply means collection of goods already purchased from different sources at some common point. Some concern asssemble goods in big lots, grade them and give them their own brand names.

(4) Selling. Selling is an indispensable part of marketing. The purpose of all marketing activities is to sell the products of the firm. Selling enables the firm to achieve its objective of satisfying the needs of the customers. Selling means finding the customers and transferring them the goods for value or consideration. It is the process whereby goods finally go to the customers to meet their wants. For selling its products, a firm has to perform a number of functions like informing the buyers and making concerted efforts to create demand for its products. Advertisement, salesmanship and other sales promotion activities are widely used to create demand and increase sales. Selling also involves the choice of the channels of distribution. A firm may decide to sell its products directly through a net-work of its branches or by executing mail orders, or through middlemen, particularly wholesalers and retailers.

Selling has become a very complicated function of marketing these days. There are a large number of substitutes available in the market and there is severe competition in the market. A firm has to devise such a marketing strategy that enables it to sell its products. He has to keep in touch with the buyers to inform them the goods points of its products and get orders from them. Selling also involves market research of its prospective customers and their demand for its products and also to know how best it can compete effectively with the rival firms in the market.

(5) **Packing, Packaging and Labelling.** Packing means wrapping, compressing, filling or crating of goods for the purpose of protection of goods and their convenient handling. Bulky materials like cotton and jute are compressed into bales, liquid materials like wine and squash are placed in bottles and cans. Heavy goods are crated and fragile goods are placed in boxes or special containers. Packing is essential for placing various kinds of goods in appropriate packages. Good packing not only means greater attention of the customers but also increases the durability of the product.

Package means a case, container, wrapper or other receptacle for packing goods in. Packaging is concerned with designing and producing or appropriate packages for a product. The significance of packaging has increased these days because of severe competition in the market and rise in the standard of living of the people. Good packaging protects the product on its route from the seller to the buyer and in some cases even during its life with the user. Packaged goods are generally more convenient to handle. Packaging facilitates the sale of a product. It acts as a silent salesman of the manufacturer, particularly at a place where there is widespread use of self-service, automatic vending and other self-selection methods of retail selling. Sometimes, package are duly sealed to ensure products of right quality to the customers. In the absence of sealing duplicate products may be distributed to the consumers by the unscrupulous dealers.

Packaging increases the utility of branding a product. The brand name and mark can be printed on the packages and it may be used for advertising the product. The packaged goods also do some sort of self-advertisement. The package advertising copy lasts as long as the product is being used in its packaged form. The user is every time exposed to the message on the label whenever he uses the product.

Packaging can also be used for giving information about the benefits and uses of the product. Finally, packaging gives identification to a product. This helps in popularising the brand name of the product and increasing its sales volume.

Labelling means putting identification marks on the package. The label is an important feature of a product. It is that part of a product which contains information about the producer of the product. A label may be a part of a package or may be a tag attached directly to the product. The label is used to communicate brand, grade and other information about the product.

(6) Storage. Generally, there is a time gap between the production and consumption or use of goods. Goods produced today will not be sold immediately. Thus, there is a need for storing the goods. Storage involves making of proper and adequate arrangements for retaining the goods in perfect order while they are despatched to the buyers. Storage makes available the goods when they are required. Thus, it creates time utility. Storage may also create place utility if goods are stored at different places. When goods are stored in different parts of the country, demands of various regions can be met immediately. Storage enables a firm to carry on production in expectation of the demand in the future.

A warehouse may be defined as a place used for the storage or accumulation of goods. Warehousing is a necessary business activity to carry on production and distribution on a large scale. Warehouses help the businessmen to keep their stocks in safe custody during the dull seasons. They can carry on production throughout the year and can sell their products whenever there is effective demand. Thus, warehousing creates time utility.

(7) Standardisation Grading and Branding. The term 'standard' implies a set of requirements or specifications as to the nature of product. It is a measurement of the physical characteristics of a product. Standard does not mean the product of the best quality. It only means that the product is of a specified quality. Goods of different standards are produced for satisfying the demands of different types of customers. Standardisation implies that the goods are of a specified and uniform quality.

Standardisation of goods facilities sale of goods because customers know that the goods are of certain standard. They purchase the goods of that standard which will satisfy their requirements. Standardisation also makes the task of middlemen easy. They can communicate well the characteristics of the standardised products. When goods are of standardised quality, the customers do not insist on detailed inspection, because they are convinced about the quality of the products with I.S.I. mark are very popular they carry the quality of the goods. It is important to point out that the process of standardisation is closely associated with the product features like grading, branding and packing.

Grading. Products may be classified into certain well defined classes or grades. This process is known as grading. Granding is done in accordance with the specifications set up by the standards. The established standards determine the grades of a product. When all the units of a product produced or manufactured are not of uniform quality they are classfied into different classes made up of units possessing similar characteristics of size and quality. Grading is of great help to the producers or manufacturers. It enables them to get higher price for higher grades of products. Grading also helps in directing the goods of different qualities towards the markets suited to them. If goods are not graded, there will be uncertainty about their usefulness. Moreover, ungraded goods fetch a lower price. Grading is very popular in case of agricultural products like wheat, rice, apple and mango. When goods are standardised and graded, sale by sample and description is facilitated.

Grading creates a good impression in the minds the customers because goods are presumed to be of uniform quality. The customers can purchase the goods of particular grades according to their choice. In such a case, there will be less chances of the goods being returned by the purchaser. The consumers like to buy graded products because they feel that they are being charged according to the quality of the product. Grading facilitates trading of goods in the commodity exchange. Since standardised and graded goods enjoy a ready market, they are rightly accepted as a collateral security for granting loans. Thus, grading helps in raising finance easily.

Branding. The American Marketing Association has defined a brand as a name, term, symbol or design or a combination of them which is intended to identify the goods or service of one seller or group of sellers and to differentiate them from those of competitors. A brand name consists of words, letter and/or numbers which may be vocalised. A brand mark is the part of the brand which appears in the form of a symbol, design, or distinctive colouring or lettering. It is recognised by sight and is not expressed when a person pronounces the brand. A trade mark is a legal term and refers to a brand which is registered under the Trade and Merchandise Marks Act, 1958.

Business enterprises generally use three types of branding: *(i)* symbols and marks like Lotus Ghee, Rath Vanaspati, and Four Square Cigarettes; *(ii)* special names such as Hamam soap and Chelpark ink; and *(iii)* names of the product and manufacturer like Tata

Coconut oil, Godrej Steel Furniture, Weston Television and Remington Typewriter.

Branding is essential particularly for big manufacturing enterprises. Branding helps in distinguishing a product from other similar products in the market. If brand name attains goodwill, it will serve as a useful medium of advertisement. A registered brand name and mark is a protection from imitation quality to the buyers. Brand name is highly used from advertising product and maintaining its individuality. Branded goods can also be sold on the basis of description only. Moreover, the price of a branded product cannot be easily compared with the prices of competiting goods. If a firm has one or more lines of branded goods, it can add new items to its product mix more easily than a firm selling unbranded goods.

The prices of branded products are fixed by the manufacturers and are printed on the packages. This protects the interest of the consumers because the retailers cannot charge more than the printed prices. The prices of branded goods remain fixed at different places and over a considerable period of time. They are not changed so frequently since it involves great inconvenience to the firm and a considerable cost in advertising the new price. Generally, the branded products are packed in suitable containers or wrappers which afford protection to the goods against heat and moisture and facilitates convenient handling. In short, customers derive many benefits from the branded products.

Sometimes a brand name becomes so common that it substitutes for the generic or descriptive name of the particular product. People associate the name with the product and with the producer owner of the brand. Illustrations of names which have legally become generic are Aspirin. Celluloid, Kerosene and Nylon. Business enterprises generally prefer that their brand name should not become generic because it involves huge cost in inventing and popularising the brand name. That is why the brand name is so chosen that it resembles the name of the company, *e.g.*, Glaxo is the brand of Glaxo Laboratories. Some enterprises use brand name in conjunction with the name of the company. Some enterprises also notify to the public through newspapers and other media that their patent is copyrighted. They do so by including the letter 'R' in a circle next to the brand name.

(8) Transportation. Transportation is the physical means of carrying goods from one place to another. It plays an important role in marketing. It helps in assembling and dispersing the goods. It links together the producers and consumers who are located at different places. By carrying the goods to such places where they are needed, it creates place utility. Transport also helps in widening the market. A manufacturer need not restrict his production for the local market only. The development of land, water and air transport has made it possible to sell the products both in the national as well in the international market. Improved means of transportation have facilitated large scale production and satisfying the needs of a large number of people.

(9) Pricing. The term 'pricing' is used to mean the money value of a product. A sound pricing policy is an important factor, for selling the products to the customers. The price policy of a firm should be such that it attracts all types of customers of different means. A good price policy helps in determining the varieties of a product to be made or procured so as to satisfy the demands of various customers. Determination of price is influenced by a large number of inter-related factors which keep on changing. This causes a great problem for the firm. No fixed standards can be adopted for fixing prices in different industries or in the same industry at different times. Further, the price policy must ensure that the price fixed covers at least the cost of procuring or making the product.

(10) Financing. Financing and marketing function of a business are inter-linked with each other. The marketing department has an important say on certain policies of the finance department in reagrd to cash and credit sales. Financing of customers purchasing has become an integral part of modern marketing. The provision of goods to the customers on credit basis is an important device to increase the volume of sales. A manufacturer has also to provide credit facilities to wholesalers and retailers. As a matter of fact, credit is the lubricant that facilitates the operation of the marketing machine.

Need for finance in marketing arises because of purchasing and maintaining inventories, meeting transport, storing and other expenses for running the marketing department. Marketing department also commits the finance of the enterprise in the form of credit to customers. Credit granted to users for the purchase of goods for personal and family consmption is known as 'Consumer Credit' and credit extended to middlemen is known as 'Trade or Mercantile Credit'. Liberal credit increases the volume of sales. Granting of credits involves risk of bad debt. Whenever credit is granted steps should also be taken to ensure prompt collection of overdue accounts. Generally, a separate section known as credit and collection department is created by the large firms. The credit-worthiness of the prospective buyer is determined before granting him the credit facility. Cash discount is also offered to the customers to stimulate them to buy goods on cash basis.

(11) Risk-Taking. Risks are involved in almost all stages in the marketing process. Right from the product planning, there are chances of risk due to changes in demand and supply conditions, loss in storage and transport, loss due to natural hazards and other risks. In fact, risk is part and parcel of the business. Risk taking or risk bearing in marketing refers to financial risk inherent in the ownership of goods held for an anticipated demand, including the possible loss due to a fall in prices and the losses from spoilage, depreciation, obsolescence, fire and floods or any other loss that may occur with the passage of time.

Risks in business can be calssified as under:

(a) **Time Risk.** Risk arises out of time element in production because of the fact that the production is done in advance of sales. There is the risk that when a thing is produced, it may not be possible to sell it at the price that will cover the cost of making it.

(b) **Place Risk.** It arises due to difference in prices of the same product at different places. If prices at a place are lower, a businessman may purchase goods from the cheaper market and sell them in the dearer market. There is risk of price changes. But this risk has been reduced because of improved means of transport and communication.

(c) **Demand Risk.** Most things are produced or procured in anticipation of demand. The manufacturer, the wholesaler and the retailer, each goes ahead on the basis of forecast of what the market requires, hoping that his judgment will prove correct. But demand may be down and prices fall with the result that losses are incurred instead of profits.

(d) **Competition Risk.** Risk also arises because of competition in the market. The competitors may unexpectedly offer better or cheaper products. It will affect the sales of other competitors who cannot offer better or cheaper products.

(e) **Natural Risk.** Drought or excessive rains may spoil the farmer's crops. Fire may burn down a factory with all its contents. Trainwreck or shipwreck may cause loss of goods in transition.

(f) **Human Risk.** Human risks arise due to man made factors such as theft, dishonesty, pilferage, bad debts, riots, strikes, lock-outs etc. Risk may also be caused by technological changes.

(g) **Political Risk.** Political risk is caused by political factors like changes in ministry, changes in governments, and changes in Government economic policies. Risks may also arise due to unhealthy relations with the neighbouring countries.

(h) **Minimisation of Risks.** It is very difficult to eliminate all the business risks completely. Some of the risk can be avoided by taking precautionary measures. For instance, risk of fire may be prevented by constructing fire proof buildings, risk due to theft may be prevented by taking the necessary safety measures and risk due to dishonesty may be avoided by appointing honest persons. There are certain risks which can be minimised through proper planning and forecasting. For instance, risks arising due to changes in demand, prices, fashions and tastes of the people, etc. can be minimised through proper marketing research. Competition risk can be avoided through business combination.

There are certain risks which can be transferred to others. An example of the transfer of risk is the process of hedging, and method or risk transfer accomplished by buying and selling for future deliveries, whereby dealers or manufacturers protect themselves against a decreasing or increasing market price between the time they buy a product and the time they sell it. Hedging involves simultaneous purchase or sale for spot delivery and purchase or sale for future delivery. Another device of shifting risk is insurance. Under a contract of insurance, in consideration of a specific payment (the premium) by one party the second party agrees in a contract to idemenify the first part to a certain limit for a specified loss which may or may not occur.

MARKETING PLANNING

Marketing Planning is the combination of two words—Marketing and Planning. Therefore, to understand the meaning of Marketing Planning, it is necessary that the meaning and definition of these two words must be understood separately. The details in this regard are as under:

Planning is the process of deciding the future actions. What to do?, How to do? When to do?, Who to do?, Why to do?, Where to do?, etc. are the questions to be decided by the process of planning so that pre-determined objectives of the enterprise may be achieved successfully and economically and future uncertainties may be minimised. Planning is also regarded as a process of selecting for best possible alternative from among the various alternatives available for the solution of a given problem. The term 'Planning' has been defined by many eminent authors. Some of the important definitions are as follows:

James L. Lundy, "It means the determination of what is to be done, how and where it is to be done, who will do it and how results are to be evaluated."

M.E. Hurely, "Planning is deciding in advance what is to be done. It involves the selection of objectives, policies, procedures and programmes from among alternatives."

George R. Terry, "Planning is a method or techniques of looking ahead, a constructive reviewing of future so that the present action can be adjusted in view of the established goals."

On the basis of analytical study of above definitions, it can be concluded that planning is the process of deciding future action. It involves the selection or organisational objectives, policies, procedures and programmes. It also involves the selection of best possible alternative from among the various alternatives available for the solution of a given problem. Planning is an important activitiy of management to get success in a venture, it is necessary to forecast and to decide the policies and programmes for it.

After making the separate study of the words—Marketing and Planning it can be concluded that Marketing Planning is a part of the process of overall planning of a business and industrial enterprise. Marketing Planning includes sales forecasting, determination of marketing objectives, and the formulation of maketing programmes and policies for the achievement of these objectives. The term 'Marketing Planning' has been defined by many eminent authors. Some of these important definitions are as follows:

> *American Markeing Association,* "Marketing planning is the work of setting up objectives for marketing activities and of determining and scheduling the steps necessary to achieve such objectives."

On the basis of analytical study of above definition it can be concluded that Marketing Planning is a continuous process in which the marketing objectives of an enterprise are decided and marketing programmes, policies, and procedures are determined for the performance of different marketing activities, such as—marketing research, product planning and development, advertisement and sales promotion, physical distribution and after sale services, etc. The process of marketing planning involves product policy planning, price policy planning, physical distribution policy planning and sales promotion policy planning. Marketing planning is a liability of marketing department. Marketing department is divided into many sub-departments and separate managers are appointed to look after all these sub-departments.

OBJECTIVES OF MARKETING PLANNING

Marketing Planning is the base of marketing management. The object of marketing planning is to make the best possible utilisation of all the human and physical resources of an enterprise so that pre-determined marketing objectives of the enterprise can be achieved. Marketing Planning helps in establishing effective co-ordination between various activities of the enterprise, brings certainly in its marketing activities, checks the wastages and brings economy in managerial efforts. However, the objects of marketing planning in an enterprise can be described as follows:

(1) **Helpful in Forecasting.** Forecasting is the essence of planning. The main object of marketing planning is to formulate marketing plans on the basis of sales forecasting. Thus, marketing planning provides the base for sales forecasting.

(2) **To Minimise Future Uncertainties.** Future is very much uncertain. An expert marketing manager is one who can forecast the future circumstances and prepare necessary plans and policies. Marketing planning provides base for the analysis of present circumstances and past trends so that the future circumstances may be forecasted and the plans to achieve pre-determined objectives may be prepared. Thus, marketing planning helps in minimising the future uncertainties, as far as possible.

(3) **Helpful in Co-ordination.** Co-ordination is the essence of marketing management. To achieve any success in the efforts of organisation, it becomes necessary that all the efforts must be very well co-ordinated. Marketing planning helps in co-ordinating the activities of all the departments of the enterprise. Marketing planning co-ordinates the activities not only of its own department but it helps in co-ordinating the activities of all the departments of the enterprise.

(4) **Helpful in Control.** Marketing planning is also an important tool in the hands of management to control the activities of the enterprise. With the help of marketing planning, the objectives are set up, the results of actual performance are measured and compared with pre-determined standards and the variances, if any, are analysed and corrective measures are adopted.

(5) **A Check Upon Wastage.** Marketing planning determines the objectives of the enterprise, decides the plans and policies, and prepares programmes, and procedures and, thus controls the activities of an enterprise in a very

efficient manner. All the efforts are made to get the maximum results with the help of minimum efforts.

(6) **Helpful in Management by Objectives.** Management by objectives is the latest approach of management. Under this technique, top executives of the enterprise take the decisions only in respect of the key problems. Problems of routine nature are solved at junior level of management. It is marketing planning which makes a difference between the problems of key nature and that of routine nature. Thus, marketing planning helps in management by objectives.

(7) **Helpful in Maintaining Healthy Competition within Enterprise.** The process of marketing planning determines marketing objectives and prepares marketing plans, programmes, and policies. It also determines the duties, responsibilities and power of all the employees of the enterprise very specifically. All the employees of the enterprise try to achieve their objectives.

(8) **Helpful in Facing Competition.** It is the time of cut throat competition. A business and industrial enterprise can be successful only if it can read the policy of its competitions and may prepare itself to face the challenges created by its competitors in the market. The process of planning helps in achieving this object very successfully. It does not concentrate only upon the activities of the enterprise but it keeps a close eye upon the policies and strategies of its competitors so that appropriate actions may be taken at proper time and the competition may be faced successfully.

(9) **Helpful in Providing Maxiumum Satisfaction to Consumer.** The process of marketing planning concentrates upon providing best possible satisfaction to the consumers. The interests of consumers are duly protected. All the best efforts are made to provide the goods and services of best quality at reasonable prices and at the time and place most suitable to the consumers. It also provides effective after

sale-services. All the activities of the enterprise go around the satisfaction of needs and wants of consumers.

(10) Helpful in Increasing the Efficiency of Employees. The process of marketing planning helps in increasing the efficiency of the employees of the enterprise also. It sets the individual objectives for all the employees, measures the results of their individual performance and evaluates this performance in the light of their individual objectives. It increases the feeling of responsibility among the employees. They try their best to achieve their objectives and they make their best efforts to get the best results. It helps in increasing their efficiency.

ELEMENTS OF MARKETING PLANNING

The process of marketing planning involves the performance of many activities. All the activities which are performed in the process of marketing planning are known as the elements of marketing planning. Main elements of marketing planning may be described as under:

(1) Determination of Objectives. Every business and industrial enterprise is established for the achievement of some specific objects and all the activities of the enterprise are performed for the accomplishment of these objects. Marketing activities are also performed with the same objects. Therefore, setting up of the objectives is the very first step of the process of marketing planning. It is the duty of top marketing executives to set the marketing objectives of the enterprise. They explain these objectives to all the members of staff and then determine the individual objectives of all the members of staff and inspire them to achieve their individual objectives.

These objects may be determined for long term as well as for short-term. The objectives must be very specific and clear and these must be clearly defined to all the concerned employees.

(2) **Forecastings.** Second element of the process of marketing planning after the determination of marketing objectives of the enterprise is to forecast different aspects to facilitate the achievement of these objectives. Forecasting is the art of estimating future on the basis of analysis of past data and present circumstances. On the basis of sales forecasting, quantity of a particular product to be produced, amount of finance required, and type of employees to be recruited, can be decided.

(3) **Policies.** Policies are the general statements of understanding created for the attainment of objectives. Policies indicate the manner in which the employees of an organisation will work in a particular situation. A policy establishes the boundaries which provide general direction in which managerial actions will take place. Policies provide guidance to the subordinates in proper discharge of their responsibilities. Policies also help in establishing co-operation among them. They also help the management in maintaining effective supervision and control. Thus, it is essential that an organisation must decide its policies well in advance.

(4) **Procedures.** A procedure is the specific manner in which the actions are to take place and the works are to be performed. A procedure is a sequence of steps to be undertaken by an enterprise to enforce a policy and to achieve its pre-determined objectives. Procedures define the way in which a particular work will be performed so as to ensure that whosoever performs it, will do it in the uniform manner. Marketing activities of the organisation require the determination of specific procedures through which the activities will be performed. These procedures must be in accordance with the objects and circumstances of the enterprise. These must be flexible so that necessary changes may be made according to the need.

(5) **Rules.** A rule is a definite and rigid plan that specifies what is to be done or not to be done in a particular situation. A rule is a plan which cannot be deviated, no flexibility can be allowed from rules. Thus, rule is a specific guide to actions and permits no discretion or judgement. Rules are different from policies because policies are framed for the benefit of the enterprise while rules are only the simple form of plans. Policies decide the sequence of activities to be done, while rules do not decide any such sequence. Rules must be decided well in advance in respect of all the marketing activities to be performed and all the best efforts should be made to get these rules followed.

(6) **Programme.** A programme is prepared to execute the planned works. A programme is considered as a brief plan to do a particular work. Programme must be prepared keeping in view the policies and procedures of the enterprise. Programme may be short-term or long-term, intensive or extensive, general or specific. It defines the steps to be taken, resources to be used, time limit for each step and the persons liable to execute a plan. A programme is a sequence of the activities which aim at implementing the policies of the enterprise so that pre-determined objectives may be achieved. Thus, a programme is a mixture of objectives, policies, procedures and rules.

(7) **Schedule.** Schedule determines the time limit for each activity. In the field of marketing right activity at the right time is the key to get success. Specific schedules must be determined for the programmcs of advertisement and sales promotion. It must be decided well in advance that how much quantity of a particular product will have to be delivered at what time and at which place. Strict schedule must be determined for every acitivity of marketing and schedule must be strictly followed.

(8) **Strategies.** A strategy is a particular type of plan which is prepared to adjust with other plans. It represents the

decisions to initiate certain actions for the accomplishment of pre-determined objectives. It seeks to meet some specific problems, *e.g.*, price reduction by competitions, slump in demand, strike by employees, shortage of the raw material or power problems etc. Plan and policies have to be changed according to the change conditions. Strategies help in adjustment with the changed conditions and implementing the plans in such conditions. Strategies depend upon the situations and problems occurring within and outside the firm. Strategies are framed for various functional areas of a business or industrial undertaking, *e.g.*, marketing strategies, financial strategies, production strategies and personnel strategies etc.

(9) Budgets. A budget is a financial plan. It establishes the limits within which the goals must be achieved. A budget is a very important tool of planning in the modern industrial age. Budgets may be of different types, such as—cash budget, purchase budget, sales budget, production budget, overheads budget etc. The activities of an enterprise can be controlled effectively through these budgets. Therefore, budget is a tool for maintaining effective control. A budget is always prepared for the future. It can never be prepared for the past. Because of this element, budget is considered to be a part of planning process.

MARKETING PLANNING SYSTEM

The system of marketing planning depends upon the type of marketing organisation adopted in the enterprise. Different business and industrial enterprises adopt different types of marketing organisation and the system of marketing planning is adopted in accordance with their marketing organisation. For convenience, the sturcture of the marketing organisation can be divided into four parts—*(I)* Function-oriented Marketing Organisation; *(II)* Product-oriented Marketing Organisation; *(III)* Market-oriented Marketing Organisation; and *(IV)* Customer-oriented Marketing Organisation.

Depending upon the type of marketing organisation structure, the system of marketing planning can also be four types as follows:

(A) Marketing Planning in the Function-oriented Marketing Organisation. Under this system of marketing organisation, the whole marketing department is divided into different sub-activities, namely, marketing research, product planning and development, advertisement and sales promotion, physical distribution, sales and after-sale-departments. All these sub-managers prepare separate plans for their sub-departments and they send their proposals to the marketing manager. Marketing manager scrutinises and analyses these sub-plans and prepares an integrated marketing plan for the whole enterprise. Main sub-plans prepared under this type of marketing organisation relate to the following marketing functions:

(1) ***Product Mix Plan.*** This plan relates to the estimate of expansion, contraction and modification of product line so that the changes in demand of product may be met successfully and timely and marketing objectives may be achieved.

(2) ***Sales Force Plan.*** This plan relates to the planning of efforts of selling force of enterprise. It includes reorganisation of sales territories, necessary adjustments in the number of selling employees, training to selling employees, motivation and inspiration to the selling employees etc. The aim of this plan is to make the efforts of sales force of the enterprise more effective.

(3) ***Distribution Channels Plan.*** This plan relates to the functions of physical distribution of the goods and services. It includes the selection of channels of distribution and the number of such channels. It also includes the formulation of policy in this regard.

(4) ***Advertising and Sales Promotion Plan.*** This plan relates to the determination of policy and preparation of programmes relating to advertisement and sales promotion. It includes the preparation of advertisement budget, selection of media of advertisement, determination of the

message of advertisement and the selection of methods of sales promotion. In addition to this, it also includes the division of advertisement and sales promotion efforts according to products, customers and market segments.

(5) **Pricing Plan.** Determination of price is perhaps the most important and sensitive issue of all the marketing functions. The price determined by the enterprise must be reasonable from the point of view of customers and beneficial from the point of view of enterprise. This plan includes the determination of price of the goods and services keeping in view the situation of money inflation, money deflation and competition.

(6) **Marketing Research Plan.** This plan relates to the efforts of marketing research in an enterprise. It includes the evaluation of effectiveness of marketing efforts of the enterprise so that necessary changes may be made in these efforts. It also includes the study of consumer behaviour and the study of changes in the conditions of market.

(7) **Marketing Organisation Plan.** This plan relates to the efforts of co-operations and co-ordination. It establishes effective co-ordination between various departments of the enterprises effective co-ordination between various departments of the enterprise so that the plans, and programmes of the enterprise may be implemented effectively and easily.

(8) **Physical Distribution Plan.** This plan relates to the efforts of physical distribution of the goods and services. It includes the determination of the selection of means of transportation so that the goods and services may be made available to the consumers at minimum of the transportation.

(II) **Marketing Planning in the Product-oriented Marketing Organisation.** Product oriented marketing organisation is the type of marketing organisation in which different marketing plans are prepared, different marketing policies are formulated and different marketing programmes are fixed for different products. Under this type of marketing organisation, separate marketing objectives are determined for every product and individual marketing efforts are decided for the achievement of these objectives. Under this system, different plans are prepared for different products relating to marketing research product planning and development, advertisement and sales promotion, physical distribution, sales, and after sale services.

(C) Marketing Planning in the Customer-oriented Marketing Organisation. Customer-oriented marketing organisation is the marketing organisation in which all the customers of the goods and services being produced by an enterprise are divided into different groups on the basis of their characteristics and different marketing plans and determined for every group of customers. Individual marketing objectives are determined for every group of customers and different marketing policies are prepared and different marketing programmes are fixed for all the groups of customers so that these marketing objectives may be achieved. The plans of advertisement and sales promotion are prepared keeping in view the individual characteristics of the all groups of customers and all the marketing efforts of the enterprise are devoted to meet the demand and requirements of these groups of customers.

(D) Marketing Planning in the Market-oriented Marketing Organisation. Marketing-oriented marketing organisation is the type of marketing organisation in which marketing plans are prepared from the point of view of different segments of market. These plans relate to the determination of individual marketing objectives for every segment of market. Different marketing policies are determined and different marketing programmes are fixed for every segment so that these objectives may be achieved. Different plans are prepared for advertisement and sales promotion efforts for every segment keeping in view the situation of competition in the related segment.

❐

2

Developments in Marketing

The concept of social marketing is concerned with the health and happiness of customers and well being of society. Such concept put questions the firm that does an excellent job of providing service and satisfying the consumers for their wants in this way the firms are caring the society .According to Kotler. "The societal marketing concept holds that the organisational task is to determine the needs, wants and interests of target markets and deliver the satisfaction more effectively and efficiently than competitors in a way that preserves the consumers and society well being". The firms which adopt the societal marketing concept make the marketing decisions in an ethical and socially responsible manner. They must consider not only the short term needs of customers but also the welfare of every one affected by their operation. For instance; people want sufficient economical energy to heat or cool their houses; on other side people also have realised the adverse effects of toxic water, oil spills and acid rain. To meet both the short term needs of buyers and the long term welfare of society; a firm has to balance the interests of the customers.

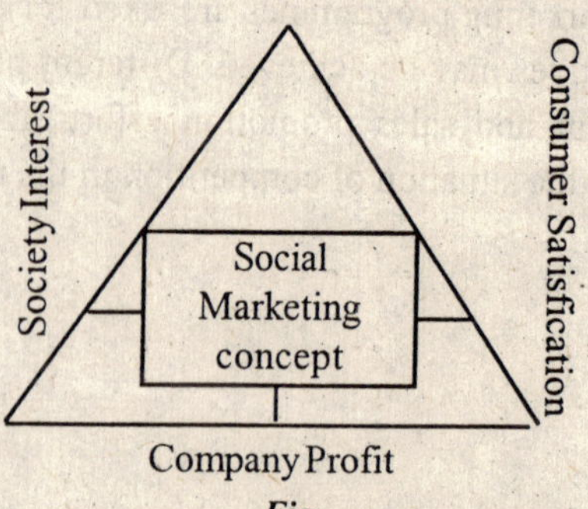

Fig.

Many firms are opting thse societal marketing concept by preserving resources or developing the products which are not harmful to the enviornment and in this way they are practicing green marketing. This concept is very difficult to implement because it requires firms to place the needs of society ahead of the goals of the organisation. Take an example—building of any new project which do not create pollution the atmosphere may decrease a firms profit. But many of the firms are thinking and feeling that in the long run they can not survive if they do not think about the welfare of society.

Importance of Social Marketing

The task of social marketing organisation to findout needs, wants interests and to provide the satisfaction to consumer of society effectively and efficiently than other competitors in the market. The social marketing concept calls upon marketers to balance the considerations and marketing policies prevelent in the market. Company profits, consumer satisfaction and public interest are the main considerations. The companies began to recognise the longterm improtance to satis consumers wants and introduce the market concept. Many companies have achieved notable sales and profit gains through adopting and practicing the social marketing concept.

Societal marketing is an important concept in business. The main purpose of business from society point of view is to produce products and provide service for exchanging for money by which needs of man can be fulfilled of same social goal. A business firm is an economic institution of society and the businessmen and the marketers are the members of society and their actions and peformances are for the consumers who are also members of our society. In this way a business is something which has oriented society In this way a business is something which is a basic necessity. Henry Ford once said that he wanted to produce more cars in the interest of society than profit. It is society which provides the necessary infra-structure facilities, security and opportunities for business. So the marketing policies and objectives of business should be framed in a way that would contribute literally to the social well-being.

Basic Elements of Social Marketing

1. Consideration of Social Impact. A business must be assessed not only on the profitability aspects but also on the overall efforts or the actions of the buisness in society.

2. Satisfaction to Human Needs. By the business marketing concept the main aim at the satisfation of human needs, its main stress is based on product. In social marketing; the marketing techniques are based on the attainment of satisfaction of human needs. The techniques must be used for achieving society's satisfaction as a whole *e.g.*, selling water, housing facilities, edible products etc.

3. Extention of Ideas on Marketing to Social Fields. Marketing should be used as an instrument to achieve the goals of society. For example, marketing techniques can help in attaining socially desirable goals—increased education, environmental awareness, population control etc.

ETHICAL MARKETING AND ORGANISATIONAL FACTORS

Marketing ethics is the moral evaluation of marketing activities and decision as right or wrong. This behaviour is judged as ethical or unethical on the basis of principles of behaviour established by society, interest groups, organisation management, competitors and individuals. It is a function of mutual trust among individuals and organisations. An ethical violation makes contninuous trust in marketing exchanges difficult if not possible. There we can see the costs resulting from unethical behaviour in the form of reduced sales or loss of goodwill. Ethical considerations continue to capture the spotlight because of well-publicised cases of unthical practices in politics, sports, businesss and religion. Ethical behaviour often goes unnoticed while unthical conduct receives a great deal of media attention. Reporting on the thousands of ethical decisions individuals make daily is difficult if not possible.

The businesses do not understand how people make decisions when faced with ethical dilemmas. How people form thier ethical standards and what causes them to encourage in unethical behaviour may help business reduce the unethical activities. The following factors influence a person's ethical behaviour:

(1) **Moral Philosophies.** It is a set of principles which directs the right and moral way to behave. Normally the masses term all these principles their families, society and education imparted to them. Moral pholosphies can be divided into utilitarian and humanistic categories.

Utilitarian philosophy seeks the maximum satisfaction to the target number of individuals. A particular activity achieves the greatest good for the greatest number can be determined by a social cost benefit analysis in which the sum of all costs of a particular action is substracted from the sum of all the profits. If the result is positive, the action under consideratin is considered ethical and if the result finds negative form then this action is unethical.

On other side people and organisation follow the humanistic philosophy which is focused on individuals rights and values. If the potential of product poses harmful to any worker or customer then it is taken off the market.

(2) **Organisational Factors.** In the competitive world of business it is believed to get the secrets of competitors at any cost and rate. It is in fact unhealthy and therefore unethical profit. Many successful business houses loses tenders, contracts, offers done the leakage of inside information.

In order to get the work done, gifts and tips to the key executives be given. In this way the finance officer has to pass the payments to parties. Here the power might be misused by delay tactics to get the payment in time the business parties give annual gifts/festival valuable gifts.

To make favours is another unethical tactics which is rapidly increasing in the society. Favouring goes on the basis of cost, colour, creed, sex, blood relations, son/ daughter of social consideration. Such practice leads to break the norms set by the laws and in this way the high position officers use their powers and achieving result is not good.

(3) **Marketing Environment.** The comman ethical problem faced by the marketers is of conflict interest. Such conflict arises when an individual acts to further his/her own selfish concerns rather than the long term interest of the organisation. For example, when bribe is taken in the form of gifts, payments etc. obtain the new customers or to satisfy the customers; a conflict of interest occures. Communications in the form of advertising may pose ethical problems in the marketing environment. False advertising and personal selling tactics are unthical and create consumer dissatisfaction.

In the world of business corruption is practiced with invisible art of cunning. It is unfortunate that a business house supports and justifies such corrupt practices that it is a worldwide phenomenon. The practices of corruption make the environment of business unfit for society, it directly put impact on the mind of consumers and due to such practices the reputation of business is hurt when it is exposed among the masses. For a good marketing environment the interest of organisation should be kept in mind for the betterment. If the marketing environment is not fit than the whole show will be spoiled.

LEGAL ASPECT OF MARKETING

Marketing decision cannot be taken without taking into account the developments in political and legal field. The viability of business depends upon the ability with which it can meet the challenges out of political and legal enviornment of a country is influenced by political stability, organisation, government's intervention and constitutional provisions affecting business, foreign policy etc.

Following are the legal enactments of marketing environment:

* The Prevention of Food Adulteration Act of 1954.
* The Agricultural Produces (Grading and Marketing) Act of 1937.

* The Drugs Act of 1940 and the Drugs Control Act of 1954.
* The Standard Weights and Measures Act of 1956.
* The Monopoly and Restrictive Trade Practices (MRTP) Act of 1969.
* The Company's Act.
* The Essential Commodities Act of 1955.
* The Trade Marks and Merchandise Marks Act of 1958.
* The Display of Prices Order of 1963.
* The Packaged Commodities (Regulation) Order, 1975.
* The Consumer Protection Act of 1986.
* I.D.R. Act.
* Import and Export Trade Control Act.

Some of the important acts are disscussed in brief to highlight the Acts regarding marketing:

1. MRTP Act. The MRTP Commission, under this Act, is empowered to enquire into: *(i)* any restrictive trade practice upon receiving a complaint of facts from any trade of consumer's association or Central and State Governments or upon its own knowledge and information and *(ii)* any monopolistic trade practice upon a reference by the Central Government or upon its own information.

Twin objects of the Act are "*(1)* To ensure that the operation of the economic system does not result in the concentration and economic powers to the common detriment and *(2)* to prohibit such monopolistic and restrictive trade practices as are prejudicial to public interest."

After investigation the report of the MRTP Commission, the Central Government may make order for any of the following measures: *(a)* regulating the product, supply distribution or control of any goods or service and also fixing of price *(b)* prohibiting monopoly undertaking to continue any such act any more; *(c)* fixing the standards of the products; and *(d)* declaring unlawful any agreement which may lead to monopolistic practice, etc.

According to the Act, monopolistic trade practice means a trade practice which has, or is likely to have, the effect of—

- Maintaining prices at an unreasonable level by limiting, reducing or otherwise controlling the production, supply or distribution of goods of any description or supply of any services or in any other manner.
- Limiting technical development or capital investment to the common detriment or allowing the quality of any goods produced, supplied or distributed, or any service rendered, in India to deteriorate.
- Unreasonably preventing or lessening competition in the production supply or distribution of any goods or in the supply of any services.
- Increasing unreasonably the cost relating to the production, supply or distribution of goods or performance of any service or increasing unreasonably the prices or the profits also treated as monopolistic trade practices.

2. Import and Exports Trade Control Act. This Act states about India's imports and exports policies. The import policy seeks to *(i)* maintain prices in the local markets by importing the necessary supplies; *(ii)* protect the domestic capital goods industries by charging higher taxes on imported capital goods; and *(iii)* ban imports of non-essential consumer goods, similarly, the export policy of India seeks to : *(i)* raise the export marketing of value-added items, *i.e.*, finished goods rather than raw materials of semi-finished products; *(ii)* fix a floor price for certain goods in which inter-se competition is severe among Indian manufacturer-exporters; and *(iii)* impose restriction on export trade when the supply in the domestic market is insufficient to meet the demand.

3. I.D.R. Act. The Central Government under this Act may secure equitable distribution and availability at fair prices of any article relatable to any scheduled industry and may provide for; *(i)* controlling the prices; *(ii)* regulating by licences, permits, or otherwise the distribution, transport, disposal, acquisition, possession, use or consumption of any such article; *(iii)* prohibiting the withholding from sale of goods ordinarily kept for sale; *(iv)* fixing by agreement a controlled price; *(v)* regulating or prohibiting any class of commercial or financial transactions which are likely to be detrimental to public; and *(vi)* requiring persons engaged in the distribution and trade and commerce to mark the goods with sale prices, etc.

The Development Councils constituted under this Act may suggest, among others, measures for: *(i)* better marketing, *(ii)* better distribution and sale of goods and *(iii)* standardisation of products which would be satisfactory to the consumer.

4. Essential Commodities Act. Under this Act, the Central Government may exercise the powers same as those stated under the I.D.R. Act above with respect to the control, production, supply and distribution of commodities and of trade and commerce, in certain specified essential commodities including coal, textiles, drugs, sugar and foodstuffs, etc., in the interests of the general public.

Legal environment is determined by the help of laws and court decisions which put pressure on the business and marketing managers.

MARKETING SERVICES

A service is any act or performance that one party can offer to another that is essentially intangible and does not result in the ownership of anything. Its production may or may not be tied up to a physical product. A service is an intangible product that provides benefits to consumers and often involves human or mechanical effort.

The term of service is rather general in concept, and it includes a wide variety of services. Services vary as to whether they are equipment based (automated car whases) or people based (windows washing). Some services require the client's presence. Service differ as to whether they meet a personal need (personal services) or a business need (business services).

There are the business and professional services such as advertising, marketing research, banking insurance, computer-programming, legal & medical advice. There are services which are provided by professionals but consumed for reasons not of business, rather for leisure, recreation, entertainment and fulfilment of other psychological and emotional needs such as education, fine arts etc.

Characteristics of Services

Services have five characteristics which affect the design of marketing programme:

(1) **Intangibility.** The primary characteristic that distinguishes services from other products is intangibility. Unlike physical products, they cannot be seen tasted, felt, heard or smelled before they are bought when you buy sugar, you can feel it, see it, touch it, smell it and see it. Teaching is a most intangible service. But by travelling in aeroplane has both tangible and intangible aspect *i.e.*, the benefit which we are deriving is a service and in a particular plane in which we fly has some tangible aspect. The goods & service continuum highlights the fate that most of the services are in reality a combination of both tangible & intangible aspects. There are only a few truly pure tangible products or pure intangible services.

(2) **Inseparability.** In case of 'products' or 'physical products', the activities of the production and distribution are separated from the act of consumption. Thus, a computer, chocolate, shoes and the like are produced in anticipation of demand and are sold as and when they are demanded. While on the other hand, in case of services, the production, the distribution and the consumption are taking place simultaneously. In most cases, the service cannot be performed unless the customer is present or drectly involved in the production process. Therefore, service cannot be separate from the person of firm providing it. A plumber has to be physically present to provide a service and alike. The service encounter cannot be completed successfully unless customers have the skills needed to participate in the transaction.

(3) **Heterogeneity.** Most services are performed by people, and people are not always consistent in their performance. This inconsistency or variation in performance is referred to as the heterogeneity of services. Performance may vary from one individual or service to another within the same organisation, or in the service one individual provides from day to day and from customer to customer. The doctor who gave you his complete attention in your last visit may behave a little differently the next time. Many people take their automobiles to a favorite mechanic at a certain service station because of his better service. But even a favourite mechanic may provide inferior service in the next visit. Thus services are much more difficult to standardize than tangible goods.

(4) **Perishability.** Services can not be stored and therefore perishable in nature. A company selling goods would deal the problem through inventory control. But service not fully utilized represent a total loss. For example, empty seats in movie's theatre in one show and due to heavy rush many people returned in another show, heavily booking in trains in peak seasons and empty seats in other days shows fluctuating demand pattern which aggravates the perishabiliy characteristics of services.

(5) **Ownership.** When you buy a product you become its owner—be it a pencil, book, shirt, refrigerator or car. In the case of a service, you may pay for its use but you never own it. By buying a ticket you can see the evening film show in the local cinema theatre; by paying wages you can hire the service of a chauffeur who will drive your car; by paying the required charges. You can have a marketing research firm survey into the reasons for your product's poor sales performance, etc. In case of a service, the payment is not for purchase, but only for the use or access to or for hire of items or facilities.

A service is purchased for the benefits it provides. If we closely examine the reasons why products are purchased, we find that they are bought because they provide certain intangible benefits and satisfactions.

Developing Marketing Strategies for Services

Like marketer of tangible goods, service marketer must strive to satisfy consumers by developing a marketing-mix for the target market.

Product Strategy. The marketing of services can be success only if there is a proper match between the service product from the customer's view point and the supplier's view point. To have a proper match, as a marketer, it is essential to analyse the following services.

- the customer benefit concept
- the service concept
- the service offer
- the service forms and
- the service delivery system.

Promoton Strategy. Because services are intangible-dominant products and therefore difficult to advertise. That's why, advertising of services should emphasize tangible cues, or symbols of the services that are more easily perceived and understood by the consumers.

Pricing Strategy. The intangible nature of services makes establishing prices difficult.

Hotels & airlines offering lower rates in off-season and lower telephone charges for outstation calls after peak hours are examples of how pricing strategy can be used to offset the perishable characteristics of services. Higher the intangibility, more difficult to calculate cost, such as doctors', lawyers' fee when fees settled sometimes through negotiation. On the other hand, services like drycleaning based on tangible component, easier to calculate the cost as a unit basis and have a uniform price policy. The above pricing based on market-oriented pricing while bank charges, electricity & water charges, rail or air fare etc. either controlled by Govt. or industry associations and are cost-based pricing.

Distribution Stategy. Due to special features of services namely 'intangibility' and 'inseparability', they cannot be stored, transported, stocked and hence poses a distribution constraint since they are able to serve only a limited localised market. The other characteristic of services which affects the distribution strategy is the fixed location of services such as universities, restaurants and hospitals which necessitates the customer to go to the service location.

Other service industries make use of different types of marketing intermediaries. Travel agencies for instance, help facilitate exchange between consumers and airlines, hotels etc. ATMs serve as electronic intermediaries for financial services. Master cards and VISA credit cards have enabled banks to extend their credit services to consumers in widely dispersed geographic area.

INTERNATIONAL MARKETING

International Marketing grows and prospers because of certain economic and political factors. The existence of global marketing over many centuries justify its existence. Some of the industrially advanced nations enjoy huge production capacity and surplus of goods. National market becomes inadequate to them. They must export so that their economies develop and expand. The need for international marketing is universally accepted because it is beneficial to all the countries. More than ever before international marketing has become important, now, because fastest means of transport and communiation has well-linked all the countries. The following factors necessitate international marketing:

(i) **Rapid Industrialisation.** Countries are economically dependent on one another. Every country has to import certain goods and also to export so as to pay for imports. The third world countries are dependent on the western countries for superior technology to achieve faster economic growth. International marketing has become prominent because of international interdependenec and growing industrialisation.

(ii) **Cost Benefits.** Due to certain favourable factors, some countries can produce certain commodities with low cost of production. International marketing is favoured by all in order to enjoy the comparative cost benefits. International marketing becomes the only option to exchange goods and export such goods where the countries enjoy cost benefit. A country will import such goods which either it cannot produce or will produce at a higher cost.

(iii) **Raised Standard of Living.** There is consciousness all over the world and people desire to raise the standard of living through the consumption of best quality goods procured from nook or corner of the world. International marketing also mobilises foreign investments, superior technology and international understanding. The standard of living of the people can be raised only by enabling them to consume quality products at reasonable prices, no matter from where they are procured. Even perishable goods are marketed within minimum possible time due to well-organised network of transport and communiation.

(iv) **Fulfils Economic Needs.** The increase in the rate of population growth has brought pressure on the Government to fulfil economic needs of growing number of its people. In order to provide basic amenities and luxuries to the increasing population imports and exports become obligatory. The growth of international trade is certainly because of increasing world population.

(v) **Cultural Exchanges.** Peaceful co-existence to a very great extent depends on economic, social and cultural exchanges. International relations can improve when people move to different countries on goodwill visits. Cultural differences separate the countries from one another. This gap can be well connected through international trade and exchange of culture.

(vi) **Maintaining International Prices.** It is not possible that varying prices will prevail in international marketing for long. Various countries market their goods at competitive rates. The comparative cost benefits enjoyed by one country in a particular item can be shared by other countries.

(vii) **Helps both Developed and Developing Countries.** International marketing is also required to narrow the gulf between advanced countries and less developed or developing countries. Even advanced nations must export their surplus so that under-developed countries can obtain their requirements. In turn, advanced countries must provide concessional terms so that developing countries have no option but to import superior technical known-how from developed countries. It is through international marketing that industrially advanced nations provide assistance to developing countries in their struggle towards economic growth. International marketing improves economic relations and reduces the chances of international conflicts.

Advantages and Benefits of International Marketing

International Marketing has number of advantages. Some of these briefly summarised below:

(i) Availability of goods which cannot be produced in the home country due to geographical factors and other natural limitations.

(ii) Proision of better standard of living to citizens by providing them with wide variety of goods and services.

(iii) Rational allocation of resources and the best use of the resources available at the international level.

(iv) Industrial development of the country, provision of massive employment opportunities to the people and full utilisation of natural resources available.

(v) Benefits of comparative cost difference as suggested in the theory of comparative costs. The benefits of division of labour and specialisation at the international level are also available through international marketing.

(vi) Interantional economic, political and cultural co-operation and world peace.

(vii) Social and cultral exchanges between different countries of the world.

(viii) Rapid expansion of tertiary sector which includes transport, insurance and shipping.

(ix) Special benefits during the period of emergency like famines and floods.

(x) Removal of deficit in the balance of trade and payments of participating countries through export promotion and import subsitution.

(xi) Effective utilisation of surpluse domestic production, introduction of new varieties of goods, improvement in the quality of production and promotion of mutual co-operation among countries.

(xii) Easy availability of foreign exchange for import of capital goods, modern technology and other essential requirements.

It may be noted that the above mentioned advantages or benefits are available only when international marketing is reasonably free from various restrictons and regulations. Unfortunately, almost all countries have imposed various restrictions on the free movement of goods. Such commercial restrictions are undesirable as they restrict the scope of free and fair international marketing.

PROBLEMS FACED BY INTERNATIONAL MARKETS

International marketing is a complex, difficult and intricate process in comparison to domestic marketing. There are differences due to different political entities, tariff, policies, restrictions, monetary system and other barriers.

The complexities caused by many factors, create following problems before the international marketing:

(i) **Trade Pattern Variations.** When one enters the international market, he has to deal with the existing trade patterns among the various countries of the world. The policies of the different countries, that govern their import and export should also be considered. These patterns, obviously impose restrictions on the international trade and the task of the international marketer becomes that of solving the problems through experience and expertise for attainment of the objectives in the best interest of the firm as well as its country.

(ii) **Different Regulatory Measures.** Now a days, every country wants that exports should be more than the import to maintain a favourable balance of payments. Furthermore, the trade patterns of a country are designed to serve the national purpose of achieving better trade position and in this it wants to export manufactured goods, surplus natural resources, agricultural commodities and avoids the import of such commodities it can be made available in the domestic market by the domestic manufacturers. This imposes certain restrictions on the trade with other countries. For this various barriers, as tariff (custom duties), quota restrictions. foreign exchange restrictions, technological regulation, state trading, preferential regulations, are brought into operation. All these present sever problems before the few and unrestricted flow of international trade.

(iii) **Unbalanced Development of Developing Countries.** Therc is a vast difference between the level of technological advancement and the developing economics. In contrast to the developing economies developed countries, have sophisticated technology capable of exploiting raw-materials and other resources and converting these into finished products. Whereas, the developing economies depend upon their old and outdated techniques of production, incapable of locating and exploiting all the economic resources available in the country. Such countries face problems due to their lopsided development and what actually happens is that, these countries export raw materials in the international market, which are converted into finished products by the developed economies and then again sold to the developing economies. The developed economies sell these commodities at the price which is always higher than their intrinsic value. A firm belonging to an under-developed economy suffers from this drawback of lopsided development.

(iv) **Economic Groupings of International Level.** There is a continuous and rising tendency among the nations to form unions at the international level, with the view of safeguarding their economic interests. Thus, the member countries of groups are in a better position than any other individual non-member economy. The union like ASEAN, COMECON, EEC etc are some, which have in built growth and free flow of international trade in the contemporary world.

(v) **National Development Policy.** Every country aspires to attain self-sufficiency by exploiting its raw-material and other resources to the optimum. This aspiraton of self-sufficiency in industrial development, has resulted into the creation of many trade barriers on the free flow of international trade. Other countries must consider their trade barrier while framing their strategy. A country aspiring rapid development, implements strategy of importing capital goods and improves restrictions on the imports of less significant consumer goods to avoid, as much as it can, the deficits in trade.

(vi) **Procedural Complexities.** There is no common procedure relating to import and export, and every country has its own procedures, documents and practices relating to international trade. These are complex and difficult essentialities of international marketing these days, which pose, problems before the international marketing.

In addition to these problems, there are some more problems like, the fact that still, the business and industry have not fully recognised the value and importance of export trade. Again there are problems caused by inflation, high prices as well as black marketing. In the recent years the management of our national economy has been very bad to the extent that it has failed to supply for its own needs.

FACTORS AFFECT THE ENVIRONMENT OF INTERNATIONAL MARKETING

There is difference between various international markets as it differs from the domestic markets. The diversity in the environments of these factors are to be considered before planning any strategy of international marketing.

Follwing are the factors that act as determinants of the international marketing policies:

(I) Cultural Factors

Social values become the distinguishing factor between domestic and international marketing. Before stepping in the international market in any way, it is essential to understand the cultural dynamics of these foreign markets. The marketer must consider the cultural factors of the country in which it wants to enter in the international marketing. Culture has a broad meaning. According to M.J. Herks Kovits, "culture may be viewed as the sum total of man's knowledge, beliefs, arts, morals, loves, customes and any other capabilities and habits acquired by man as a member of society". To be more precise, culture is the, "distinct, way of life of a group of people, their complete design for living". Man has tried to solve the problems by borrowing from other cultures the various alternatives and by adopting it according to his environment and what is more appropriate for his society.

The borrowing by one society from another society is a process which is systematic and unending. It rather goes on inter-stingly. The adoption of a borrowed system or techniques is restricted to the environment of the society which is borrowing. This is why one product which is radically acceptable by one society is not liked by another society. In the like manner, a technique of selling workable in one society may not be successfull in another society. These differences occur because of differences in the way of living, customs, habits, beliefs, morals etc.

The existence of subculture *i.e.*, a culture within a nation's culture, is again a matter that attracts serious thought. Sub-culture arises due to differences existing within a culture. For instance in India, there is a distinction between the northern and the southern part of the country. Sub-cultures, may exist in the geo-political boundaries and sometimes they spread across all the political boundaries. For example, Bangladesh is very much like the West Bengal in India, as far as the cultural similarities are concerned. For the point of view of international marketing these differences between cultures and sub-customs, are very important because of their influence on the marketng plan as well as on the decisions about the selection of these markets. The demand for a product, influenced by cultural factors, must be ascertained to achieve success in the field of international marketing.

A marketer willing to enter an international market, must study following aspects of cultural background of a foreign market.

(a) **Material Culture.** This includes technology and economic aspects of that country.

(b) **Social Institutions.** This includes the consideration of social organisation, education system, and political system of the foreign country. The belief and family system and its kinds is also to be considered.

In additional to these, the Aesthetic part of culture including graphic and plastic art, folk lore, folkways and mores, music, drama, dance, etc. are also the aspect to be given consideration. And the last but not the least, is the language of the foriegn market.

Regarding culture, the changes that often take place in every society from time to time must also be considered as these caste effective impact on various aspects of peoples life. A firm desirous of entering international market must consider these factors and it should also evaluate the degree of influence and involvement of these factors, on the decision of international marketing policies.

There exists a feature of resistance of the cultural change. This reflects a certain degree of surprise on and apprehension about new products, ideas, and techniques. The degree and extent of this resistance differ from economy to economy. It has also been noticed that changes affecting the very basic structure of the culture face maximum resistence.

There is also a tendency, commonly present in all economies, to regard foreign goods as the things of social status. One more reason for the indication towards foreign products is the inferior nature of the domestic products, this feature is more common to the developing economies.

Thus for a successful international marketing, proper understanding of the culture is essential.

(II) Political Considerations

Political environment is another factor affecting the foreign market. It is necessary for an international marketer to assess the political environment since this affect has success as well as existence in such markets.

The study and assessment of the political environment include the following:

(a) Political Systems. The type of government *i.e.*, whether it is Socialistic, Capitalistic, Democratic etc must be analysed, since the philosophy of the government is reflected in its policies.

(b) Philosophy of the Government. It is essential to study government's philosophy in particular about, policy towards private sector and foreign business. Generally, the governments of the target foreign countries, specify their priority areas in which foreign business is encouraged.

Many rules exist in the different countries. For example in india Foreign Exchange Regulation Act 1973, specifies guidelines for foreign private investment.

Infact, the government's philosophy towards foreign capital goes under change with the change of the party in power at a given period of time. From all this view points, it is essential for an international marketer, to assess the philosophy of the government in power, as well as the long run political prospectives.

(c) **Permanency and Stability of the Policy of the Government.** It is necessary to examine the extent of permanency and stability of government policy of the target foreign market. The marketer must always be careful about such changes in policy that lead to its destabilisation. It also involves the assessment of the long-run predicability of the governments policy.

The policy of a government in the field of trade may be rendered unstable, because of any one of the following factors:

(i) Change in Governments.

(ii) Grow.ng aspirations of nationalism.

(iii) Shifting of political parties reaching the government at different levels. Due to certain causes, the products become politically vulnerable.

The attempt of the international marketer should be to minimise it.

(III) Economic Factors

An international markerter should assess the level of economic development of the concerned country. Since the level of development of the countries is not the same, so marketer must act according to making his best contribution to the economic development. It is also essential to assess the economic aspirations of the concerned countries. The factor of 'market potential' should always be kept in mind while studying the levels of economic development of a country.

A marketer should study following indications, in regard:

(a) Gross National Product.

(b) Per Capita Income.

(c) Purchasing power of the consumers.

(d) Rate of economic growth.

(e) Level and degree of industrialisation.

(f) The form of marketing channels and related infrastructure.

These factors play tremendous role in chalking out the marketing strategy of the firm deciding to enter the international marketing arena.

In addition to these factors, an interantional marketer should also study the policies, programmes and objectives of the international economic institutions like GATT, UNCTAD, UNIDO, IMF, World Bank, Asian Development Bank etc.

GREEN MARKETING

The firms which are accepting the societal marketing concept which do not harm the environment is called or considered Green Marketing. It involves the developing products and packages which are less harmful for the environment. It includes many areas which control the pollution for example. Procter and Gamble Company are producing the containers which are less harmful for our environment. In this way green marketing will provide benefit from better relations with consumers, suppliers, regulators and other firms in Industry. For successful green marketing programme a company must have the commitment of top management as well as in an internal environment that encourages employees to act as environmentalist. Many companies have established new positions such as vice president of environment, health and safety. Others reward employees for reducing waste or developing such kinds of products which are not much harmful for the environment. In this rapid growing industries era the pollution became a major challenge for us. Due to the mass production, the industries are demanded, one side we have benefits but other side we have to face the monster of pollution. The industries and top management are trying their best by acheiving new avenues in their field to put less harm by their industries. As individuals become more committed to the environment, green product will gain a competitive edge. But because environmental claims have to be used to mislead consumers, some firms find it difficult to successfully launch the green marketing programme. Successful green marketing requires being as precise as possible to enable consumers to understand the claims made in the message. As a result of all this same firms have retreated from making environmental claims about their products, even though they continue to develop products and packages that are good up to some extent for the environment. Pricing is also a big concern; since green products typically cost more than competing brands. Consumers prefer green products when they are readily available and their price and quality are similar to that of products.

Green Consumerism

The products demanding immediate eco-marketing are toilet soap, textiles, packages, paper, paints pesticides, drugs etc. These consumer goods with ecomark labels can spur the demand for Green Consumerism which is the prime aim of Ecomark Scheme. After that we can take other consumer goods like lubricating oil, petrol, wood substitutes, plastics, cosmatics, batteries, agricultural products etc. to get the ecomark stamp. The successful operation of the ecomark rests on the following assumptions:

(1) The consumers are environmentally conscious and are writing to buy them, and they are ready to exercise a choice if alternatives are available.

(2) Many products which can be demonstrated to be environment friendly and can be ecomarked.

(3) The manufacturers are also having environmental awarness and show their keen interest in the ecomark.

The Central Pollution Cotnrol Board of India is the final authority to implement ecomark scheme on voluntary basis. For example we do not have even soaps/detergents (not using phosphates) to be sold under ecomark stamp.

Implications for Marketers of Green Marketing

The various issues involved in green marketing may eventually imply a change in the prevailing quality of living standard and in the basics of consumer behaviour. Stocks, hosiery and clothing will for example be of higher quality, last longer and not need daring or mending too often ! But the customer will pay more for convenience, reflecting the value of the time that this convenience affords him or her. He or She may consume more quality but less quantity.

Forecasters suggest that consumers may return to demanding product attributes favouring quality, reliability, durability and safety. This change in behaviour reflects the beginning of a rejection of the "throw away society". The concept of the throwaway society is increasingly seen as untenable and unsustainable.

Sustainability is seen as a key issue within green marketing. A fundamental question is whether the marketing process is environmentally sustainable, or does it exploit that environment on an irrecoverable basis? For instance:

(a) Tropical deforestation, short term ranching, soil erosion, flooding and desertification; Or

(b) The planting of tropical or temperate hardwoods; the use of properly managed hardwood forests for furniture and construction materials (etc.); proper replanting to maintain eclogy and habitat.

The issue of sustainability can be placed within the context of consumption. Sustainability may become a key benefit required with the attribute set considered appropriate for any partıular usage requirement.

Some Key Principles for 1990's Green Consumer

Given the rapidly increasing awareness on the part of the general public of the importance and urgency of the green issues summarised above, Elkington and Hailes identify some key principles for the 1990's green consumer. These are that in general, the Green Consumer should avoid products (or services) which are likely to:

- endanger the health either of the consumer or of others;
- cause significant damage to the environment during manufacture, use or disposal;
- consume a disproportionate amount of energy during manufacture, use or disposal;
- cause unnecessary waste, whether because of over-packaging, an unduly short useful life or because they are not suitable to reuse or recycle;
- use materials derived from threatened species or from threatened environments;
- involve the unnecesary use of, or cruelty to animals, whether this be for toxicity testing or other purposes;
- adversely affect other countries, particularly in the Third World.
- The more widely these basic principles are promoted and understood by the general public as consumers, the greater will be the effect on consumer behaviour, and the greater the resulting impact on the product-marketing strategies pursued by suppliers to consumers and industrial markets.

Environment consciousness, and green consumer behaviour are likely to diffuse through consumer, then industrial markets in the west at an increasing rate showing an increasingly potent "casade effect". This increasing public awareness and propensity to act in an environmentally conscious manner will simply reflect the wider socio-cultural and political climate as it develops in response to a (potentially) deteriorating environmental context, over-population (etc.).

CYBER MARKETING

It is always advisable that before beginning a market campaign we have to develop a market plan. If the process is adopted accordingly the positive marketing results can be obtained. In this respect cyber marketing is not different than the conventional media. Normally people are very busy trying to get a product out of the door and to devote enough time for planning. This side cyber marketing is changing rapidly and it is really very hard to plan when our marketing vehicle moves so much. First of all the first step is to quickly develop a cyber marketing plan. We can have the information from soap to nuts but it is useful only when we write a comprehensive plan.

To get the objectives of cyber marketing we have to find out what we want to have online. Will you use cyberspace to. Other functions instead of or in addition to try to generate sales such as investor relations, customer service or recruiting new employees. Do you want to market to existing customers; prospects or both. When you answer the above question, you will have your cyber marketing objectives. These objectives should explain which parts of cyber space you use and which tactics are used by you. This is totally electronic/digital marketing which can be done only by educated customers (having the knowledge of computers or cybershops).

Following are some Marketing outline for the development of Cyber Marketing Plan:

(1) Successful cyber-Marketing sites

(2) Cyber marketing information resources

(3) Internet Market research

(4) Internet News Resources

(5) Internet Advertising

(6) Searchable Archieves

(7) Tracking New Commercial Sites

(8) Internet Commerce Organisations

(9) Internet People Demographics

(10) Promoting your electronic storefront

(11) Electronic Payment Systems

(12) Internet Market Makers

(13) Online Shopping & Electronic Commerce

(14) Internet computer Demographics.

No good plan goes without a time line. Different people may have different ideas about how detailed these should be. For example dates for content completion promotion launches, online seminars etc. From the list of your milestones, you can be as detailed with dates and events as you feel it necessary.

After deciding where is cyber space you want to set up shop, determine what kind of information or content will help you achieve your objectives. The technical design and limitations of some parts of cyberspace will determine how your content will look, and so be sure you become familiar with the different elements of cyberspace. What information can you give them about your product or company that they can't get in traditional marketing channels. What information will you provide that will be more reliable to people than typical ads and brouchers. What content can you provide that is not related to your product, you will draw people to your areas. After that decide what you want, who will be responsible for content and in appropriate proportion. Will it be Marketing Sales or ad agency? Can they deliver the materials you need to change you online areas regularly to build repeat traffic? will customer Service or Human Resources develop content? How many people will need to oversee content development and managing your online areas? What outside resources will you need, such as internet providers, website designers writers etc?

The above mentioned tips for cyber marketing plan are dependent for successful implementation of cyber space. This marketing can bedone by the educated customers only. It is proved very costly and beyond the reach of poor customers.

There are seven aspects of traditional marketing that can be effected by cyberspace. Following aspects are considered as tactics for cyber marketing.

1. **Educating Your Market.** It includes giving customers and prospects an in-depth understanding of your product or service, your company or your industry. Many people are more likely to buy a product when they fully understand how it works. This works whether you sell industrial

plastics or cakes which are prepared according to an "old family recipe."

2. **Public Relations.** There is a multiple of magazines and newspapers that are publishing online. Work with both the journalists who use cyberspace, and the online publications to get coverage for your company.

3. **Direct Response Promotions.** This may seem like splitting hairs, but there is a difference between promotions that help build brand awareness or loyalty, and promotions that induce people to take a specific action, and preferably right now (buy a product, pick up literature). You may have a greater need for direct response promotions to help you rise above the resulting marketing noise level.

4. **Research and Product Development.** One of the most overlooked benefits of cyberspace is its research potential. Feedback can make the biggest difference in a company's ability to be profitable. This can be feedback from customers, the market in general, others in your industry, and even your competitiors. Cyberspace can deliver more feedback than you know what to do with.

5. **Product Demonstration and Distribution.** This is an effective way to build people's comfort levels so they'll be more inclined to buy your products or services. Distribution goes hand in hand with demonstrating products because, if you can demonstrate your wares online, prospects should be able to receive them right then when they're highly motivated to buy. It you can't physically deliver products on the Net, at least have a system in place so they can place an order and receive confirmation that the order has shipped.

6. **Service and Support.** If you decide to provide customer service and support online, you should develop tactics to make this happen. You may want to consider activities such as special offers to shift customers from telephone to online support, or incentive programs for customers who regularly volunteer to help others online.

When developing tactics in this area, consider support for people other than customers. For example, you can support your field sales people or resellers and make sales presentations casier and more effective. Rather than lug around tons of marketing materials, sales people can modem into your online area during a presentation to access the data they need.

7. **Building Brand Awareness and Loyalty.** You want to build a community of customers who are loyal to your product (brand). Besides customers, you want as many surfers as possible to know what your product and company have to offer.

   Your brand marketing tactics may consist of promotions and creative sponsorships, but they can also include aggressive hyperlinking of your Internet information with other sites.

RELATIONSHIP MARKETING

Relationship marketing is the practice of building long-term satisfying relations with key parties-customers, suppliers, distributors—in order to retain their long-term preference and business. Smart marketers try to build up long-term, trusting, "win-win" relationship with valued customers, distributors, dealers, and suppliers. They accomplish this by promising and delivering high quality, good service, and fair prices to the other parties over time. Relationship marketing results in strong economic, technical, and social ties among the parties. It also cuts down on transaction costs and time. In the most successful cases, transactions move from being negotiated each time to being a matter of routine.

The ultimate outcome of relationship marketing is the building of a unique company asset called a marketing network. A marketing network consists of the company and all of its supporting stakeholders: customers, employees, suppliers, distributors, retailers, ad agencies, university scientists, and others with whom it has built mutually profitable business relationships. Increasingly, competition is not between companies but rather between whole networks, with the prize giving to the company that has built the better network. The operating principle is simple. Build a good network of relationships with key stakeholders, and profits will follow.

The basic purpose of marketing is customers delight with permanent customers for the business. In other words, the old customers should repeat orders with the firm. This requires building strong relationship between the seller and the buyer. Philips Kotler has coined the term 'relationship marketing' to signify the need of building good rapport between the business and its customers. The marketer who knows how to build and manage strong relationship with the key customers can secure plenty of future sales from such customers.

Relationship marketing is most appropriate with those customers who can influence the company's future to a great extent. For instance, a small number of customers may, account for 80 per cent of the company's sales. Sales persons working with such customers should build strong relationships by offering personalised attention and service through increased social contacts. Relationship marketing shall pay an important role in future.

Relationship marketing involves the following steps :

1. Identification of key customers who will influence the firm's future prospects.
2. Assignment of a relationship manager to each key customer.
3. Preparation of detailed job descriptions for all relationship managers.
4. Development of annual customer relationship plans.
5. Co-ordination and review of the performance of relationship managers.

Key Principles of Relationship Marketing

To understand customer relationship marketing, we must first examine the process involved in attracting and keeping customers. Figure shows the main steps in the customer-development process. The starting point is suspects, everyone who might conceivably buy the product or service. The company looks hard at the suspects to determine who are the most likely prospects—the people who have a strong potential interest in the product and the ability to pay for it. Disqualified prospects are those whom the company rejects because they have poor credit or would be unprofitable. The company hopes to convert many of its qualified prospects into first-time customers, and then convert those satisfied first-time customers into repeat customers. Both first-time and repeat customers may continue to buy from competitors as well. The company then acts to convert repeat customers into clients—people who buy only from the company in the relevant product categories. The next challenge is to turn clients into advocates, customers who praise the company and encourage others to buy from it. The ultimate challenge is to turn advocates into partners, who the customer and the company work actively together. At the same time, it must be recognized that some customers will inevitably become inactive or drop out, for reasons of bankruptcy, moves to other locations, dissatisfaction, and so on. The company's challenge is to reactivate dissatisfied customers through customer win-back strategies. It is often easier to reattract ex-customers than to find new ones.

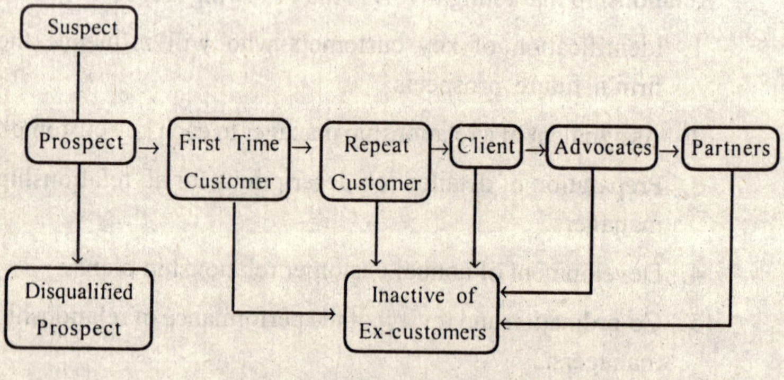

Fig. The customer-Development Process

Source : Philip Kotler, Marketing Management

Developing more loyal customers increases the company's revenue. However, the company has to spend more to build greater customer loyalty. Development of customer loyalty will be more profitable in some business than in others. How much should a company invest in customer-relationship building, so that the costs do not exceed the gains? We need to distinguish five different levels of company investment in customer-relationship building:

(1) **Basic Marketing.** The salesperson simply sells the product.

(2) **Reactive Marketing.** The salesperson sells the product and encourages the customers to call if he or she has any questions, comments, or complaints.

(3) **Accountable Marketing.** The salesperson phones the customer a short time after the sale to check whether the product is meeting the customer's expectations. The salesperson also asks the customer for any product or service improvement suggestions and any specific disapportionments. This information helps the company continuously improve its performance.

(4) **Proactive Marketing.** The company salesperson contacts the customer from time to time with suggestions about improved product uses or helpful new products. (Kraft U.S.A.'s sales reps used to limit their customer efforts to devising promotions in supermarkets, now they are more proactive, offering research and tips for improving a store's profits.)

(5) **Partnership Marketing.** The company works continuously with the customer to discover ways to effect customer savings or help the customer perform better. (General Electric has stationed some of its engineers full time at Paraxair, Inc. to help boost Praxair's productivity.)

❐

3

Marketing and Consumer Research

Marketing research evokes different images in different people's minds. Some quota it with consumer interviews; some think of it as sales forecasting or sales analysis; to others it represents obtaining reactions to new product ideas or models. Different companies even use different terms. Some call it sales research, other refers to it as commercial research, business research, or commercial intelligence. Marketing research is the more generally used term, however, and it is the broad term that encompasses a wide spectrum of fact gathering and analytical activities. There are about as many definitions of market research as there are active market researches today, but they all have one thing in common; Market Research is the arm of marketing that finds out things and thereby lays the basis for marketing strategy. It is concerned with the facts of what people buy, when they buy, where they buy.

The American Marketing Association defines marketing research as: "The systematic gathering, recording and analysis of data about problems relating to marketing of goods and services".

According to Kotler, "Marketing research is the systematic design, collection analysis and reporting of data and findings relevant of a specific marketing situation facing the company.

The key word in the above definition is 'systematic'. This is the difference between research and hapahazard gathering of findings. For a study/research to be systematic there must be two qualities in the least. First, it should be orderly so that the measurement have accuracy and their is a fair cross-section. Second, it should be impartial in analysis and interpretation.

Now for a research to be systematic it should be planned in advance. Moreover to complete it, it should be interpreted. We thus arrive at a definition of Marketing Research; "Marketing research is the planning of and systematic gathering, recording, analysis and interpreting data about problems (or opportunities) relating to the, marketing of goods and services".

CHARACTERISTICS OF GOOD MARKETING RESEARCH

Having examined marketing research procedure, we can now advance five characteristics of good marketing research.

(i) ***Interdependence of Models and Data.*** Competent marketing researchers recognise that the facts do not speak for themselves but rather derive their meaning from models of the problem. The attempt to guide their search for information on the basis of useful decision model to help the executive.

(ii) ***Research Creativity.*** At its best, marketing research develops innovative ways to solve problem.

(iii) ***Scientific Method.*** Competent marketing research is characterised by an attempt to follow the scientific method: careful observation, formulation of hypotheses, prediction, and testing.

(iv) ***Value and Cost of Information.*** Competent marketing researchers show concern for measuring the value of information against its cost. Value/cost is a consideration when the marketing research department chooses which research projects to conduct, which research design to use and whether to gather more information.

(v) ***Multiple Methods.*** Competent marketing researchers shy away from overreliance on anyone method, preferring to adapt to the method to the problem rather than the other way around. They also recognise the desirability of the

simultaneous gathering of information in different ways to give greater confidence than anyone method would provide.

SCOPE OF MARKETING RESEARCH

Here will again consider another definition of marketing research. Clark and Clark define marketing research as: "The careful and objective study of product design, markets and such transfer activities as physical distribution, warehousing, advertising and sales management". Thus the scope of marketing research lies in its variety of applications. They may be summarised as follows:

(i) ***Business Economics and Corporate Research.*** Short range forecasting, long range forecasting, pricing (policies and strategies) studies, studying business trends, and MIS, etc.

(ii) ***Sales and Market Research.*** Measuring market potential, analysing market shares, determining market characteristics, sales analysis, sales quotas and territories, test marketing audits and distribution channels.

(iii) ***Product Research.*** Acceptance of existing products, acceptance of new products, packaging competitive products etc.

(iv) ***Advertising Research.*** Advertising effectiveness, copy research, media research, etc. Thus, marketing research has a broad area of application which describes its scope. The main purposes of marketing research to a marketer are planning and control, but, one point that must be stressed here that a marketer (or a marketing manager) has always limitations in terms of resources (staff and money) and time. There may be a number of problems or decisions to face and due to the above limitation only critical problems areas should be identified and given priorities for research.

IMPORTANCE OF MARKETING RESEARCH

Marketing research plays a key role in the entire marketing process. It helps the firm in market measurement, assessment of market potential and development of sales forecasts. It also helps the firm to acquire better understanding of the consumer and the marketing environment.

It aids the formulation of the marketing mix. As a matter of fact, decision-making on each element of the marketing mix, like products and service mix, distribution mix, promotion mix and pricing policy, relies heavily on marketing research findings. For example, through marketing research, the firm can appraise the profitability of a particular ad campaign, customer acceptance of a particular product, effectiveness of the middlemen, etc. Marketing research can significantly help each and every function of marketing.

FUNCTIONS OF MARKETING RESEARCH

The scope of marketing research in any modern, large-sized enterprise is two-fold in character;

— Routine problem-analysis and

— Non-routine problem analysis.

Before we proceed with a discussion of these, it is essential to clarify the relationship and the difference between marketing research and marketing information system (MIS). The job of MIS is to supply reliable, timely and pertinent marketing information. On the other hand, problem analysis is the main function of marketing research. Marketing research too generates and utilises marketing information but its purpose is research and problem solving. In other words, whereas MIS consists of an ongoing collection of marketing information, marketing research uses MIS for tackling and analysing specific marketing problems.

Marketing research assists a variety of tasks such as sales forecasts, assessing market potentials, assessing the reactions of customers and dealers to company's products, services and sales policies such activities belong to the category of routine problem analysis.

The non-routine problem analysis is the more important part of the marketing research job. It also calls for the more creative research efforts.

MARKETING RESEARCH PROCEDURE

Marketing research undertaken in the effort to understand a marketing problem better. The value of the results depends upon the skill with which the marketing research project is designed and implemented. Effective marketing research involves the following five steps: problem definition, research design, field work, data analysis, and report presentation and implementation.

(i) Problem Definition. The first step in the conduct of research calls for a careful definition to the problem. If the problem is stated vaguely, if the wrong problem is defined, or if the user of the research are not made clear, then the research results may prove useless to the manager.

The poor definition of the problem is often the fault of the manager requesting the study. Thus a top administrator in the U.S. Postal System might ask the market research manager to research public attitudes toward the postal system. The marketing research manager has a tight to feel uneasy about the assignment. It is too general. It is not clear how much interviewing should be done of home users and business users or what aspects of the postal system they should comment on. This kind of research is called exploratory research and is mostly warranted in situations where the organisation's ignorance of the market place is substantial. Yet research is generally more efficient when the problem and the alternatives are well defined—the cost of research is generally related to the total amount of information gathered, while the value of research is associated only with the proportion of information that is useful.

(ii) Research Design. The problem definition stage should lead to the development of a dear set of research objectives, stated in writing if possible. The marketing research manager faces a choice among many alternative ways to collect the information that will satisfy the research objectives. The manager must decide on the data collection method, research instrument and sampling plan.

(iii) Field Work. After the research design has been completed, the research department must supervise, or subcontract, the task of collecting the data. This phase is generally the most expensive and the most liable to error. Four major problems arise:

(a) ***Interviewer Bias.*** Interviewers are capable to introducing a variety of biases into the interviewing process, through the mere fact of their age, sex, manner, or intonation. In addition; there is the problem of conscious interviewer bias or dishonestly.

(b) ***Refusal to Cooperate.*** After finding the designated individual at home, the interviewer must interest the person in cooperating.

(c) ***Respondent Bias.*** The interviewer must encourage accurate and thoughtful answers.

(d) ***Not-at-homes.*** When no one is home, the interviewer must either call back later or substitute the household next door.

(iv) Data Analysis. The fourth step in marketing research procedure is to extract meaningful information from the data, and there are four steps in this process. The first is to calculate relevant averages and measures of dispersion. The second is to cross-tabulate the data to produce goodness of fit tests. The fourth is to apply multivariate statistical techniques to the data an the hope of discovering important relationships. The most important multivative techniques are described below:

(a) ***Multiple Regression Analysis.*** Even marketing problem involves a set of variables. The marketing researcher is interested in one of these variables, such as sales, and seeks to understand the cause(s) of its variation over time and or space. This variable is called the independent variables. The researcher hypothesises about other variables, called independent variables, whose variations over time or space might contribute to the variations in the dependent variable. When one independent variable is involved, the statistical procedure is called simple regression; when two or more independent variables are involved. The procedure is called multiple regression.

(b) ***Discriminant Analysis.*** In many marketing situations the dependent variable is classificatory rather than numerical. Consider the following situations:

An automobile company wants to explain brand preferences for Chevrolet versus Ford.

A detergent company wants to determine what consumer traits are associated with heavy, medium, and light usage of its brand.

A retailing chain wants to be able to discriminate between potentially successful and unsuccessful store sites.

In all these cases, two or more groups to which an entity (person or object) might belong are visualised. The challenge is to find discriminating variables that could be combined in a perceptive equation to produce better than-chance assignment of the entities to the groups. The techniques for solving this problem is known as discriminant analysis.

(c) ***Factor Analysis.*** One of the problems faced in many regression and discriminate analysis studies is multi collinearity—high intercorrelation of the independent variables. The idea in multiple regression is to use variables that are truly independent, both in the sense that they influence but are not influenced by the dependent variable and in the sense that each independent variable is independent of the others. The simple correlation of efficient (or all pairs of variables will reveal which variables are highly inter correlated, and the analyst has the option of dropping one from each pair. Another approach is to factor analyse the set of inter correlated variables in order to derive a smaller set of factors that are truly independent of each other. Factor analysis is statistical procedure for trying to discover a few basic factors that may underlie and explain the intercorrelations among a larger number of variables. In the marketing area, factor: analysis has been applied to determining the basic factors underlying attitudes toward air travel, alcoholic beverages, and the clustering of medical program types.

(v) Report Presentation and Implementation. The last step is the preparation, presentation, and implementation of a report presenting the major findings and recommendations coming from the study. The report should begin with a short statement of the problem and the major findings. This should be followed by an elaboration of the findings and technical appendices. The report should be discussed and decisions made on the basis of the findings.

LIMITATIONS OF MARKETING RESEARCH

Inspite of the undoubted value of marketing research, it is important to recognise that marketing research has definite limitations.

The danger of accepting too literally the findings of the research designed to predict what consumers will do under certainties of circumstances. While some techniques have often proved accurate, no technique can guarantee accuracy all the time. In reaching decisions, therefore, marketing managers must use the findings of predictive research along with their own experience and judgement, as well as the expedience and judgement of others on their marketing staff. We were surveying the role of research in decision making, two marketing research managers reported that their managements relied too heavily on marketing research, that they attempted to substitute research findings for executive judgement. Such wholehearted reliance on research in just as wrong as not using research at all.

If the management decision to be made is important, and if the research findings run contrary to the judgement of marketing management, the market test usually is available as a device to determine the correct course. Market testing is a management too that is used far too little by many companies.

When marketing research findings support the judgement of the marketing management team, the marketing manager can feel more confident in his decisions. When research disagrees with executive judgement, it should serve as a warning flag that says, 'Go slow; check further'.

Rarely are there completely right or wrong actions in marketing. Most decisions are made with the expectation that one course of action will produce more profits than another. The findings of many research studies do not indicate a clear-cut course of action; they reveal only that the company will do about as well going in one direction as in another. Other studies clearly indicate that a proposed course of action will be bad or good. New product acceptance, for example, is difficult to predict in advance because so many unknown factors will affect the buy or no-buy decisions at the time they will be made by the prospective buyer. But careful research can nearly always spot a loser and can usually predict a winner.

Properly conceived and executed, marketing research is a termendous aid; yet it is no substitute for management judgement.

CONSUMER RESEARCH

The basis of Consumer Research lies in the fact that mass production and consumption have brought about a standardization in the habits and the tastes of the mass of the people. It has therefore, become possible to examine the habits of a whole market by conducting tests upon small samples.

The uninitiated may be sceptical. It is an affront to our dignity and our belief in our own individuality, to be informed that we are in fact, just one of a herd and that the habits by which we live our lives- and the urges which motivate them—are paralleled by those of the vast majority of our fellow citizens. Whether we like it or not, however, there is overwhelming evidence, not only in the United Kingdom, but throughout Western Europe and the United States of America, that this standardization of taste and living habits exists. It has been accentuated in the last decade or so by a blurring of the boundaries of what were once described as working- and middle-class incomes.

If he is to know his consumer, therefore, the Marketing Manager must know about Consumer Research. He must understand the techniques employed in the selection of test-samples of the population, know how interrogations are carried out and how the mass of information derived from research interviews is coded, classified and pnally presented in the form of statistics. He must understand not only how these statistics are arrived at but how to interpret them and use them as a basis for his marketing decisions.

It is unfortunate that the credibility of the methods used in the conduct of mass surveys should have been put in question by the apparent failure of opinion polls to predict correctly the outcome of elections, both in the United States of America and in Britain. It must be realized, however, that opinion research differs considerably from consumer research. The opinion researcher will, for example, ask people their opinion on a topical controversial issue of the day. Direct questions seeking an opinion rather than a fact may not produce a truthful answer. Respondents may offer an opinion regardless of whether they hold it or not, rather than admit to not having any opinion at all. Similarly, when people are asked how they intend to vote, it is easy for a misleading set of answers to be obtained. There are those who will say that they intend voting for Mr A or Miss B, but when the time comes their opinions may have altered or they may not even trouble to vote at all.

The consumer researcher, however, is dealing not with opinions, but with behaviour. One of the factors which has been established by Market Research organizations over many years, both here and abroad, is the general honesty of ordinary people. When asked to provide facts about how and when and where they do their shopping and the uses to which they put the products which they buy, the great majority of people tell the truth to the best of their knowledge. The main hazard for the researcher is not, indeed, the deliberate lie but inaccuracies which can creep in due to mistakes caused by poor memory. Because this problem is recognized, however, steps are taken, in both the formulation of questions and in interviewing methods, to overcome the difficulty.

We can, therefore, forget the possible shortcomings of the opinion polls, recognizing the additional hazards under which they must work. Our purpose is to consider the credibility of the results of consumer surveys where people are, in the main, invited to respond to a series of questions regarding their buying habits and the uses to which, they put the various types of merchandise in which the survey is interested.

USES OF CONSUMER RESEARCH

Increasing sophistication of marketing methods generally has led to a more sophisticated approach to the question of consumer needs. Whereas Consumer Research was, at one time, solely concerned with establishing the how, the why and the when of the purchase of goods or services, it is now more interested in the use made of them by the ultimate consumer. Indeed, research now concentrates a people's composite activities as distinct from a single activity or process.

We have already referred to the importance of identifying new consumer needs in order to formulate new products and services to satisfy them. It is by a study of the behaviour patterns of people that their unrecognized needs may be established. Modern research endeavours to discover how people live and work in their homes, the times of day at which they take their meals and the particular meals at which they eat certain foodstuffs. Efforts are made to find out how kitchen equipment is used and the part it plays in the general activity of for example, the preparation of a meal or dealing with the family laundry. The finding of research of this nature is a guide not only to the future design of such equipment but also to their methods of promotion and presentation to the buying public.

Consumer Research seeks to establish the total number of potential consumers for a given product and then to subdivide them by sex, age group, marital status, occupation, social class and geographical location. Bearing in mind that a consumer is not necessarily the same as a customer, it is the function of Consumer Research to find out who actually buys the product in question and where it is bought: at the corner shop, or the co-operative store, at a chemist's or a grocer's or at a multiple store. Finally, it seeks to establish when the product is used and how it is used.

DISCOVERING HOW THE CONSUMER'S NEEDS CAN BE SATISFIED

Apart from identifying the consumer to whom we aim to sell our product, the findings of Consumer Research will indicate the kind of product which the consumer is more likely to buy because it will more exactly satisfy his need.

The types of domestic equipment which consumers possess will have an effect upon their use of products in their homes. The optimum size of food storage containers should relate to the size and shape of the storage area of the most popular sizes of domestic refrigerators: the market for humidifiers must relate to the number to homes in which central heating is installed; the market for bathroom fittings is dependent upon the number of dwellings which have bathrooms. Such examples seem self-evident. What may be less evident are those factors which determine the extent of a market. Can one assume that the market for tubular garden furniture is limited to the number of homes with gardens? What about the needs of caravan-owners, many of whom doubtless live in apartments without even a window-box. In assessing the optimum size for a motor-car, for example, there are many facets of the consumer's needs which must be studied. A model aimed at the middle-management executive in the £3,000-£5,000 per annum income bracket must be large enough to provide an adequate status symbol. It must also fit into his garage. He will probably live in a modern house in a modern suburb and have a garage of a standard size. If the car one hopes to sell to him is two inches too long and he cannot close the garage doors he may change his mind and order another make which is just the right size.

Consumer Research can indicate to the Marketing Manager the preference of consumers. Why is one brand of washing-up liquid preferred to another? Is it the quality of the product, its utility, the design of the package or its promotion—its brand image which evokes a favourable response?

It can also alert the manufacturer to possible changes in the market brought about by changes in consumers' needs. It must be remembered that no market ever remains static. It is constantly undergoing change. A product, popular and in great demand today, may be dead inside two years. Similarly, a market can decline and ultimately disappear as the fickle public whim changes. In today's trading conditions, when society, both at home and abroad, is undergoing major changes in its behaviour, its standards and its ambitions, the Marketing Manager must for ever be on the look-out for the advent of new consumer needs which conflict with the current demand for his particular product or service. Thus the popularity and comparative cheapness of foreign travel creates and satisfies a demand and in so doing tends to absorb some of the surplus purchasing power which might otherwise have been spent, for example, on new house furnishings.

Sometimes, Consumer Research can come up with surprises for the Marketing Manager. He may discover that his product is being used, by some consumers, for purposes for which it was not originally intended. Such knowledge may enable him to promote this new need and thus expand the size of his market. Consumer Research will also provide evidence of the consumer's views on competitive products and their performance. What is it about a particular competitive product that the housewife prefers?

The Marketing Manager must be careful in the inferences which he makes from Consumer Research. The wrong inferences will lead to the making of wrong decisions. The value of statistics prepared as the result of research surveys depends entirely on the interpretation put upon them and the use made of this additional knowledge. It is easy to misread a set of statistics. The researcher should ensure that the figures the produces are correctly defined; but the Marketing Manager would be well advised to take nothing at its face value. He should check the sources from which the figures have been obtained to make sure that the definitions used are correct.

METHODS OF CONSUMER RESEARCH

There are three main methods used in Consumer Research. These are: desk research; field research; motivation research. Each method has a part to play in providing the Marketing Manager with a picture of the men and women who will consume his product or use his service.

Desk Research

The starting point for any form of market research is that which can be done—as the name implies—seated at one's desk. There are masses of statistics prepared by government departments, trade associations and market research consultants readily available to the would—be researcher and which he can consult without stepping outside his own office. Before we consider these, however, let us take a look at information which is likely to be at the Marketing Manager's elbow; namely, the records kept by his own company. All trading organizations keep records of one form or another, such as customers' accounts, turnover figures, product sales totals, sales area turnover figures and salesmen's commission records.

(a) Company Statistics. All of this statistical information can provide useful guidance for the formulation of marketing decisions. It may require arranging and analysing. One may have to go back over a period of five years or so, and seek some relationship between products and product groups in terms of volume and turnover. The company's sales figures should provide a barometer to indicate seasonal fluctuations. Indeed, any major fluctuations in turnover must have a cause and the discovery of that cause may well indicate some characteristic of fluctuating consumer needs or buying habits.

Customer Research in the industrial goods field can begin with a similar examination of company records. Since individual customers are identifiable, they can be categorized according to the products they use as well as the after processes to which the products are put. Existing information, rearranged in this manner, can tell one a great deal about the market in which one is operating as well as highlighting factors which hitherto may have been obscured.

(b) Trade Statistics. Statistics relating to the pattern of production and consumption in a particular trade or industry are usually available, in a classified form, from the appropriate trade association. Trade directories, year books, trade periodicals and the financial press are additional sources of market information.

In addition, there are in the United Kingdom, as in most other industrialized countries in Europe and North America, firms who specialize in the provision of trade and technical information. They can provide market research services and will under take to furnish to subscribers up-to-date information on market growth and trends.

(c) Government Statistics. The United Kingdom government provides, through Her Majesty's Stationery Office, a very considerable amount of statistical information of value to trade and industry.

Field Research

Although desk research will provide the Marketing Manager with a great deal of general information with regard to general economic trends, it is unlikely to provide him with any guidance on the consumer's reactions to his own specific range of products or to those of his immediate competitors. It is this kind of research which is vital if one is to pursue a fully consumer-orientated marketing policy.

(a) Consumer Sampling. The foundation of the sample method in consumer research relies on two factors. The first, to which we have already referred, is that the vast majority of people interviewed in a survey will give answers which are true to the best of their knowledge. The second is that it is usually possible to establish that the sample is, within fairly acceptable limits, representative of the whole.

It is important that one should understand the importance of this second factor. Upon the degree of probability which exists in any survey will depend the credibility of its findings. If there is reasonable doubt that !he sample which is being examined is not representative, then it will be better to abandon the project and start again; because a wrong sample will produce wrong results which could be disastrous for those who may decide to act upon them.

How certain can one be that any sample is truly representative of the whole?

Let us consider, for a moment, a typical example of sampling, frequently undertaken by businessmen when entertaining their more important clients. When they order a bottle of wine they will, in the first instance, be shown the bottle with its cork intact. This enables them to be assured that the description on the label coincides with the particular vintage which they have ordered. Subsequently, the wine waiter will uncork the bottle and pour a small sample of its contents into the host's glass for him to taste and test. Now, this conventional method of approving wine is based on the overwhelming probability that the sample which is taken is representative of the whole of the contents of the bottle.

Few consumer surveys are quite so undeniable! Indeed, in an effort to overcome this problem, market researchers have developed a number of methods all aimed to achieve the highest degree of representativeness compatible with reasonable economy.

We have already referred to the possibility that false statements made by individual respondents could have a detrimental effect upon the value of the survey. In practice, however, it has been found that a false statement in one direction is usually cancelled out by an equally false statement in the other. Where it is discovered, in a survey, that a high proportion of false answers have been given to a specific question, it is usually because that question has been badly phrased. Note that I say obviously false answers. When we come to consider the preparation of questionnaires it will be seen that the series of questions put to respondents can be designed in such a way that untruthful answers can be pinpointed without much difficulty.

The obvious advantage of the sampling technique compared with a total survey of the whole market is that the cost of the sample survey is much smaller. However, since the size of the survey will have a direct bearing on its cost, it will be dependent upon the budget which has been allocated. The ideal sample is a microcosm of the entire population. It should be noted that the words population or universe refer, in market research parlance, to the sub-section of the actual population which one is investigating. A universe, therefore, may be the total number of school teachers, or the total number of families with two cars.

It is the composition of the sample that is more important than its size. It should be remembered that the researcher is not trying to establish a large or a small sample upon which to carry out his survey but one of optimum size. If for example, one intends to survey a whole country, one would arrange about 2,000 interviews for the sample. This figure, however, would apply equally to countries with such divergent population sizes as, let us say, the United Kingdom, the United States of America, or Germany or Holland. Where the universe is uniform it is often possible to work with a smaller sample, but it must remain a true cross-section of the population.

Where the universe is not uniform, the researcher will probably divide it up into sections or strata which are uniform. It will be appreciated that when this occurs the size of the sample which is decided upon will depend upon the size of the smallest sub-section. This is because no sub-section can contain too few respondents. However, this could lead to the necessity of interviewing such a large number of respondents that the entire survey would be hopelessly uneconomic.

Let me explain this with an example. Let us say that we select a sample containing 2,000 interviews in order to study the buying habits of a universe of, say, 750,000 people. In order to represent adequately the views of the various categories of people which make up that universe, 50 persons have been included to represent those with an income in excess of £10,000 per annum. Now it must be obvious that 50 is too few to reflect adequately the variety of viewpoints, personal interests and buying habits of the highly paid section of the universe.

The problem is, that if we were to double the quantity of the £10,000-a-year people the whole sample would have to be doubled. That would be very expensive. The way round this problem is to double only the number of highly paid people and increase the sample to 2,050 interviews. A correction is made to the final results when the figures which relate to the answers given by the wealthy respondents are halved. Thus the proportions are maintained and the final results derived from the survey are not distorted. This device is known as weighting the results.

There are various methods of selecting samples for consumer surveys. Those most frequently employed are the probability, the random and the quota systems. In practice, researchers often use hybrid methods to suit the type of research in which they are engaged.

(b) The Probability System. Using the grobability system, the researcher prepares a list of the names and addresses of the entire universe which he proposes to survey. He discovers these names in city and trade directories, telephone directories or professional list. Copies of electoral rolls, obtainable from local authorities, are also used. Once his list is complete, the researcher sets out to select a representative sample in a uniform basis. Thus, if he intends to work with a sample of 5 per cent of the universe, he will select one name in twenty. He will not merely select 5 per cent of the list of names, because to do so would fail to ensure that the spread of names was even.

The researcher must be on his guard lest bias should enter into his sample. It has been found, for example, that people with the same initial letter to their names are not free from bias.

Since uniformity is the essence of this particular method, the interviewers employed to carry out the survey are not allowed to choose the people to be interviewed. Were they to do so, this could introduce bias because, naturally, each interviewer will be biased, to some extent, in the kind of person she selects.

There are a number of problems with the probability system of surveying, Researchers find difficulty in getting a list of all the names and addresses which make up the universe, which is not surprising. Electoral rolls and other published lists of names quickly become out of date. Also, the time spent in selecting respondents from these lists is expensive.

A further problem is that, to maintain the uniformity of the survey, a person whose name has been selected on the list must be interviewed. The pattern of uniformity will be broken if a neighbour is substituted. At first glance this may seem like pedantry carried to excess. On second thoughts, however, it will be seen that the way of life and, therefore, the buying habits of the woman who is frequently out and, therefore, difficult to get hold of, will be different from those of the woman next door who, on the contrary, is readily available simply because she is nearly always at home.

(c) The Random System. The Random System is a simplification of the above. It does not require a complete register of the population which is being surveyed. Small areas of the country are selected at random and in each of these districts one particular address is chosen, also at random, as the starting point of the interviewer's route. Calls are then made at every house in the street whose number ends in a randomly chosen unit. The interviewer then moves to the next street which has been chosen on a random basis and the process is repeated.

A modification of this method is to list, in the first instance, all the districts in the country, urban and rural, and then to select, on a random basis, a limited number of districts for the conduct of interviews. Within those districts houses will be selected at random. Thus the geographical scatter of the homes which have been selected for interviewing is reduced without causing any reduction to the representativeness of the sample.

(d) The Quota System. A further modification and the method most frequently used for consumer surveys is known as the Quota System. Here, the first stage is to decide upon the size of the sample which will be taken and then to stratify the universe. This stratification-or dividing into sections—will be carried out on the basis of age, sex, marital status, income group, occupation, and the size of the town, suburb or village in which the respondents live.

When this has been completed, the entire sample is divided by the total number of interviewing days which are considered necessary to complete the survey. For example, if we assume that an interviewer can complete twenty interviews in a day and that the total number of questionnaires to be: filled out numbers 2,000, the sample will be divided into 100 parts. Each interviewer is then given a quota, in this case twenty persons, whom she must find and interview. She is entrusted with the task of selecting her own respondents, but these must fit closely the various categories the researcher will stipulate, based on the stratification of the universe already carried out.

The Quota System is not considered to be as representative as the Probability or Random methods, but it is much cheaper to operate. The costly listing of the entire universe is eliminated and the interviewer does not have to make recalls to interview specific people not at home at the time of her first visit, as is the case in the other two methods.

(e) The Use of Consumer Panels. One of the major drawbacks to all the above methods of personal interview surveys is that they do not provide a means of supplying continuous information on the buying habits of the respondents.

The Marketing Manager needs, in addition to research reports on specific consumer reaction, some form of permanent consumer audit by means of which he can monitor the buying habits of the respondents, their degree of loyalty to any particular brand and when that loyalty comes to an end and they change to another brand. He also needs some means of gauging consumer reaction to advertising and promotion, not only of his own product, but of those of his competitors as reflected in possible changes to buying patterns.

To provide this continuous information, panels are set up of respondents, selected either randomly or by the quota method, and who are prepared to supply information on their shopping activities over a considerable period of time.

A housewife panel for consumer products would normally consist of about 2,000 respondents, representing as closely as possible a cross-section of the universe under scrutiny They would usually be recruited by personal interview and thereafter communicate with the market research organization by post. They are supplied with a diary in which they are asked to keep a record of all their purchases of certain branded goods. The information required is usually fairly simple, consisting of the name of the brand, the packet size (where this is applicable), the price paid and name of the shop where the product was purchased. At the end of each week (or month) the housewife returns her diary to the market researcher and receives a new one for the subsequent period.

Consumer panels are seldom maintained by single business organizations. The cost of setting them up and maintaining them is very high. They are usually run by market research organizations to provide research data for a group of product manufacturers.

Cost is not the only problem. Researchers have constant difficulty in maintaining a panel once it is set up. The number of housewives prepared to undertake this work is limited and many find it tedious. Too high a turnover of respondents, however, will reduce seriously the very continuity which is the whole purpose of the panel. Furthermore, some housewives find that the task of writing the simple details of their purchases in a diary is difficult. However, those with a low degree of literacy cannot be eliminated from the sample because the semi-literate members of the universe have to be represented.

Perhaps the greatest problem with regard to consumer panels is the danger of bias creeping in simply because the respondents, by undertaking panel membership, cease to be fully representative. They can no longer think and act in quite the same way as other housewives when they go shopping. The significance of their choice of purchases will introduce a degree of self-consciousness not experienced by the hundreds of thousands of other housewives whom they are intended to represent.

(f) Interviewing Methods. The basis for the sampling of respondents in a consumer research survey is to ask them to provide answers to a questionnaire. There are several different methods of approaching respondents, including the personal interview, group interviews, the use of postal questionnaires and telephone interviews.

1. *The Personal Interview.* It is not surprising that the personal interviewer, approaching respondents at their homes, in

the street or at work, achieves a much greater response than any other survey method. The interviewer can by her presence, encourage the respondent to answer each question in the questionnaire and she can assist her by explaining the reasons for the survey and the importance which attaches to the respondent's contribution. Mistakes made in answering questions or misunderstanding of the meaning of questions can be dealt with at the time, thus reducing considerably the number of spoiled questionnaires which would have to be disregarded at the editing stage.

A good interviewer can add considerably to the response she obtains from her interviews by the assessment she makes of the individual respondents. She is often provided with a special form in which she can enter comment of this nature.

The drawback to the personal interviewer method is that it is expensive—Apart from remuneration there is the question of travelling costs, which can be considerable, particularly when a sampling method is being employed which may involve the interviewer in a number of recalls upon respondents. Even with the quota system, which avoids such recalls, the interviewer may have to devote considerable time to finding respondents who have the desired characteristics-age, sex, income bracket, occupation-to fit into her quota. The interviewers themselves must be carefully selected. Apart from all considerations of suitability one must take account of the fact that the interviewer is a personality who will have her own ideas and opinions which, however detached she may try to be, must create some bias.

2. *Group Discussions.* Some researchers select a small group of respondents representing a cross-section of the universe to be surveyed and invite them to attend a group discussion. Such gatherings are usually chaired by an experienced

interviewer who, instead of conducting interviews, puts a number of points to the meeting to provoke discussion.

The resulting conversation can be recorded on tape for subsequent examination by the research team. They are concerned not only with what the respondents have to say but the way in which they say it. By such means the broad opinions of a representative group of housewives may be considered; but the information gathered has, of course, no statistical use.

3. *Postal Surveys.* The conduct of a postal survey which eliminates the need for trained interviewers is obviously much cheaper than systems requiring the employment of paid inter-viewers. There are, however, a number of problems.

The questionnaire sent out to respondents through the post cannot be as comprehensive as that used for a personal interview. Since there will be no interviewer at hand to explain the questions they must be put in an elementary manner and require as little writing as possible on the part of the respondent. The normal method is either to frame questions which require a simple 'yes' or 'no' answer, or to provide several alternative answers to each question and respondents are asked to put a mark against the one they consider applicable.

One of the main difficulties with the use of postal questionnaires is that only about one person in ten will take the trouble to respond. Furthermore, the fact that they have taken this trouble, whereas the other nine out of ten have not, suggests that they are probably not typical of the universe they are supposed to represent.

Various devices are employed to encourage respondents to respond. Sometimes a free gift is attached to the questionnaire and the researcher hopes that the respondent will feel obliged to complete and return the questionnaire.

Like all unsolicited direct mail approaches-of which this is but a specialized category—the accompanying letter of explanation must be concocted in such a manner that the respondent is urged to make the necessary effort to read and complete the questionnaire and post it back. This letter must explain the purpose of the survey in terms which the respondent will under—stand and, ideally, which will excite some interest on his part. It is sufficient to say her that postal surveys form an important part of mail order trading and are frequently used to gain market reaction to new products and new selling techniques as well as the creation of mailing lists.

4. *Telephone Surveys.* Having far less application than the postal survey, market research by telephone has been used to question consumers with regard to purchases of cars, domestic appliances and various types of household goods. It is a method used more widely in the United States where a far greater number of households possess a telephone than is the case in Britain.

   The method is comparatively cheap, immediate responses can be obtained and the interviewer can telephone a large number of respondents in a fraction of the time it would take to make personal visits to their homes.

   There are major drawbacks. Since the possession of a telephone is very far from being universal, respondents reached in this manner will not be typical for many types of surveys. The number of questions which can be put to respondents is, once again, extremely limited. Attempts to establish their age and occupation are likely to meet with an immediate rebuff. Generally speaking, people do not like being telephoned by complete strangers asking them questions and, more often than not, a semi-hostile response is likely to be encountered.

Motivation Research

In all the methods of consumer research which we have so far discussed, the researcher has been establishing ways and means of discovering how people behave in relation to certain products. The questions put to respondents in the probability, the random and the quota systems, and by means of the consumer panel, refer to the make of product they have purchased, the retail outlet from which the purchase has been made, the date and the time of the purchase and the quantity of the product which they have bought. Such information, reduced to statistical form, provides the Marketing Manager with important guidelines on the state of the market and its likely trends and also on the situation of his own product and the products or his competitors within that market.

In spite of this abundance of information, however, one essential question is still left in the air This question is: why does the consumer behave in the way he does?

Upon reflection, it will be apparent that none of the research methods so far discussed can answer this question adequately. We have seen that ordinary people will, on the whole, provide truthful answers with regard to their purchasing habits for a wide range of the goods and services which they buy. When it comes to the question of why they purchase particular products, from a particular retail outlet at a particular time, accurate answers are far more difficult to achieve. For one thing, the motives which prompt a considerable proportion of purchasing behaviour are entirely subjective and it might be difficult for the respondents themselves to offer any logical explanation. Secondly, people's motives for wanting to buy certain products or to use certain products in certain ways, their preferences for one brand as against another, for shopping in one type of store as against another, are rooted in habits or mental attitudes which, even if they were recognized by the respondents, they would often not wish to divulge to the research interviewer. If pressed to provide explanations for their actions, they would in all probability, take refuge, consciously or subconsciously, in evasion or falsehood.

It has therefore, long been recognized that research into the motives of consumers—or, as it has come to be called, motivation research—is a specialized field and demands specialized methods of approach on the part of the researcher.

Motivation Research originated in America. It was found that purchasing behaviour of consumers resulted from influences which could be divided into two groups. The first of these was external influences, such as the size of the family being catered for, the social class to which they belonged, the appeal of the product in its physical form—such as its size, shape, taste or smell—and its emotive appeal by means of advertising and promotions. The second group consisted of internal influences such as the consumer's personality characteristics, acquired knowledge, moral standards, superstitions and religious beliefs.

To tap this subterranean flow of motives the consumer researcher has turned to the field of clinical psychology and has adopted and adapted a number of its techniques. The methods used in Motivation Research are considerably more expensive than conventional methods of consumer research. Respondents are asked to submit themselves to various types of psychological tests such as word association, sentence completion and cartoon tests. These are all designed to establish subjective reactions to certain stimuli, as a result of which—it is claimed—the researcher can classify the pattern of their behaviour.

It is hardly surprising that a method of research intended for commercial purposes which relies upon methods still at the pioneering stage of medical research should not receive universal acceptance in the business world. Indeed, considerable scepticism exists as to the value of motivation research. Apart from doubts as to the validity of its methods, a major drawback is that, in general, it does not lend itself to statistical treatment.

Motivation Research is a complex subject. It is still very much in the stage of innovation and there can be little doubt that, as science delves deeper and deeper into man's mental and emotional processes, there will be greater opportunities for, and confidence in, the motivation methods of consumer research.

The Construction of Questionnaires

All forms of consumer sampling, with the exception of certain types of motivation research, have as their basis a list of questions which the respondent is invited to answer. The construction of a questionnaire is, therefore, a vital part of the research process. The success of a survey will depend as much upon the way in which the questionnaire has been prepared as upon all the other factors we have already considered.

The market researcher will, in the first instance, wish to know exactly what information the Marketing Manager requires and secondly, how he wishes that information to be presented to him. Armed with this knowledge, he will be able to prepare a series of questions for respondents to answer which will be strictly relevant to the purposes of the survey.

In drawing up his questionnaire, the researcher will take account of four main considerations:

1. The general subject of the survey
2. The classification of respondents
3. The provision of control questions
4. Questions designed to establish the information required.

When approached by an interviewer and asked to provide answers to a questionnaire, the majority of people will wish to know something about the survey before they accept. They are likely to ask for whom the survey is being conducted and what is its purpose. Although the respondent has a perfect right to request and to receive such information, disclosure of the name of the sponsor and the purpose for which the survey is being conducted, can, on occasion, be undesirable from the sponsor's point of view. If, for example, one is surveying a market in which one is not currently active, but into which it is intended to enter as part of a diversification programme, such information is obviously highly confidential. To disclose one's hand to competitors at such an early stage could have serious consequences.

There are other reasons why a manufacturer may not wish to have his name disclosed to respondents. If the men and women who are being interviewed are aware that the survey is being conducted on behalf of the manufacturers of a particular brand, this is likely to cause some bias to enter into the way in which they answer the questions. According to the make-up of the individual, there could be a tendency not only to over- or under-criticize the product in question, but also to read into the questions interpretations which do not apply.

To overcome these difficulties it is not uncommon for researchers to omit the name of the sponsor firm from the questionnaire. Alternatively, companies with unknown—and therefore, innocuous—names are founded specially so that their names can be shown on questionnaires and cited to respondents on demand.

Similar problems arise with the question of the title of the survey. Here again, in the interests of security, or to avoid introducing unnecessary bias into respondent's answers, it may be desirable to avoid an exact statement of purpose. This can be achieved by the use of a general rather than a specific title. In his efforts to avoid the disclosure of confidential information regarding his client, the researcher must be equally careful not to mislead the public by stating to respondents things which are not true.

To assist classification and to enable comparisons to be made from the answers of various sub-groups of respondents, it is normal for the first set of questions to establish facts about the person being interviewed, such as:

1. Sex.
2. Age.
3. Marital status.
4. Occupation.
5. Membership of professional organization/trade union, etc.

6. The occupation of the head of the household.
7. Does the family own the house it lives in?
8. Is it rented?
9. Is there a telephone?
10. At what age will the children in the household, if any, leave school?
11. What is the family income?

It will be seen that some of these questions intrude deeply into the respondent's personal and financial affairs and the problem of truthful or untruthful replies has to be faced. Sometimes researchers put such questions at the end of the questionnaire in the belief that by the time this stage has been reached the interviewer will have succeeded in establishing a friendly relationship with the respondent, thus reducing his or her natural suspicison or feeling of embarrassment.

Researchers are often divided on the controversial question of whether or not the name of the respondent should be recorded. There is a strongly held opinion that a guarantee of anonymity allows the respondent to relax and generally produces more truthful replies.

The researcher's next consideration, before he prepares his questions on the general subject-matter of the survey, is to decide upon the number and nature of the control questions which he will incorporate into his questionnaire. Control questions aim to check the accuracy of the respondent's answers to the standard questions. Where an answer to a control question is at variance with the answer given to a standard question, it is apparent to the researcher that incorrect replies have been recorded. When this occurs the entire questionnaire will be eliminated from the survey.

Care must be taken in the wording of the control question. If it merely repeats the original question it is likely to be answered in the same vein and no control will have been achieved. To be effective it must broach the same subject as the standard question but from a different point of view.

In deciding upon the wording of questions and their sequence in the questionnaire, the researcher must bear in mind the mental attitude of the respondent. He, or she, has been approached by the interviewer, who has explained what the survey is about, that they have been selected by pure chance and are; therefore, representative of public opinion and to invite their co-operation in providing answers to certain questions which will contribute to the success of the project. It is important that the confidence of the respondent should be established as quickly as possible as this will enable him to relax and to co-operate in the interview.

The work of the interviewer in achieving this desirable state of affairs will be assisted by the way in which questions are worded and the sequence in which they appear on the form. As soon as the introductory questions, which establish the respondent's characteristics, have been dealt with, it is important to move on to questions dealing with the substance of the survey and which are likely to engage the respondent's interest. One question should succeed another in a logical sequence because this enables the interest to be maintained and avoids the irritation which can occur when the respondent is asked to switch his mind from one topic to another to answer questions which may appear aimless in their intent.

One of the major problems of consumer surveys which are concerned with people's behaviour rather than their opinions, is their dependence upon the memory of respondents. We have said before that, generally speaking, the public is prepared to co-operate in research of this nature and wrong answers are seldom given intentionally. However, questions which relate to such mundane matters as the last time one purchased a certain brand of washing powder are hardly likely to stimulate the memories of most people, and the housewife must be forgiven if she cannot remember the price she paid for it or the shop where she bought it. Experience has shown that, for the best results, one should seek information about goods bought only the day before. Slightly less reliable results will be achieved from enquiries made into purchases of a week before. If one seeks to take the respondent back over a period of two weeks or more, answers of doubtful accuracy can be expected.

As to the type of questions to be used in questionnaires, these fall, generally, into three categories:

(a) Dichotomous Questions

(b) Multiple Choice Questions

(c) Open-ended Questions.

Questions which can only be answered by the words 'Yes' or 'No' are called dichotomous questions. Where these are used in a questionnaire; it is usual to state the alternatives and add spaces for 'Don't know' and 'No answer'. Researchers like dichotomous questions. They make the work of interviewing much easier and also simplify the counting of results. An example of a dichotomous question is 'Did you go abroad for your holiday last year?'

A multiple choice question is one which admits several alternative answers. When these are used in a survey, the alternative answers are provided and usually the respondent is invited to choose the answer with which he agrees. Again, statistical analysis is simplified. A multiple choice question will ask: 'If you went abroad for your holiday last year did you travel by *(1)* scheduled airline, *(2)* charter flight, *(3)* boat and rail, *(4)* boat and by car?'

The open-ended questions provide for much greater latitude on the part of the respondent. He is invited to answer the question in his own words and the interviewer enters that answer on the form. An open-ended question will ask: 'Why did you go abroad for your holiday?'

Care must be exercised in the use of words in questionnaires. They should be kept as simple as possible. It must be remembered that, in the majority of surveys, a cross-section of the population will be interviewed and this must, of necessity, include people of the lowest intelligence and education as well as the highest. Every word which is used should have a precise meaning, because if the respondent is in any doubt as to the meaning of the question which is put to him, he is liable to give a genuinely mistaken answer. Unfortunately, many of the words in the English language have more than one meaning or a different meaning in different parts of the country.

That enemy of the researcher, namely bias, can be introduced unwittingly to a survey by the use of ill-advised questions. If you ask a housewife: 'Do you give your children a cooked break-fast every morning?' she may well imagine that to answer in the negative would suggest that she was failing in her duty as a mother. A better approach would be to say: 'Some children like a cooked breakfast; others have no appetite first thing in the morning. Do your children like a cooked breakfast or do they not like a cooked breakfast?'

Once all the questionnaires in the sample have been completed, the researcher is faced with the task of processing the information he has obtained. The first step is to edit the questionnaires. Editors are appointed, whose job it is to check every questionnaire to make sure that correct answers have been given. This is achieved by means of the control questions which have been inserted for this very purpose. Researchers refer to the 'Triangle Clause' which consists of three related questions within a questionnaire each of which approaches the same subject from a slightly different angle. If it is found that one of the answers to these questions contradicts another, it can be assumed that the answer which has been given to the third question decides the issue.

Having ensured that the information which appears in the questionnaire is satisfactory, the editor applies code numbers to each answer. Where dichotomous and multiple choice questions are used throughout a questionnaire, these are usually coded in advance. The open-ended questions are rather more difficult to classify. They are often grouped and tabulated by hand and those answers which do not fall into any convenient group are placed under a miscellaneous heading.

Finally, the coded answers are tabulated, by hand, by means of punched cards or by use of a computer. From the figures thus produced, the market researcher prepares his statistical tables.

In this chapter, we have considered, in some detail, the methods employed by consumer research and, more particularly, the conduct of sample surveys. In the majority of small and medium-sized commercial firms it is unlikely that the Marketing Manager will become directly involved in the details of consumer research. It is specialized work and few companies have their own market research departments. Even where such departments do exist within the business organization, it is normal practice for the conduct of field research to be undertaken by outside agencies. These can be either independent firms or the market research departments of advertising agencies.

Independent organizations differ very considerably, according to their degree of experience and the nature of the work in which they specialize.

Market research departments of advertising agencies usually specialize in advertising research. There has been an increasing tendency, however, for the advertising agency to attempt to provide a complete marketing service to clients and this has involved them in various branches of consumer research. The general practice is to undertake the organization of a consumer survey, but to sub-contract to outside agencies the work of interviewing, editing and tabulating. The final report on the survey is then presented by the advertising agency's own market research, specialists.

❑

4

Marketing Analysis and Selection

Following environments must help us in understanding marketing environment.

Demographic Environment

The first environmental force to monitor is population because people make up markets. Marketers are keenly interested in the size and growth rate of population in different cities, regions, and nations; age distribution and ethnic mix; educational levels; household patterns; and regional characteristics and movements. We will examine the major demographic characteristics and trends and illustrate implications for marketing planning:

(i) **Worldwide Explosive Population Growth.** The world population is showing "explosive" growth. It totalled 5.4 billion in 1991 and is growing at 1.7% per year. The world population explosion has been a major concern of governments and various groups throughout the world. Two factors underlie this concern. The first is the possible finiteness of the earth's resources to support this much human life, particularly at living standards that represent the aspiration of most people. *The Limits to Growth* presented an impressive array of evidence that unchecked population growth and consumption would eventually result in insufficient food supply, depletion of key minerals, overcrowding, pollution, and an overall deterioration in the quality of life. One of its strong recommendations is the worldwide social marketing of family planning.

The second cause for concern is that population growth is highest in countries and communities that can least afford it. The explosive world population growth has major implications for business. A growing population means growing human needs, but it does not mean growing markets unless there is sufficient purchasing power. If the growing population presses too hard against the available food supply and resources, costs will shoot up and profit margins will decline.

(ii) Population Age Mix Determines Needs. National populations vary in their age mix. At one extreme is Mexico, a country with a very young population and rapid population growth. At the other extreme is Japan, a country with one of the world's oldest populations. Products of high importance in Mexico would be milk, diapers, school supplies, and toys, whereas Japan's population may consume more adult products.

Marketers are increasingly indentifying age groups within age groups as possible target markets. Each group has a known range of product and service needs and media and retail preferences, which helps marketers fine-tune their market offers.

(iii) Geographical Shifts in Population. The 1990s is a period of great migration movements between countries and within countries. As a result of the collapse of Soviet Eastern Europe, nationalities are reasserting themselves and trying to form independent countries. The new countries are making certain ethnic groups unwelcome (such as Russians in Latvia, or Muslims in Servian Yugoslavia), and many of these groups are migrating to safer areas. As foreign groups enter other countries for political sanctuary, some of the local groups start protesting. In the United States, there has been opposition to the influx of immigrants from Mexico, the Caribbean, and certain Asian nations.

(iv) Household Patterns. The traditional household is thought to consist of a husband wife and children (and sometimes grandparents). In the United States today, the traditional household is no longer the dominant household pattern. Today's households include *single live-alones, adult live-togethers of one or both sixes, single-parent families, childless married couples, and empty nesters.*

(v) Education Groups. The population in any society falls into five educational groups illiterates, high school dropouts, high school degrees, college degrees, and professional degrees.

(vi) Ethnic Markets. Countries vary in their ethnic and racial makeup. Japan is at one extreme where almost everyone is Japanese; and the United States is at the other extreme, with people from virtually all nations.

(vii) Shift from a Mass Market to Micro-markets. The effect of all these changes is to fragment the mass market into numerous micro-markets, differentiated by age, sex, ethnic background, education, geography, lifestyle, and so on. Each group has strong preference and consumer characteristics and is reached through increasingly targeted communication and distribution channels. companies are abandoning the 'shotgun' approach that aimed at a mythical 'average consumer and are increasingly designing their products and marketing programmes for specific micro-markets.

Demographic trends are highly reliable for the short and intermediate run. There is little excuse for a company's being suddenly surprised by demographic developments. The Singer Company should have known for years that its sewing machine business would be smaller families and more working wives; yet it was slow in responding. Companies need to list the major demographic trends, their probable impacts, and what actions they should take.

Technological Environment

The most dramatic force shaping people's lives is technology. Technology has released such wonders as penicillin, open-heart surgery, and the birth-control pill. It has released such horrors as to hydrogen bomb, nerve gas, and the submachine gun. It has also released such mixed blessings as the automobile, video games, and white bread. One's attitudes towards technology depend on whether one is more enthralled with its wonders or its horrors.

Every new technology is a force for "creative destruction". Transistors hurt the vacuum-tube industry, xerography hurts the carbon paper business, autos hurt the railroads, and television hurts the newspapers. Instead of old industries moving into the new, many fought or ignored them, and their businesses declined.

The economy's growth rate is affected by how many major new technologies are discovered. Unfortunately, technological discoveries do not arise evenly through time-the railroad industry created a lot of investment, and then there was a dearth until the auto industry emerged; later radio created a lot of investment, and there was a death until television appeared. In the time between major innovations, the economy can stagnate. Some economists believe that the current economic flatness of the global economy will continue until a sufficient number of new major innovations emerge.

In the meantime, minor innovations fill the gap. Freeze-dried coffee probably made not one happier, and antiperspirant deodrants probably made no one more attractive, but they do create new markets and investment opportunites.

Each technology creates major long-run consequences that are not always foreseeable. The contraceptive pill, for example, led to smaller families, more working wives, and larger discretionary incomes—resulting in higher expenditures on vacation travel, durable goods, and other things.

The marketer should watch the following trends in technology.

(i) Accelerating Pace of Technological Change. Many of today's common products were not available 30 years ago. John F. Kennedy did not know personal computers, digital wristwatches, video recorders, or facsimile machines. Alvin Toffler, in his *Future Shock*, sees an accelarative thrust in the invention, exploitation, and diffusion of new technologies.

(b) **Varying R & D Budgets.** The Unted States leads the world in annual R & D expenditure ($74 billion) but nearly 60% of these funds are still earmarked for defense. There is a need to transfer more of this money into researching material science, biotechnology, and micromechanics. Meanwhile Japan is increasing its R & D expenditures much faster and is now spending $30 billion, mostly nondefense, with a good portion exploring fundamental problems in physics, biophysics and computer science.

(c) **Unlimited Innovational Opportunities.** Scientists today are working on a startling range of new technology that will revolutionize our products and production processes. The most exciting work is being done in biotechnology, solid-state electronics, robotics, and material sciences. Scientists today are working on AIDS cures, happiness pills, pain killers, household robots, totally safe contraceptives, and nonfattening tasty nutritious foods. In addition, scientisits also speculate on fantasy products, such as small flying cars, three-dimensional television, and space colonies. The challenge in each case is not only technical but commercial namely, to develop affordable versions of these products.

(d) **Increased Regulation to Technological Change.** As products become more complex, the public needs to be assured of their safety. Consequently, government agencies have expanded their powers to investigate and ban potentially unsafe products. Thus the Federal Food and Drug Administration had issued elaborate regulations on testing new drugs, with the result that industry-research costs are higher, the time between idea and introduction has been lengthened from five to about ten years, and much drug research has been driven to countries with fewer regulations. Only recently have changes been made to accelerate new drug approvals. Safety and healthy regulations have also increased in the area of food, automobiles, clothing, electrical appliances, and construction. Marketers must be aware of these regulations when proposing, developing and launching new products.

Marketers need to understand the changing technological environment and how new technologies can serve human needs. They need to work closely with R & D people to encourage more market oriented research. They must be alert to un-desirable side effects of any innovation that might harm the users and create consumer distrust and opposition.

Natural Environment

The deteriorating condition of the natural environment is bound to be one of the major issues facing business and the public in the 1990s. In many world cities, air and water pollution have reached dangerous levels. There is great concern about industrial chemicals creating a hole in the ozone layer that will produce a "green house effect, namely a dangerous warming of the earth. In Western Europe, "green" parties have vigorously pressed for public action to reduce industrial pollution. In the United States, several leaders—including Kenneth Boulding, the Erlichs, the Meadowses, and Rachel Carson—documented the amount of ecological deterioration, while watchdog groups such as the Sierra Club and Friends of the Earth carried these concerns into political and social action (see Marketing Environment and Trends 6-3).

Marketers need to be aware of the threats and opportunities associated with the following trends in the natural environment:

(i) **Shortage or Raw Materials.** The earth's materials consist of the infinite, the finite renewable, and the finite nonrenewable. *An infinite resource*, such as air, poses no immediate problem, although some groups see a long-run danger. Environmental groups have lobbied for a lab of certain propellants used in aresonal cans because of their potential damage to the ozone layer of air. Water is already a major problem in some parts of the world.

(b) **Increased Cost of Energy.** One finite nonrenewable resource, oil, has created serious problems for the world economy.

(c) **Increased Levels of Pollution.** Some industrial activity will inevitable damage the quality of the natural environment. Consider the disposal of chemical and nuclear wastes, the dangerous mercury levels in the ocean, the quantity of DDT and other chemical pollutants in the soil and food supply, and the littering of the environment with nonbiodegradable bottles, plastics, and other packaging materials.

Economic Environment

Markets require purchasing power as well as people. The available purchasing power in an economy depends on current income, prices, savings, debt, and credit availability. Marketers must pay close attention to major trends in income and consumer-spending patterns.

Nations vary greatly in the level and distribution of income. A major determinant is the nations industrial structure. Four types of industrial structures can be distinguished:

(1) Subsistence Economics.

(2) Raw-Material Exporting Economics.

(3) Industrializing Economics.

(4) Industrial Economics.

MICRO AND MACRO COMPONENTS OF MARKETING

The term 'marketing' can be defined from two viewpoints-micro and macro *i.e.*, firm's point of view and national point of view.

Micro-Marketing. It may be described as the process of formulating and implementing such strategies by a firm (*viz.* product development, pricing, promoting and distributing) that ensures flow of need satisfying goods and services at a profit. According to Kotler "Marketing is a social and managerial process by which individuals and groups obtain what they need and want through creating, offering and exchanging products of value with others". Marketing is a human activity directed at satisfying needs and wants through exchange process.

The American Marketing Association defines marketing as "the performance of business activities that direct the flow of goods and services from producer to consumer or user". According to this definition marketing comprises a wide range of activities *e.g.*, designing, pricing, promoting and distributing goods and services.

In the words of Stanton, "marketing is a total system of interacting business activities designed to plan, price, promote and distribute want satisfying product and services to present and potential customers."

The analysis of this definition reveals the following points:

(a) Marketing is an integrated system. It is not an activity but the sum total of several activities. It is the result of interaction of many activities.

(b) The ultimate aim of marketing is to satisfy human wants. In other words, marketing is consumer-oriented.

(c) Marketing is successful only when it yields maximum profits in the long run.

The concept of micro-marketing reveals two significant aspects. First, marketing must ensure need satisfying goods and services. It should begin with the customer and not with the production process. Secondly, marketing rather than production should determine what products are to be made. These two aspects suggest that consumer is at the centre of all marketing activities. "The aim of marketing should be to know and understand the customer so well that the product or service sells itself."

Macro-Marketing. In a broader sense, marketing may be viewed as a complex system of organisations and processes by which a nation's resources are distributed amoung the people to satisfy their needs and wants. Here the focus is on the total system rather than on the activities of an individuals firm.

Macro-marketing is concerned with how effectively a society uses its resources and how fairly it allocates its output of goods and services. Macro-marketing is responsible for effective performance of the following functions.

1. ***Information Function.*** Under an efficient marketing system there should exist a network of information that links together producers and consumers. If the productive sector has to meet the changing needs of the consumer in a cost efficient manner, the provision of accurate and timely information is vital. For example, it is often complained that producers of agricultural products do not know what the market will pay for the product when harvested. Further, lack of information on supply and demand makes the product dear in some place and cheap in some other places. This cause losses not only to sellers but to buyers as well.
2. ***Equalising and Distribution Function.*** There is always an imbalance in supply and demand for many products. This imbalance is primarily due to geographical and temporal separations. Adjustments are required in holding stock and their equitable releases geographically and at required times. It is true that in such cases transport costs and/or storage costs are incurred but the price variations in many case reveal that such extra costs are offset by price differentials. An efficient distribution system is also capable of maintaining price stability in the long run showering advantages on buyers and sellers as well.
3. ***Centralised Exchange Function.*** In primitive economies markets tend to be mainly physical locations called central

markets, where buyers and sellers meet face to face and exchange goods and services. As the economies grow the exchange process has to be widespread to satisfy the growing demand in width and depth. They may need middlemen/intermediaries as the producers as the producers may not be able to ensure supply throughout.

From the foregoing analysis it is evident that no economy can achieve its objectives and goals without an effective macro-economic system. This is true irrespective of the fact that one is a planned or a market-directed economy. The recent changes that were initiated in Soviet Russia and China are drawing their economies more closer to market economies. In a still broader view, macro-marketing is viewed as a "fundamental societal process which neceesarily and inherently evolves within a society to facilitate the effective and efficient resolution of the society's needs for exchange of consumption values.

DECISION MAKING PROCESS

Decision making is the most important task of a manager of a business and industrial enterprise. If decision making process is divorced from the functions of management, the management process will be meaningless, useless and impractical. The fact is that a manager is a person who takes decisions. In the words of *John Mc/ Donald*, "a buisness manager is a professional decision maker."

While establishing the business enterprise, many decisions have to be taken as to—What will be the nature of business? At which place the business will be started? What will be the amount of capital invested in the business? What will be the area of activities of business? etc. After the establishment of business enterprise, many decisions are required to be taken for the successful operation of enterpise as to—What should be the quantity of production? What should be the quantity of raw-materials to be purchased? From where the raw materials should be purchased? Where the sales must be made? What price should be fixed? What should be the policy of credit sales? how many and of what qualifications of employees should be appointed? What should be personnel policies? etc. In addition to all these, some more decisions are to be taken as to—Whether the production of a particular commodity should be discontinued? Whether a particular branch should be closed? Whether a particular area of sales should be dropped? Whether the business should be dissolved? etc. Thus, various decisions are required to be taken at various levels at various time, and for various purposes right from the establishment of enterprise to the dissolution.

In the words of Peter F. Drucker, "Every activities of management depends upon decisions. *Prof. Earnst Dale* has commented upon the importance of decisions making in the words, "Managerial decision means the decisions which are taken in the course of managerial activities such as planning, organisation, direction, staffing, rennovation and control etc."

Above discussion makes it clear that the decisions are taken in every field of managerial activities. Truely speaking, main function of a manager is to take the managerial decisions and the structure of managerial activities depend upon the managerial decisions.

TECHNIQUES OF DECISION MAKING

There are two techniques of decision making—(A) Traditional Method; and (B) Scientific Method. These methods are described in detail as follows:

(A) Traditional method. This method of decision making is based upon the method of systematic diagnosis. As in the old time a doctor used to treat his patient on the basis of symptions of disease. In the same manner, the business managers decide some definite solution for some definite problems on the basis of their experiences. Wherever that situation arise, they take the decisions according to their predetermined solution. But this method of decision making is not based on scientific analysis. This method is losing its popularity these days because a definite solution cannot be applied at all times.

(B) Scientific Method. Under this method of decision making, a scientific process is applied for taking decisions. *Peter F. Drucker* has described this process as under:

(1) ***Ascertaining the Problem.*** The problem must be ascertained carefully before deciding its solution. Therefore, the very first task in the process of decision making under this method is to understand the problem fully and deeply unless we understand our problem , we cannot solve it. For example, if the sale of enterprise are decreasing and the decisions are to be taken to increase the sales, it becomes necessary that the reasons for the fall in the sales must be diagnosed. There may be many reasons for this fall as—fall in quality of the products, increase in price, fall in customer services, lack of advertisement lack of co-operation of salesmen, heavy competition, etc. Before taking any decision for this problem, the reason for to fall in sales must be established and then the efforts must be made to solve the problems. Therefore it is of vital importance that before making decisions, the problem and the cause of problem must be carefully examined.

(2) ***To Analyse the Problem.*** After understanding the problem, second important step of the decision making process is to analyse the problem. For the analysis of problem, the co-operation of reasearch and development department must be taken. Analysis of problem involves the following:

(i) Who should take the decision?

(ii) What information would be required before taking decision?

(iii) How the decision must be made?

(iv) Who must be informed of the decision?

(v) How can the required information be obtained?

(vi) Who can must be consulted before making decisions?

(3) ***Development of Alternative Solutions.*** After ascertaining and analysing the problem, all the possible alterantives are developed for the solution of problem. All the possible alternatives may be as follows:

(i) To reduce the selling price of product.

(ii) To improve the quality of product.

(iii) To advertise the product incentively.

(iv) To arrange for more effective distribution of the product.

(v) To change the look or packing of product so that it may attract the attention of customers.

(vi) To provide a better after-sale-services to the consumers.

(vii) To discontinue the product.

(4) Selection of the Best Alternative. This is the most important step of the process of decision making. After developing all the possible alternatives and studying them thoroughly, an attempt is made to select the best possible alternative. While making such selection, certain points must be considered. *Petter F. Drucker* laid down the following criteria for such selection:

(i) Economy of Efforts. We must try to choose the alternative in which we can get the maximum results by putting our minimum efforts.

(ii) Risk. Risk is an essential part of the business activities and every decision involves some or the other risk. The only think we can do and we must do is to take the measures to minimise the risk.

(iii) Limitation of Resources. While making a decision the availability of resources to implement the decision must be duly considered. If we take a decision which cannot be implemented because of the lack of resources, it will be useless. Therefore, the limitation of resources must be considered and the decision must be taken keeping in view the available resources.

(iv) Timing. Timing is a very important factor while making a decision. We must take the right decision time. A decision taken at a wrong time is useless even if it was the best. Therefore, the time as an element must be considered important.

(5) To Convert the Decision into Effective Action. A decision is not an end in itself. It is only a means to achieve an end. It is of no use to take even the best possible decisions, if it is not implemented. Therefore, all the efforts must be made for getting the decision implemented. For such implementation, following procedure may be adopted:

(i) Managerial executive must be delegated to required authority to implement the decision.

(ii) Effective communication system must be adopted to communicate the decision to the concerned employees.

(iii) The acceptance of employees must be obtained on the particular decisions so that they may contribute their whole-hearted efforts to implement it. All the necessary steps must be taken to implement the decision.

(6) Following up the Decision. Decision making process is not completed, if the decisions are not effectively followed. It will be of hardly any use to the enterprise, if the decisions are taken and implemented, but not followed. The effectiveness and the uses of decisions can be evaluated only, if it is properly followed. Actual results must be compared with the decisions made and the points of variations must be determined. The reasons for such variations must be established and corrective measures must be taken to remove such variations.

The process of decision making can be made clear with the help of the following chart:

Process of Decision Making

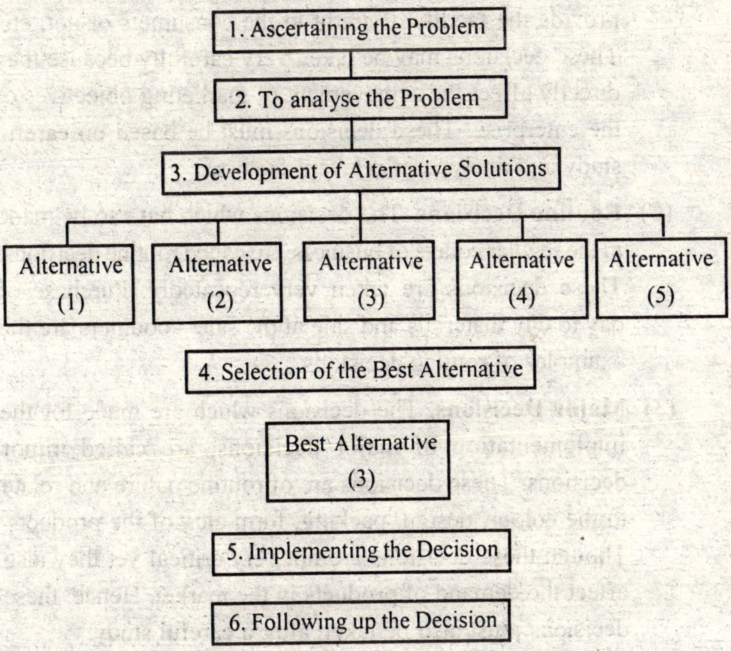

TYPES OF MARKETING DECISIONS

A marketing manager has to take various decisions in the course of discharge of his duties. These decisions aim at achieving pre-determined marketing objectives of the enterprise. Marketing decisions are very critical because the achievement of marketing objectives and the success of an enterprise depends upon these decisions. Marketing decisions define the scope of marketing activities of the enterprise. These also define the duties, responsibilities and power of the employees of the enterprise. Marketing decisions may be of many types as follows:

(1) Major Decisions. Major decisions are considered to be pillars of the marketing activities of an enterprise. Such decisions affect the product line of the organisation or the quality of production or key policies of the organisation. Some examples of major decisons may be as—whether to produce a new product or not; whether to continue the production of an existing product or not; whether to provide the facility of credit to the consumers or not; etc. These decisions may be taken very carefully because they directly affect the achievement of marketing objectives of the enterprise. These decisions must be based on careful study and analysis of relevant factors.

(2) **Routine Decisions.** The decisions which have to be made in the regular course of business, are called routine decisions. These decisions are taken very repeatedly. Purchase of day to day materials and sale at the sale—counters are the examples of routine decisions.

(3) **Major Decisions.** The decisions which are made for the implementation of major decisions, are called minor decisions. These decisions are of routine nature and relate to the colour, design, packing, form etc., of the products. Though these decisions are not very critical yet they also affect the demand of products in the market. Hence, these decisions must also be taken after a careful study.

(4) **Rare Decisions.** Rare decisions are the decisions which are not taken regularly and repeatedly. Such decisions are taken only in specific conditions. The examples of such decisions may be to change the advertising agency, to change the organisational structure, to change the channels of distribution and to change the sales organisation, etc.

(5) **Vital Decisions.** The decisions which affect marketing efficiency and profitablity of the organisation, are called vital decisions. For example, a decision to purchase a new plant or to develop the capacity of the old plant are the examples of vital decisions.

(6) **Recurring Decisions.** The decisions which are made repeatedly at different intervals, are called recurring decisions. These decisions relate to the usual matters of organisation. Decisions of determining sales quota of various

middlemen, advertising etc., are the examples of recurring decisions.

(7) Very Risky Decisions. Decisions involving great risk, are called risky decisions. The success or failure of an enterprise largely depends upon the effectiveness of such decisions. Example of such decisions may be to decide the pricing policy of the enterprise to change the price of products, to appoint a marketing executive, etc. These decisions must be taken by the Top Management.

(8) Policy Decisions. The decisions which decide the marketing policy of enterprise, are called policy decisions. The examples of such decisions are—selection of channels of destribution, selection of media of advertisement, selection of methods of sales promotion, etc. These decisions play an important ole in the success or failure of an enterprise. Therefore, these decisiosn must be taken by the Top Management and based upon sound marketing research.

(9) Less Risky Decisions. Decisions which involve comparatively, minimum risk or no risk, are called less risky decisions. These decisions are taken by the heads of concerned departments. These decisions relate to the appointment of sales representatives, change of colour or packing of products, etc.

SPECIAL CHARACTERISTICS OF MARKETING DECISIONS

Though thc proccss of decision making is very critical in itself because the decisosn taken by the management of an enterpise determine the success or failure of the efforts of enterprise. If the decisions taken are correct, feasible and practical, the efforts of the enterprise will produce desired results and if the decisions are not correct and practical, the results of the enterprise will not be fruitful. It makes it necessary that the decisions must be taken by experienced and intelligent officers of the enterprise a critical and analytical study of the circumstances. The proces of decision making, when we talk of marketing decisions, is much more sensitive because marketing decisions are the most important decisions in an interprise. Marketing decisions determine the scope of marketing activities of the enterprise. The image of the enterprise and the success of its marketing efforts depend upon the nature of marketing decisions. Some of the important characteristics of marketing decisions may be summarised as follows:

(1) **Human Behaviour Oriented.** Marketing decisions are primarily the decisions related to human behaviour. The success of such decisions depends entirely upon the study of human behaviour. Main aim of a marketing manager is to provide maximum satisfaction to the consumers so that the object of earning the maximum profits may be achieved. This aim can be achieved, if the marketing manager understands the behaviour of his consumers. He must try to understand the quality what his consumers may like; the quanity what his consumers can buy; the price what his consumers can afford; the packing, form, colour and labelling, what his consumers may prefer. In addition to this, he must understand the time and place of distributing the goods and services, the channels of distribution the media of advertisement and the method of sales promotion etc.

(2) **Complexity.** Marketing decisons are much more complex than other decisions of the enterprise because marketing managment is a new concept and the techniques of decision making in the field of marketing have not developed properly. Another great difficulty in taking marketing decisions is of the frequent changes in the habits, tastes, and behaviour of consumers. As human behaviour is complex, the process of marketing decisions becomes complex.

(3) **Organisation Effect.** Marketing decisions cannot be free from the effect of organisational conditions and situations. If the enterprise is well managed and all the decisions are taken by responsible and efficient executives, the marketing

decisions will also be sound and practical. Such marketing decisions will contribute in the achievement of marketing objectives of the enterprise.

(4) **Rationality.** As marketing decisions affect the decisions of other departments also and as the success of whole of the enterprise depends upon marketing decisions, it becomes imperative that marketing decisions of the enterprise must be taken carefully and cautionsly. The decisions must be based upon deep and analytical study of all the relevant conditions and situations.

(5) **Long-run Effect.** Another important characteristics of marketing decisions is that these decisions do not affect the activities of marketing department only. These decisions affect the decisions and activities of all other department of the enterprise because the activities of the whole enterprise depends upon marketing decisions. For example, a decision to start the production of a new product does not require the changes in marketing activities only, it requires necessary changes in other departments also, such as—production, personnel and finance, etc. Therefore, marketing decisions are very important for the organisation.

(6) **Birth to New Decisions.** A very important characteristics of marketing decisions is that some of the marketing decisions give birth to many new decisions. A decision to start the production of a new product will give birth to many new deicions, such as—Quality of product; quantity of product; Media of advertisement; Method of sales promotion etc.

PROCEDURE MARKET SEGMENTATION

The procedure of market segmentation consists of following steps:

1. Survey Stage. The researcher conducts exploratory interviws and focus groups to gain insight into consumer motivations, attitudes, and behaviour. Using these findings, the researcher prepares a formal questionnaire to collect data on:

A. Attributes and their important ratings.

B. Brand awareness and brand ratings.

C. Attitudes towards the product category.

D. Product-usage patterns.

E. Demographics, psychographics, and mediagraphics of the respondents.

2. Analysis Stage. The researcher applied factors analysis to the data to remove highly correlated variables. Then the researcher applies cluster analysis to create a specified number of maximum different segments.

3. Profiling Stage. Each cluster is now profiled in terms of its distinguishing attitudes, behaviour, demographics, psychographics, and media-consumption habits. Each segment can be given a name based on a dominant distinguishing characteristic. Thus in a study of the leisure market, Andreasen and Belk found six market segments: passive homebody; active sports enthusiast, inner-directed self-sufficient, culture patron; active home body; and socially active. They found that performing arts organisations could sell the most tickets by targeting culture patrons and socially active people.

This market-segmentation procedure must be repeated periodically because market segments change. For example, Henry Ford assumed that only price mattered. General Motors subsequently outpaced Ford by introducing car brands aimed at different income segments.

The hierarchy of attributes also reveals customer segments. Those buyers who first decide on price are price dominant; those who first decide on the type of the car (*e.g.*, sports, passenger, station wagon) are type dominant; those who first decide on the car brand are brand dominant; and so on. One can go further and identify those who are type/price/brand dominant, in that order, as making up a segment; those who are quality/service/type dominant as making up another segment; and so on. Each segment may have distinct demographics. This reasoning is called market-partitioning theory.

The Hendry Corporation of New York has built a brand-choice forecasting system based on identifying the primary partitioning attributes used by buyers.

STRENGTHS AND LIMITS OF MARKET SEGMENTATION

The chief strength of market segmentation lies in the better understanding of consumer needs, behaviour, and expectations because when information is gathered segment-wise it is more precise and pointed and, therefore, easily and effectively usable. Decisions based on such inforamtion are prone to be more effective.

On account of divergence in the character of different market segments, formulation of the marketing-mix for the aggregate of market will be irrelevant for attaining marketing and corporate objectives. As such, when information is gathered segment-wise about market forces—consumers and competitors and is used for marketing-mix formulation, there emerges an effective mix of marketing inputs capable of attaining objectives. The product development is compatible with consumer needs, product pricing matches consumer expectations and promotional programmes are in tune with consumer willingness to receive, assimilate and positvely react to communications. In substance, the strength of market segmentation lies in matching products to consumer needs that augment consumer satisfaction and firm's profit position.

However, the major limit to the use of market segmentation arise from the inability of a firm to take care of all the segmentation bases and their numerous variables. If each one of these variables is assigned weights and is inter-related, then the number of market segments may run into thousands. For example, a market segment carved out on the basis of region may be further subdivided in terms of sex, age, family size, education, occupation, income levels, religion, ambitions, gregariousness and host of other personality traits. If such a segmentation process is taken to its logical end, it may boil down to one consumer—one segment ratio. It is so because "the market is not a single cohesive units; it is a seething, desparate, pullating, antagonistic, infinitely varied sea of differing human beings—every one of them as distinct from every other one as fingerprints; every one of them living in circumstances different in countless ways from those in which every one of them is living".

In a country like India with a large population and wide geographic, demographic and socio-economics differences described in the subsequent pages, it becomes as formidable managerial task to subdivide market into tiny market segments so as to take care of consumer differences. Still, the strengths of market segmentation outweight its limits and offer considerable opportunities a firm may, therefore, adopt the following four criteria to segment its market:

A. **Market Potentia.** Each market segment must be large enough to justify the investment required to market the product in it.

B. **Demand.** The market segment must have the economic ability to buy the product or service. Simply wishing or wanting it may be relevant for firm's long-range strategy, but for the present it may not hold much relevance.

C. **Accessibility.** The market segment should be sufficiently homogeneous in terms of geography, demography, and socio-economic characeristics to enable the firm to reach it efficiently.

D. **Need.** The market segment should want the product or service. Alternatively, it should have the potential of being educated to want it. For example, illiterate village women-fold as a market segment may not want or have less chances of being educated enough.

SELECTION OF MARKET SEGMENTS

Having evaluated different segments, the company must now decide which and how many segments to serve. That is the problem of target market selection. The company can consider five patterns of target market selection:

1. **Market Specialization.** Here the firm concentrates on serving many needs of a particular customer group. An example would be a firm that sells an assortment of

products for university laboratories, including microscopes, oscilloscopes, Bunsen burners, and chemical flasks. The firm gain a strong channel for all new products that this customer group could feasibly use. The Downshift risk would occur if university laboratories suddenly had their budgets cut and reduced their purchases.

2. **Full Market Coverage.** Here a firm attempts to serve all customer groups with all the products that they might need. Only large firms can undertake a full market coverage strategy. Examples would include IBM (computer market), General Motors (vehicle market), and Coca-Cola.

   Large firms can cover a whole market in two broad ways, namely, through undifferential marketing.

C. **Selective Specialization.** Here the firm selects a number of segments, each objectively attractive and appropriate, given the firm's objectives and resources. There may be little or no synergy between the segments, but each segment promises to be a money maker. This strategy of multisement coverage has the advantage of diversifying the firm's risk. Even if one segment becomes unattractive, the firm can continue to earn money in other segments.

D. **Product Specialization.** Here the firm concentrates on making a certain product that it sells to several segments. An example would be a microscope manufacturer that sells microscopes to university laboratories, government laboratories, and commecial laboratories. The firm makes different microscopes for these different customer groups but avoids manufacturing other instruments that laboratories might use. Through this strategy, the firm builds up a strong reputation in the specific product area. The downside risk would occur if microscopes were supplanted by an entirely new technology.

E. **Single-Segment Concentration.** In the simplest case, the company selects a single segment. Volkswagen concentrates on the small-car market, and Richard D.

Irwin on the economics and business texts market. Through concentrated marketing, the firm achieves a strong market position in the segment owning to its greater knowledge of the segment's needs and the special reputation it gains. Furthermore, the firm enjoys operating economics through specializing its production, distribution, and promotion. If it captures leadershp in the segment, the firm can earn a high return on its investment.

At the same time, concentrated marketing involves higher than normal risks. The particular market segment can turn sour.

EVALUATION OF MARKET SEGMENT

In evaluating different market segments, the firm must look at factors, namely segment size and growth, segment structural attractiveness:

A. Segment Size and Growth. The first question to ask is whether a potential segment has the right size and growth characteristics. The "right size" is a relative matter. Large companies prefer segments with large sales volumes and often overlook or avoid small segment. Small companies in turn avoid large segment because they require too many resources.

Segment growth is normally a desirable characteristics, since companies generally want growing sales and profits. At the same time, competitors will rapidly enter growing segments and depress their profitablility.

B. Segment Structural Attractiveness. A segment might have desirable size and growth but lack profit potential. Porter has identified five forces that determine the intrinsic long-run profit attractiveness of a market or segment. The company has to appraise the impact on long-run profitability of five groups. Industry competitors, potential entrants, substitutes, buyers, and suppliers. The five threats they pose are as follows:

(i) ***Threat of Intense Segment Rivalry.*** A segment is unattractive if it already contains numerous, strong, or aggressive competitors. The picture is even worse if the

segment is stable or declining. If capacity additions are done in large increments, if fixed costs are high, if exit barriers are high, or if competitors have high stakes in staying in the segment, these conditions will lead to frequent price wars, advertising battles, and new-product introductions and will make it expensive for the companies to compete.

(ii) ***Threat of Growing Bargaining Power of Buyers.*** A segment is unattractive if the buyers possess strong or growing bargaining power. Buyers will try to force prices down, demand more quality or services, and set competitors against each other, all at the expense of seller profitability. Buyers' bargaining power grows when they becomes more concentrated or organized, when the product represents a significant fraction of the buyers' costs, when the product is undifferentiated, when the buyers' switching costs are low, when the buyers are price senstive of low profits, or when the buyers' can integrate backward. In defense, sellers might select buyers who possess the least power to negotiate or switch suppliers. A better defence consists of developing superior offers that strong refuse.

(iii) ***Threat of Growing Bargaining Power of Suppliers.*** A segment is unattractive if the company's suppliers are able to raise prices or reduce quantity. Suppliers tend to be powerful when they are concentrated or organisation, when there are few substitutes, when the supplied product is an important input, when the switching costs are high, and when the suppliers can integrate forward. The best defenses are to build win-win relations with suppliers or use multiple supply sources.

(iv) ***Threat of New Entrants.*** A segment is unattractive if it is likely to attract new competitors who will bring in new capacity, substantial resources, and a drive for market-

shares growth. The question boils down to whether new entrants can easily get in. they will find it hard if there are high barriers to entry coupled with sharp retaliation from incumbent firms. The lower the barriers to segment's attractiveness varies with the height of the entry and exit barriers. The most attractive segment to be in is one on which entry barriers are high and exit barriers are low. See fig. given below. Few new firms can enter the industry, and poor-performing firms can easily exit. When both entry and exit barriers are high, profit potential is high but is usually accompanied by more risk because poorer-performing firm stay in and fight it out. When entry and exit barriers are both low, the firms easily enter and leave the industry, and the returns are stable and low. The worst case is when entry barriers are low and exit barriers are high: here firms enter during goods times but find it hard to leave during bad times. The result is chronic overcapacity and depressed earnings for all.

Entry Barriers \ Exit Barriers	Low	High
Low	**Low stable returns**	**Low risky returns**
High	**High stable returns**	**High risky returns**

(v) Threat of Substitute Products. A segment is unattractive when there are actual or potential substitutes for the product. Substitutes place a limit on the potential prices and profits that a segment can earn. The company has to watch closely the price trends in the substitutes. If technology advances or competition increases in these substitute industries, prices and profits in the segment are likely to fall.

BASES FOR SEGMENTING MARKETS

Different variables are used to segment consumer markets. The variables fall into two broard groups. Some researchers try to form segments by lòoking at consumer characteristics. They commonly use geographic, demographic, and psychographic characteristics. Then they examine whether these customer segment exhibit different needs or product responses. For example, they might examine the differing attitudes of 'professionals, "blue collars," and other groups toward, say, "safety" as a car benefit.

Other researchers try to form segments by looking at consumer responses to benefits sought, use occasions, or brands. Once the segments are formed, the researcher sees whether different consumer characteristics are associated with each consumer-response segment. For example, the researcher might examine whether people who want "quality" versus "low price" in buying an automobile differ in their geographic, demographic, and psychographic makeup.

The major segmentation variables are shown in following Table.

Variable	*Typical Breakdown*
1	*2*
A. GEOGRAPHIC	Pacific, Mountain, West North Central, West South Central, East North Central, East South Central, South Atlantic, Middle Atlantic, New England
Region	
City or Metro size	Under 5,000; 5,000—20,000; 20,000—50,000, 50,000—100,000; 100,000—250,000; 250,000—500,000, 500,000—1,000-000; 1,000,000—4,000,000, 4,000,000 or over
Density	Urban, suburban, rural
Climate	Northern, southern
B. DEMOGRAPHIC	
age	Under 6, 6-11, 12-19, 20-34, 35-49, 50-64, 65+

Contd.

1	2
Gender	male, female
Family size	1-2, 3-4, 5+
Family life cycle	Young, single; young, married, no children; young, married, youngest child under; young, married, yougest chilf 6 or over; older, married, with children; older, married, no children under 18; older, single; other.
Income	Under Rs. 10,000, 10,000-15,000, 15,000-20,000, 20,000-30,00 and over.
Occupation	Professional and technical managers, officials, and proprietors; clerical, foremen; operatives; farmers; retired, students; house-wives; unemployed.
Education	Grade school or less; some high school; high school graduate; some college; college graduate.
Religion	Catholic, Protestant, Jewish, Muslim, Hindu, other.
Race	White, black, Asian
Nationality	American, British, French, German, Italian, Japanese.
C. BEHAVIOURAL	
Occasions	Regular occassion, special occasion
Benefits	Quality, service, economy, speed
User status	Nonuser, ex-user, potential user, first-time user, regular user.
Usage rate	Light user, medium user, heavy user.
Loyalty status	None, medium, strong, absolute.
Readiness stage	Unware, aware, informed, interested, desire-ous, intending to buy.

Contd.

1	2
Attitude towards product	Enthusiastic, positive, indifferent, negative, hostile.
Major Segmentation	Variables for consumer Markets
D. PSYCHOGRAPHIC	
Social class	Lower lowers, upper lowers, working class, middle class, upper middles, lower uppers, upper uppers.
Lifestyle	Straights, swingers, longhairs.
Porsonality	Compulsive, Authoritarian, ambitious.

A. Geographic Segmentation. The geographic location of prospective customers may affect their need and willingness to buy a particular product, Dimensions used for geographic market segmentation include:

(i) Region

(ii) Urban, suburban, rural

(iii) Climate

(iv) City size

(v) Population density

Different locations in the market place frequently have sufficient variations in consumption patterns to justify geographical market segmentation. These variations may result from differing cultural heritages or topography and have signficant implicants for the marketer of some products. Furniture manufacturers, for example, find that consumer style preference vary among different geopgraphic sections of the United States. The consumer in the South shows stronger preference for traditionally styled furniturre than does not Midesterner, and Far Western consumers have a preference for furniture styles incorporating oriental influences. Other examples of distinctive regional preference are found in food, clothing, floor covering, paint, and housing. Climatic differences among regions can also have an important marketing impact. Manufactures of outerwear sell heavier coats in the Northeast and Midwest than in the Southeast and Southwest and more rainwear in the Pacific Northwest.

Segmentation by degreee of urbanization—based on whether buyers reside in urban, suburban, or rural areas—differentiates buying behaviour for many products. Although suburban is not as important in most countries as it is in the United States, the urban versus rural differentiation is an appropriate segmentation base in most parts of the world.

City size is another useful segmentation base. For example, some very expensive luxury products serve such a limited share of the total market that only major population centres have sufficient potential buyers to justify distribution. Thus, Rolls-Royce is distributed only a few major cities throughout the world. Still another geographic factors influencing use of this segmentation base is population density. Population in Japan is so dense in many areas that people have gardens large enough to use mechanized garden equipment. Japanese parking problems are so serious that prospective buyers of automobiles must prove that they have access to suitable parking spaces before they are issued permits to buy their cars.

B. Demographic Segmentation. Demographic segmentation consists of dividing the market into groups on the basis of demographic variable such as age, gender, family size, family life cycle, income, occupation, education, religion, race, and nationality. Demographic variables are the most popular bases for distinguishing customer groups. One reason is that consumer wants preference, and usage are often highly associated with demographic variables. Another is that demographic variables are easier to measure than more other types of variables. Even when the traget is described in non-demographic terms (say, a personaility type), the link back to demographic characteristics is necessary in order to know the size of the target market and the media for reaching it efficiently.

C. Behavioural Segmentation. In behavioural segmentation, buyers are divided into groups on the basis of their knowledge, attitude, use, or response to a product. Many marketers believe that behavioural variable are the best starting point for constructing market segments.

(i) ***Occasions.*** Buyers can be distinguished according to occasions when they develop a need, purchase a product, or use a product. For example, air travel is triggered by occasions related to business, vacation, or family. An airline can specialize in serving people for whom one of these occasions dominates. Thus charter airlines serve people who fly for group vacation.

Occasion segmentation can help firms expand product usage. For example, orange juice is most usually consumed at break fast. An orange juice company can try to promote drinking orange juice on other occasions-lunch, dinner, midday. Certain holdays—Mother's Day and Father's Day, for example-were promoted partly to increase the sale of candy and flowers.

In additional to product-specific occasions, a company can consider critical events that mark life's passages to see whether they are accompanied by certain needs that can be met by product and/or service bundles. The occasions include marriage, separation, divorce; acquisition of a home; injury or illeness; change in employment or career; retirement; and death of a family member. Among the providers that have emerged to offer services of these critical occasions are marriage, employment, and bereavement counselors.

(ii) ***Benefits.*** A powerful form of segmentation is to classify buyers according to the different benefits they seek from the product. One of the most successful benefit segmentations was reported by Haley, who studies the toothpaste market. Haley's research uncovered four benefit segments: economy, medicinal, cosmetic, and taste. Each benefit-seeking group had particular demographic, behaviouristic, and psychographic characteristics. Each segment also favour certain brands. A toothpaste company

can use these findings to focus its current brand better and to launch new brands. Thus Procter & Gamble lauched Creast toothpaste offering the benefit of "anticavity protection" and became extremely successful " Anticavity protection became its unique selling proposition.

(iii) ***Usage Rate.*** Markets can also be segmented into light-medium-, and heavy-user groups of the product. Heavy users are often a small percentage of the market but account for a high percentage of total consumption.

A product's heavy users often have common demographics, psyhographics, and media habits. The profit of heavy beer drinkers shows the following characteristics: working class; ages 25 to 50; heavy viewers of television, particularly programmes. These profiles can assist marketers in developing price, meassage, and media strategies.

Social marketing agencies face a heavy-user dilemma. A family-planning agency would normally target poor families who have many children, but these families are also the most resistant to birth control messages. The National Safety Council would target unsafe drivers, but these drivers are the most resistant to safe-driving appeals. The agencies must consider whether to go after a few highly resistant heavy offenders or may less-resistant light offenders.

(iv) ***User Status.*** Market can be segmented into groups of non-users, exusers, potential users, first-time users, and regular users of a product. Thus bloods banks must not rely on only regular donors to supply blood. They must recruit new first-time donors and contact ex-donors, and each will require a different marketing strategy. The company's position in the market will also influence its focus on attracting potential users, whereas firms will focus on attracting current users away from the market leader.

(v) ***Loyalty Status.*** A market can be segmented by consumer-loyalty patterns. Consumers can be loyal to brands (Coca-

Cola), stores (Sears), and other entities. Suppose there are five brands: A, B, C, D, and E. Buyers can be divided into four groups according to their brand loyalty status:

Each market consists of different numbers of the four types of buyers. A brand-loyal market is one with a high percentage of hard-core brand-loyal buyers. Thus the toothpaste market and the beer market are fairly high brand-loyal markets. Companies selling in a brand-loyal market have a hard time gaining more market share, and companies that enter such a market have a hard time getting in.

A company can earn a great deal by analyzing loyalty in its market. It should study the characteristics of its own hard-core loyals. Colgate finds that its hard-core loyals are more middle class, have larger families, and are more health conscious. This pinpoints the target market for Colgate.

By looking at customers who are shifting away from its brand, the company can learn about its marketing weaknesses and hope to correct them. As for switchers, their numbers are growing. The company can attract them by running frequent sales; however, they may not be worth attracting.

(vi) ***Attitude.*** Five attitude groups can be found in a market-enthusiastic, positive, indifferent, negative and hostile. Door-to-door workers in a political campaign use the voter's attitudes to determine how much time to spend with the voter. They think enthusistic voters and remind thm to vote; they try to win the votes of indifferent voters; they spend time trying to change the attitudes of negative and hostile voters. To the extent that attitudes are correlated with demographic descriptors, the political party can more efficiently locate the best prospects.

(vii) ***Readiness Stage.*** A market consists of people in different stages of readiness to buy a product. Some are unware of

the product; some are aware; some intend to buy. The relative numbers make a big difference in designing the marketing programme. In general, the marketing programme should be adapted to the different stages of buyer readiness.

D. Psychographic Segmentation. In psychographic segmentation, buyers are divided into different groups on the basis of social class, lifestyle, and/or personality. People within the same demographic group can exhibit very different psychographic profiles:

(i) ***Social Class.*** We showed that social class has a strong influence on the person's preference in cars, clothing, home furnishing, leisure activities, reading habits, retailers, and so on. Many companies design products and/or services for specific social classes.

(ii) ***Personality.*** Marketers have used personality variables to segment markets. They endow their products with brand personalities that correspond to consumer personalities. In the late fifties, Fords and Chevrolets were promoted as having different personalities. Ford buyers were identified as "independent, impulsive, masculine, alert to change, and self-confident, while Chevrolet owners were conservative thrifty, prestige-conscious, less masculine, and seeking to avoid extremes." Westfall found evidence of personality differences between the owners of convertibles and nonconvertibles, with owners of the former appearing to be more active, impulsive and sociable.

(iii) ***Lifestyle.*** That people's product interests are influenced by their lifestyles. In fact, the goods they consume express that lifestyles. Marketers are increasingly segmenting their markets by consumer lifestyles.

Companies making cosmetics, alcoholic beverages, and furniture are seeking opportunities in lifestyle segmentation. At the same time, lifestyle segmentation does not always work; Nestle introduced a special brand of decaffeinated coffee for "late nighters," and it failed.

PATTERNS OF MARKET SEGMENTATION

Markets consist of buyers, and buyers differ in one or more respects. They may differ in their wants, purchasing power, geographical locations, buying attitudes, and buying practices. Any of these these variables can be used to segment a market.

Figure A. shows a market of six buyers. Each buyer is potentially a separate market because of unique needs and wants. A seller might design a separate product and/or marketing programme for each buyer. For example, Boeing manufactures airplanes for a limited number of airlines customers and customizes its product for each. This ultimate degree of market segmentation, called customized marketing, is illustrated in Figure.

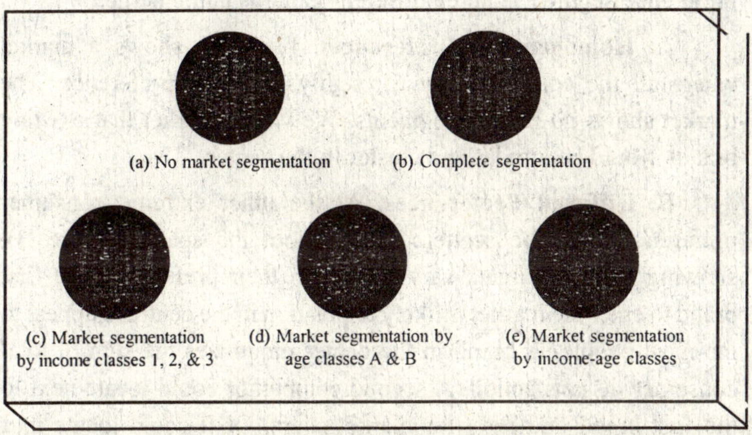

Fig. A

Most sellers will not find it profitable to "customize" their product for each buyer. Instead the seller identifies classes of buyers who differ in their broad product requirements and/or marketing responses. For example, their seller might discover that income groups differ in their wants. In figure a number is used to identify each buyer's income class. Lines are drawn around buyers in the same income class. Segmentation by income results in three segments the numerous segment being income class-1.

On the other hand, the seller might discover pronounced differences between the needs of younger and older buyers. In figure a letter (A) or (B) is used to indicate each buyer's age. Segmentation by age class results in two segments, each with three buyers.

Now both income and age might influence the buyer's behaviour towards the product. In this case, the market can be divided into five segments: Figure shows that segment 1A contains two buyers and the other segments each contain one buyer.

Earlier, we segmented a market by income and age, resulting in different demographic segments. Suppose, instead, we ask buyers how much they want of two product attributes (say, sweetness and creamings in the case of ice cream). The aim is to identify different preference segments. Three different patterns can emerge.

A. Homogeneous Preferences. Figure A shows a market where all the consumers have roughly the same preference. The market shows no natural segments. We would predict that existing brands would be similar and cluster in the center.

B. Diffused Preferences. At the other extreme consumer preferences may be scattered throughout the space (Figure B), showing that consumers vary greatly in their preference. the first brand to enter the market is likely to position in the centre to appeal to the most people. A brand in the center minimizes the sum of total consumer dissatisfaction. A second competitor could locate next to the first brand and fight for market share. Or it could locate in a corner to attract a customer group that was not satisfied with the center brand. If several brands are in the market, they are likely to position thorughout the space and show real differences to match consumer-preference differences.

C. Clustered Preferences. The market might reveal distinct preference clusters, called natural market segments [Figure (C)]. The first firm in this market has three options. It might position in the centre hoping to appeal to all groups (undifferentaited marketing). It might position in the largest market segment (concentrated marketing). It might develop several brands, each positioned different segment (differentiated marketing). Clearly, if the first firm developed only one brand, competitors would enter and introduce brands in the other segments.

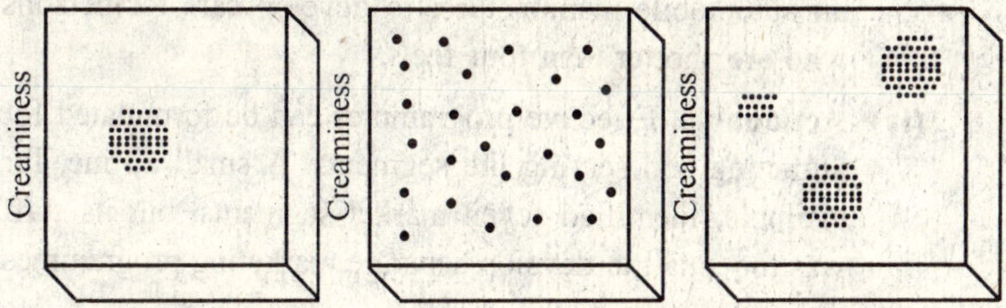

(A) Homgeneous Preference (B) Diffused Preference (C) Clustered Preference

MAIN CHARACTERISTICS OF MARKET SEGMENTS

There are many ways to segment a market. Not all segmentations, however, are effective. For example, buyers of table salt could be divided into blond and brunet customers. But hair colour is not relevant to the purchase of salt. Furthermore, if all salt buyers buy the same amount of salt each month, believe all salt is the same, and want to pay the same price. This market would be minimally segmentable from a marketing point of view.

To be maximally useful, market segments must exhibit five characteristics:

(i) Measurable. The size, purchasing power, and profile of the segments can be measured. Certain segmentation variables are difficult to measure. An illustration would be the size of the segment of teenage smokers who smoke primarily to rebel against their parents.

(ii) Accessible. The segments can be effectively reached and served. Suppose a perfume company finds that heavy users of its brand are single women who are outlate at night and frequent bars. Unless these women live or shop at certain places and are exposed to certain media, they will be difficult to reach.

(iii) **Substantial.** The segments are large and profitable enough to serve. A segment should be the largest possible homogenous group worth going after with a tailored marketing programme. It would not pay, for example, for an automobile manufacturer to develop cars for persons who are shorter than four feets.

(iv) **Actionable.** Effective programmes can be formulated for attracting and serving the segments. A small airline, for example, identified seven market segments, but its staff was too small to develop separate marketing programmes for each segment.

(v) **Differentiable.** The segments are conceptually distinguishable and respond differently to different maketing-mix elements and programmes. If married and ummarried women respond similarly to a sale of fur coats, they do not constitute separate segments.

DETERMINANTS OF BUYER BEHAVIOUR

It is obvious that the social environment provides stimulus to buyer behaviour and psychological frame intervenes in the input processing. The intervening variables in the consumer's decision-making process have been divided by Howard and Shetch into endogenous and exogenous variables. According to them endogenous variables include motivation, perception and learning, whereas the exogenous variables include personality, social class, culture, organisation, and financial status of an individual. The former are found within the individual and condition his/her mind and the latter are located within his decision-making environment and influence him.

It is important for a marketer to understand all these variables so as to know as to why a consumer, behaves in the manner he/she does and how his/her mind is conditioned and influenced. One of the best way to get an explanation of this behaviour is to study the various factors and theories of consumer behaviour as derived from the behavioural sciences, namely, economics, psychology and sociology. Some of these have been discussed here:

Economic Determinants

Economists were the first to advance formal explanations of buyer behaviour. In addition, their studies of income and personal consumption and the concept of discretionary income help us to understand buyer behaviour. Generally, economists visualize the market as being made up of homogenous segements of supply and homogenous segments of demand. Economic theory describes humans as rational buyers who have perfect information about the market and use it to obtain optimum value for their buying effort and money. Price is regarded as their strongest motivation. They compare all competing sellers' offerings and, since all are alike in every respect, they buy the one with the lowest price. Above all, the economic person's behaviour is rational. Under these circumstances his or her buying choices are predictable and yield maximum value.

In some situations this model of the economic person helps us to understand and even predict consumer buying behaviour. It explains why a consumer may select the food store with the most or best "weekend specials" for his or her Friday shopping trip. It explains why a special on brand X may attract customer who normally buys brand Y. It also explains why a consumer, having decided to buy a new Ford station wagon, visits several Ford dealerships to get the best trade in the price. However, for the most part, decison making by individuals is far too compelx to reduce to the simplistic model of economic person. Although this model may explain, for example, why a buyer chooses one.

In striving for a realistic explanation of buyer behaviour, we must discard one assumption that pervades the concept of economic person—that markets are homogenous. Heterogeneity, not homogeneity, characterizes markets. The entire notion of market segmentation is based on the realization that not all buyers are alike—that they differ in numerous and distinctive ways. Further more, this heterogenity is evident on both the supply (sellers') and demand (buyers') sides of every market. Essentially, then, the overal marketing problem of the total economy is to match heterogenous segments of supply with heterogenous segments of demand.

This idea is consistent with those economic theories that explain competition among sellers by emphasizing innovative competition, product differentiation, and differential advantage. The position occupied by every firm engaged in marketing is in some respects unique. Each is differentiated from all other by the characterisics of its products, its services, its geographic location, or its particular combination of these features. Therefore, each firm's survival requires that it presents, to some group of buyers, a differential advantage over other suppliers. Any marketing organisation makes sales to a core market composed of buyers who prefer this source and to a fringe market made up of buyers who find the source acceptable, at least for occasional purchase. A firm's hard-core market is that segment composed of brand loyal buyers. The farther one goes from the core, out to the fringes, the less brand loyalty is shown by buyers, to the point where brand name is of little importance. The core market concept has special meaning for the firm that wants to increase its market share, since this normally means that it must concentrate its markting efforts in areas where its fringe overlaps that of another firm's. The key point is that, for a firm to increase its market share, it must expand at the fringes.

Numerous economic factors influence consumers in the ways in which they spend their incomes for personal consumption. In this section we examine a few of the more important uncontrollable economic factors, that is, those that individual firms cannot influence to any significant extent:

(a) Disposable Personal Income. Goods and services are produced for purposes of consumption; purchasing power is used to convert production into consumption and disposable personal income (*i.e.*, what people have to spend or save after they have paid their taxes) represents potential purchasing power in the hands of consumers. In most years, however, people do not spend all their income. Disposable personal income is used both for personal consumption spending and for saving.

Personal consumption spending tends both to rise and fall at a slower rate than does disposable personal income. But in inflationary periods, such as throughout most of the 1960s and 1970s, and well into the 1980s, spending sometimes rises faster than income. Generally however, in years of higher income, a lower proportion is spent and higher proportion is saved. In years of lower income, the proportion spent tends to increase while that saved declines.

(b) **Size of Family and Family Income.** Size of family and size of family income affect spending and saving patterns, but infortunately, little research has been reported on these relationships, and what studies have been done are relatively old. Two studies are cited here to illustrate the type of research that can provide useful information concerning spending behaviour as it relates to size of family and family income. The Wharton study disclosed that in urban families with lower incomes, average personal consumption spending exceeded income. it also showed that the average propensity to consume declined rather rapidly as income rose above the poverty level.

Findings of Researchers imply that significant changes occur in a family's spending and saving pattern as it moves from one income bracket to another. They also indicate that changes in the distribution of all the families in a population, relative to income brackets, may bring about significant changes in marginal propensities to consume and to save.

(c) **Consumer Credit.** Availability of consumer credit influences the pattern of consumer spending. Through credit, which allows one to buy now and pay later, a consumer commands more purchasing power than that represented by his or her current income. Availability of credit has been a key factor in the rapid growth of the markets for mobile homes, boats, camping trailers, and the like.

(d) **Consumers' Income Expectations.** The incomes that consumers expect to receive in the future have some bearing on their present spending patterns. In particular, spending for automobiles, furniture, major appliances, and other expensive items tends to be influenced by consumer's optimism or pessimism about future income.

(E) **Consumer's Liquid Assets.** Consumer buying plans are influenced, especially those for "big-ticket" items, by the size of their holdings of liquid assets—that is, cash and other assets readily convertible into cash, for example balances in checking and savings accounts, shares in savings and loan associations, deposits in credit unions, and holdings of government bonds and readily marketable stocks and bonds. Even though a consumer may buy with current income, the freedom with which he or she spends is influenced by his or her accumulation of liquid assets. Retired and unemployed individuals may use liquid assets to buy everyday necessities. Other consumers may use liquid assets to meet major medical bills and other emergencies.

(f) **Discretionary Income.** A family with money left over after buying such necessities as food, clothing, shelter, and transportation has discretionary income.

Even small fluctuations in income cause sharp repercussions in consumer's purchases of durables. This traces partly to the fact that consumers can postopone or speed up their purchase of such durables as automobiles, furniture, and major applicances. If a family is temporarily short of income, it can use the old refrigerator for another year or so. Or, if it finds itself suddenly with more discretionary income, it may replace the refrigerator this year instead of next. The quick response of durable goods expenditures to income changes traces also to the wide use of instalment credit in financing such purchases. Consumers are willing to increase instalment debt when income is rising and are reluctant to incur additional indebtedness when income is declining. Lenders are also more agreable to debt creation in prosperous times. Purchases of nondurables and services which are much less postponable than purchases of durables, react less violently to changes in income.

Sociological Determinants

Sociologists view marketing as involving the activities of groups of people motivated by group pressures as well as by individual desires. Their studies of sociological influences have emphasized the signficance of reference groups, the individual's concept of social role, the diffusion process, and social class as influences on hunan behaviour. These studies have demonstrated the importance of social factors in analyzing and influencing consumer behaviour.

(a) **Reference Groups.** The people with whom an individual regualrly associates exert strong influences on his or her beahviour. He or she must conform at least partially to their standards of beahviour to gain group acceptance. An individual's behaviour is also influenced by groups with whom he or she has little regular contact but with whom he or she identifies closely. Both types of groups are called reference groups, which include family and peer groups, social groups, and others, such as religious fraternal organisations.

(i) ***Primary Groups.*** These groups, fundamental in determining the social nature of the individual, are groups of people engaged in intimate, face to-face contact and cooperation. The most pervasive and traditionally the most influential primary group is the family, but with the emergence of the modern small, two-generation family, much of this influence has passed to other primary groups, particularly peer groups. Peer groups are composed of individuals who spend considerable time together and are of fairly common age and social background. Among children, these are often play groups; among adults, they include neighbourhood and community groups. Other groups with varying degrees of socializing influence are religious, educational, and political institutions and work groups.

Each individual may hold membership in several different primary groups. At work one may be a part of a close-knit, friendly group of co-workers. As a Church member, one may or may not have close personal contacts with other members. As a member of social or fraternal organisations, one may be a part of still other primary groups. Any of these groups is classified as a peer groups if it is sufficiently homogeneous. Purely social groups are most likely to qualify. Some peer groups transfered national boundaries; scientists and professional people often identify strongly with counterparts in other nations. The peer groups has the greatest influence on the individual as a consumer because the group's general interests and mode of life are most nearly like his or her own.

(ii) ***Individual's Concept of Social Role in Groups.*** The way in which a person sees his or her role in the social groups in which he or she holds membership is important in explaining the person's motivation, A "rugged individualist" may enjoy establishing a reputation as one who set his or her own patterns of behaviour within existing group norms of acceptable conduct. Individualism was once a common mode of beahviour in the united States and is still important in some nations. Group behaviour has since evolved and become more important in the United States. The newer mode of behaviour requires close conformity to group norms. The group-oriented individual is anxious to fit into the behaviour patterns of his or her peers. What they do, the individual must do. This does imply, however, that the individual's pattern of behaviour is rigidly frozen. Groups norms may change, and the individual adjusts his or her behaviour accordingy. The

group-oriented individual is seldom motivated by the traditional appeal of "being an innovator" or "leading the pack." To be motivated to action, one must first be persuaded that the suggested action is accepted by one's peers as the proper thing to do.

(iii) ***Significance of Reference Groups to Marketing.*** Knowledge of reference group and their influences makes it easier to explain why consumers behave in particular ways and-more important to marketers-to predict their behaviour. It explains, for example, why two groups of young people in the same community-one, high school seniors, and the other, college freshmen—adopt different styles of dress or other behaviour even though they are nearly the same age and come from similar family backgrounds. Even within a college freshman group, different reference groups dictate wide variations in dres and behaviour. Even the same individual behaviour differently at different times as he or she identifies with different reference groups. A young executive, for example, may dress and act conservatively when on the job and in other contact with businesss associates, but off the job he or she may be a sportscar racing buff and behave and dress very differently.

(iv) ***Influentials.*** An influential is a person who serves as an opinion leader of a group. Such opinion leaders are not confined to a single social class; they are found at all levels of society. Outwardly, influentials and those they influence (*i.e.*, others in the same social groups) are very much alike—they have similar incomes, occupations, family backgrounds, and so on. According to one sociologist, an individual's influence is related to; *(1)* who one is, *(2)* what one knows, and *(3)* whom one knows. For example, an unmarried girl may be a fashion leader because of who she is; and older woman

her group's cooking expert because of what she knows; and a man his group's political leader because of whom he knows, not only in the group but also outside it.

Influentials play key roles in marketing. If an influential tries or uses a product, his or her followers are prone to do the same. Marketers, therefore, often target their promotional efforts to reach influentials and, through them, reach their followers by word of mouth or other subtle influences exterted by the influentials.

(b) **The Diffusion Process.** The social process of spreading information about new products or services to persuade consumers to accept them is known as diffusion. Studies of the diffusion process reveal that most users do not adopt an innovation simultaneously. The first groups to adopt an innovation is made up of a small number of "innovators." They are soon copied by another groups, who, although not venturesome enough to try first, want to be among the early users. Gradually, members of other groups adopt the innovation until it finally reaches market saturation. For a dramatically new product, such as television, the entire process may take ten years or more.

Fig. 'B'. The diffusion process is visualized as curve approching a normal distribution, with 16 per cent of the consumers in the combined innovator and early adopter groups, 34 per cent each in the early and late majority groups, and 16 per cent in the laggard group. It is important to identify target market segments at each stage in the diffusion process. In the intial phases of market introduction, for instance, effort and money may be wasted if the marketer tries to cultivate the entire market all at once.

The various adopter groups exhibit marked differences. The innovators are usually the youngest and have the highest social status and wealth; they are frequently cosmopolites and have professional, business, and personal contacts outside their own immediate social circles. Those in the early adopter groups are generally influentials but their contacts are restricted largely to their own local group, they enjoy high status within their own social groups, and they are usually younger than those in the groups followings. Those in the early majority group are the most deliberate; they will not consider buying a new product until a number of their peers (innovators and early adopters) have done so. Those in the late majority have below-average income and social prestige and are older than members of earlier groups. Laggards have still lower incomes and social status; by the time they buy a new product, the earlier groups are often already trying something newer.

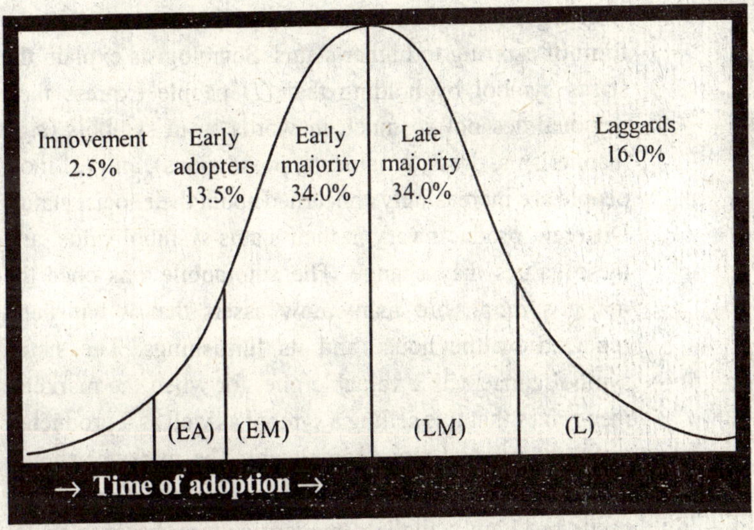

Fig. 'B' Classification of Adopter Groups

(c) Social Classes. Every society classfies its members according to some social hierarchy. All have people who occupy positions of relatively higher status and power. Most sociologists divide American society into three broad, roughly defined classes; the upper, middle, and lower classes. W. Lloyd Warner, on the basis of studies in three American towns, set up a hierarchy of six social classes; upper upper, lower upper, upper middle, lower middle, upper lower, and lower lower. Under Warner's system the class status of each person is ascertained by asking his or her equals, superiors, and inferiors to rank the person. This dependence on the ratings of others has been the main criticism of the Warner system. The ordinary citizen does not think in terms of this complex hierarchy and, when asked to classify his or her fellow citizens into the six groups, he or she shows little agreement with other who are asked to do the same thing.

(d) **Status Symbols.** Despite difficulties in classifying individuals by social class, most sociologists agree that the twin urges for self-expression and self-betterment take the form of aspiring to higher status. Sociologists explain the status symbol by holding that *(1)* people express their personalities not so much in words as in symbols (*e.g.*, mannerisms, dress, ornaments, possessions), and *(2)* most people are increasingly concerned about their social status. Different products vary in their status sysmbol value, and these values may change. The automobile was once the major symbol, but many now assert that it has been replaced by the house and its furnishings. The status symbol concept is a valuable one, for when the marketer recognizes that it is selling a symbol as well as a product, it views its product more completely. The marketer should understand not only how the product satisfies certain needs but how it fits into modern culture, because social classses exhibit differences in life-style."

Cultural Anthropological Determinants

Every culture evolves unique patterns of social conduct. Analysis of these patterns help in explaining the buying behaviour of individuals. Thus, the Japanese culture provides for certain patterns of eating, of dress, and social interaction; the Arbain culture provides for different patterns and both are different from those prevalent in the United States. Many aspects of American culture and subcultures within the United States are unique, including the roles of ethnic groups, religion, women in society, leisure time, and fashion as well as the population composition itself.

(a) **Religions.** Whereas the predominant religions of some nations stress passive acceptance of life, the Christian and Jewish religions, which comprise the basic religious heritage of American society, emphasize the perfectibility of people and their environment and, hence, encourage them to improve themselves and their way of life. Therefore, the production and consumption of goods are acceptable activities because they contribute to these goals. Within the American Judeo-Christian religious pattern, however, there are many individual sect and creeds. And although they share similar feeling about the overall social roles of production and consumption, consumption patterns of selected foods, beverages, and apparel very considerably among them. In other nations, religion has a different impact. Hinduism, for example, with its passive acceptance of one's role, affects consumption patterns in India.

(b) **The Role of Women.** Roughly one-half of adult American women work and have incomes of their own; labour-saving appliances provide the other half with more time free of domestic responsibilities and, hence, more time for shopping. American women has either sole or major responsibility for making many kinds of purchases and exert increasing influence on all buying decisions. As the women's movement has gathered strength, increasing numbers of women take active rather than passive roles in society—this trend has great signficance to marketing, especially in the choice of advertising themes. Throughout the world, women's role varies from a very small but growing place of women in Arab countries to the place of near equality in Scandinavia.

(c) **Ethinic Groups.** The United States is a melting pot of cultures and peoples, but this blending has not been complete. An identifiable American national culture has emerged, but it has not equally permeated all portions of society or all geographic regions. There is, for example, an African influence not only in the Deep South but wherever black people have moved in large numbers, a Mexican influence in the Southwest, a Scandinavian influence in Minnesota and the Pacific Northwest, and a Cuban and Puerto Rican influence in many cities, including Miami, Chicago, Washington, D.C., New York, and Philadelphia. Although ethnic differences tend to decrease with each generation in the United States, their continuing existence helps to explain differences in consumer motivation and behaviour that would not exist in a country with a population of common cultural heritage. Yet there are also nations which have multiple cultural heritages that remain distinct for generations, as, for example, Switzerland. In such nations, marketing plans must take into account variations in the different cultures.

(d) **Fashion.** The role of fashion in American society has been growing in importance. With widespread ownership of television sets, not to mention rising circulations of magzines and newspapers and the increasing mobility of consumers, fashion news is disseminated in minimum time. The time span covered by the appearance of a new fashion, its adoption by a few pacesetters, its rise to popularity, and its subsequent decline is becoming progressively shorter. At the same time, expansions in discretionary income permit consumers to spend more in their attempts to satisfy the desire for change. Since there are increasing numbers of group-oriented people and fewer individualists more importance has been placed on conforming to fashion changes.

(e) **Leisure Time.** Increasing number of people have greater amounts of leisure time, and this is reflected in changes in value and the way of life. Instead of buying an expensive car to impress friends, a consumer may buy an economy model in order to buy a boat, shop, or fishing equipment. New homes are planned to simplify participation in leisure-time activities. People have ceased being producers for much of their lives and have become active consumers for the products and services that go along with increasing leisure. The old Puritan dictum that "For Satan find some mischief still for idle hands to do" is being overthrown, but the Puritan influence still remains in the United States. People refer to "active" leisure rather than just to "leisure"—the active disassociating leisure from the guilt-loaded idea of 'loafing.''

(f) **Population Composition.** Most of the population growth throughout the world is in metropolitan areas, but the United States, it is in the suburbs rather than in the cities themselves. This trend has marketing significance because the subordinate often represents a different market than the city dweller. The suburb retains much of the character of a small town—thus, neighbourhood and local social group strongly influence individual consumption patterns.

The population composition of the central core cities has been changing to a predominantly low-income and poverty-level group of consumers. At the same time, an increasing proportion of central-city residents are members of minority groups—from 1960 to1980, for instance, New York's black population more than doubled. Low-income and ghetto groups are often served by different marketing institutions than those serving others; recent studies have raised questions as to whether such groups are being served adequately. One counter trend should be mentioned: the "back-to-the-city movement," a social phenomenon evident in certain large cities that can be traced to the increased giving inconveniences resulting from the extreme sprawling of sub urban areas.

Psychological Determinants

There have been three major approaches to the development of a psychological theory of human behaviour: the experimental, the clinical, and the gestalt. Experimental psychology has concentrated upon physiological tensions or body needs as motivational forces and has experimented with both human beings and animals. In clinical psychology, the basic physiological drives are examined as they are modified by social forces. Gestalt psychology, often called social psychology, regards the individuals and his or her enviornments as an indivisible whole and considers individuals behaviour as being directed toward various goals. Each approach adds to our understanding of human behaviour, but thus far no single psychological theory of consumer motivation is completely adequate or satisfactory in explaining buyer behaviour. Consequently, marketing has borrowed those theoretical concepts that seem most applicable.

(a) **Attitudes and Learning.** Studies of learing and the related areas of recognition recall, and habitual response have furnished markets with several keys to understanding consumer behaviour. Concept borrowed from learning theory help in answering such questions as these; How do consumers learn about products offered for sale? How do they learn to recognize the recall these products? By what process do they develop buying and consuming habits?

The current trend in psychological thinking is to look at the total experience of the individual and to consider learning as a process in which total functions are altered and rearranged to make them more useful to the individual. Particualr external stimuli do not always activate predictable responses, because motives and other factors internal to the individual also affect responses. What does this mean for the marketer? Simply that the buyer is influenced not only by external stimuli—for example, the marketer's promotion—but also by internl factors.

(b) **Motiation—Various Explanations of Buyer Behaviour from Clinical Psychology.** Clinical psychology has evolved from the pioneering work of Signmund Freud. The principal motivation research techniques in marketing trace to concepts originally developed by clinical psychologists. Among the most important of these concepts are as follows:

1. ***The Unconsicous.*** This concept was championd by Signmund Freud, the founder of psychoanalysis. According to him, the mind contains ideas and urges—some conscious and some beneath the threshold of consciousness but all influencing behaviour. People are not consciously aware of all their motives and this explains why consumers are often unable to articulate their real reasons for buying or not buying. Recognizing the existence of the unconscious mind, motivation researchers use indirect approaches, such as depth interviewing. More conventional research approaches, such as direct questioning, have been unsuccessful in providing data sufficiently reliable to justify predictions of consumer behaviour. Practical marketers, of course, have long known that there are often wide discrepancies between what people say they will buy and what they actually do buy.

2. ***Free Association.*** The principle of free assoicaiton, which traces to Freud and is used extensively in psychoanalysis, has also been put to use by motivation researchers in their development of indirect research techniques. As Newman says, "The basic idea is that if a person gives up the usual logical controls he exercises over his thoughts and says whatever comes into his mind at the moment in the presence of a skilled listner, unconscious feelings and thoughts can be discovered." Thus, an application of the principle of free association is found in in-depth interviewing, many of the techniques of which take the form of word association tests, in which respondents are asked to give the first word that comes to mind for each of a list of unrelated words. Given the word rain, for example,

the respondent might reply drop. Among the many marketing applications of word association tests are those of screening possible names for new products, measuring the penetration of advertising appeals, and approximating the market shares of different competitors.

3. ***Rationalization.*** This concept relates to the mental processs of finding reasons to justify an act or opinion that is actually based on other motives or grounds than those stated, although this may or may not be apparent to the rationalizer. In advertising, rationalization may often by capitalized upon by providing readers or listeners with a plausible, acceptale reason for buying in situations where they may be unwilling, consciously or unconsciously, to admit the real reasons. The prevalence of rationalization in our society explains why such direct quesions as "why did not buy this?" or "What were your reasons for buying?" so often fail to uncover the real buying motives. Thus, when it is suspected that rationalizing is a factor in consumer behaviour, indirect research approaches, such as depth interviewing, are used.

4. ***Projection.*** This concept concerns the reaction that occurs when a person, seeing someone else facing a certain problem or situation, assumes that the other person's reactions would be the same as his or her own. In other words, he or she ascribes his or her own motives to the other person. Putting the projection concept to practical use, motivation researchers have designed projective techniques (*e.g.*, the stimulus picture) that provide a means for uncovering consumers' hidden or unconscious motives and attitudes.

Other Associated Concepts

It is true that the human mind working at the unconscious and subconscious levels is an important determining factor in consumer behaviour. Nevertheless, there are other important factors assoicated with the consumer personality which exert considerable influence on his purchasing decisions. These factors include the following:

(i) **Perception.** We have learnt that a person is motivated to act when an appropriate stimulus is offered. But there is an intervening factor in between stimulus and response. The response is dependent on the way the stimulus is interpreted by the person towards whom it is focussed. Kerby has described such interpreted stimuli as perception. He further says that a wide range of things that can happen to either stimuli, the observer or the situational elements, will cause two people receiving what appears to be precisely the same stimulus to interpret it differently. People behave in response to a need, but the specific response will be determined, in a large measure, by the individual's assessment of the benefits it will produce, which almost inevitably is an interpretational matter. Therefore, according to Britt "the various ways in which the consumer perceives products and services play a large part in his behaviour in the market place". A consumer may perceive satisfaction-delivering attributes in a product whereas an other may not. It may be so on account of the product's image in the market place notwithstanding technical superiority of the competing brands.

(ii) **Personality Traits.** While highlighting the personality in consumer behaviour, psyhologists with interest in marketing, have often referred to the contributions of personality traits. According to Britt, every one has a very personal and unique way of responding to his environment. In fact, our ways of behaving are usually sufficiently unique to enable other individuals to describe us fairly accurately as talkactive, shy, bold, timid or otherwise. When our friends use such adjectives in speaking about us they are referring to our behaviour traits. Personality traits have been defined as "those characteristics that account for difference among people and that are predictive of their behaviour". More specifically, a trait has been defined as "any distinguishable, relatively enduring way in which one individual differs from another". Thus, behaviour of every individual is different from another and can be identified in terms of certain unique characteristics called traits. These personality traits have been classified in a variety of ways depending upon the type of personality measurement techniques used.

(iii) Attitude. Like personality traits attitudes of consumer also influence the buying behaviour of people. A loook at the buying decisions process shown in Fig. makes it clear that the decision depends upon the pre-disposition of the consumer. The predisposition, whether positive or negative, towards a product may be explained with the help of his attitude towards that product or the company promoting it. Allport has defined attitude as " mental or neural state of readiness organized through experience, exerting a directive or dynamic influence upon the individual's response to all objects and situations, with which it is related. Simply stated, attitude may be described as a predisposition of a person to act or react in a certain manner towards an object or stimulus, say, a person or product. Psychologists have recognised two major components of attitude, namely, cognitive and affective. The cognitive component consists of knowledge or beliefs about an object while the affective component consist of the way a person feels towards an object. An attitude may be either cognitive or affective or both. When it is a combination of two, it is relatively more stable.

Nevertheless, conflict in a person's attitudes does exist at times. This makes prediction of behaviour difficult. Notwithstanding, an understanding of attitudes provides a useful guide to consumer behaviour. It is often said that atttidues, even if accurately known, do not provide an infallible guide to consumer beahviour. In this reagrd, Kerby has pertinently remarked that "a guide does not have to be infallible to be useful. Rather, the fact that behaviour does not invariably follow attitudes is a complication with which marketers must cope".

(iv) Self-Concept. Still another concept relevant to the study of consumer behaviour is that of self-concept or self-image. According to it, an individual's behaviour is conditioned by his own image as viewed by himeslf or the manner in which he wants others to see him. The view of Self inlcudes not only one's physical being but evaluations and definitions of Self in terms of strength, sophistication, fairness honesty, etc.

(v) Gestalt Approach. Gestalt psychologists believe that an individual perceives products and ideas as parts of the whole instead of isolated and segregated segments. It is based on the premise that the 'total is different from that sum of its parts'. The term gestalt means 'form' or 'configuration'. The Gestalt theory states that stimuli area perceived in relation to the ogranisation of one's experiences. Also, every person tends to organise parts of information and ideas into whole so as to respond to stimuli. It is so because perception based on parts differs from that based on the whole. Therefore, marketers should attempt to avoid action which by itself may not be negative but becomes so when combined with other parts of actions already initiated or likely to be initiated. It is so because consumer will not think of only one action of marketers but the totality of the actions. For example, a marketer has built up his image as the one who sells highly priced quality products through prestigious stores for high-income groups consumers. If this marketer goes in for periodic reduction sales then his consumers would add this information to other parts and organise another whole or gestalt which may not be compatible with their self-image. Thus, the marketer would not tend to lose his clientale on account of a mis-fitting part which by itself is not harmful but becomes so when combined with others.

(vi) Cognitive Dissonance. Largely based on the gestalt approach, the Theory of Cognitive Dissonance was propounded by Festinger. This theory is based on the premise that a person strives towards consistency (consonance, agreement, equilibrium) wihtin his cognitive structure (set of beliefs about products, people, events, and other objects) and attempt to reduce tension so as to make life comfortable'. Inconsistency (disharmony, frustration) which has been called dissonance by Festinger, is a state of psychological tension/anxiety which may result from any decision, say, purchase of a product. It has, therefore, been also called post-decision anxiety.

This theory centres around the idea that if a person knows various things that are not psychologically consistent with one another, he will, in a variety of ways, try to make them more consistent.

NEED SATISFACTION AND BUYER BEHAVIOUR

Psychological studies indicate that human activity, including buying behaviour, is directed toward satisfying certain needs. Not only individual acts in the same way in the effort to fulbill these needs; the actions of the each not only depend upon the nature of the needs themselves but are also modified by the individual's particular environmental and social background. The motivation for any specific action derives from the tensions built up to satisfy needs, needs that frequently lie beneath the threshold of consciousness. Whatever action the individual takes is directed toward reducing these tensions.

Although clinical psychologists have not agreed on a single list of needs.

The different lists available show more agreement than disagreement. In one list, illustrated in Figure above 'A', Maslow enumerates needs in their order of importance for most people with

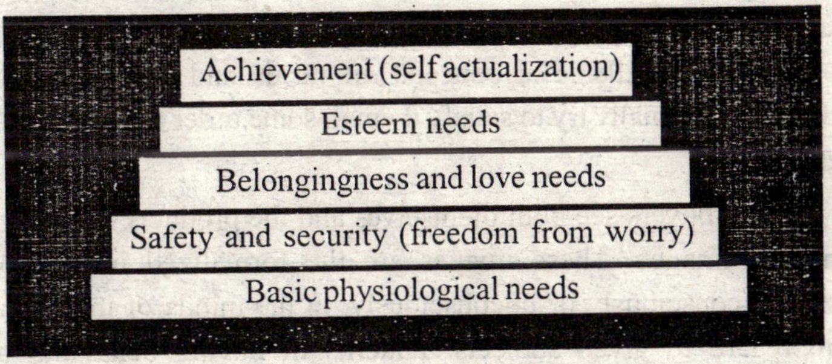

Fig. A Maslow's hierarchy of needs

the most basic needs at the bottom of the figure. According to him, an individual normally tries to satisfy the most basic needs first and, satisfying these, he or she is then free to devote his or her efforts to the next one shown on the list. Each category of need on the Maslow list is described as follows.

(i) **Basic Needs.** The needs to satisfy hunger, thirst, sleep, and so forth. These are the most basic needs, and until they are satisfied, other needs are of no importance.

(ii) **Safety and Security Needs.** In modern society, these needs are more often for economic and social security rather than for physical safety.

(iii) **Belongingness and Love Needs.** The need for affectionate relations with individuals and a place in society is so important that its lack is a common cause of maladjustment.

(iv) **Esteem Needs.** People need both self-esteem, a high evaluation of self, and the esteem of others in our society. Fulfilment provides a feeling of self-confidence and usefulness; nonfulfilment produces feelings of inferiority and helplessness.

(v) **Achievement Need.** This is the desire to achieve the maximum of one's capabilities. Although it may be present in everyone, its fulfilment depends upon prior fulfilment of the more basic needs.

Often the marketing success of a brand depends on its ability to satisfy several needs at once; motivation research techniques are available to identify the strength or weakness of a product in terms of the needs it fulfills. The concepts of needs and the theory that individuals normally try to satisfy them in some order are specifically significant.

They buyers see both themselves and the products they buy in terms of images. These images are the formalized impressions residing, consciously or unconsciously, in the minds of individuals with regard to given subjects. Patterns of buying behaviour are influenced by the images that consumers have of different products, particular brands, companies, retail outlets, and of themselves, Because images affect consumer buying behaviour, marketers take them into account in drafting promotional plans and programmes. Differences among individuals, products, brands, and the like result in different images, and motivation research is used not only to identify the nature of images but also to detect the implications for marketing action:

(a) **Self-image.** The self-image is the picture that people have of them-seles-the kind of people they consider themselves to be and the kind of people that they imagine others consider them to be. Different people have different kinds of self-images, and this gives rise to market segmentation along psychological lines. For instance, the woman who sees herself primarily as a good housewife and mother exhibits a different total pattern of buying behaviour from that shown by the woman who sees herself as a social leader or professional careerist. It many buying situations an individual prefers to buy those products and brands whose images appear consistent with his or her self-image. However, the power of the self-image as a buying influence varies from individual to individual and even within the same individual as he or she makes different buying decisions at different times.

(b) **Brand Image.** The brand image, another stereotype, results from all the impressions consumers receive, from whatever sources, about a particular manufacturer's brand. In the minds of consumers familiar with a particular brand, there tends to be considerable consistency in the brand image or, as it is sometimes called, the brand personality. For competing brands there are in the minds of consumers distinctive images. Similarly, retail stores exhibit distinct images or personalities, as do corporations.

Consumers' appraisals of the distinctivness of a brand's physical attributes not only affect the brand image but also have important implications for marketing. When consumers believe that the brand is physically different from competing brands, the brand image centers on the brand as a specific version of the product.

TYPES OF BUYING BEHAVIOUR

Consumer decision making varies with the type of buying decision. There are great differences between buying toothpaste, a tennis racket, a personal computer, and a new car. Complex and expensive purchases are likely to involve more buyer deliberation and more participants. Assael distinguished four types of consumer buying behaviour based on the degree of buyer involvement and the degree of differences among brands.

(1) Dissonance Reducing Buying Behaviour. Sometimes the consumer is highly involved in purchase but sees little difference in the brands. The high involvement is again based on the fact that the purchase is expensive, infrequent, and risky. In this case, the buyer will shop around to learn what is available out will buy fairly quickly becase brand differences are not pronounced. The buyer may respond primarily to a good price or to purchase convenience. For example, carpet buying is a high-involvement decision because it is expensive and self-expressive; yet the buyer may consider most carpet brands in a given price range to be the same.

After the purchase, the consumer might experience dissonance that stems from noticing certain disquieting features of the carpet or hearing favourable things about other carpet. The consumer will be alert to information that might justify his or her decision. In this example, the consumer first acted, then acquired new beliefs, and ended up with a set of attitudes. Here marketing communications should aim to supply beliefs and evaluations that help the consumer feel good about his or her brand choice.

(2) **Complex Buying Bahaviour.** Consumers go through complex buying behaviour when they are highly involved in a purchase and aware of significant differences among brands. Consumers are highly involved when the product is expensive, bought infrequently, risky, and highly self-expressive. Typically the consumer does not know much about the product category and has much to learn. For example, a person buying a personal computer may not know that attributes to look for. Many of the product features carry no meaning : "16K memory", "disc storage", "screen resolution", and so on.

This buyer will pass through a learning process characterized by first developing beliefs about the product, then attitudes, and then making a thoughtful purchase choice. The marketer of a high-involvement product must understand and information-gathering and evaluation behaviour of high-involvement consumers. The marketer needs to develop strategies that assist the buyer in learning about the attributes of the product class, their relative importance, and the high standing of the company's brand on the more important attributes. The marketer needs to differentiate the brand's features, use mainly print media and long copy to describe the brand's benefits, and motivate store sales personnel and the buyer's acquaintances to influences the final brand choice.

(3) **Variety—Seeking Buying Behaviour.** Some buying situations are characterized by low consumer involvement but significant brand differences. Here consumers are often observed to do a lot of brand switching. An example occurs in purchasing cookies. The consumer has some

beliefs, chooses a brand of cookies without much evaluation, and evaluates it during consumption. But next time, the consumer may reach for another brand out of boredom or a wish for a different taste. brand switching occurs for the sake of variety rather than dissatisfaction.

The marketing strategy is different for the market leader and the minor brands in this product category. The market leader will try to encourage habitual buying behaviour by dominating the self space, avoiding out-of-stock conditions, and sponsoring frequent reminder advertising. Challenger firms will encourage variety seeking by ofering lower prices, deals, coupons, free samples, and advertising that presents reasons for trying something new.

(4) **Habitual Buying Behaviour.** Many products are bought under conditions of low consumer involvement and the absence of significant brand differences. Consider the purchase of salt. Consumers have little involvement in this product category. They go to the store and reach for the brand. If they keep reaching for the same brand, it is out of habit, not strong brand loyalty. There is good evidence that consumers have low involvement with most lowcost, frequently purchased products.

Consumer behaviour in these cases does not pass through the normal belief/attitude/behaviour sequence. Consumers do not search extensively for information about the brands, evaluate their characteristics, and make a weighty decision on which brand to buy. Instead, they are passive recipients of information as they watch television or some print advertisements. Advertisement repetition creates brand familiarity rather than brand conviction. Consumers do not form a strong attitude toward a brand but select it because it is familiar. After purchase, they may not even evaluate the choice because they are not highly involved with the product. So the buying process is brand beliefs formed by passive learning, followed by purchase behaviour, which may be followed by evaluation.

Problems in Studying Buyer Behaviour

It has to be made clear at the outset that there is no unified, well defined, tested and universally established theory of buyer behaviour. What we have today are certain ideas propounded for describing buyer behaviour. In their approach and content these ideas vary widely from one another. Some of these ideas have taken their cue from economics, others from psychology, and yet others from several of the social sciences simultaneously. These concepts have been developed after extensive study and research. Individual firms have conducted studies; professional researchers have also studied the subject on their own. All these studies have contributed to a heavy assortment of information on buyer behaviour. But a universally accepted theory of buyer behaviour is yet to emerge. It is with an understanding of these limitations that we have to proceed further with the topic.

Buyers needs and desires are innumerable. And they vary from security needs to aesthetic needs. These needs and desires are often at different stages of emergence and actualization. Some are latent, some are manifest, some are dominant. The buyer has his own ways and plans of meeting these needs. Some of these needs are within his means. He can easily meet them. Some are too costly for him. He may keep postponing the purchase.

And this buyer is exposed today to a world of information—about new products, new services, new uses for existing products, new ideas and new styles. His attitudes towards this bombardment of information is also peculiar. He might ignore certain pieces of information, whereas he may actively seek out some other information. He may read a certain message, but may not disgest it. He may merely overhear some message about some product and it may get registered in his mind. In other words, he filters the information in a rather unconscious manner. His perception is partial, in the sense that he perceives and retains what he would normally like to perceive and retain. This selective perception is actually his defense mechanism against the information explosion to which he is constantly exposed.

And when he takes a buying decision, there is no rigid rule to bind him. Sometimes, the decision is taken on the spot. That does not necessarily means it is an irrational decision. Sometimes he may decide after making a long search, after evaluating the various alternatives available, and after reassuring himself with the experience of those who have already purchased the product. Still, he may find later that his purchase was impulsive or even foolish! He may go to a shop after having taken the decision to buy a product. Still he may not buy. For no apparent reason, he may postpone the purchase or even drop the very idea of purchasing.

The very essence of buyer behaviour study is the recognition of the fact that the buyer is a complex person, influenced by the social environment in which he lives, his family, his society, his neighbours, his friends, his job, his colleagues-everything leaving some imprint on him, influencing him in this day-to-day life. His purchases and consumption are carried out within the larger context of his day-to-day living. And his role as a buyer is not distinct from his role as a human being. Buyer behaviour, after all, is only a specific aspect of general human behaviour and is therefore as complex as general human behaviour.

SIGNIFICANCE OF CONSUMER BEHAVIOUR

When a person gets his pay-packet at the beginning of each month he sits down with his wife and prepares the family budget after carefully apportioning amounts to different items of expenditure. However, after a trip to the market with his family, he finds that the whole 'exercise in rationality' (budget) had been futile as the purchases made by him are not compatible with the budget items. On recapitulation and analysis, he finds that it was his wife, son, daughter and even he himself who were responsible for this deviation. All of them had made a contribution in making this budget upside down. The deviation was attributed to the arousal of new needs on account of new produts displayed, better packages, better credit facilities, charming saleswomen/menship and also beacause a nouyeau riche neighbour was buying some particular article. While making purchases, the son had a friend's dress in his mind, the daughter had her class teachers' new lipstick in her mind, the wife was thinking of a particular sari she had seen at a party, and he himself was overawed by his neighbour's choices. This whole behaviour of a person (s) while making purchases may be termed as consumer behaviour. It has been defined as "the process whereby individuals decide whether, what, when, where, how and from whom to purchase goods and services'.

In this process, the consumer deliberates within himself before he finally makes a purchase move. This deliberatin relates to many variables and is aimed at solving consumption problems. Amongst these problems, the first and foremost is to decide whether to spend money or to save it. Once a decision is taken to spend money, the second problem is to decide what to buy because the needs are multiple and resources scarce. Therefore needs are to be ranked in terms of priority. The subsequent consumption problems relate to the place from where to buy, the mode of purchase—large/small quantities, cash/credit purchases and the like—and, last, the seller/shop from whom to buy.

This whole consumption behaviour consists of both physical and mental activities. The physical acitivities involve visiting a shop, examining product, selecting products or eating/drinking outside; that is, the actual act of consumption. Mental activities, on the other hand, involve deliberations within and forming of attitudes, perceiving communication material and learning to prefer a particular brand of product.

Consumer Behaviour and Consumption Behaviour

Consumer behaviour relates to an indiviudal person (micro behaviour), whereas consumption behaviour relates to the mass or aggregate of individuals (macro behaviour). "The study of consumer behaviour always focuses on the decision processes of the individual consumer or consuming unit, such as the family. It includes all the efforts to describe and explain one or more act of choice either at a given time or over a period of time. In contrast, the study of consumption behaviour is concerned with the description and explanation of the behaviour of aggregates of consumers or consuming units, again at a given time or over a period of time. The subject matter of consumption behaviour parallels at the aggregate level to that of consumer behaviour.

Consumer Behaviour and Buyer Behaviour

The area of consumer behaviour includes activities of both ultimate and industrial consumers. The former is the end-user of the product/service whereas the latter is only an intermediate user who adds further value to the product/service before it is consumed by the end-user. When behaviour of both the kinds of buyer is under reference, the term used to denote it is "buyer behaviour'. When the behaviour of only end-users is under reference, the term 'consumer behaviour' is used to denote it.

The relevance and importance of understanding consumer behaviour is rooted in the modern marketing concept. In order to operationalise this concept, management attempts to solve some consumption problems of consumers. However, no business can possibly help consumers solve their consumption problems unless he understands them and unless he makes an attempt to comprehend the buying process and the factors influencing it.

Consumer behaviour is dynamic. Therefore, it is necessary to continuously study, analyse and understand it and monitor this understanding to the marketing management so that effective decisions can be taken in respect of products, price, promotion and distribution. The profit position of a product hinges on the kind of predisposition-positive/negative—that a consumer has developed towards it. It is essential to study and analyse it in order to understand why he/she has developed such a predisposition? Besides, the Indian marketing conditions in particular the role of the Government and the steadily emerging consumer movement, necessitates that marketers in India must understand consumer behaviour—their needs, aspirations, expectations and problems. It will be extremely useful in exploiting marketing opportunities and in meeting the challenges that the Indian market offers.

Thus, in substance, it may be said that in the interest of effective marketing decisions, marketers must develop an understanding of their consumer's behaviour, the buying process and the factors influencing this process.

STAGES OF CONSUMER BUYING PROCESS

In order to understand consumer behaviour, it is first essential to understand the buying process. During the last two decades, numerous models of consumer behaviour depicting the buying process have developed. All these models treat the consumer as a decision-maker who comes to the market place to solve his consumption problems and to achieve the satisfaction of his needs. Amongst all these models the one given by Howard and Sheth is the most comprehensive and largely approved. However, as the Howard-Sheth model is a very sophisticated model.

A simple model is composed of three stages—'Input-Process-Output'. Input is a stimulus. It is provided by two sets of stimulus variables, namely, the firm marketing efforts and the social environment. The firm's marketing effects are designed to positively expose, inform and influence consumers. These efforts include product/service itself, advertising, price strategies, distribution network, and in fact all marketing functions. For example, when a company introduces a new brand of detergent powder or a television set, it may run a series of radio commercials with supporting press advertisements. The social environment serves as a non-commercial source of consumer information and influence which is not under the direct control of the firm. It includes reference groups and individuals, family members, social class and castes, culture, and the like. Both these stimulus variables influences consumer and the buying process.

Stages of Buying Process

The buying process is compared of a number of stages and is influenced by an individual's psychological framework composed for the individual's personality, motivations, perceptions and attitudes. The various stages of the buying process are described here:

(1) **Need Recognition.** Need recognition means awareness of a want, a desire or a consumption problem without whose

satisfaction the consumer normally builds up tension. For example, a busy housewife may feel the need for a washing-aid on account of her desire to find more time to spend with her children. This recognition of the need for a washing-aid might activate her to search for some aid may be manual or mechanical-say, a washerman/woman of a washing machine. Nevertheless, it is possible that she might be already aware of some such product (aid) before she recognised its needs. In order to accept this possibility, the arrow head between need recognition and product awareness stages has been reversible and a path is included to indicate movement from the need-recognition stage directly to the interest stage.

(2) Product Awareness. In this stage, the consumer is exposed to the existence of a product that may satisfy a need. This awarness may be on account of the search carried out by the consumer himself/herself or because of a firm's communications through advertising or salesmanship or through social environment. This awareness may be neutral or active. When no need is currently recognised by a consumer the awareness is neutral because there is no immediate interest in it. When a consumer is already aware of a product and subsequently recognises a need, then the product awareness is active, and immediately converted into interest. In our example of the housewife requiring a washing-aid there was already a need recognition for a washing-aid. When she was exposed to a press advertisement or radio commercial about a particular washing machine her interest in it was aroused.

(C) Interest. Interest may be viewed as a state of mind that exists when a consumer perceives a need and/or is aware of alternative products capable of satisfying that need. Consumer interest is indicated in the consumer's willingness to seek further information about a product. At this stage the consumer is actively involved in the buying process and pays attention to the product. However, if he loses interest during this involvement, his/her attention will be diverted and the buying decision process will break down. In our example of the housewife requiring a washing-aid, she may look for further information about these machines ones she became aware of such machines. The kind of information she may look for is about the alternative washing machines available in the market-place, their relative price, operational efficiency, warranty and service facilities.

(4) **Evaluation and Intention.** Once interest in a product (s) is aroused, a consumer enters the subsequent stage of evaluation and intention. The evaluation stage represents the stage of mental trial of the product. During this stage, the consumer assigns relative value-weights to different products/brands on the basis of the accumulated stock of product information and draws conclusions about their relative satisfaction—giving potential. After this evaluation, the consumer develops the intention either to purchase or reject the product/brand. The final purchase will, however, depend on the strength of the positive intention—that is the intention to buy. In our example of the housewife, after arousal of her interest in washing machines, she will compare the stock of information she has accumulated for the different washing machines in the market and then evaluate the value of each one of them before she develops the intention to buy. However, if she feels that a washerman/woman would serve the need then she may altogether reject the idea of buying any washing machine.

(5) **Output.** Output is the end result of the inputs of consumer behaviour. It emerges after these inputs are duly processed by the consumer. Output is composed of purchase and post-purchase behaviour.

(6) **Purchase.** Purchase is a consumer commitment for a product. It is the terminal stage in the buying decision process that completes a transaction. It occurs either as a

trial and/or adoption. If a consumer is buying something for the first time then from the behaviour viewpoint it may be regarded as a trial. This trial enables him to accumulate experience about the product purchased. If this experience is positive in terms of satisfaction derivation, then repeat purchases may occur otherwise not. For example, when a new brand of bathing soap is introduced in the market, the consumer may buy it for the first time as a trial. However, repeat purchases will occur only when he is satisfied with its performance. But the possibility of a trial-purchase is not available in all cases. In the case of consumer durables such as scooters, refrigerators and the like, a trial is not possible, because once a product is purchased, it has to be adopted and repeatedly used. Adoption means a consumer decision to commit to a full or further use of the product. In our example of the housewife, the washing machine is not open for trial purchase; it will have to be adopted only.

(7) Post-purchase Behaviour. Post-purchase behaviour refers to the behaviour of a consumer after commitment to a product has been made. It originates out of consumer experience regarding the use of the product and is indicated in terms of satisfaction. This behaviour is reflected in repeat purchases or abstinence from further purchase. If product-use experience indicates satisfaction then repeat purchases will occur, otherwise not.

FACTORS AFFECTING THE CONSUMERS BUYING BEHAVIOUR

There are many factors which affect the behaviour of consumers. These factors may broadly be divided into two parts—(I) Economic Factors; and (II) Psychological Factors. The details in this regard are as follows:

(I) Economic Factors

Economic factors are the factors which affect financial conditions of a consumer. Some of the important economic factors affecting the behaviour of a consumer are as follows:

(1) **Personal Income.** Income of a consumer is the most important factor affecting his demand. A consumer has to fulfil his unlimited wants within his limited sources of income. If the income of the consumer is high, his demands will be more.

(2) **Consumer's Credit.** The increase or decrease in demand is also affected by the facility of credit available to the consumers. If the facility of credit is available to the consumers, their demands will increase.

(3) **Family Income.** Family income of a consumer also effects his purchasing power. If the family of a consumer is living below the poverty line, his demands will be very limited. On the other hand, if the family of a consumer is happy and prosperous, his demands will be more.

(4) **Expectation of Income.** If a consumer expects an increase in his sources of income in future, his demands may be more. On the other hand, if a consumer expects a fall in his sources of income in future, his demands will be limited.

(5) **Discretionary Income.** Discretionary income means the income which is left after meeting all the necessities. Such income can be used by the consumers at their own discretion. This type of the income will increase the purchasing power of consumers.

(6) **Government Policies.** Goernment policy, particularly the rates of taxes in the country, affects consumer behaviour to a great extent. If the rates of income tax in the country are high, the purchasing power of the consumers will be low. Low rates of income tax can help in increasing the demand of consumers.

(II) Psychological Factors

(1) **Basic Needs.** Every Consumer has some basic needs which he wants to fulfil first of all. These needs may differ from person to person and from time to time. *Prof. A. H. Maslow* has described basic needs of a consumer as

follows—*(i)* Physical; *(ii)* Safety; *(iii)* Love; *(iv)* Prestige; and (v) Self-ego. Prof. Maslow stated that a consumer wants to fulfil his needs in this order.

(2) **Learning Theory.** Learning theory is very important to study the behaviour of a consumer. With the help of this theory, the marketers may understand the motives for the satisfaction of which, a consumer purchases a product. According to this theory, following factors affect the behaviour of a consumer:

(i) ***Motivation.*** There are many buying motives which affect the behaviour of a consumer to a great extent. These motives may be categories as emotional, rational, natural and learnt.

(ii) ***Repetition.*** Continuous touch of a consumer with a product helps in increasing his knowledge about the product. For example, continuous advertisement of a product for a long time increases the knowledge of consumer about the product and the consumer are inspired to consume such product.

(iii) ***Group Influence.*** Group influence also affects the behaviour of a consumer. For example, if a prestigious person of the society or if a rich person starts to consume a particular product, many other persons will start to consume the same product.

(iv) ***Conditioning.*** The condition of a product also affects the behaviour of consumers. For example, if the packing of a product is very attractive, some new consumers may purchase the product for this reason also.

(3) **Image.** Image is the thinking of consumers about a particular product. This image affects their buying behaviour to a great extent. Image may be of many types such as self image, product image, brand image etc.

(4) **Clinical Psychology.** Clinical psychology includes following two factors:

(i) ***Rationalisation.*** Rationalisation means to study the reasons for which the consumers buy a product. Every consumer is a rational and makes rational purchasings, So, a marketer must study these reasons.

(ii) ***Unconsciousness.*** Unconsciousness is the stage of a consumer when he is not in a position to explain the reasons for which he buys a product. A marketer has to be much more vigil and careful about the study of behaviour of such consumers.

After making a study of the factors affecting the behaviour of consumers, a question arises as to which factor affects the behaviour of a consumer more. Some scholars are of the opinion that economic factors play more important role in determining the behaviour of consumers while some other scholars think that psychological factors play much more important role in this direction. The fact is that both the factors play equally important role in determining the behaviour of consumers. Therefore, a marketer must make a deep study of both the economic and psychological factors affecting the behaviour of consumer. Advertisement programme of an enterprise must include both the factors, as far as possible.

❑

5

Promotion Decisions

In marketing management, it is the communication process, that forms the basis for promotional activities. A marketer's promotional measage must be received by those making up market targets, if the goals are to be achieved.

The word "Communication" is dervied from the Latin word "Communis," meaning common. There is communication only if there is "commoness" in the words or symbols used by both the sender and the receiver *i.e.*, message must mean one and the same thing to both. Communication means "sharing of meaning." Implicit in this definition is the notion of transmission of information, because sharing necessitates information. Communication is concerned with who says what to whom, through which channel, and with what effect. Such a communication may be made through written or spoken words or through gestures of some type.

MARKETING COMMUNICATION PROCESS

Generally, marketing communication is undertaken to pass on the message of a product or sale to the ultimate consumers. Thus, there are three elements in this process.

(a) the receiver There are four groups of receivers:

(i) Consumers

(ii) Sales supporting personnel, *viz.*, wholesalers, retailers, etc.

(iii) Other members in the functional areas, *viz.*, finance, transport, etc.

(iv) Government/Institutional agencies.

(b) the source	Producer/seller from where the Inforamtion originates.
(c) the message	The literal/oral/visual form of the message.

One aspect needs special mention here. When we say flow of information, it is not a 'one-way traffic', but it is a both-way traffic. It is desirable and essential that each element in the flow of messages acts as both sources and receiver, so that return flow of communications, called 'feedback', is accomplished.

Advertising is meant to pass on an information to the prospective customers. It is one of the most powerful elements in the promotion mix. It is stated that advertising, though impersonal in character, could create profound influence in persuading prospects to become customers. It is true that advertising carries only a message to the consumers and does not substantiate the consumers with any physical attributes.

As pointed out earlier advertising essentially means spreading of information. From the earliest days, men have proclaimed by word of mouth or in writing the virtue of goods which they have produced. The word originated from a Latin term "advertire" which means "to turn to". The dictionary meaning of the term is "to give public notice or to announce publicity".

John Hobson of the Hobson Bates Agency, UK, remarked, "People do not buy things; they buy the satisfaction, both objective and subjective, that those things are going to deliver to them personally. It is a fact that a shop windows or window display can only display the goods. It takes advertising to display the satisfactions. Advertising is thus a kind of "window display of satisfactions". Satisfaction, in turn, is purely psychological in nature. It is the psychological element that is "tickled" through advertisements.

ELEMENTS OF COMMUNICATION

According to Crane a communication process requires only three elements or stages a message, a source of this meassage and a receiver. But some more elements have also been added to it so that five distinct stages are recognised in communication.

At the first stage, the information sources originates the communication, *i.e.*, there must be a person with idea to communicate. For instance, the marketing executive may have ideas, information instructions, to communicate to his subordinates, sales force and the target markets.

The Second stage is that of encoding, *i.e.*, the idea to be communicated is translated in a language or medium of expression, either through written or spoken words or into a gesture of some sort (through show of hands, waving of arm, or dimming the bright lights.)

In the third stage, the message carrying the idea is carried from one point to another or one individual to the other either by print media or sound wave.

In the fourth stage, the receiver decodes *i.e.*, interpretes the message in the light of his experience or termes of reference.

In the fifth stage, the receiver acts as per the message received.

Besides these, there are two more elements which are normally present in the communication system. One is the noise, which consists of extraneous disturbances interfering with communication (such as noise made by children, or that by the ringing of a door bell or some other disturbance like thundering of clouds etc.) The other is the "feedback" *i.e.*, the receivers' acceptance or action. Feedback gives an idea whether and to what extent the message has been received or learnt by the receiver. Feedback may take any form a nod, an expression of interest or anger, or a smile or acceptance of the message by conduct.

PROMOTIONAL MIX

Promotion is an important part of the marketing mix of a business enterprise. It is the spark plug of the marketing mix. It is a process of communiation involving information, persuation, and influence. It includes all types of personal or impersonal communication with customers as well as middlemen in distribution. The purpose of promotion is to inform, persuade and influence the propsective customers. Personal selling, advertising publicity and sales promotion are widely used to inform the people about the availability of products and create among them the desire to buy the products. Non business enterprise can market its products unless it undertakes promotional activities effectively. The prospective customers have to be informed about the product its features, utility and availability. The need for promotional activities has increased because of stiff competition, widening of market and rapid changes in technology and tastes of the customers.

The term 'promotional mix' is used to refer to the combination of different kinds of promotional tools used by a firm to advertise and sell its products. The main promotional tools or activities which make up promotion mix are personal selling, advertising, publicity and sales promotion. These are also known as elements of promotion mix.

In the modern business world, big business firms cannot depend upon a single promotional tool. They have to make use of all the promotional tools in different degrees depending upon the nature of produce, nature of competition and kinds of customers. The marketing manager is supposed to decide about the use of various promotional activities and allocate budget for them. while taking a decison about promotion mix, two factors need adequate consideration. Firstly, a combination of promotional activities are to be used because any promotional tool, used alone, may not prove fully effective.

Secondly, all promotional tools are not of equal importance and their importance may change with the change in business environment.

There is no tailor-promotional mix for a firm. Every firm has to design its own promotional mix, *i.e.*, to determine, the various promotional tools to be used for promoting the sale of its products. The most striking feature of the promotional tools is their cross-substitutability. They represent alternative ways to influence buyers. This substitutability calls for treating various promotional tool in a joint decision framework. Promotional strategy is determined by the product market strategy and over-all marketing strategy. Various combinations, types and degrees of personal selling, advertising and other promotional tools are brought together into a promotional mix to develop the promotional strategy. For each component of the promotional mix, management has to set objectives, determine policies and formulate strategies.

Scope of Promotion Mix

Promotion encompasses all the tools in the marketing mix whose major role is persuasive communication. Two best known form of promotion are personal selling and advertising. They are also the most important forms in terms of cost and market impact. Most of the firms use personal selling as an important part of promotional programme and it is commonly supported by advertising. Other forms of promotional tools are publicity and sales promotion. The four components, namely, personal selling, advertising, publicity and sales promotion, make up the promotion mix of a firm. A brief discussion of these components is given below:

1. **Advertisng.** Advertising is an imporant from of promotion. It involves transmiting standard message to a large number of intended receivers. Advertising is any paid form of non-personal presentation and promotion of ideas, goods or services of identified sponsor. The message which is disseminated is known as advertisement. Advertisement is a paid form of communication which is resorted to by an identified sponsor.
2. **Publicity.** Publicity is any non-paid mention of an organition of its products in the news media. It is non-personal stimulation of demand for a product by planning commercially significant news about it in a published medium or obtaining favourable presentation of it upon radio, television or stage that is non-paid for by the sponsor.
3. **Personal Selling.** Personal selling is the process of assisting and persuading a prospective buyer to buy a commodity in a face to face situation. It involves direct and personal contact between the seller or his representative with the prospective buyer. Personal selling is by far the major promotional method used to increase profitable sales by offering want satisfying products to the people.

4. **Sales Promotion.** Sales promotion includes all those activities, other than the three discussed above, they stimulate consumer purchasing and dealer effectiveness. The examples of sales promotion are: distribution of samples, coupons, premium on sale, trading stamps, displays, shows and exhibitions, holding contests, increasing public relations, etc. sales promotion techniques are designed to supplement and co-ordinate personal selling and advertising efforts:

   (1) ***To Spread Information.*** The main purpose of promotional activities is to inform the prospective customer about the availability, characteristics and use of a particular product.

   (2) ***To Stimulate Demand.*** Promotional activities create awaraness and build people interest in new products and new technology.

   (3) ***To Differentiate the Product.*** Promotion helps in differentiating a particualr product of the firm from the competing products of their firms. A business firm can supply data revealing how its product compares with other products.

   (4) ***To Highlight the Utility of Product.*** Promotion helps in letting the people know the utility of the new product. It also tells them how the concerned products will be helpful in satisfying their certain demand.

   (5) ***To Stabilise Sales.*** In the modern age of competition, it is an important purpose of promotional activities to help in stabilising sales volume by reassuring the customers about the quality and price of the product. It is very much possible that a customer using a particular brand of a product may buy another one next time because the other brand is advertised so heavily.

DETERMINANTS OF PROMOTIONAL MIX

The managerial decision about the promotional mix of a firm is influenced by the following factors:

1. **Stage of Product's Life.** The stage of a products' life cycle is an important determinant of promotion mix. During the introduction stage, the customers are to be informed about the availability of the product and educated about its benefits and uses. That is why, most of the firm made use of all kinds of promotional activities to launch their products successfully. After the product has been launched, advertisement and publicity are more important to create continued patronage of the customers, to create a good image of the product and its manufacturer and to meet competition in the market. But during the last stage of the product when its sales are declining, it may be decided to make drastic cuts as pormotional efforts.
2. **Availability of Funds.** The allocation of funds by the top management for the promotional activities must be kept in mind by the marketing manager while determining the promotional mix of a firm. A firm with huge promotional budget can spend as all promotional activities. But a firm with financial constraints will be selective in the use of promotional activities. Personal selling is cheaper and more effective in the short-run. Advertisement in reputed magzines and journals is very costly, but can attract the status conscious customers toward the product of the firm.
3. **Nature of Market.** Nature of market and customers determine, to a great extent, the promotional mix of a firm. For instance, if the customers are concentrated in a particular locality, personal selling is likely to be more effective. But if they are scattered widely in different parts of the country, advertising publicity, sales promotion and personal selling—all are necessary to push up a product. Advertisement and publicity are also important to attract the status-conscious customers.

4. **Nature of Product.** The type of promotional mix will differ depending upon the nature of the product. In case of sale of consumer's goods, advertisng, publicity and sales promotion are necessary in addition to personal selling. But in order to push up industrial goods, personal selling is much more effective because its market is easily identifiable, products are often made to specifications and a great deal of pre-sale and after-sale services are required to sell and install the product.

OBJECTIVES OF PROMOTIONS

There are three specific objectives of promotion:

(a) To Communicate,

(b) To Convince, and

(c) To Compete.

It has been pointed out that communication is the basis of all marketing effort. In fact, it involves much in addition to the stimulation of sales. Moreover, most marketing communications are promotional.

It is not enough merely to communicate. Ideas must be convincing so that action (purchase) would follow. In other words, distribution of information should be capable of producing marketing results.

A good product, an efficient channel, and appropriate price are not enough by themseleves. Communicaton and convincing elements should supplement to offer contrasts to the efforts of competitors. It may even be stated that the competitive characteristics of promotion defines its vital role in marketing strategy.

Communication is a necessary element in everyday and in every walk of life. People communicate for many reasons. A dynamic society cannot be there without sufficient modes of communication. Members of the society seek amusement, ask help, give help, provide information, all through some form of communication developed over centuries.

Promotion is the mode of communication adopted by business community for achieveing certain specific objectives. From the point of view of a seller such communications may become necessary to modify consumer behaviour and thoughts and/or to reinforce existing behaviour of consumers.

Thus, the objectives of promotion are as under:

(i) to provide information to prospective customers about the availability, features and uses of products.

(ii) to stimulate demand by creating awareness and interest among customers,

(iii) to differentiate a product from competitive products by creating brand loyalty,

(iv) to stabilise sales by highlighting the utility of the product.

Promotion has often been the target of criticism. Some opine that "promotion contributes nothing to society", and for some others "promotion forces consumers to buy products they cannot afford and do not need", and so on. It may be true that promotion can certainly be criticised on many of its aggressive and compelling factors. But it should also be recognised that it plays a crucial role in modern soceity, particularly in business, economic and social spheres of influence.

The objectives of promotion are illustrated in the following chart:

Hierarchy of effects	*General behavioural objectives*	*Specific behavioural objectives*	*Selected promotional mix elements*
1	*2*	*3*	*4*
Awareness ↓ Knowledge	Provide information	Obtain consumer recognition, gain consumer knowledge of product atrributes	Advertising, Publicity, Point of Purchase and Window displays

Contd.

1	*2*	*3*	*4*
↓ Linking ↓ Preferences ↓	Develop positive attitudes and feelings	Obtain favourable Attitudes, gain preference for brand	All media advertising, publicity and personal selling
Conviction ↓ Purchase	Stimulus and retain desires	Sustain strong consumers preference, maintain continued purchase	P.O.P. displays, special offers, direct mail, personal selling

KINDS OF PROMOTION

1. Information Promotion. All promotions, essentially, are designed to inform the target market about the firm's offerings. Informative promotion is more prevalent during early stages of product life cycle. It is a necessary ingredient for creating primary demand. Such type of promotion is needed as the consumers make their purchases only if they are convinced about the product benefits. This could be done only with the help of communications and such communications are usually information-oriented and not sales-oriented, Naturally, this will help the consumer in this intelligent buying.

2. Buyer Behaviour Modifications. The effect of promotion is measured through the modification in consumer beahviour. The repeated advertisements and constant personal selling methods are designed to achieve this goal.

3. Persuasive Promotion. The basic purpose of promotion is to persuade people to buy. But many do not accept this goal, as it would involve high-pressure selling but essence of all promotion is persuasion. It is designed to stimulate purchase and to create a positive image in order to influence long-term buyer behaviour. Except on certain occassions promotion is not intended to create immediate response. Moreover, when the product enters growth stage persuasion becomes the primary goal of any kinds of promotion.

4. Reminder Promotion. This goal is adopted when the product reaches maturity stage. Insisting and emphasising brand names and product features in competitive terms is the central aim of reminder promotion. It simply serves as a "memory jogger".

PROMOTIONAL ACTIVITIES

After the product has been planned, the channels of distribution and physical distribution of the product decided, and the price structure evolved; the next step is to decide upon the promotional activities that the firm may follow. It has rightly been said that "nothing happens until somebody sells something." This gives in a nutshell the philosophy of promotional activities. The promotional activities are concerned with : *(a)* informing the people about products' distinctive want-satisfying characteristics and its availability; *(b)* reminding people periodically about the product and its role; and *(c)* persuading the people/prospective buyers that make people to do what they might not otherwise do what they don't really want to do.

Promotion may be defined as "the coordination of all seller initiated effort to set up channels of information and persuasion to facilitate the sale of a good or service or the acceptance of an idea". In other words promotion refers to activities and processes designed to change or reinforce behaviour and/or ideas through communication. Promotion is telling and selling.

Selling, Promotion and Sales Promotion

Promotion is an exercise in information, persuasion and influence. These three are inter-related in the sense that to "inform is to persuade" and if "a person is persuaded he is informed," "Selling and promotion" are often used synonymously. Selling has been defined as "the personal or impersonal process of assisting and/or persuading a prospective customer to buy a commodity or a service or to act favourably upon an idea, that has commercial significance to the seller." On the other hand, "promoton" is the all inclusive term representing the broad field-advertising, personal selling, and sales promotion. "The promotional mix, therefore, deals with coordination of the sales force acitivities, the advertising programmes, and other promotional efforts, which may include packaging, branding, direct mail solicitation, point of purchased display, premiums, holding trade shows and exhibitions, use of samples of gifts."

It may be noted that "promotion" and "sales promotion" are different. Promotion is a very wide term including, advertising, personal selling. sales promotion and other promotional tools that can be devised to reach the goals of the sales programme. On the other hand, "sales promotion" is only a part of it. Sales promotion has been defined as activities other than personal selling, advertising and publicity, that stimulate consumer purchasing and dealer effectiveness, such as displays, shows and expositions, demonstrations, tension of each trade. Under instalment payment seller is to take overhead risks of bad debts and in order to minimise these higher prices are charged. Instalment system is limited to persons of good reputation and various non-recurrent selling efforts not in the ordinary routine." In retailing sales promotion is interpreted to cover "all methods of stimulating customer purchasing including personal selling, advertising and publicity. The important function of sales promotion is to serve as a bridge between advertising and personal selling to supplement and co-ordinate efforts in these two areas. The main purpose of promotion is to attract customers, awaken their dormant demand and stimulate them to act in the desired manner. Thus, establishing and maintaining communications with large market segments are the main tasks of promotional activities.

Objectives of Promotional Activities

The need for promotional activities has been recognised by the marketer for more than one reason. First, the physical separation of the consumers and producers, and an increase in the number of potential customers, have been significant to communication system.

Second, improvements in physical distribution facilities have expanded the area limits of the markets with which establishment of communication system becomes a necessity.

Third, a large number of wholesalers and retailing middlemen have developed between the producers and the users, which has necessitated that not only the consumers be informed about the benefits of the product, but also the middlemen need be informed about products. These middlemen, in turn, should also communicate with the retailers and consumers.

Fourth, when sale begins to decline, either due to preference for a new product brought out by the competitor, or a total dislike for it, promotion works as a stimulant to restore the demand for the existing product. It is needed to maintain the high material standard of living and the high level of employment.

Histya and Will put the objectives of promotion under three heads.

(1) Demand objectives, the idea of which is to influence, stimulate, maintain and create demand for a product.

(2) Communication objectives which aim at creating awareness, providing information to the customer and retailers about product features where products can be obtained, and what the products are capable of doing or achieving brand preferences.

(3) Specific objectives *i.e.* performance objectives which provide specific information about a product and which influence the decision of purchasing by the customer.

PROMOTIONAL PLANNING PROCESS

A crucial element from the cost point of view is promotion expenses. Not only huge amounts are to be spent on promotion, its controlling aspect is difficult. Hence, planning is essential in of promotion. The logical stages of promotional planning processes are as follows:

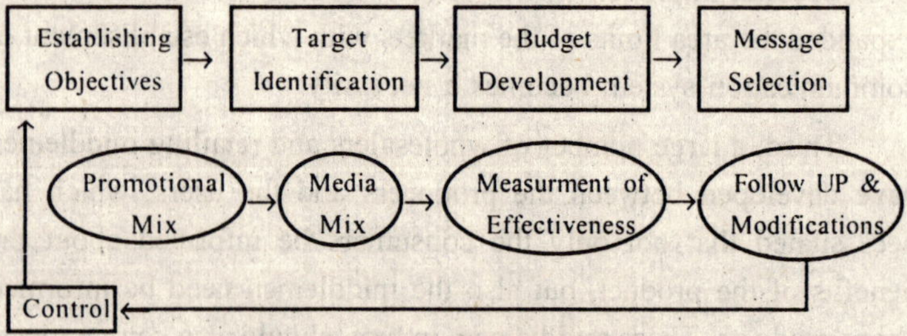

Fig. Promotional Planning Process

A separate and independent promotion plan has no place in a marketing-oriented company. Within the marketing plan for a particular product, there will be objectives that can best be achieved through promotion. But it much depends on how the resources could be used between different variables. For instance, there are different tools such as 'advertising, personal selling, sales promotion', etc. Usually five basic steps are followed in planning promotional activities:

1. Problem definition,
2. Definition of detailed objective,
3. Design of promotion mix,
4. Detailed planning, and
5. Monitoring and evaluation.

Promotional mix for the sake of discussion could be divided into three categories: Personal selling, Advertising and Sales promotion activities.

Factors Affecting Promotion Mix

While determining the promotion mix of a business firm, the following factors should be considered:

(i) Nature of Product. Different products require different tools of promotion. In case of industrial goods (like plant, machinery, equipment, etc.) personal selling is most effective because a great deal of presale and after sale services are required to sell and install the product. Such products are often made to specifications and the market is well identified. On the other hand, advertising and publicity are more important in case of consumer goods, particularly low priced convenience goods for daily use. In case of these goods the buying decisions are generally made at the point of purchasing and no installation is required.

(ii) Stage of the Product's Life. During the introduction stage the main aim or promotion is to create primary demand by emphasising the product's features, utility, etc. Therefore, a combination of advertising and publicity is required. During the maturity stage, advertising and personal selling are needed to ensure continued patronage of customers and to meet competition. During the decline stage, drastic cuts have to be made in the promotional efforts and sales promotion can be used to push up sagging sales.

(iii) Nature of Market. Number of location of customers exercise considerable influence on promotion mix. If the number of potential buyers is small and the customers are concentrated in a particular locality, personal selling is likely to be more effective. Where the members of customers is large and they are scattered widely in different parts of the country, advertising, personal selling and sales promotion all are required to sell the product. Type of customers also influences managerial decisions on promotion mix. Educated, urban and institutional customers require different types of promotion as compared to illiterate rural and household customers.

(iv) Availability of Funds. The promotional budget of the firm is an important determinant of promotion mix. If the funds available for promotional activities are large, a combination of all promotional methods can be used. But in case of financial constraints the firm has to be selective in use of promotional tools. Personal selling is cheaper and more effective in the short run. Advertising is costly but can attract a large number of customers.

(v) **Readiness of Buyer.** Different tools of promotion are effective at different stages of buyer readiness. At the awareness stage, advertising and publicity are more effective. At the comprehension stage advertising and personal selling play a greater role. During the conviction stage, personal selling is most effective. Personal selling and sales promotion are effective at closing the sale stage. Thus, advertising and publicity are more effective during the early stages of the buying decision process whereas personal selling and sales promotion are more effective during the later stages.

(vi) **Nature of the Technique.** Each technique of promotion has its unique features which must be understood before deciding the promotion mix. Advertising is an impersonal and mass method of promotion. It is a pervasive medium and colour and sound can be used to amplify the expression. Therefore, advertising can be used for both building a long term image of the product and for generating quick sales. Personal selling involves face to face presentation and is, therefore, more effective in cultivating relationships and building buyers' preference. Sales promotion offers incentives and induces buyers to buy now. It can create a quick response and boost sagging sales. Public relation enjoys high credibility and can be used to supplement the other tools of promotion.

(vii) **Promotional Strategy.** Promotion mix depends to a great extent on whether a company chooses a push or pull strategy to create sales. In a push strategy, the manufacturer includes his dealers to carry the product and promote it to consumers. Personal selling and trade promotion are more suitable to this strategy. On the other hand, a pull strategy involves inducing consumers to ask dealers to carry the product. Advertising and consumer promotion are more appropriate for full strategy.

PERSONAL SELLING

Personal Selling means the performance of actual selling acitivity. Personal selling is quite direct and personal. Personal selling involves oral conversation between seller and buyer for the purpose of making sales. Ultimate purpose of personal selling is to sell the goods to their ultimate buyers by bringing right goods and services into contact with the right customers. Therefore, personal selling is said to be the 'Back-bone of Marketing'. The term 'Personal Selling' has been defined as under :

Richard Buskirk, "Personal selling consists of contacting prospective buyers of products personally."

William J. Stanton, "Personal selling consists in individual personal communication, in contrast to mass relatively impersonal communication of advertising, sales promotion and other promotional tools."

Amercian Marketing Association, "Oral presentation is a conversation with one or more prospective purchasers for the purchase of making sales."

On the basis of analytical study of above definitions, it can be concluded that personal selling involves oral conversation between seller and buyer (when they come in contact with one another). The seller wants to convince the buyer of the goods and services which he wants to sell. When the buyer is convinced, he purchases these goods and services.

Thus, it is clear that personal selling is the most important of all the marketing efforts of an enterprise because through personal selling the consumers are encouraged to buy the product.

PROCESS OF PERSONAL SELLING

The activities involved in the selling process vary from salesman to salesman and also with selling situations. No one method is used by the two salesmen. Generally, the following process is utilised in selling a product:

(1) **Prospecting and Evaluating.** Prospecting consists in developing a list of potential customers. The first step in

the sales process is to discover the names of prospects from several sources such as the company's sales records, consumer's information requests from advertisements, other customers newspaper announcements, public records, telephone and trade directories, who's who, yearbooks, and trade association list.

After developing the prospect list, a salesman evaluates each prospect to determine whether the prospect is able, willing, and authorized to buy the product. On the basis of this evaluation, names of some prospects may be deleted, while others are deemed acceptable and may be ranked in relation to their desirabilty or potential.

(2) **Approaching the Consumer.** This is most critical step because the prospect's first impression of the salesman may be a lasting impression that has long-run consequences. One type of approach is based on referrals; the salesman approaches the prospects and explains that an acquitance as associate, or a relative has suggested the call. The 'cold courses' is an approach in which the salesman calls or potential customers without their prior consent. 'Repeat contact' is another common approach, when making the contact, the salesman mentions a prior meeting. What type of approach would be suitable, depends upon the salesman's preferences, the product being sold, the firm's resources, and the characteristics of the prospect.

(3) **Preparing for the Sale.** This step consists in finding and analysing information regarding prospects's specific product needs, current brands being used; feelings about other available brands and personal characteristics. This information is used in selecting an approach and in creating a sales presentation. The more information about a prospect that a salesman has, the better able he is to develop an approach and presentation that precisely communicates with the prospect.

(4) Making the Presentation. During the sales presentation, the salesman must attract and hold attention of the prospect in order to stimulate interest and convince and arouse desire for the product.

To attract such attention, the salesman should talk to the prospect briefly about the product either by asking a question that interests him or by display of some material, such as a sample, or by allowing the prospect touch, hold, or actually use the product. Demonstration may also be given about the product so that the prospect gets more involved.

(5) Overcoming the Objections. There are certain objections which can be anticipated and their answers formulated before the sales interview takes place. There are other objections which cannot be anticipated because they are usually related to the procedures of a particular business. For these objections, the following methods may be used:

1. Direct denial method (also called the "head-on or contradiction" method), under which the salesman should never contradict the buyers' observation. In such method, the salesman should keep in mind these guidelines; *(a)* He should not be offensive, rather he should smile; *(b)* The retail sales clerk should not attempt this method because he is seldom in a position to keep the customers; *(c)* The type of customer must be kept in mind so that his feelings may not be hurt; *(d)* It should not be used if the objection has any 'ego' involvement in it.
2. The Boomerang method (also called the translation method), is so called because the object raised by the prospect often comes back at him as a valid reason for buying the product. This method is useful in meeting excuses that are not strongly backed by facts. It is effective only when the salesman is skilled in applying this technique.

3. Indirect-dential method (also known as "yes but method or 'sidestepping the question method), is most widely used method. It is a method of compromise because both salesman and prospects "bend" a little. They admit to each other that they both are right, but there is the other side of the problem to consider also.
4. Compensation method, which merely acknowledges the validity of an objection, but points out some advantage that is supposed to compensate for the objection, such as lower price, or special care of the product.
5. The Pass-up method, is one where the salesman smiles and tries to passover the objection especially when the objection is of trivial nature that it does not deserve a careful or thoughtful answer.
6. The question method, under which the salesman asks questions regarding objections, so that further analysis be made. The "reason objections" are answered with the word why because why reopens the discussion and the possibility of making a sale.

The salesman, while using any of these methods of handing objections, must be sure that he is applying the right method in such particular situation.

6. **Closing the Sale.** This step is the climax of the selling process in which the salesman asks the prospect to buy the product or products. "He who wins the last battle wins the war" is truly applicable to a salesman foreclosing in the test of every salesman. Inadequate preparation, poor impression, failure in meeting objections or wrong approach on the part of the salesman may come in his way. Buyer's fears and the salesman's attitude are two important obstacles of closing the sale. The sale must be closed only when the salesman knows hat the customer is prepared for it. The close of the sale depends upon the conditions, personality for the parties and the nature of the goods.

Some of the effective ways of closing the sale are: *(i)* to take it for granted, *(ii)* offer some inducements, *(iii)* telling business stories how others have benefitted by the purchase of the products, *(iv)* fear of loss, *(v)* stressing minor but interesting details, and *(vi)* marketing a straight request for an order.

The salesman may employ a "trial close" by asking questions that assume the prospect will buy the product, *e.g.* he might ask the potential customer questions about financial terms, desired colours, or sizes, delivery arrangements, or the quantity to be purchased. The prospects reactions to such questions usually indicate how close the prospect indirectly respond that they will buy the product without having to state those sometimes difficult words "I'll like it". A salesman should try to close at several points during the presentation, because the prospect may be ready to buy.

7. **Following up.** After a sale is closed,, it should be properly followed. The salesman should ensure that the delivery instructions given by the customer are properly followed. The salesman must visit the customer often to learn what problems or questions have arisen regarding the product "After sales service" should be punctual, quick and satisfactory.

Characteristics of Personal Selling

On the basis of above definitions of personal selling, following characteristics of personal selling may be enumerated—*(i)* Seller and buyers come in direct contact with one another. *(ii)* It involves oral conversation between seller and buyers regarding quality, price, characteristics, use etc., of the product. *(iii)* In personal selling, seller wants to convince the buyers about the goods and services which he want to sell. *(iv)* It involves the sale of goods and services personally. *(v)* It is most effective tool in increasing the sales. *(vi)* It helps in providing many important information to the enterprise regarding market. *(vii)* It is oldest method of sale of goods and services.

Functions of Personal Selling

Some of the important functions of personal selling may be summed up as under:

(i) To sell the goods to new and old customers;

(ii) To demonstrate the goods before customers;

(iii) To remove the doubts and confusions of customers about products;

(iv) To provide after-sale-services to the customers;

(v) To instruct the customers for the use of product;

(vi) To advise the customers on certain matters;

(vii) To maintain the record of sales;

(viii) To prepare long-term and short-term marketing programmes;

(ix) To train new salesman;

(x) To slove the problems of selling force.

MERITS OR ADVANTAGES OF PERSONAL SELLING

Some of the important merits or advantages of personal selling are as under:

1. **Helpful in Getting New Customers.** Personal selling helps in discovering and getting new customers. In personal selling, salesmen concentrate upon attracting the attention of new customers and encouraging them to buy the goods.

2. **Helpful in Removing the Doubts and Confusions of Customers.** Personal selling is the only tool of all the marketing efforts of an enterprise through which doubts and confusion of customers may be removed because buyers and sellers come into personal contact in personal selling.

3. **Helpful in the Demonstration of Products.** Personal selling demonstrates the products before customers. It provides an apportunity to the customers to see the practical use of the product and to understand it thoroughly.

4. **Helpful of Communication.** Personal selling is the most effective tool of communication between buyers and sellers. It communicates new products and their new uses to the customers. It also communicates the problems, doubts and grievances of customers to the management.

5. **Helpful in the Improvement of Product Specifications and Services.** As personal selling is the tool through which selllers come to know about the problems and grievances of customers, it provides an opportunity to them to know the defects of the products, and thus, it provides an opprotunity to impove product specifications and services.

6. **Helpful in Real Sale.** Advertisement and sales promotion are the tools which encourage consumers to buy a particular product while personal selling is the tool which actually sells the product to them.

7. **Helpful in Non-selling Activities.** Personal selling is helpful not only in the sale of goods and services but also in many non-selling activities, like—marketing research, sales forecasting, after-sale-services to the consumers and removal of the problems and grievances of consumers etc.

8. **It Provides Social Inspiraction.** Personal selling brings seller and buyer close to each other. They become friend to each other. Salesman behaves not only as a salesman but also as a friend, and guide with the customers believe upon the advice of salesman.

DEMERITS OR LIMITATIONS OF PERSONAL SELLING

Personal selling, though very useful in selling the goods and services of the enterprise, cannot be said to be free from limitations.

Some of the important demerits and limitations of personal selling are as under:

(1) Increase in the Cost of Sales. Enterprise has to spend heavy amount on travelling allowances, commission and salaries of its salesmen. It increases the cost of sales which is added to the price of products.

(2) Difficulty of Reporting at Right Time. Personal selling can be effective only when the salesman reports at the time when the buyer is in a position to purchase, it is very difficult to know this time correctly and to report at this time. Thus, it has been the experience that the proper time of selling becomes a question.

(3) Lack of Efficient Salesmen. Success of personal selling depends exclusively upon the ability, capability and experience of salesmen. Qualified, trained and experienced salesmen are not available in required number or are available at very high cost. Thus, availability of trained and experienced salesmen is another important limitation of personal selling.

ADVERTISING

Advertising consists of those activities by which usual and oral messages are addressed to selected public for the purpose of informing and influencing them to by the products or services or to act or to be inclined favourably towards ideas, persons, trademarks or institutions featured. As contrasted with publicity and other forms of propaganda, advertising messages are identified with the advertiser either the signature or oral statement, further advertising is a commercial transaction involving pay to publishers, broadcasters on others whose media employed.

"Advertising is paid, non-personal communicating various media by business organisations, non-profit organisations and individual who are in some way identified in advertising message."

Clearly advertisement includes the following forms of messages. The out-door boards, our street cards, bus and train cards and in circular of all kinds whether distributed by mail, by person, through tradesmen or by inserts in packages, dealer help materials and efforts, store signs, house organs where picture used by advertising messages or signature of the advertiser.

Labels, toys and other literature accompanying merchandise are also deemed advertising, because they may reasonably be said to fall within the definition of advertising given above. Writers sometime includes these items.

In the foregoing paragraph, the informative aspect of advertising has been stressed. Though the basic purpose of advertising is to bring the advertised product as well as its features and uses to the notice of consumers, it has begun to be used for a number of other allied purposes now:

1. In the existence of intense competition has given rise to what may be described as competitive advertising. In other words, advertising is undertaken these days not only to inform people about of product, but is used also to maintain the demand for an existing product and to add to existing demand by weaning people away from rival products in the market. To take a concrete case, when the bottlers of Coca-Cola found a strong rival in Pepsi cola, they changed the tone and emphasis of their advertisements and began to emphasise that only 'it is real'.
2. Large-scale advertising is often undertaken with the objective of creating or enhancing the goodwill of advertising company. Thus, in turn, increases the market receptiveness of the company's product and help the salesman to win customers easily.
3. Advertising is used as a means to demand creation. Many needs of the people are the creations of advertising. Actually advertising seeks to channelise the surplus incomes of the people towards those products which are not included among the basic necessities of life. In this process, it makes people conscous of the need not something without which they had been living so far. This consciousness is

turned into desire, and an ardent desire, when the advertisevement continues to rub in the need for a product.

4. It follows from the above that advertising may be used with a view to preparing ground from a new product that is proposed to be introduced in the market. Most of the cinema advertisements are designed to serve this purpose. By the time a film starts its run at a theatre, the poeple are already prepared to receive it. That explains the gate-crashing and the heavy rush at the box office right on the opening day of picture. The readers would recall how ground is prepared for the opening and how enthusiastically the people rush to see it in the first week of its run.

FUNCTIONS OF ADVERTISING

Advertising has become an essential marketing activity in the modern era of large-scale production and severe competition in the market. It performs the following functions:

(1) It promotes the sale of goods and services by informing and persuading the people to buy them. A good advertising campaign helps in winning the new customers both in the national as well as the international market.

(2) It helps in the introduction of new products in the market. A business enterprise can introduce itself and its products to the public through advertsiing. No new enterprise can make an impact over the prospective customers without the help of advertising. Advertising enables quick publicity in the market.

(3) Advertising facilitates large-scale production. Advertising encourages production of goods on mass because the business firm knows that it will be able to sell on a large-scale with the help of advertising. Mass production reduces the cost of production per unit by making possible the economical use of various factory of production.

(4) It stimulates research and development activities. Advertising has become a competitive marketing activity. Every firm

tries to differentiate its product from the substitutes available in the market through advertising. This compels business firm to do more and more research to find new products and their new uses. If a firm does not engage in research and development activities, it will be out of the market in the near future.

(5) Advertising educates the people about new products and their uses. Advertising message about the utility of a product enables the people to widen their knowledge. It is advertising which has helped people in adopting new ways of life and giving up old habits. It has contributed a lot towards the betterment of the standard of living of the society.

(6) It sustains press. Advertising provides an important source of revenue to the publishers of newspapers and magazines. It enables to increase the circulation of their publications by selling them at lower rates. People are also benefited because they get new publications at cheaper rates.

(7) It buildes up the reputation of the advertiser. Advertising enables a business firm to communicate its achievements and its efforts to satisfy the cusotmer's need to the public. This increases the goodwill and reputation of the firm which is necessary to fight comptition in the market.

OBJECTIVES OF ADVERTISING

A crucial step in any management effort is the establishment of operational objectives. In order to determine criteria for decision-making and measurement standards for evaluating the advertising effort, management must first establish advertising objectives. But, there is a wrong feeling that the effect of advertising could be measured in terms of product sales. Reaching the sales goal alone is not an indication of advertising effectiveness. Because, many other factors influence product sales including product availability, price, etc.

It is the this connection that the principle of DAGMAR becomes relevant. The DAGMAR—Defining Advertising Goals for Measured Advertising Results—approach defines an advertising goal not as a sales quota but as a specific effect on a target audience. In terms of the effect produced, an advertisement can either make the consumer aware of the existence of a product, provide the consumer with information about it, convince the consumer of the product's advantages over competitive offerings, or actually encourage the consumer to purchase the product.

As pointed out earlier, the purpose of advertising is nothing but to sell something—a product, a service or an idea. The real objective of advertising is effective communication between producers and consumers. In other words, the ultimate purpose underlying all advertising is 'increased awareness'. In marketing. The specific objectives of advertising are as follows:

(i) To make an immediate sale.

(ii) To increase market share.

(iii) To modify existing product appeals and buying motives.

(iv) To inform about new product's availability or features or price.

(v) To increase the frequency of use of a product.

(vi) To build primary demand.

(vii) To introduce a price deal.

(viii) To inform about a product availability.

(ix) To build brand recognition or brand insistence.

(x) To help salesmen by building an awareness of a product among retailers.

(xi) To create a reputation for service, reliability or research strength.

(xii) To increase the number or quality of retail outlets.

(xiii) To build overall company image.

(xiv) To effect immediate buying action.

(xv) To reach new areas or new segments of population within existing areas.

(xvi) To develop the overseas market.

As pointed out earlier, effective advertising management requires the establishment of goals as the first step. These goals will provide a basis for planning and evaluating advertising efforts. The objectives can either be communciation goals or sales goals. In a way, both are complementary. A communication goal would be to convey information or to maintain 'top of the mind awareness'. This is done by informing, persuading and reminding the potential customers.

KINDS OF ADVERTISING

Advertising may be classified into the following categories:

1. **Product Advertising.** Normal characteristic of advertising is to create primary demand for a product category rather than for a specific brand. It is wrongly believed that product advertising must stress on brand name. This is based on the feeling that a good image often enhances the effectiveness of product advertising. Naturally, the stress is laid on the brand. However, in practice, most companies were successful in marketing the product image by using the brand names (*e.g.*, Dalda, Dettol, Horlicks). In short, where the company tries to sell its product or services through advertising it may be referred to as product advertising.

2. **Selective or Competitive Advrtising.** When a product enters growth stage of the life cycle and when competition begins, advertising becomes competitive or selective. Here, the goal of advertising is to influence demand for a specific product or service. Often, promotion becomes less information and more emotional during this phase. Advertising may begin to stress subtle differences in brands, with heavy emphasis on 'brand name recall'. Pricing also will be use as a key promotional weapon as products become very similar.

3. **Institutional Advertising.** Where the objective of advertising is to project the image of a compnay or its services, it takes the form of an institutional advertising. These advertisements are not always directed only to consumers. Instead, it may be aimed at many of the various sets of public (shareholders, creditors, etc.). It is not at all product-oriented, but is designed to enhance the image of the company.

4. **Primary Demand Advertising.** It is intended to stimulate primary demand for a new product or product category. It is heavily utilised during the introduction stage of the product life cycle.

5. **Comparative Advertising.** This is a highly controversial trend in competitive markets that is recently noted. Such types of advertising stress on comparative features of two or more specific brands in terms of product/service attributes. This method is adopted in the maturity stage when similar products fastly appearing the market constitute a stiff competition. Comparative advertising delivers information not previously available to consumers''. When comparative advertising appears it reveals the intensity of competition in the market.

6. **Shortage Advertising.** When shortage in the supply of products occurs, advertising often disappears into the background. A concrete example is found in the case of petroleum products that since the oil crisis in 1974, virtually advertising for these products ceased. But the intelligent marketers have found that advertising is still a viable marketing tool during times of shortage. This is what is termed as sortage advertising. In such kinds of advertising new promotional objective may be incorporated such as:

   (a) educating the user of more efficient means of utilising the product, thus reducing the demand;

   (b) to reduce customer pressure on the sales force;

(c) improving goodwill; and

(d) making appeal to save resources.

7. **Co-operative Advertising.** When manufacturers, wholesalers and/or retailers jointly sponsor and share the expenditure on advertising, it takes the form of co-operative advertising. Such advertising would carry the names of all the parties involved. From the point of view of the customers this is beneficial as they could get the articles directly from the authorised outlets. For example, the manufacturers of cars undertake this type of advertising.

8. **Non-Commercial Advertising.** These are usually published by charitable institutions preferably to solicit general and financial help (*e.g.*, collection of donations or sale of tickets.)

9. **Direct Action Advertising.** Advertising that stresses and persuades immediate buying of the product is known as direct action advertising. Direct mail advertising is capable of achieving immediate action to a large extent.

10. **Commercial Advertising.** It is also termed as business advertising. As the name suggests such advertising is solely meant for effecting increase in sales. Usually the following forms of commercial advertising are recognised:

    (a) Industrial advertising—this is exclusively used for selling industrial products.

    (b) Trade advertising—advertising relating to a trade.

    (c) Professional advertising—undertaken by professional people such as doctors, accountants, etc.

    (d) Farm advertising—exclusively used for selling farm products such as fertilisers, insecticides, farm implements, etc.

Some kind of specialisation is found in all the above forms of advertising. Hence all these forms could be commonly called selective advertising.

MAIN MEDIA OF ADVERTISEMENT

Advertising media are the means to transmit the message from the advertiser to the particular class of people. A manufacturer can select any one or more of the following media of adverstisement to promote his sales:

1. Newspaper. A newspaper is generally a daily publication containing news and opinions about current events and feature articles. The improtance of newspaper is obvious from the fact that newspaper reading is a common habit of most educated people these days. Besides daily newspapers, there are bi-weekly and weekly newspapers also. Newspapers reach almost every place and are read by all kinds of people. Therefore, newspaper can be used as a medium of advertisement with great advantages. While selecting a newspaper for this purpose, an advertiser has to take into consideration the strength of circulation, the class of readers it serves, the geographical region over which it is popular and the cost of space. Newspaper advertising has many advantages. Firstly, a newspaper has large circulation and a single advertisement in a newspaper can reach a large number of people. Secondly, continuous advertisement is possible because a newspaper is published daily. An advertiser can repeat his advertisement either daily or weekly. Thirdly, newspapers provide flexibility in advertising in the sense that advertisement campaign can be initiated and stopped quickly. One day's notice is sufficient for this purpose.

Newspaper advertising has certain limitations also. Firstly, the life of a newspaper advertisement is very short. Moreover, people devoted only an insignficant part of their day's time in reading the newspaper. Thus, advertisements are likely to draw the reader's attention only casually. Secondly, newspaper advertisement is successful only when the people to be communicated are educated. Thirdly, newspapers cannot be used for coloured advertisements since they are printed in black and white. Because of this, they may fail to help the customers in identifying the product at the point of purchase.

2. Outdoor Advertising. Outdoor advertising includes the use of poster displays, bill board displays and electrical displays. Posters are fixed or pasted on walls at important public places so that they may intercept the people on their way to work and back home. Painted or bill board displays involve the advertisements directly painted on the boards meant for that purpose. They are quite big in size and are fixed at outstanding locations like busy markets and crossings. Painted displays take the form of painted walls when the message is painted on the walls. Electrical display involves the use of electrical lights or neon tubes to attract the attention of people particularly during night. Generally, a short message is illuminated in tubes of different colours so that it is conspicuous and attractive. Electrical displays are fixed at heavy traffic centres.

Outdoor advertising is highly flexible and low cost medium. It is very useful for advertising consumer products because advertising can be displayed at various crowded crossings. Outdoor advertisement attracts the attention quickly and requires less time and efforts on the part of the readers. Moreover, a complete picture of the product can be advertised through outdoor displays. Business concern also use bill boards near the actual side of the business. The recent trend in outdoor advertisement is the use of public transport vehicles for advertising purposes.

3. Direct Mail Advertising. Direct mail is probably the most personal and selective of all the advertising media. Direct mail is used to send the message directly to the customers. For this prupose, the advertiser has to maintain a mailing list and the mailing list can be expanded or contacted by adding or removing names from the list. But a limitation is posed by the difficulty of getting and maintaining a good mailing list.

Advertisements that are sent by direct mail may be in the form of circular letters, leaflects folders, calenders, booklets and catalogues. Circular letters, folders, calendars, books catalogues. Circular letters are sent to the prospective customers to inform them about the merit of the product and to create their interest in the product. Booklets and catalogues contain the information about the products advertised.

Information about the terms of sale and price of diffrent varieties of the product is given to the prospective customers through catalogues. Mail advertising has a personal appeal since it is addressed to a particular person. The message can be changed whenever the need arises. It also maintains secrecy in advertising. The competitors do not get the information about the advertised material. The main drawback of mail advertisement is that it is not suitable for all types of products and it has a limited coverage.

4. Film Advertisement. Films are also an important medium of advertisement. Business concerns usually get a short motion picture prepared and distribute it to different cinema houses for displaying it before the commencement of the regular shows or during the period of intermission. Such films are accompanied by running commentary to explain the features, uses and superiority of the product. But film advertisement can be adopted only by the well established firms. Since it involves high cost, small business firms can get cinema slides prepared for display in the cinema halls. Film advertisement is very effective since it combines spoken worlds and visual presentation of pictures. It also helps in selective advertisement. A trade can advertise his product only in a particular locality if he wants to attract the local customers only. The major drawback of film advertisement is that it is usually ignored by the people. Only a few persons are present in the hall before the start of the film and during the interval, and they too are busy in talking.

5. Television. Television is the latest and fastly growing medium of advertisement. It makes its appeal through both eye and ear. Products can be demonstrated as well as explained as in film advertisement. Television is a very costly medium of advertisement and can be made use of by the well established companies only. Another limitation of television advertisements is that once it is presented, its back reference is not possible as in the case of radio advertisement.

6. Magazine. Magazines or periodicals are an excellent medium of advertisement when a high quality of printing and colour is desired in an advertisement. Magazine advertisements can be directed towards a particular class of people and thus they avoid wasteful expenditure on advertising. Many specialised magazines or journals are published which can be used for transmitting the message to the particular class of customers. Magazine advertisements attract greater attention of the people since they are read more carefully and at greater leisure. The life of the magazine advertisements is longer. Magazines are preserved for a long period of time and are read time and again. Since advertisement copy presented in a coloured form, it creates and better image of the product advertised. Exact picture can be portrayed to enable the customer to identify the product at the point of purchase.

Magazine advertisements have certain less favourable characteristics also. Magazine advertisements are to be prepared and sent for publication well in advance. It is not possible to make the last minute change in the advertisement copy. Magazine advertisements are costlier than the newspaper advertisements since their circulation is small. Small circulation is also another drawback of magazine advertising.

7. Radio. Radio advertisements are gaining greater popularity these days. advertisements are broadcast from the transmitting stations of the commercial service of All India Radio and picked up by the receiving sets owned by the public. Radio advertisements are normally broadcast along with popular programmes of music. Even the sponsored programmes of interviews and plays can be broadcast over the radio.

Radio advertisements carry an effective appeal and cover numerous listeners of different tastes. People can listen to them even when they are busy in other activities. Radio advertisement also reach the illiterate people who cannot read newspapers and magazine advertisements. Radio also provides selectivity to some extent because advertisements can be included in different programmes meant for different types of people. In short, radio advertisements are very much suitable for the promotion of mass scale consumer goods. But demerit of radio advertisement is that it is non-visual. Sometimes, the message is not understood properly by the listeners. Moreover, the message may be missed by many listeners. In order to remove this drawback, many big advertisers give the same advertisement daily in different programmes.

8. Speciality Advertising. Many business firms offer speciality articles to the persent and prospective customers. These articles may be diaries, pen holders, desk trays, key chains, purses, paper weights, cigarette case and calendars. The name and address of the advertiser is printed in or inscribed on the sepciality items. They also bear the brand name of the firm. Since these articles are of daily use, they have greater capacity to remind their users about the brand name of the firm offering such articles.

9. Window Display. Windows display is an on-sight method of advertising. Goods can be exhibited in artistically laid out windows at the shop fronts or at important busy centres like railway stations and bus stops. Large show rooms are organised by the big manufacturers and wholesalers in the main market to advertise their products and attend to the queries of the prospective customers. The retailers also organise attractive display of certain goods in the windows of their shops. Window displays are very popular with the retailers since they help in informing the customers the types of goods available with them.

The main objectives of windows display is to draw the attention of the public and arouse their interest in the products displayed. Almost all the manufacturers insist that their products should be displayed at the retail shops. If a product is displayed properly at the point of purchase by the customers, it can make many customers to buy it. Many people having no preference for a particular brand may discover a particular brand quite appealing and attractive and may purchase it. Thus, window display creates the demand for the product. Windows display acts as a silent salesman. In order to achieve the purpose of windows display, cleanliness and a well furnished appearance for the window are essential. Articles should be arranged in a systematic way and, if possible, price tags should also be attached with the articles. It is also better if window displays are changed regularly to make the customers look at the displays every time they visit the shop.

SELECTING THE ADVERTISING MEDIA

For the purpose of choosing the appropriate medium or media of advertisement, following factors should be taken into consideration:

1. **Nature of Product.** Nature of the product to be advertised has an important bearing on the medium of advertisement. Product should be classified in a two broad categories, namely, consumer goods and industrial goods. Consumer goods can be advertised in newspapers. magazines, radio and television and through outdoor displays. But industrial goods can be advertised profitably in the specialised trade, technical and professional journals.
2. **Objectives of Advertising.** The objectvies of the advertising programme are very important in determining the choice of advertising media. The objective may be introduction of new product, to increase demand of an existing product or to avoid competition by the rivals. If advertising is to be carried on a mass scale, to have big impact in the short and long-run, a combination of various advertising media may be chosen. Sometime advertisements are inserted in the newspapers and magazines to complement the readers in order to enchance the goodwill of the advertiser.
3. **Nature of Market.** Nature and extent of market can be determined by various factors like geographical region, size of population and the purchasing power of the population. The market may be either local or national. Film advertising and outdoor advertising are more suitable for local products. Newspapers are the most suitable for advertising products which can be sold throughout the country.
4. **Life of Advertisement.** Outdoor displays and magazines and direct mail have sufficiently longer life, but the life of newspaper, radio and television advertisements is very

short unless they are repeated regularly. Therefore, the advertiser should also take into consideration the duration for which he wants to create the impression in the mind of the prospective customers.

5. **Media Used by Customers.** The choice of advertising media also depends upon the media used by the competitors. If a product is being advertised in a newspaper, the producers of its substitutes will find it better to advertise them in the same newspaper. This practice has become more common these days in order to fight competition in the market.
6. **Type of Audience.** If the message is to be conveyed to illiterate or less literate people, radio, television and cinema advertisement will serve the purpose in a better way. Newspapers, magazines, displays and direct mail may be used to convey the message to the educated people. Since different language are popular in different regions, advertisements in different languages may be given to popularise the product.
7. **Financial Consideration.** The cost of advertising media is an important consideration and it should be considered in relation to, *(a)* the amount of funds available, and *(b)* the circulation of the media. In the first instance, the amount of funds available may dictate the choice of a medium or a combination of media of advertisement, and on the second account, the advertiser should try to develop some relationship between the cost of the medium and its circulation. The cost-benefit analysis will enable the advertiser to take right decision in regard to selection of the advertising media.
8. **Circulation of Media.** If the media have greater circulation the message of the advertiser will reach a larger number of people. It may be mentioned that newspapers have the widest circulation, but other media have limited and selective circulation.

BENEFITS OF ADVERTISING IN THE FIELD OF MARKETING

Advertising broadens the knowledge of the consumer. With the aid of advertising, consumer find and buy necessary products without waste of time. This speeds up the sales of commodities; the efficiency of labour in distribution increases; and the cost of selling diminishes, it is an accepted fact that without market stimulus of heavy advertising, consumers might have waited another sixty years for the product evolution that took place in less than ten years—it took, after all, over sixty years from the invention of the safety razor before the first acceptable stainless steel blade appeared in the market.

These words are more than enough to testify the potentialities of advertising in the field of modern marketing. The benefits of advertising may be narrated as follows:

Benefits to Manufacturers

1. It increases sales volume, On the one hand, it reduces the cost of production and, on the other, increases profits.
2. It helps easy introduction of products into the markets.
3. Retail price maintenance is possible.
4. It helps to establish a direct contact between manufacturers and consumers.
5. It helps to create an image and reputation not only of the product but also of the advertiser.

Benefits to Wholesalers and Retailers

1. Easy sale of the products is possible since consumers are aware of the product and its quality.
2. It enables them to have product information.
3. It ensures more economical selling.
4. It increases the rate of the turnover of stock.
5. It supplements the selling activities.
6. The reputation created is shared by the wholesalers and retailers alike.

Benefits to Consumers

1. Advertising stresses quality and very often prices. This forms an indirect guarantee to the consumers. Furthermore, large-scale production assured by advertising enables the seller to sell the product at a lower cost.
2. It helps them to know where and when the products are available. This reduces their shopping time.
3. It provides an opportunity to the customers to compare the merits and demerits of various substitute products.
4. Modern advertisements are highly informative.
5. This is perhaps the only medium through which consumers could know the varied and new uses of a product.

Benefits to Salesmen

Salesmanship is incomplete without advertising. Advertising serves as the forerunner of a salesman in the distribution of goods:

1. Introducing the product is made easy.
2. The contact established with the consumer by a salesman is made permanent through advertising.
3. The salesman can weigh the effectiveness of advertising when he makes a direct contact with the customers.
4. Advertising prepares necessary ground for a salesman to begin his work. Hence sales efforts are reduced.

Benefits to the Community

1. Advertising, in general, is educative in nature. In the words of the late President Roosevelt of the USA, "Advertising brings to the greatest number of people actual knowledge concerning useful things; it is essentially a form of education—and the progress of civilization depends on education."
2. Advertising leads to large-scale production creating more employment opportunities.

3. Newspapers would not have become so popular and so cheap if there had been no advertisements. The cheap production of newspapers is possible only through the publication of advertisements. In other words, it is the advertising revenue that makes the newspapers live.
4. It initiates a process of creating more wants and their satisfaction resulting in a higher standard of living. For example, advertising has made more popular and universal the uses of such inventions as the automobiles, radios and various household appliances. To quote Sir Winston Churchill, "Advertising nourishes the consuming power of man. It creates wants for a better standard of living.... It spurs individual exertion and greater production."
5. It assures employment opportunities for the professional artists.

Objections Against Advertising

Advertising has also been subjected to a number of objections mainly because it has been misused by a few people to serve their own ends, overlooking the business interests. An examination of some of the forceful objections will be of interest:

(a) Multiplication of Needs. It is said that advertising compels people to buy things they do not need. Human instincts, like desire to possess, to be recognised in the society, etc., are provoked in order to sell products. Sometimes, various types of appeals are advanced to arouse interest in the product. Sentiments and emotions are played upon to gain customers. To say this would not, however, be correct in as much as advertising cannot force anybody to buy a thing which he considers unnecessary.

(b) Misrepresentation of Facts. Through misrepresentation of the benefit a product will give, goods of no real value are sold. Tall claims are made by the advertisers to tempt people to take such actions as go purely to their advantage and cause tremendous loss to the consumer. Even adulterated food and medicines are marketed, which by no stretch of imagination can benefit anybody. By sheer exaggeration of facts, demand for the merchandise advertised is created without much difficulty even when the commodities carrying greater worth or satisfaction are already therein the market. Such unscrupulous actions of a few tell upon public confidence in advertising.

(3) **Consumer's Deficit.** While advertising leads to increased satisfaction from commodities already in use, it also creates discontent in the minds of many people who are tempted to purchase some commodities but are not able to do so because of insuffficient purchasing power. Such discontent is obviously not very desirable from the point of view of society particularly if it affects a large majority of people.

(4) **Wastage of National Resources.** A more serious objection against advertising is that it is used to destroy the utility of goods before the end of their normal period of usefulness. New models of automobilies with nominal improvements are, for instance, advertised at such high pressure that the old models have to be discarded long before they become useless. Not that merely, the most advertised products are delicate, fragile and brittle. In the U.S.A., there is evidence of a marked decline in the quality and durability of cars, furniture, rugs, television sets, refrigerators, etc. That appears to be the way of which the increased demand created through advertising can be sustained. The same is true of dresses, funiture and other products. From the point of view of the commnity it is a waste of resources. "The natural resources, capital equipment and labour energy which go into the production of new items to take the place of the discarded ones amount to waste when measured in terms of social well-being."

(E) **Increased Cost.** There is a great deal of controversy as to whether advertising leads to increase in the cost which the community has to pay for a product. In a sense it is true since expenses on it form a part of the total cost of the product. But at the same time it would be wrong to infer that if the advertising costs were cut down the goods would necessarily be cheaper. Advertising is, no doubt, one of the items of costs but it is a cost which brings savings in its wake on the distribution side. On the manufacturing side, it is one of the factors that made large-scale production possible and anyone would agree that large-scale production leads to lower costs.

(F) The 'Monopoly Argument'. An objection which is most commonly raised against advertising is that it tends to develop monopolies.

THEMES OF ADVERTISEMENT

Different advertisers use different themes or central ideas to influence the instincts of different kinds of people. Some of the important themes are as follows:

1. **Prestige.** This theme is used to popularise luxurious item like motor-car, refrigerator and furniture. Their possession acts as a symbol of prestige to their holders.
2. **Comfort.** This theme is used to advertise products like fans, airconditioners and refrigerators, etc. as such products help to make the life comfortable.
3. **Health.** Health is the central idea used to advertise foodstuffs and patented medicines.
4. **Beauty.** This theme is very popular with the manufacturers and dealers of cosmetics, toilet soaps and perfumes.
5. **Parental affection.** This idea is used for advertising products meant for children like toys, baby triscycles, baby foods, and baby dresses, *e.g.* "Brightways treat your children beautifully."
6. **Achievement.** Many big organisations use this theme to advertise their products. For instance, Gedore Tools manufacturers advertise "Earning over Rs. 12 crores in foreign exchange from 45 countries."

7. **Fear.** This theme is used by Insurance Companies to stimulate people to go in for insurance against death, accident, loss through fire, flood, burglary and so on. The traffic police also make use of this theme to caution the people *e.g.*, "Avoid the agony of an accident."

8. **Patriotism.** Certain firms advertise a product on the basis of the theme of nationalism, *e.g.*, the slogan. "Made from Indian materials with Indian Technology." influences the attitudes of the people who believe in purchasing goods made in India only.

9. **Economy.** This theme is generally used for clearance sale or as a part of sales compaign on a mass scale.

REQUISITES OF A GOOD ADVERTISEMENT

Advertisement has become a specialised job these days. Whatever might be the medium of advertisement chosen, and advertisement copy should fulfil the following requirements:

1. It must Attract the Attention of the People. The advertisement copy must be drafted in such a way that it is able to draw the attention of the people to whom it is addressed and create their interest in the product, service or idea. If it cannot do this, all expenditure on advertising will go waste. The following methods may be adopted in order to attract the attention of prospective customers: .

(i) By using picture and drawing of the product being advertised alongwith an illustration of the use of the product *e.g.*, a young lady washing clothes having a package of 'Surf' by her side.

(ii) By using attractive headlines. The main headline should be as short as possible so that the reader or listener may remember it, *e.g.*, "Merri makes meri mood", "Campa Cola, the only one", "Mothers who care use Dalda". The headlines are generally in the form of slogans as given in the above illustrations. Sometimes the headlines may be quite lengthy and take the form of a quotation *e.g.*, "If you are leaving your wife, do it in broad day light (and do it on a weakned)" by Air India, "Our actions, our words more than anything else reflect who we are. Our culture is important, preserve it" by Weston Electronics Limited. In many cases, the headline contains the quality of the product being advertised, as for instance, "Power packed Vim Clorex gives you total cleanness."

(iii) By providing artistic borders and plenty of blank space around the actual cording. This helps in separating the advertisement text from the rest of the material and to compel the reader to pay attention to it. Sometime the goods words in the copy are underlined.

(iv) By using question headline *e.g.*, "Wouldn't you wish for a happy old age?" by Life Insurane Corporation of India, "Can you get a better Refrigerator than a Gem?" by General Equipment Merchants Ltd.

(v) By giving price quotation. If it is thought that the price is low and will attract the attention of the people.

(vi) By inserting coupens for free literature or gifts.

2. It must Suggest Something to the Reader or Listener of the Advertisement. An advertisement can suggest to the reader either the necessity to him/her of the product advertised or the superiority of the product advertised. If simple slogans can be used to make suggestions to the readers, they will be more useful, *e.g.* "Take care of your tomorrows, save with Oriental Bank". Bring out the silky softness and lustre of your hair with deep-action Palmolive Shampoo. An ad copy will not be effective if it does not suggest the people that the product advertised will solve their problems or give them increase satisfaction.

3. It should Aim at Educating the People for which it is Meant. It should suggest new uses of the product in question and the mode of using it *e.g.*, method of using a medicine, method of preparing a dish and so on. It should educate the people in the way of using the existing product, the sources from where the product can be had, services available alongwith the product, price and so on.

4. It must have a Conviction Value. A suggestion made by the advertiser in the advertisement copy must be backed by convincing arguments. It should not, in any case, leave an impression in the mind of the people that the qualities of the product have been exaggerated in the advertisement. Similarly, vague generalisations cannot convince the people. There are many ways of convincing the prospective customers through the advertisement. An illustration of the product being tested for quality may be used. It will simplify the task of communication the product message to the people. The quality of the product may be advertised in the form of a slogan to convince the people *e.g.*, Anacin relieves pain faster as it is microfined" and "Kissan products are automatically processed." Some advertisers use the tool of 'money back guarantee' to convince the people regarding the quality of the product.

5. An Advertisement should Create a Need for the Product in the Mind of the People and Make them Buy the Product. An advertisement is effective if it appeals the instincts of the readers and induces them to take the desired action. The advertisement should appeal the various instincts inherent in man like self-preservation, parental and self-display. Self-preservation instinct deals with preservation of oneself, one family and belonging. Parental instinct deals with love and affection of parents with their children. Instinct for self-display deals with dresses and other things which add to the personality of a person. The purpose of influencing the instincts is to motivate him to buy the product advertised.

6. It must Make the People Remember or Retain the Message. The advertisement copy must retain the attention of the people in it. The impression created in the mind of the reader or listener must be such as likely to be remembered by him for long time afterwards. This can be achieved if short and spectacular slogans are made use of in the advertisement. The trade mark or brand of the product is repreated in the advertisement time and again, as for instance, Hamam, Saridon, Limca and Chelpark. Care must be taken to see that the same advertisement should not be repeated for such a large number of times that the people start neglecting it. In order to retain the interest of the people, the advertisement copy should be given new forms all the while identifying the trade mark and qualities of the product.

SELECTION OF MEDIA

Advertising medium is a means through which advertisers communicate their message to likely customers to influence them with a view to know and decide about the product or service advertised.

According to Brennan, "The term media embraces each and every method that the advertiser has at his command to carry his message to the public." Advertising media may be defined as "the physical means whereby a manufacturer of goods or utilities or a purveyor of services tells the consumer about his product or services."

FACTORS AFFECTING SELECTION OF MEDIA

Selection of particular media is a matter of prudent calculation. It costs money and unless correct selection is made most of the money spent on it can be wasted without any result. The advertiser is generally confused by the number and variety of the advertising media and at times finds it very difficult to make a final and very satisfactory selection. As there is no single good road which leads to it, the media for an advertising campaign should be based on certain principles. Some general observations can, however, be made. The media of advertisement should be tested with reference to:

(1) **The Number of People Influenced by it.** Every media has a general circulation and an effective circulation. The general circulation is made up of the total number of people who read or subscribe to the media. The effective circulation is the number of prospective consumer or customers who read it and the number of those who influence sales, though they may not buy themselves. Sometimes two or more periodicals circulate among the same people. Therefore, merely adding together the total circulation of

these journals does not give a true idea of the number of persons reached. From 10 to 15 per cent of those people may be reading both or all of the periodicals. This duplication, however, is not necessarily wasted where frequent repetition is desired it is an advantage but when it is desired to reach a large number of people who can and will buy and this need for repetition is not urgent, duplication should be avoided, where possible.

(2) **The Condition Under which People are Influenced.** The reader's mood at the time he reads the advertisement helps in determining his receptivity to suggestions. One would not expect to find people particularly receptive to advertising for a medicine when they are well and healthy, or to an advertising for correspondence courses when they are holidaying or to an advertisement for a tour through Kashmir when it is midwinter. Similarly, certain periodicals are usually read by people at times when they are more receptive to certain kinds of suggestions than to others. When this is known, it is better not to advertise in these periodicals the kind of things that people would not be interested in at the time they usually read them.

(3) **The Class of People Influenced.** People who are to be influenced may be classified in any way but the classification of media will depend upon the nature of the product and its market. Mass population may be divided into different groups by their social standing, by the kind of work they do, by their income; and by their educational standard and religion, by sex and age, etc. They may also be divided into urban and rural groups, by the districts and states in which they live. The main thing is to determine which of the groups gives the most workable classification and then use those in defining the market and the people to be reached by the advertising media.

(4) **The Reputation of the Media.** Few newspapers or periodicals are regarded more important and of better

standard than others by the public and the tendency is for this regard to be passed on to the advertising efforts carried by these periodicals. The claims of advertisements appearing in papers with a good reputation are more likely to be believed as compared to the advertisements appearing in papers of a lower standard. The general quality of the advertising usually appearing in any paper with good idea of its prestige or standing with other advertisers will be the general public.

(5) **Objective of the Advertisement.** Media choices are influenced by the purpose of a particular advertisement and by the goal of the entire campaign. For instance, if an advertisement is to be made for the selection of salesmen for industrial users, direct mail method may be used. If it is made to induce people to act spontaneously, radio or newspapers may be utilised.

(6) **The Cost of Space.** The larger the circulation the higher are the rates charged. Further preferred positions are charged at higher prices and so is the case with advertisements in colour. Many monthlies charge on the basis of a full page or a half or a quarter page. It may be noted that advertisement is cheaper in the long run if it is continuously given. The cost of advertising media should be considered in relation to *(i)* the amount of funds available, and *(ii)* the circulation of the media. If the funds available are small radio or television cannot be used.

(7) **Requirements of Message.** The media which is most suitable for the presentation of the message to the customer is always preferred. For example, floor coverings, sanitary wares, women's apparel are generally best presented in pictorial form, and radio may not be a good media for these products. Insurance service cannot be properly presented by outdoor media, for its handbills or circulars may be effective.

(8) **Time and Location of Buying Decision.** A media which reaches the prospective customer, as near as possible to him and at a particular time, can be best chosen for products like groceries, dairy and bakery products, or gasoline etc.

Before choosing a particular media, the advertising manager should analyse and study each available medium in the light of above criteria. Each factor must be given due consideration and compared with others before a final decision is made.

METHODS OF EVALUATION OF ADVERTISEMENT EFFECTIVENESS

Every body knows that some advertisements are more effective than others. However, the extremes in effectiveness between advertisments that cost the same amount of money did not become apparent until we had adequate measuring sticks. Mayer points out that businessmen probably know less than ever before about the efficiency of their sales promotion efforts. Counts to forces encouraging the growth of copy testing are others that can limit its growth. Four of the most difficulties are the following:

1. Good research is expansive and time consuming serve large agencies budget several hundred throusand dollars a year per copy testing an expense no usually passed directly to the client. Even more discouraging to advertising people is the delay in getting results. They want quick answers to their questions.
2. Certain creative people have objected both publically and privately to copy testing as it is practiced today. (This statement does not mean that all creative persons feel this way, because many are enthusiastic boosters of copy testing). They have expressed concern about the just of certain writers and account people to ape the 'best read' of "highest roted" ads. They feel that creative people are taking research findings to literacy. Then, too, some creative people mistakenly suspect that copy testers are trying to interfere with their creative efforts. They believe that

consumers are so computer and unpredictable that no method of research can measure accurately the effort of an individual ad. By and large, these fears are not well-founded, few copy testers claim the omniscience about which creative people sometimes complain, few of them attempt to write the ads. The known as well as the creative people that this is amplest business, but they also believe current methods of research are better than no research at all.

3. Advertising people are understandably consumed by the apparant disagreement among the researches themselves regarding the validity of the different method of measuring audience response. The disagreements are sometimes decidedly heated and occasionally are worked as public forums. However, these disagreements often turn out to be about details rather than about basic approach.

4. There is the almost insurmountable task of isolation the effects of advertising from those of the many other variables that produce a sale. A sale seldom is made in such a tarified atmosphere that the advertising researcher can point to the advertisement and say "This advertisement produced that sale." The intervening of the variables discourages many from even trying to unravel them. Many however do not give up but instead concentrate their efforts on certain measurable factors—such as readership, recall consumed opinion, belief, or disbelief, attention, comprehensive registration of message and change in attitude. They are assuming, of course that what they measure has a positive relation to ultimate sale.

The managerial responsibility in the area of advertising does not cease with the execution of the advertising programme. A management of concerned with goal achievement and performance excellence also attempts to evaluate the results of all managerial endeavour in this area.

The needs for evaluating effectiveness of advertising arises for a number of reasons some of which include the following:

(1) It is not necessary to ascertain the saturation point of advertising—the point, beyond which advertising produces negligible sales response—so as to reshuffle communication-mix and marketing-mix to produce a tangible sales respnose.

(2) On account of the dynamic nature of market, it is necessary to identify and isolate the effect of different components of the marketing-mix so as to ascertain the relative contribution of each against the targeted contribution.

(3) It is also necessary to have some measure of the impact of alternative media, copy and layout.

(4) It is necessary to have some measure of the impact of advertising on sales so that the size of succeeding advertising appropriations may be intelligently determined.

The time consumed, the expense and the uncertainty involved in most testing mean that the market must concentrate on the particularly important problems that he feels, he can measure with some enactures. Most of these have to do with the message or with the media.

In this case of message research, the tester may wonder as to the degree "what is said", is important in the ultimate effectiveness of the message and to what extent how "it is said", is important. This dilemma had led researchers to put more and more emphasis on completed advertising alternatives (Campaigns or sets of advertisement) and somewhat less on the testing of individual advertising components. Advertisers are becoming increasingly concerned with the sales effectiveness of strategy. A versus strategy. B this is a reflection of improved method of evaluating alternative strategies both in the temporary and in the field of improved electronic equipment for processing the data quickly and accurately. Of course, there is still much questioning of which appeal will communicate the message best.

What test is best depends on the question of what it is you want to find out. One method will be best for one type of problem, another for a different type. One method will be perfectly satisfactory for a sought idea of which one communicates best, for something more precise, you may have need a more elaborate method.

Perhaps the most useful approach is to consider the various types of test and to attempt to assess the condition under which each will be most useful. One useful and commonly used method of classifying them is to divide them into two general classes pre-testing, which is conducted before the advertising is exposed to an audience and post-testing which is done after exposure.

Another method of classifying tests is in terms of limited objectives and sales-objective tests. Although most persons would like to know the sales effectiveness of a proposed message or media plan, many contend that in practise we have to settle for some communication (such as awareness and recall) we can reasonably expect that the more effective an advertising message is in communicating the more effective it will be in getting the product among the most important communications criterion are the following:

1. **Awareness.** Did the test increase awareness of the message, product, theme and so on?
2. **Recall.** Can the respondents recall something that can be related to the specific meassage or medium?
3. **Attitudes and Opinions.** Was the persons attitude changed as a result of the advertisement.
4. **Belief.** Does the consumer believe what is said in the advertisement?
5. **Inquiries.** Which ad produced the most inquiries?

MEASURES AND METHODS

There are broadly two measures of advertising effectiveness, namely, sales response and communication response. These are described below:

1. Sales Response. There can hardly be a better measure of advertising's effectiveness than the sales response it generates. Sales response refers to the amount of sale which may be attributed to the advertising input. The following methods may be used to determined the sales response:

(a) ***Satistical Studies.*** In statistical studies, an attempt is made to find out the co-efficient of correlation between advertising expenditures and the sales revenue over a period of time, usually the financial year, which may indicate the positivity or negativity of relationship. The advertising expenditure data may relate to the current year or past years or both; the past year's data may be taken into account so as to consider the cummulative effect of advertising.

Alternatively, simple or multiple regression studies may be carried out to determine the impact of advertising expenditure on sales. The multiple regression study incorporates measures of the levels of other variables (other than advertising) during the peirod so as to isolate the net effect of advertising.

(b) ***Mathematical Models.*** Mathematical models may also be used to measure the sales response to advertising expenditures. In the USA, for example, two outstanding studies using historical data have been conducted employing such models. These are referred to as the Palda and Telser studies. In the Palda study the distributed lagged model was used whereas in the Telser study the Markov Probability brand switching model, whose parameters were estimated by least squares techniques, was employed.

(iii) ***Little-group Method.*** M/sArthur D. Little Inc., a consulting firm in the USA, has contributed these concepts for determining sales response to advertising the sales decay constant, the saturation level, and the response constant.

These concepts are defined as follows:

(a) *Sales-Decay Canstant.* In the absence of promotion, sales tend to decrease because of product obsolescence, competitive advertising and other factors. Under relatively constant market conditions, the rate of

decrease is, in general, constant, that is, a constant percent of sales is lost each year.

(b) *Saturation Level.* It refers to the practical limit of sales that can be generated, and represents the fraction of the market that a particualr advertising campaign can capture. It indicates the point beyond which sales generation is negligible on account of additional advertising outlay.

(c) *Problems.* The sales response to advertising, as determined by any of the above methods, is certainly an appropriate measure of an advertising's effectiveness. But the whole exercise is replete with problems and difficulties which discourages its use.

2. Communication Response. The problems described above considerably discourages management to attempt an evaluation of advertising in terms of sales response. Nevertheless, it is possible to evaluate advertising in terms of its communication effect on target consumers. The theory behind evaluating the communication effect is that the advertisement effectively communicates also generates sales and induces other desired action at consumer level. Therefore, communication effect indirectly indicates sales effect. The communication response is usually measured in terms of advertising's influence on consumers' knowledge, beliefs, and convictions as indicated by readership, listenership, memory and attitudes. "Many advertisers feel that the links between sales and advertising are too tenuous, complicated, and long term to permit measuring the direct impact. They feel instead that the more short-term communication effects of given advertisements should be measured." According to a study, the "behavioural and attitude and opinion measures, as predictors of future sales behaviour, are the best measures of the sales effectiveness of an individual advertisement".

The taks of evaluating communication effect is usaully divided into two parts, namely, pre-testing and post-testing. Pre-testing is concerned with assessing communication-effectiveness of an advertisement before its presentation to target consumers while post-testing is concerned with assessing effectiveness after its presentation to target consumers. It is with the post-testing that we are concerned here. The usual methods adopted to evaluate communication effort of advertising are described here under:

(i) ***Enquiry Test.*** In the enquiry test, the number of consumer enquiries produced by an advertising copy medium is considered a measure of its communication effectiveness. Therefore, the number of enquiries is the test of the effectiveness which can be produced only when the advertising copy/medium succeeded at attracting and retaining reader viewer attention. To encourage consumers to enquire, the following techniques are employed.

(ii) ***Recognition Test.*** Recognition test is based on memory. It attempts to measure effectiveness by determining to number of people who have read/seen the advertisement. For this purpose, a survey of readership/listenership is carried out by a band of interviewers. A sample of readers/listeners is selected and shown different advertisements including the ones being tested and asked to identify them. The sample is also asked to indicate whether he/she has seen different components of the advertisement. In this test, that copy is considered more effective which is recognised by larger number of readers/listeners.

(iii) ***Attitude Test.*** In conjunction with recognition and recall tests, effectiveness may be evaluated by attitude test also. Attitude test attempts to measure the impact of advertisement. Positive attitude and opinion indicates the effectiveness of the advertisement.

A review of the above method reveal that no one methods is perfect and, therefore, usually a mix of these methods is developed to evaluate the effectiveness of advertising. However, the ultimate choice of methods would largely depend on the unique needs of a company, the resources and information constraints and the outlook and training of the executive involved in the work.

❒

6

Product Decisions

The product policy of a firm is one of the most important aspect of its operation. It is concerned with establishing objectives and guidelines which determine the nature and extent of the goods and services that the firm decides to market to its target customers. It covers existing as well as new goods and services. For the success of a firm, it is of utmost importance to plain its product, product mix. Successful marketing operations are built around two essential elements—Product and Markets. In other words, the essence of marketing is the bringing together products possessing want satisfying capabilities with markets made up of potential customers having particular funds.

A product may be defined as a bundle of utilities consisting of various product features and accompanying services. The bundle of utilities or the physical and pyschological satisfactions that the buyer receives is provided by the seller when he sells a particular combination of product features and associated services. Customer does not buy merely the physical and chemical attributes of a product. He is really buying want satisfaction. He will buy a product which will offer him expected satisfaction. Thus brand, package, label, price, status of manufacturer and distributor and services offered to the customer constitute a part and parcel of a product. It should be noted that what a buyer buys is mixture not of goods and services, but rather of expected physical and psychological satisfactions. Therefore, the term 'product' should not mean the physical product itself but the total product including brand, package, label, price, status of manufacturer and distributor and services offered to the customer in addition to the physical goods.

According to Philip Kotler, "A product is anything that can be offered to a market for attention, acquisition, use of consumption; it includes physical objects, services, personalities, place, organisations and ideas." A product has many other dimensions besides its physical appearance. In fact, product like an onion with several layers and each of the layers contributes to the total product image. Philip Kotler is of the opinion that a product has three layers or dimensions which must be distinguished. As shown in Fig., these dimensions are: *(a)* core product, *(b)* formal product, and *(c)* augmented product.

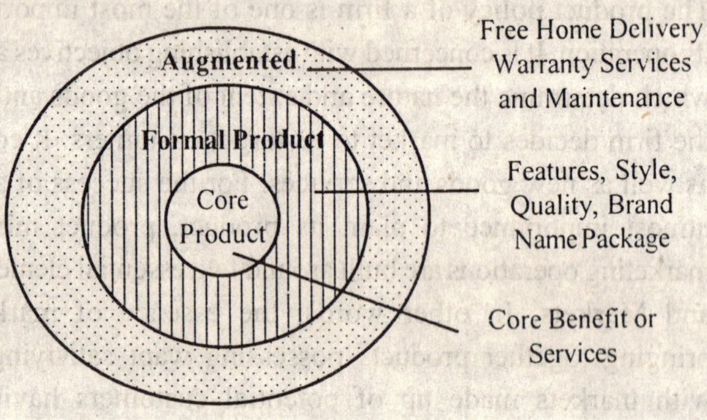

Fig. Dimensions of a Product

A. Core Product. It is the fundamental dimension of a product as it represents of bundle of benefits to its prospective buyer. The core product answers the question : "What is the buyer really buying?" For instance, a woman buying a washing machine is buying comfort and not a mere collection of drum, beater and nuts and bolts for their own sake; and a woman buying a lipstick is buying hope and not a set of chemical and physical attributes for their own sake. The basic job of a market is to sell the core benefits.

B. Formal Product. It is the larger packaging of a core product. It is what the target market recognises as the tangible offer. For isntance, washing machines, lipsticks, motor cars, televisions, etc., having the following attributes; *(a)* features, *(b)* style, *(c)* a level of quality, *(d)* a brand name, and *(e)* packaging. Services ahve also got features which are generally intangible. Thus, services like auto repair, electricity supply, management consultancy, psyhological counselling and medical advice are all products.

C. **Augmented Product.** It is a broader conception of the product. It represents the totality of benefits that a person may receive or experience in getting the formal product. The augmented product of a T.V. distributor is not only T.V., but also delivery, free installation, warranty, and service and maintenance. This dimension of the product is very important for a firm operating in a competitive market. The firm that develops the right augmented product will be able to attract more customers and servive in the competitive market.

KINDS OF PRODUCT

Product or goods can be classifed into two broad categories depending upon the use for which they are meant. These categories are: *(I)* consumers' goods and *(II)* industrial goods:

I. Consumers' Goods

Consumers' goods are meant for final consumption by the ultimate consumers. Bread, butter, TV sets, cosmetics and garments are all consumer goods. On the other hand industrial goods are meant for use in the commercial production of other goods or in connection with carrying out some business activities. Machine tools, iron-ore, and electronic computers are all industrial goods. It should be noted that all goods cannot be classifed exclusively as consumers' goods or indusrial goods. For example, typing paper is used for both personal and business correspondence and therefore is both a consumers' and an industrial goods. The distinction between consumers and industrial goods is necessary in order to understand the behaviour of their purchasers. The purchasers of industrial goods have an altogether different approach as compared to the purchasers of consumers' goods.

Consumers' goods can be further classified into convenience goods shopping goods, and speciality goods. a brief description of these is given below:

(i) Convenience Goods. These include items which the consumers buy frequently, immedaitely, and with minimum shopping efforts. Cold drinks, cigarettes, magazines and newspapers, drugs and most grocery items are the examples of convenience goods. These goods are non-durables *i.e.*, they are consumed or used up rapidily. At the time of buying these goods, the habit of the consumer dominates his behaviour. He does not take much item in marking the buying decision.

(ii) Shopping Goods. These include items which consumers select and buy after making comparisions on such criteria as suitablity, quality, price and style. In case of a shopping goods, a substantial number of consumers habitually make shopping comparisons before they take a buying decision. Furniture items, dress materials, shoes, and how should appliances are the examples of shopping goods. A shopping goods is durable and is used up slowly. The consumer has to compare different stores offerings and devote considerable time and effort to take the buying decision.

(iii) Speciality Goods. As the name implies, the consumers have to make a special purchasing effort to purchase speciality goods. Items in this category must possess unique features or have a number of brand names or both. Fancy goods, stamps and coins for collectors and prestige brands of men's suits may be termed as speciality goods. The consumers are already aware of the product or brand they want and they are willing to make a special purchasing effort to find the outlet handling it. Thus, in case of speciality goods, the consumers do not compare the desired sepciality goods with others. But they may take considerable time in deciding to start the special search required because goods are often in the luxury price class.

II. Industrial Goods

Industrial goods are those meant for use in making other products or for rendering a service in the operation of a business organisation. For a comprehensive analysis, industrial goods may be classified on the basis of use (instead of buying habits as in case of consumers goods) into five categories, namely, raw materials, fabricating parts and materials, installations, accessory equipment and operative supplies. A brief description of these are given below:

(i) **Raw Materials.** Raw materials are those industrial goods which will become part of another physical product and which have received no processing at all than that necessary for economy or protection in physical handling. Raw materials may be divided into natural products: Minerals, land, and products of the forests and the seas: and agricultural products: Wheat, cotton, tobacco, fruits, live-stocks and animal products such as eggs and raw milk. Raw materials are usually graded for standardised quality.

(ii) **Fabricating Materials and Parts.** These are partial or complete items which become part of the final product. They have already been processed to some exent. Fabircating materials undergo further processing, *e.g.*, pig iron going into steel, yarn being woven into cloth, leather being shaped into shoes, and flour becoming a part of cake or bread. Fabricating parts are assembled with no further change in form *e.g.*, spark plugs in an automobile, barrel of a rifle and buttons on a coat.

(iii) **Accessory Equipment.** Accessory equipment includes industrial goods usually less expensive and having shorter life than installations. They are required for the manufacture of final product though they do not form part of the finished products, *e.g.*, portable drills, hand tools, work-lift trucks, etc. these items are highly standardised.

(iv) **Installations.** Installations are long-life and expensive major equipment of an industrial user. These are necessary for further production of goods, but they do not form part of those products, *e.g.*, heavy machinery, diesel engines, trucks, factory sites and production lines.

(v) Operating Supplies. Operating supplies are short-lived and low priced items usually purchased with a minimum of effort. They are the 'convenience goods' of industries. They do not have a signficant impact on the long run profitability of an organisation. Supplies include floor wax, lubricating oils, heating fuel and office stationary like pins, pens, pencils, papers, etc. Operating supplies do not become a part of finished product.

Distinction between Industrial Goods and Consumer Goods

Industrial goods and consumer goods are two broad divisions of manufactured goods. But they show latent differences which are evident from the following definitions given by the American Marketing Association.

"Consumer goods are destined for use by ultimate consumers or households and in such forms that they can be used without commercial processing." Against this industrial goods are defined as "those goods which are destined to be sold primarily for use in producing other goods or rendering severice as contrasted with goods destined to be sold primarily to be ultimate consumer." These definitions *prima facie* bring out two differences. Firstly industrial goods are not meant for consumption, so their buyers are different from the buyers of consumer goods. Secondly, further processing is required in the case of industrial goods before they can be finally consumed.

In the industrial products the customer is well informed and know the relative merits of a particular product, alternative sources of supply and also the various competitive products available.

But this classification is not an air-tight compartment. An industrial product may serve the two markets simultaneously. For example, a typewriter may be used in industrial concern and it may also be used for personal purpose. In the later case it is pure consumer product.

Differences in the Marketing of Industrial and Consumer Goods

However the marketing remains 'the same, yet there are important differences in marketing the industrial product and marketing consumer products. The prime difference in marketing of those goods is nature of their demand. The demand of consumer goods is 'original' while that of industrial goods is 'derived'. The industry is to supply the goods according to the wants of actual consumers or users. It means that the demand of industrial product is derived from the demand of consumer products in which the industrial products may play an important part in making.

Again the knowledge and sophistication of customers varies according to whether the goods are industrial goods or consumer goods. The industrial buyer is well informed of the relative merits and demerits of the alternative success of supply of various competitive products. Moreover the number of customers of industrial product is small as compared to the number of consumers of consumer products. Therefore, in marketing industrial products, greater emphasis is placed on personal selling through salesmen whereas in marketing the consumer products, emphasis is laid on mass marketing and hence most of the selling has to be one through advertising.

PRODUCT LINE

Product line refers to a group of products that are closely related because they satisfy a class of needs, are used together, are sold to the same customer groups, are marketed through the same type of outlets, or fall within given price changes in product line or product item naturally changes the product mix and vice versa. The following are instances where the product mix is altered. (Product mix consists of all the different product lines a firm offers.)

(a) Product Modification. It is the process by which the existing products are modified to suit the changing demand on account of fashion changes. Such a decision is required at a time when the product is in the maturity stage of the product life cycle. Product modificaton may be defined and deliberate alteration in the physical attributes of product or its packaging.

(b) Product Elimination. There are some products which cannot be improved or modified to suit the market needs. Here, the profitable alternative would be to withdraw the product. The process of withdrawal is technically known as 'product elimination'.

(c) Product Line Modification. Product line is altered or modifed through the following methods:

(i) Product Line Contraction. This is also known as "Contraction of Product Mix." It is a method by which a fat and long product line is thinned out. It is also termed as 'Simplification'. The decision to reduce the product items might be due to the purposeful act of the management to suspend the production of unprofitable products. Marketing problems also compel the manufacturers to withdraw certain items.

Product line contraction is a major decision from the point of view of management. "Many sick or marginal products never die; they are allowed to continue in the company's product mix until they fade away." These products will, in course of time, eat away the profits earned by the other products. The decision to give away a product often results from changes in the market. Market saturation makes a product unprofitable. Products also may be abandoned, even though still profitable, if the management feels that the same resources could yield a higher profit from other products. Thus, the process of avoiding or stopping the production of a particular product is called simplification. It is also termed as Product Line Contraction. From this viewpoint it is opposite of diversification. In spite of the advantages, most managements are shy and do not accept "Product pruning" programmes. R.S. Alexander categorically states, "But putting products to death—or letting them die—is a drab business and often engenders much of the sadness of a final parting with old and tried friend." The reasons for this are partly logical and partly sentimental.

(ii) Product Line Expansion. It is just the opposite of the above and is referred to diversification. To utilise the marketing opportnities a firm may have to expand breadth and depth of its product line. The expansion of the product line is undertaken by increasing the lines and/or items of products. New lines may be related or unrelated to the present products. For example, manufacturers of radio sets may start producing television sets and tape-records.

Diversification, by definition, means that something new will be added. It may be new products, new markets, new technologies or even a new company. Generally, it means adding a new product (not various qualities of the same product) to the existing product line or mix. For example, if a fan manufacturing company starts producing sewing machines, it is a case of diversification. It does not mean that the new product should be complementary or an allied product to the existing one. It may be a product which may be entirely distinct and different from the existing products. The term is applicable not only to production but also to selling. For instance, if a wholesaler dealing in engineering goods starts selling simultaneously confectionary items, it is also a case of diversification. Some of the reasons for such a change are:

(1) There is a technological development in the process of production,

(2) New markets are to be created,

(3) There is a constant threat for the existing product due to abrupt changes in fashion,

(4) The advantage of the reputation of the company's name and its existing products to be spread to other products,

(5) The spare capacity of the factory is to be fully utilised.

Diversification is profitable only in the large companies which are "multimarket and multiproduct". Further, such companies must have financial resources supported by a well-organised management. Diversification of products, to a very large extent, is capable of preventing recessionary trends entering the industry. The usual way in which diversification is brought about is by means of mergers like one company acquiring another.

Hindustan Machine Tools offers a good example in this regard. Started as a company manufacturing various machine tools (lathes, drillling machines, etc.), it moved into the field of watch-making. Their diversification process continues and their latest entry is in the field of manufacturing printing presses and electric bulbs.

(iii) Changing Models or Styles of Existing Product. Continuous changes in fashion, desires and needs of the consumers compel the management to review the existing products and their style.

For example, some time ago, a cigarette manufacturing company used to sell two varieties of cigarettes. One variety was popular in South India while the other dominated the North Indian markets. The company withdrew one variety and tried to popularise another. Quite contrary to this, another cigarette manufacturing company, that had only a medium variety, introduced other varieties in the market. This kind of problems arise mainly because of the fundamental fact that 'different individuals have different tastes'.

(iv) Quality Variations. In contrast to the above, under certain circumstances a manufactuer is forced to produce differing qualities of a particular product. Even if the quality of the product is good, a single quality may not be enough to retain the market. For example, manufacturers of pens invariably market pens of different varieties with varying quality at different prices.

In the matter of quality, the manufacturers of consumer goods particularly speciality goods and convenience goods, face the problem of changing the quality often to suit the market.

PRODUCT MIX

In the modern age a producer produces a number of products so that the needs of maximum number of consumers may be satisfied, maximum sales may be made and maximum profits may be earned. As the needs, wants, tastes and likings of all the consumers are different, they can not be satisfied with a single product, therefore, different product of different characteristics are offered to different consumers so that the enterprise may capture a goods share in the market. All the product being produced by an enterprise are known as Product Mix. Thus, product mix is the composite of all the products offered for sale by a business and industrial enterprise. It is necessary to understand the meaning of the term product item and product line before coming to the definition of the term product mix.

Product item means a specific product of certain specifications, such as—Lux Soap, Colgate Toothpaste, Facit Typewriter, H. M. T. Watch, Rath Vanaspati, Televista Televiosion and Bajaj Chetak Scooter.

A product line is a group of different product items, closely related with each other. All the products of a product line are clsoely related with each other either because they satisfy a class of needs, or used together, or are sold to the same group of customers, or are sold through the same channel of distribution, or are within same pricing range. Toothpaste. Watch, T.V., Scooter, Typewriter are the examples of a product line. Here, it is appropriate to note that a particular brand of a poduct is a product item and all the brands of the same product are included in product line.

Product Mix is the composite of all the products offered for sale by a business or industrial enterprise. The term 'Product Mix has been defined by American Marketing Association as, "Product Mix is the composite of products offered for sale by a firm or a business unit." For example if an enterprise manufactures or deals with different varieties of Soap. Oil, Toothpastes, Toothbrush, etc., the group of all these product is called 'Product Mix'.

On the basis of above discussion, it can be concluded that a single product item is called as a product item. All the product items of the same group are collectively known as a Product Line and all the product lines manufactured or distributed by an enterprise are collectively known as 'Product Mix'.

FACTORS AFFECTING THE PRODUCT MIX

Following are the factors which affect the Product Mix of an enterprise:

(1) Changes in Market Demand. Purchasing power of consumer's habits, tastes, needs and wants of consumers; attitudes and preferences of consumers keep on changing from time to time. Every such change results in the change in the demand of a product. A business or industrial enterprise has to make necessary changes in its product mix in accordance with the changes in demand. For example, an increase in the income of consumers increases their purchasing power. As a result of which, the demand for inferior goods falls and the demand for superior goods increases. Keeping this change in mind, producers have to change their production. They have to decrease the production of inferior goods and increase the production of superior goods.

(2) Production Capacity. The enterprise has also to change its product mix from time to time so that the best possible results may be achieved from its resources. Such change also become necessary to improve the quality of production. For example, the product mix may be enhanced by starting the production of a by-product with the use of wastes and scraps.

(3) Marketing Capacity. Sometimes, the changes in product mix of an enterprise may be necessary to get the maximum results of marketing efforts of the enterprise. For example, if a product is not getting desired response from the market, the decision may be taken to step the production of such a product and the resources of the enterprise may be diverted to produce a new product.

(4) Competitive Policies and Strategies. An enterprise has to keep a close eye upon the marketing policies and strategies of its competitors and should make necessary changes in its marketing policies and strategies. For example, if the competitors have made any change in packing or size or colour or price etc. of their products, relevant changes should also be made in the product of the enterprise.

(5) Earn Maximum Profits. Ultimate objects of every business and industrial enterprise is to earn the maximum possible profits. Product mix of the enterprise requires to be changed for this purpose also. For example, the production of less profitable product may be stopped and the production of more profitable products may be increased.

(6) Financial Resources. Finance is the blood of all the activities of an enterprise. Availability of financial resources also necessitates some changes in the products mix of an enterprise. For example, if a particular product is continuously going into a loss, the decision may be taken to change such product. Similarly, if the financial resources of an enterprise are not adequate to carry on production of all the products, the decision may be taken to curtail a product item.

(7) Image of Producer. Sometimes, product mix of the enterprise is changed to improve the image of the producer. For example, a decision may be taken to produce the products only of high quality.

BRAND

The American Marketing Association has defined a brand as a name, term, symbolc or design or a combination of them which is intended to identify the goods and services of one seller or groups of sellers and to differentiate them from those of competitors'. A trade mark is a brand that has been given legal protection thus ensuring its use exclusively by one seller. 'Trade mark' is thus a legal term.

We are living in an age of brands. Whether in industrial goods or consumer goods, there is a proliferation of brands. Fifteen years ago in India, there were hardly 4 to 5 brands of tooth pastes. Today we have more than a dozen brands. Similarly, among soaps, one had to choose from a handful of brands. Today we have a big assortment of brands, and brand competition has development as a feature of the Indian marketing scene.

In an age of brands, the brand name is quite often the major selling tools, and the most important component of the total product offering.

Giving brand names to products facilitate an effective promotional campaign. Advertising an undifferented or unbrantiaded product becomes a difficult task. A brand name facilitates advertising and functions as a demand stimulant.

The intensive brand promotion undertaken by the marketers of various products have made consumers extremely brand conscious. These days no one asks for just tooth paste. He or she asks specifically for Binaca Fluoride, Signal, Colgate or Forhans. No woman asks for just bathing soap, she may insists on a particular brand. A man who wants a steel cupboard may straight away go in for a Godrej without thinking twice about several other brands available. The brand image developed by sales promotional measures creates different degrees of brand loyalty among consumers. The significance of the brand name on the total sales appeal is evident from the fact that several goods products have failed in the market solely due to wrong brand appeal.

In India, a brand receives such legal protection under the Trade and Merchandise Marks Act, 1958 after it fulfills the following conditions as laid down under Sections 11 and 12 of this Act:

1. It is not similar to any existing trade mark.
2. It is otherwise not entitled to protection in court.
3. It does not hurt the religious sentiments or feelings of any class or section of the citizens.
4. It does not comprise or contain scandalous or obscene matter.
5. It is not contrary to any law for the time being in force.
6. It is not likely to deceive or cause confusion.

When a brand mark is registered and legalised it becomes a trade mark. Thus registered brands are Trade Marks. In that sense all trade marks are brands but all brands are not trade marks. Trade marks is defined as a "brand or part of a brand that is given legal protection because it is capable of exclusive appropriation."—(Glossary of Marketing Terms—AMA). Thus, the trade mark is essentially a legal term protecting the manufacturer's right to use the brand name or trade mark.

BRAND CLASSIFICATION

Brands may be classified into the following three kinds:

(i) Manufacturer's Brand. A brand which is owned by a manufacturer and/or registered as a trade mark under the manufacturer's name is referred to as manufacturer's brand.

(ii) Distributor's or Private Brand. A brand which is owned by a distributor and/or registered under a distributor's name is referred to as a distributor's or private brand. It is private because the manufacturer is not identified or the product is not recognised because of him. The manufacturer simply manufactures the product and brands it as per specifications of the distributor.

(iii) Mixed Brands. A company may opt for both its own and its distributors' brands in respect of its products. It may sell some products in its own brand name and the rest may be sold to dealers under their own brand names.

Both manufacturer's and distributor's brands may be further divided on the basis of persons and region.

Products may carry an individual brand name for each product item as, for example, Hindustan Lever's Surf detergent power and Lux toilet soap or Government Soap Factory, Bangalore's point detergent powder. Products may also carry the family name of the manufacturer as for example, Tata's trucks, Modi's Continental truck Tyre or Mafetlal's Cotton Fabrics. The family name may blanket all products or there may be separate family names for different products. Sometimes products may carry just the company's name or the company's name coupled with product's own generic name as, for example, Colgate Palmolive & Co's., Colgate Tooth Paste or Lakme Lipstick or Face Cream.

Geographical coverage of a product is still another way of classifying brands. A brand is referred to as a national brand when the product is to be identified throughout the country by only one brand. For example, Hindustan Lever's Dalda brand of Vanaspati ghee is a national brand. But when a product is identified by different brands in different regions of the country, these brands are referred to as regional brands.

ADVANTAGES AND LIMITATION OF BRANDING

It is obvious from the definition of brand that its major function is to create an identification of product so that it is easily recognised and distinguished from the competitive offerings. A brand endows a number of advantages and limitations on both consumers and marketers. Some of these are described here:

Consumers' Advantages and Limitations

Advantages

(a) It is easier to lodge complaints and claims against marketers when a branded product fails to live up to its proclaimed value satisfaction. Thus, it gives to consumers both trade and legal protection against unscrupulous trade practices.

(b) There is a considerable saving of time and energy in shopping for goods because a brand render product identification much easier. The money value of this saving is significant in the industrial buying.

(c) Certain brands provide status and prestige to consumers which endow them a somewhat conspicuous pyschological satisfaction otherwise not normally available.

(d) When a product is distinguishable by its brand, consumer has an assurance of quality and consistency in the product attributes being offered.

Limitations

(a) Popularity of brands render them out of the common man's reach because they command a premium price.

(b) Consumers are often confused in product selection on account of the plethora of brands offered in the market. The confusion is confounded when all the brands carry an assurance of similar value satisfaction.

(c) Brand loyalty helps save time and energy in product selection but it discourages the consumer from trying out other new brands which may possibly be more satisfying.

Marketer's Advantages and Limitations

Advantages

(a) Brand loyalty ensures repeat and replacement purchases and considerably helps the marketers in overcoming competitive pressure.

(b) Brand as a peripheral product attribute also has significant communication value. It assists advertising and sales promotion in building up demand for product (s).

(c) Brand builds up an unique reputation for its owner which facilitates new product introduction in terms of easy and immediate recognition and favourable consumer disposition.

(d) It discourages price competition because every product item has a distinctive image and is considered an exclusive offering. It ensures marketer's independence in pricing decisions.

(e) Brand reputation ensures some kind of market control in as much as it serves as an antidote to possible retailer hostility (when their margins are reduced).

Limitations

(a) Brand imposes responsibility for maintaining consistent quality and delivering proclaimed value satisfactions. In case of failures, marketer cannot escape identification owning to brand recognition.

(b) Some products by their very nature do not lend themselves to branding. For examples, nails, rivets, pins, fruits and vegetables (unless canned.)

(c) Building up brand recognition and loyalty are very expensive. Small business cannot afford it. Thus, it helps promote market monopolies.

BRAND STRATEGIES

A company may choose any one or a combination of the above referred to classes of brands and formulate its own brand strategy. Usually, the following strategy options are available to a company:

1. **Multi-brand Product Strategy.** It refers to the practice of offering more than one brand in a product category. For example, Hindustan Lever offers Lux and Pears in its toilet soap category and Bata Shoe Company offers Ambassador and Exclusive brands of shoes in men's wear category.

2. **Single-brand Product Strategy.** it refers to the use of a single brand name for all the products sold by a company whether the brand name is that of a family, compnay or an individual. For example, the 'Erasmic' brand is put on shaving blades, shaving cream and after shave lotions manufactured by Hindustan Lever Ltd.

3. **Mixed Brand Strategy.** In this strategy, a manufacturer offers his products to consumers in his own as well as as distributor's brand names. For example, a manufacturer sells detergent washing powder both under its owns as well as its distributors' brands.

4. **Distributior's or Private Brand Strategy.** A manufacturer may opt to introduce his products under a distributor's brand name. For example, in the Indian cotton textile industry it is a common practice for dealers, usually wholesalers, to prescribe their own brand names while booking orders. Sahakari Bhandar (Super Bazar) of Bombay has been selling toilet soap, talcum powder, detergents, etc. under its own brand name Aparna.

5. **Trading-up and Trading-down Strategy.** When marketers known for marketing low-priced products introduce products with high price and presumably of higher quality, it is known as trading-up. Conversely, when marketers, introduce cheaper products than their original links, it is regarded as trading-down. When this kind of strategy is adopted has to be blended with adequate brand differentiation. Marketers, therefore, use different brands for products traded-up and traded-down so as not to alienate the current clientele.

METHODS OF DETERMINING BRAND

Some important methods of determining a brand are as follows:

(1) **On the Name of Manufacturer.** Some of the manufacturers use their own name as the brand for their products. Main reason for selecting the name of brand on the name of manufacturer is the goodwill and popularity of manufacturer. For example—all the products of Tata, Bata, Modi, Dalmia, Philips, Bajaj, Mafatlal, S. Kumar, J.K., etc., are named after the name of their manufacturers.

(2) **Special Name.** Some of the manufacturers select a special name for their products. For example—The scooters manufactured by Scooters (India) Limited are named as Vijay Super and the fans and Sewing Machines manufactured by Jai Engineering Works Limited are named as Usha.

(3) **Special Mark.** Some of the manufacturers do not give a name to their products. They select a mark for their products. For example—Rath Ghee, Khazoor Ghee, Do Tote mark Pan Masala, etc.

BRAND POLICIES AND STRATEGIES

Brand policies and strategies can be divided into three parts—*(A)* Brand Policies and Strategies adopted by Manufacturers, *(B)* Brand Policies and Strategies adopted by Middlemen, and

(C) Other Brand Policies and Strategies.Details in this regard are given below:

(A) Brand Policies and Strategies Adopted by Manufacturers

It includes the following brand policies and strategies:

(1) Marketing Under the Own Brand of Manufacturer. Under this brand policy and strategy, a manufacturer sells all his products under the brand name of his own. There are various policies under this category and a manufacturer can select any of these policies. Main policies of this category are as under—*(i)* Individual brand; *(ii)* Product line brand; *(iii)* Family brand; *(iv)* Local brand; *(v)* Provincial brand or State brand; *(vi)* Regional brand; *(vii)* National brand; *(viii)* International brand; *(ix)* Fighting brand, and *(x)* Competitive brand.

Main advantages of this brand policy and strategy are—*(i)* It increases the goodwill of manufacturer. *(ii)* It facilitates in the implementation of advertisement and sales promotion programmes of the enterprise. *(iii)* It helps in bringing stability in the prices of products of the enterprise. *(iv)* It helps in controlling the marketing activities of the enterprise. *(v)* It helps in adopting a suitable policy regarding product mix of the enterprise.

Main disadvantages of this brand policy and strategy is that middlemen do not find any existence of their own.

(2) Marketing under the Brand of Middlemen. Under this policy and strategy of brand, a manufacturer does not use any brand for his products. The manufacturer sells his products to the middlemen without any brand. Under this situation, the middlemen are free to use any brand for their products.

Main advantages of adopting this policy are—*(i)* The manufacturer has no need to concentrate upon the marketing of products. *(ii)* The manufacturer can invest his resources in the best possible manner to produce the best quality of the goods at most reasonable costs.

Disadvantages of this brand policy are—*(i)* The manufacturer has to depend upon the marketing policy and efficiency of middlemen.

(ii) The middlemen may create unhealthy competition among the manufacturers because if they get products from any of these manufacturers at cheap rate, they stop to sell the products of earlier manufacturer, *(iii)* If the middlemen are not efficient enough or they do not take appropriate interest in marketing the products of an enterprise, the enterprise may have to face a very critical situation.

(B) Brand Policies and Strategies Adopted by Middlemen

It includes the following brand policies and strategies:

(1) Use of the Brand of Manufacturer Only. Under this brand policy and strategy, the middlemen sell all the products of a manufacturer under the brand name of the manufacturer. They do not use any independent brand name for the products.

Main advantages of this policy are: *(i)* Middlemen have not to make special efforts for selling the products. *(ii)* The middlemen get full advantage of the goodwill of manufacturer. *(iii)* It increases the sales of the middlemen.

Main disadvantages of this policy is that middlemen do not find any existence of their own.

(2) Joint Use of the Brand of Manufacturer and the Brand of Middlemen. As is evident from the heading, under this policy, the products of two brand names are marketed—the products of the brand of manufacturer and the products of the brand of middlemen.

Main advantages of this policy are—*(i)* Middlemen feel that they have their own existence. *(ii)* It increases the sales of the product very high because of the use of brands of both the manufacturer and middlemen. *(iii)* The middlemen get full advantage of goodwill of manufacturers and their own goodwill. *(iv)* The middlemen feel assured that they do not depend upon the manufacturers.

Main disadvantages of this policy is that this policy is not appreciated by the manufacturers because they feel that the middlemen will concentrate upon the sale of the products of their own brand and will not pay due attention towards the sales of their brand.

(C) Other Brand Policies and Strategies

Other brand policies and strategies may be as under:

(1) **Multiple Brand Policy.** Under this brand policy and strategy a business and industrial enterprise uses different brands for its different products.

(2) **Product Line Brand Policy.** Under this brand policy the enterprise uses a single brand for all the product items of a product line. Brands for all the product lines of the enterprise are different.

PACKAGING

While formulating packaging policies and strategies, it is important for marketers to develop a packaging concept around which these are to be formulated. A packaging concept is a description of product package and the functions it is supposed to perform in respect of that particular product. The conceptualisation of package involves determining package functions and developing an appropriate mix of these functions so as to attain product objective. For example, in case of Zodiac neckties and hand-kerchieves package visibility was defined as the basic packaging concept and therefore, rigid plastic package was developed.

Classification of Packaging

(1) Family Packaging. The products of a particular manufacturer when packed in an identical way is known as family packaging. The shape, colour, size etc. of packaging will be similar for all his products. Family brands are made meaningful by using family packaging, also. In such cases packaging methods, material used for packaging the appearance etc. will be one and the same for all the products of a manufacturer.

(2) Re-use Packaging. Packaging that could be used for some other purposes by the consumers after the packed goods have been consumed is known as re-use packaging. This aspect increases the sales value of the product considerably.

(3) Multiple Packaging. It is the practice of placing several units in one container. This helps to introduce new products and increase the sales.

The various aspects of packaging are now treated as a mangement activity.

The following are the problems encountered in packaging:

(a) Cost of packaging

(b) Appearnace

(c) Kinds of designs

(d) Convenience

(e) Re-use purpose

Inspite of its various advantages, packaging has been subjected to criticism. One among them is that it adds cost. To some extent this complaint holds goods. It is true that packaging expenses definitely increase the price. But the benefits derived are sufficient to compensate the increase in cost. For example some medicines which we buy are to consumed at once. Their preservation is very important. Only a good package can render this service. So long as the product is capable of absorbing the packaging cost proportionately this criticism cannot be accepted.

In considering some of the more sophisticated uses of packaging the protective aspects of packaging should not be disregarded. Attention is therefore drawn to the following hazards against which packaging should provide a defence:

1. **Insect Attack,** *e.g.* months in clothing.
2. **Mould,** *e.g.* in canned foods, paints.
3. **Flavour** loss or change.
4. **Chemical change,** *e.g.* mental corrosion, coffee rancidity.
5. **Moisture Gain and Loss.** Many products have an optimum moisture content, *e.g.* cement, ceramic paints, frozen foods.

6. **Contamination by Dust or Dirt.** Clothing, food and fine machinery are obvious examples of products liable to damage in this way.

7. **Pilferage.** Loss through pilferage can be quite high-especially if there are many handling points.

8. **Product Loss.** Liquids and powders are highly susceptible to loss, *e.g.* powder leakage, liquid evaporation.

9. **Damage by Mechanical Handling.** Most damage occurs in the handling process and, the more frequently product are handled in the distribution process, the greater is the need for protection. One of the advantages of the liner rain and other container transport development is that they will result in less damage through handling. Damaged goods have to be replaced and are likely to cause loss and inconvenience to seller and purchases. Often slightly damaged products may not be returned, but may inhibit repeat purchase.

GROWTH AND IMPORTANCE OF PACKAGING

The growth of self-service stores and the importance of gaining distribution, shelf space and display have made packaging decisions in the field of consumer goods a highly important area of decision in regard to product policy and planning. Even in the marketing of industrial goods packaging is taking on increasing significance and extending beyond the obvious necessity of providing for production, transportation and storage.

The demand for packaging has led to an enormous increase in the range of packaging equipment and materials available. There have been spectacular increase in the use flexible packaging involving special papers, plastics and aluminium foil. New printing methods have been developed, *e.g.* flexography, by which process it is possible relatively inexpensively to reproduce photographs or artwork in a wide range of colours on a wide range of materials.

Packaging design is influenced by the cultural, social and political environment. In the USA, for example, the house wife buys approximately 90% of her weekly purchases from supermarkets and self-service shops in one day. In the UK the percentage of food purchase from self-service outlets is much lower and there is still a great deal of daily shopping. In Latin countries pre-packed foods are rather slow in sales growth. Attitudes to colour differ; white is symbolic of mourning in many far Eastern countries as opposed to purple in Latin countries.

A package should be designed to perform many functions:

(i) Provide Protection. At any stage in the distribution process and ulimately in the home or factory of the user or consumer (*e.g.* against product damage, contamination, evaporation, chemical change, pilferage): For example, surface treatment of packaging avoids deterioration of appearance after transit and/or storage.

(ii) Offer Convenience. This covers handling, storage and opening of packages at all stages of distribution, and frequently in eventual use.

(a) ***Convenience of Storage in Warehouse, Shop and House.*** In designing the package there must be a consideration of the economics of stocking large quantities of bulky, slow-moving low unit proit-margin products, and the difficulties of stacking certain carton shapes.

(b) ***Convenience in Use.*** There must be a consideration of the development of new materials and functional designs—acrosol containers, vacuum cans for vegetables, flip-top cigarette packets. New packaging ideas may lead to new products or product formulation, *e.g.* hair sprays, cheese spreads. Safety features should also be considered, as in the design of easy-opening cans eliminating the possibility of cuts and finger nail damage.

(iii) Reduce Transport Costs. This is achieved by the use of lightweight yet adequately strong materials, especially important when goods have to be transported by air.

(iv) Provide Opportunities for Re-use. The package may be deliberately designed so that it can be used for the storage of other items once the original product is consumed, *e.g.* plastic and aluminium containers. On the other hand, some packages are designed so that refills may be bought. The design may be so differentiated that only a refills of the same product can be used in the original container.

(v) Create a Favourable Product Image. The package has frequently to represent the product symbolically—to convey its buying advantages. The packaging "image" will be reinfored if there is a close tie-in with advertising and promotion.

(vi) Establish Product Differences. The package is often the major way in which narrowly differentiated products are distinguished. The difference may be in the art design, the shape or the materials used. A package can be used to convey an impression of quality differences. Gift packs are a good example of extending the range through packaging.

(vii) Establish Corporate Identity. Some companies aim at promoting individual products in their own right. Others deliberately aim at creating a company rather than product loyality, *e.g.* Heinz baby foods.

(viii) Gain Display at Retail Level. The package must be easy to arrange on shelves or racks and at the same time should attack the potential customer. Developments in print techniques, *e.g.* flexography, combined with newer packaging materials, *e.g.* poltingthylene film, have significance in this connection.

As an important peripheral attribute of product, a package has the following functions to perform:

I. Utilitarian Function. Package performs a utilitarian function by retaining and enhancing the product value of consumers in the following ways:

(a) Package protects products from deterioration, spilling, spoilage and evaporation during its transit from manufacturer to consumer.

(b) It enhances product use convenience by keeping it clean and undisturbed.

(c) It helps easy brand identification.

(d) It makes product handling easier and safe on the retail store shelves.

II. Profit Function. Package also performs a profit function in the following two ways:

(a) Consumers assigning relatively higher value to package are usually prepared to pay higher price for this product attribute. As a result, higher contribution to profit flows from package.

(b) Effective package cuts costs of handing and transportation and protects product from damage, thereby, saving a company from cuts in profits.

III. Communication Function. Package performs a commnication function by becoming an important adjunct to the components of the communication-mix, namely, advertising and sales promotion. It performs this function in the following ways:

1. It promotes product at the point of purchase and triggers impulse buying.
2. Package repeats the selling message imprinted on it before consumers when it is repeatedly handled during a series of uses. This encourages repeat and replacement purchases.
3. A change in product package design and message considerably facilitates implementation of product brand repositioning strategy of a company.
4. Package features communicate product message and motivate consumers product message and motive consumers to buy.
5. It makes product identification and differentiation both easy and effective. In a competitive market when differences in the tangible product attributes are not conspicuous, it is the package whose unique presentation makes products look different from the competing brands.

Packaging Policies and Strategies

Every producer adopts a certain policy and strategy. There may be different types of packaging policies and strategies and a producer has to select any one of these policies and strategies. Use of a particular policy depends upon the needs, requirements and circumstances of the producer. Some of the important packaging policies and strategies are as under:

(1) **Transit Packaging.** Every product has to be delivered to its real consumers. Delivery of a product from producer to consumer is the process involving many activities. One of these activities is the transportation of product from the place of producer to the place of consumers. Product must be packed in the manner that it may reach to the consumers in its original condition. Such packing of product is called transit packaging. Thus, transit packaging is that from of packaging which is meant to keep a product safe in the process of physical distribution. It is also known as distribution packaging. The materials, generally used for transit packaging are the drums, wooden containers tins, sacks of jute or hard board etc. Main stress in this type of packaging is upon the safety of product.

(2) **Consumer Packaging.** The packaging in which a product is finally delivered to its consumers, is known as consumer packaging. Material used for consumer packaging may be—a bottle of glass, a bottle of plastic, a jar, a tin, a box of plastic, a box of hard board, a box of iron, polythene bags, etc. Main stress in consumer packaging is upon the attraction of packaging. Packaging must attract the attention of consumers and it may be convenient for consumers to handle.

(3) **Product Line Packaging or Family Packaging.** When a producer uses identical packagings for all the product items of a product line, it is called product line packaging or family packaging. This type of packaging is widely used by the producers of consumer goods and generally by the

producers producing a large number of product items in a particular product line. The best example of family packaging is the packaging of shoes, Canvas Shoes, Chappals, Hawai Chappls mainly by the producers of a repute such as—Bata, Relaxo, BSC, CSC, Sona, Liberty, etc.

Main advantage of this type of packaging is easy identification of the products. It helps in getting the Brand loyalty of conumers.

(4) **Re-use Packaging.** The form of packaging in which the packages can be re-used after consuming the product, is called re-use packaging. For example—Containers of Ghee, Oil, Biscuits, Toffees, Sweets, Coffee, Medicines, etc. These packages are either of tin or plastic or glass or hard board etc. This type of packaging is very useful from the point of view of consumers because it makes the packaging easy and convenient to handle and empty packages can be re-used for some other purposes.

(5) **Multiple Packaging.** Multiple packaging is the packaging in which many products of different types are packed in a single packaging. This type of packaging is widely used by retailers because it saves their time, money and energy. Various products of different nature may be packed in a single package such as—readymade garments, towels, pen, pencils, rubber etc.

Packaging Decision

A decision taken in respect of packaging of a product, is known as packaging decision. When a producer wants to take a decision in respect of packaging of a product, he has four main points for considerations to take the decision. These considerations are as follows:

(1) **Package Design.** The very first decision taken by a producer in regard to packaging of a product, is to decide the design of packaging. Decision of design of packaging includes following five decisions: *(i)* Which type of material

will be used for packaging? *(ii)* What will be the design of packaging? *(iii)* What colours will be used on packaging? *(iv)* What will be the matter printed on packaging? *(v)* What will be the brand name and trade mark on packaging? In addition to the decision on above questions, the design of packaging is determined keeping in view the convenience of consumers and middlemen. The design of packaging must be such that it may facilitate the activities of storage, transportation, and distribution. Other factors affecting the decision of design of packaging are—nature of product, cost of packaging, size of packaging, legal restrictions, advertisement, etc.

(2) Package Cost. While taking any decision on packaging of a product, the cost of package plays an important role. The package must be selected only after considering the cost of package and its effect on the price of product.

(3) Package Size. Very important decision in respect of packaging is to decide the size of packaging. The size of packaging differs from product to product, producer to producer and time to time. In addition to it, a single product is offered by a single producer to the consumers at a single time in different sizes of packaging. The size of package depends upon the nature of product and the quantity generally purchased by cosnumers. As different consumers buy a product in different sizes, it is advisable that the product must be packed in the packages of different sizes.

(4) Package Test. When a package is decided for a product, the efforts are made to test it so that it may be assured that the package will meet the requirements of consumers. There may be four types of test for this purpose:

(i) Technical Test. Technical test is the test carried out with the purpose of testing whether the package design is proper or not for the safety of product?

(ii) *Middlemen Test.* This test is carried out with the purpose of testing the suitability of package from the point of view of middlemen.

(iii) *Consumer Test.* Consumer test of package aims at testing the package with a view whether it will be liked by the consumers or not?

(iv) *Appealing Test.* This test, tests the package whether it looks attrative or not? If a package is approved in all the four tests, it is finally decided and if a test fails at any stage, it is disapproved.

Product Labelling

Packages and their lables should give buyers accurate and up-to-date information as to the contents and necessary guidance regarding the use of the product. Packaging process completes only after giving the proper label to it. It means, the labelling is an integral part of the packaging. A label may be any thing—a piece of paper, printed statement, imprinted metal, leather—which is either a part of a package or attached to it.

Packaging, branding and labelling go together and constitute an integral part of product planning and development. Label give the proper information about the contents and use of the product. Labelling is also an important marketing decision for legal reason as well. For example, consumer interest in food labelling has increased as an aging and health-conscious population tries to toxic substances, fats and sodium. The Food & Drug Adminstration and the Consumer Product Safety Commission can require that certain products be labelled or marked with warnings, instructions, ingredients, certification and manufacturer's identification. Informed customers are essential for the efficient functioning of the free market economy. Labelling must recognise the consumer's right to be informed and so must incorporate the necessary information from the customer point of view.

Apart from the statutory information, the label should provide:

- Picture of the product
- Colour, size and appearance of the product
- Direction for use of the product
- Brand name
- Date of manufacturer and expiry date
- Name of manufacturer
- Statutory warning, if any

PURPOSES OF LABELLING

(i) A label describes the product specialities which make the product a quick-mover. Without label, it is very difficult to judge the contents inside the package.

(ii) It helps in avoiding the unwanted confusion among the competitive products availabe in the market. A small spelling mistake in case of drugs and chemicals may prove fatal to the users.

(iii) It gives sufficient information about the product to the user.

(iv) It is a strong sales total that encourages self-service operations.

PRODUCT LIFE CYCLE

The concept of product life cycle indicates that sooner or later all products die and that if management wishes to sustain its revenues, it must replace the declining products with the new ones. The product life cycle concept also indicates what can be expected in the market for a new product at various stages. Thus, the concept of product life cycle can be used as a forecasting tool. It can alter management that its new product will inevitably face saturation and decline, and the host of problems these stages pose. The product life cycle concept is also a useful framework for describing the typical evolution of marketing strategy over the product life cycle. This will help in taking sound marketing decisions at different stages of the product life cycle.

Like a human being, a product has also a certain length of life. Again, like a human being, a product has also to pass through certain identifiable stages in its life. As the life of a human being can be divided into six stages—Infant, Childhood, Youth, Adult, Old and Death, in the same manner life of a product can also be divided into six parts—*(1)* Introduction, *(2)* Growth, *(3)* Maturity, *(4)* Saturation, *(5)* Decline, and *(6)* Obsolescence. These six stages are collectively known as the Life-cycle of a product. The team Life-cycle of a product has been defined by many eminent authors. Some of the important definitions are as under:

> *Philip Kotler*, "The product life-cycle is a attempt to recognise distinct stages in the sales history of the product."
>
> *Arch Patton*, "The life-cycle of a product has many points of similarity with the human life-cycle; the product is born, grown lustily, attains dynamic maturity then enters its declining year."
>
> *Willian J. Stanton*, "From its birth to death, a product exists in different stages and in different competitive environment. Its adjustment to these environment determines to a great degree just successful its life will be.

Analytical study of the above definitions, indicates that different stages in the length of the life through which a product has to pass, are known as its life-cycle. The life of a product begins with its introduction into the market. Then the product enters into a period during which its market grows rapidly. After this, the product reaches maturity and then the stage of saturation comes. After the stage of saturation, the market of the product starts to decline and finally the life of product comes to an end.

It is important to note in this reference that the length of life-cycle differs from product to product. The Life-cycle of some products is very short such as fashionable ready-made garments. On the other band, some are the products whose life-cycle goes on upto a long period such as machine. It is also important to note that some of the products come out of the market even before passing through all the stages of their life-cycle in the same manner as some persons die in childhood or at young age.

VARIOUS STAGES OF THE LIFE-CYCLE OF A PRODUCT

A product passes through six different stages in its life-cycle. These stages can be explained with the help of following diagram:

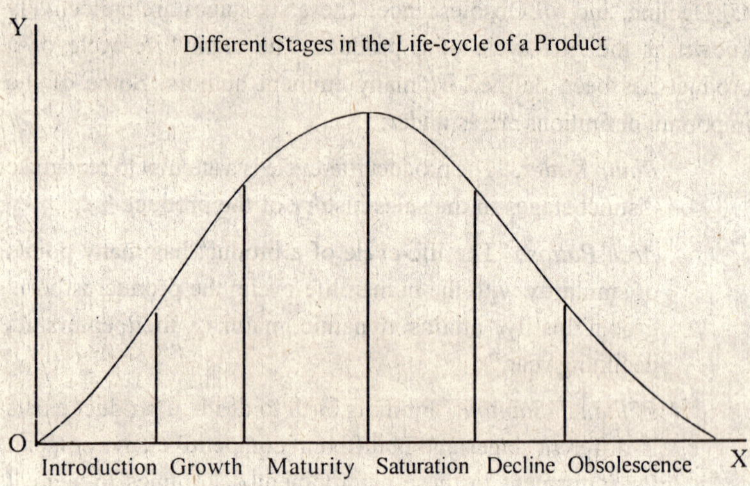

These stages of the life-cycle of a product can be explained as under:

(1) Introduction. This is the very first stage of the life-cycle of a product. At this stage, the product is introduced into the market. The product is made known to its potential consumers throught various programmes of advertisement. The quality, characteristics and utilities of the product are widely publicised in the market. At this stage, heavy expenditure is spent on the programmes of advertisement and sales promotion. As the consumers do not know about the uses of product, the sales of a product remains very low at this stage. As the product is introduced at very competitive price, the amount of profits remains very low or rather negligible at this stage. Some of the products fail to capture market at this very stage.

To get success at this stage of product, it becomes necessary that effective advertising and promotion programmes must be prepared and implemented so that uses and characteristics of the product may be convinced to the consumers. The system of physical distribution must also be very sound.

(2) Growth. This is the second stage of life-cycle of a product. Under this stage, the product gains priority and recognition among the consumers. Consumers like the brand of product and as a result of which the sales of the product increase very rapidly. Increase in sales result in the productions at large-scale and the promotion at large-scale brings many internal and external economies to the enterprise. Consequently, the cost of production comes down and the profits of the enterprise go up. Increase in profits attracts new competitors to enter into market.

In order to maintain the stage of growth for a long time, the marketer must concentrate upon programmes of advertisement and sales promotion. New and alternative uses of product must be widely communicated to the consumers. New market segments for the product must be discovered and the system of physical distribution must be made very sound. A close study of the reactions of the consumers must also be made so that necessary changes may be made in the product.

(3) Maturity. At this stage, a product captures significant place in the market. The customers like and prefer the product. Total volume of sales goes on increasing but the rate of increase in the volume of sales declines. The reason of such declines is the entrance of some new competitors into the market. At this stage, the expenditure of the enterprise on advertising and sales promotion increases so that the deamnd of product may be maintained. At the same time, the price of product should be reducted due to the increase in competition. Consequently, the rate of profits of the enterprise declines.

This stage of product is a challenge to the marketer which must be faced with strong determination and concrete efforts. The marketer must change his marketing strategies, policies and programmes keeping in view the changing circumstances of the market. He must have a close eye upon the policies and strategies of his competitors.

(4) **Saturation.** Saturation is the stage in the life-cycle of a product when total sales of the product are at the maximum possible level. The sales of the product become stagnant at this stage. This stage continues till substitutes of the product enter into the market. The production goes on increasing and the competitors try to capture the market. The costs of advertisement and sales promotion increase and consequently the profits of the enterprise decrease.

At this stage of product, the marketer must try to develop new and alternative uses of the product. Necessary developments and modifications must also be introduced so that some new consumers may start to use it.

(5) **Decline.** Decline is the stage of a product when the sales of the product start to decline. Substitute products capture the market and the popularity of old product goes on declining. The consumers prefer substitute products. This is the stage when there is a great fall in the total sales of the product and profits of the enterprise become almost nil.

At this stage, the marketer must try to find out whether there is any possibility of selling his product or not. If he finds that the possibilities of selling his product are nil, he should decide to stop the production of the product and to divert the resources of the enterprise for the production of some new products. If he finds that the possibilities of selling his product are still alive, he must go ahead to explore such possibilities and necessary changes must be made in the product according to the tastes, habits and likings of consumers.

(6) **Obsolescence.** This is the stage of death for a product. The demand of the product is almost nil and there is no effect of advertisement and sales promotion measures of the enterprise on consumers. New substitutes capture the market and the old product is practically out of the market. This is the stage when the enterprise suffers a loss and the possibilities of creating any demand for the product are almost nil.

At this state, it is advisable that the marketer should stop the production of this product and think of starting the product of some new products.

IMPORTANCE OF PRODUCT LIFE CYCLE

The concept of product life cycle is very important from marketing point of view of a producer or a marketer. The main utilities of the concept are:

1. **Life of a Product is Limited.** According to the concept the life of a product is always limited. The product will die out over a period of time irrespective of the fact, that the product had made tremendous progress during the past. Knowing this fact, management always try to improve its existing product or to develop a new product.
2. **Estimation of Profits.** The quantum and rate of profits increases or decreases with the quantum of turnover. An introductory stage, profits are negligible, then they go up and after some time they begin to fall and gradually they move to nil. Thus, the management can well predict the firm's profits in different stages of the life-cycle of the product.
3. **Marketing Programme.** Different policies, procedures, and strategies are followed in the different stage of the life cycle of a product. So, management can prepare the marketing programmes accordingly and may get success.

FACTORS AFFECTING THE LIFE-CYCLE OF A PRODUCT

There are many factors affecting life-cycle of a product. The statement of Joel Dean is very important in this regard. He said, "The length of the product life-cycle is governed by the rate of technical change, the rate of market acceptance and the case of competitive entry." Some of the important factors affecting life-cycle of a product are discussed hereunder:

(1) **Rate of Technical Changes.** Life-cycle of a product depends upon the rate of technical changes taking place in the country. If technical changes take place in the country at a very high rate, the life-cycle of the products in that country will be very limited because new and improved products take place of the old products. On the other hand, if the rate of technical changes in a country is not so high, the life-cycle of the products in that country may be longer. For example, rate of technical changes in India is lower when compared with that of the other developed countries. As a result of it, the life-cycle of products in our country is higher than that of the developed countries.

(2) **Rate of Market Acceptance.** The length of life-cycle of products in a country depends upon the rate of market acceptance in the country also. If the customers of a country accepts a new product very fast, the life-cycle of products in such country will be very limited because the customers who have accepted a product so fast, can accept another product on next day and the product may stand out of the market. On the other hand, if the customers of a country accept a product gradually, the life-cycle of products in such country may be quite long. For example, the rate of market acceptance in our country is very low and therefore, the life-cycle of most of the products in out country is quite long.

(3) **Ease of Competitive Entry.** The success or failure of a product in the market depends to a large extent upon the

situation of competition in the market. If the competitors can enter into a market very easily, the life-cycle of the product will be very short because the competitors can make the products out. On the contrary, if the competitors cannot enter into a market so easily, the life-cycle of products in such market can be fairly long.

(4) **Risk Bearing Capacity.** The enterprises having more risk bearing capacity can keep their products standing in the market for a long period because they can face all the challenges of market effectively. On the other hand, the enterprises having less risk bearing capacity are unable in facing the challenges of the market, life-cycle of their products is curtailed to short.

(5) **Economic and Managerial Forces.** Economic and managerial forces of an enterprise also determine the success of the enterprise in the market to a great extent. If an enterprise enjoys sound economic and managerial forces, the life-cycle of the product of such enterprise can be longer than that of the products of an enterprise suffering from weak economic and managerial forces.

(6) **Protection by Patent.** If the patent of a product is get registered, the life-cycle of the product can be fairly long, and if the patent of a product is not get registered, the life-cycle of the product is cut short.

NEW PRODUCT DEVELOPMENT

Product planning and development is an important function of the marketing department of any concern following consumer orientation. It includes a number of decisions, namely, what to manufacture or buy, how to have its packaging, how to fix its price and how to sell it. In case of a manufacturing organisation, the production department, will develop and produce products on the advice of the marketing department because it is the marketing department which knows better the requirements of the customers. In case of a purely trading organisation, the purchase department will purchase these products as are suggested by the marketing department.

The work of product planning and development will be performed by the marketing department itself.

Whatever may be the nature of operations of a concern, product planning and development is necessary for its survival and growth in the long-run. Every product has a life cycle and it becomes obsolete after the completion of its life cycle. Therefore, it is essential to develop new products and alter or improve the existing ones.

On the most common product planning problem relates to the addition of new products to the existing product line. Addition of new products involves generation of new product ideas, securing of various possibilities, economic analysis, product development, product testing, test marketing and developing markets. Another important problem of product planning is modification or elimination of existing products. The need for continuous modification of the product is great because society's needs are always changing, and different products must be forthcoming to fulfill them. All products have certain deficiencies for they are the result of a great many compromises. The perfect product has yet to be made. Research makes possible the reduction of these deficiencies resulting in improved products.

STAGES IN PRODUCT DEVELOPMENT

Product development does not just happen, it has to be planned. Dynamic firms plan their innovations for five to ten years in advance. They have a definite idea of exactly what product developments they want and what new product they will need to cater to the demands of their customers. Experience has proved that those firms which are most successful in developing marketable products are the ones which have formally recognised the function of planning product development. The function of planning and developing new products involves the following phases:

(i) **Generation of New Product Ideas.** The product planners must visualise new product ideas. Ideas may be contributed by professional designers, scientists, customers, sales force, dealers, competitors, etc. Ideas may also come from brain-storming sessions of management. It may be noted that the source of ideas is not so important as the firm's system for stimulating new ideas and then acknowledging them and reviewing them promptly.

(ii) Detailed Study of New Product Ideas. The ideas generated at the first sage are examined to eliminate those which have no potential or which are no capable of making any significant contribution to the marketing objectives. The ideas should be screened properly because any idea passing this stage would cost the firm both money and time.

Sources of New Product Ideas

Ideas for new products can come from any sources. *e.g.*:

(a) from research and development personnel;

(b) from markeing personnel;

(c) from associated companies in other countries;

(d) from customers;

(e) from outside technological or scientific discoveries;

(f) from employee suggestions;

(g) from brainstorming sessions of executives;

(h) from competitors;

(i) from knowledge or government needs;

(j) from individual executives;

(k) from a study of unused patents.

(iii) Commercial Feasibility. The product planners evaluate the 'extent and importance of identified markets' needs and appraise the exent to which present products fulfill them. They evaluate new ideas in the light of the company's capability with respect to scientific knowledge, technological skills and financial resources. Only the most feasible and profitable ideas are picked up for further detailed investigation. Marketing research is critical during this phase since it can reveal the changing behaviour of buyers, strategies of competitors and availability of new technological ideas.

(iv) Product Development. This phase relates to actual development of the new product based on the product data evaluation system. A programme is made for the proper development of the product. First of all precise description of the features of the proposed product should be studied. After this, selected consumers may be called upon to offer their comments on the proposed product. Decisions regarding branding, packaging, labelling, etc., are also made during this phase. When the product takes a tangible form, consumer test can be done. Consumer testing will provide the ground for final selection of the product for mass production and distribution.

(v) Testing Market. Test marketing is necessary to find out viability of marketing programme for large-scale distribution. Before the product is widely distributed, it is tried in a selected market. Customers' relation may be noted and product may be improved further, if necessary.

(vi) Commercialisation. After the test marketing gives green signal for the introduction of the product in the national market, the firm may proceed to finalise all features of the product. The marketing deaprtment will launch a full fledged production promotion campaign for mass distribution. Distribution channels will be chosen to make available the product wherever it is demanded. After this, the life cycle of the product will start.

Each of the above stages becomes progressively more expensive in terms of money and scarce manpower. But once the produce idea passes through these stages and careful analysis has been done at each stage, the chances of product failure will be reduced considerably.

SOURCES OF NEW PRODUCT IDEAS

The new product-development process starts with the search for ideas. The search should not be casual. Top management should define the products and markets to emphasize. It should state the new-product objective, whether it is high cash flow, market-share domination, or some other objective. It should state how much effort should be devoted to development breakthrough products, modifying existing products, and copying competitors' products

New product ideas can come from many sources customers, competitors, employees, channel members, and top management.

1. **The Marketing Concept holds that Customers'** needs and wants are the logical place to start in the search for new-product ideas. Hippel has shown that the highest percentage of ideas for new industrial products originate with customers. Technical companies can earn a great deal by studying a special set of their customers, the lead users, namely, those customers who make the most advanced use of the company's product and who recognize needed improvements ahead of other customers. Companies can identify customers' needs and wants through customer surveys, projective tests, focused group discussion, and suggestion and complaint letters from customers. Many of the best ideas come from asking customers to describe their problems with current products.
2. **Companies Also Rely on their Scientists,** engineers, designers, and other employees for new-product ideas. Successful companies have established a company culture that encourages every employee to seek new ideas for improving the company's production, products, and services. Toyota claims that its employees submit two million ideas annually, about 35 suggestions per employee, and over 85% of them are implemented. Kodak and some American firms give monetary and recognition awards to their employees who submit the best ideas during the year.
3. **Companies can Find Good Ideas by Examining their Competitors'** products and services. They can learn from distributors, suppliers, and sales representatives what competitors are doing. They can find out what customers

like and dislike in their competitors' new products. They can buy their competitors' products, take them apart, and build better ones. Their competitive strategy is one of product imitation and improvement rather than product innovation. The Japanese are masters of this strategy, in that they have licensed or copied many Western products and found ways to improve them.

4. **Company Sales Representatives and Middlemen are a Particularly Good Sources of New-product Ideas.** They have first hand exposure to customers' needs and complaints. They often learn first of competitive developments. An increasing number of companies train and reward their sales representatives, distributors, and dealers for finding new ideas. For example: Bill Keefer, chairman of Warner Electric Brake and Clutch requires his salesforce to list on each monthly call report the three best product ideas they heard on customer visits. He reads these ideas each month and pens notes to his engineers, manufacturing executives, and so on, to follow up the better ideas.

5. **Top Management can be Another Major Source of New Product Ideas.** Some company leaders, like Edwin H.Lard former CEO of Polaroid, take personal responsibility for technogical innovation in their companies. This is not always constructive, as when a top executive pushes through a pet idea without throughly researching market size or interest. When Land pushed forward his Polavision project (instantly developed movies), it ended as a major product failure, because the market became more interested in video-tapes as a way to film action.

IDEA-GENERATING TECHNIQUES

Really good ideas come out of inspiration, perspiration, and techniques. A number of "creativity" techniques can help individuals and groups generate better ideas.

1. **Attribute Listing.** This technique calls for listing the major attributes of an existing product and then modifying each attribute in the search for an improved product. Consider a screwdriver: Its attributes : a round, steel shank, a wooden handle, manually operated and torque provided by twisting action. Now a group considers ways to improve product performance or appeal. The round shank could be made hexagonal so that a wrench could be applied to increase the torque; eletric power could replace manual power; the torque could be produced by pushing.

2. **Morphological Analysis.** This method calls for identifying the structural dimensions of a problem and examining the relationships among them. Suppose the problem is that of "getting something from one place to another via a powered vehicle."

3. **Forced Relationship.** Here several objects are considered in relation to each other. An office-equipment manufacturer wanted to design a new desk for executives. Several objects were listed a desk, television set, clock, computer, copying machine, bookcase, and so on. The result was a fully electronic desk with a console resembling that found in an airplane cockpit.

4. **Synectics.** William J.J. Gordon felt that Osborn's brainstorming session produced solutions too quickly, before a sufficient number of perspectives had been developed. Gordon decided to define the problem so broadly that the group would have no inkling of the specific problem.

5. **Need/Problem Identification.** The preceding creatively techniques do not require consumer input to generate ideas. Nee/problem identification, on the other hand, starts with consumers. Consumers are asked about needs, problems, and ideas. For example, they can be asked about their problems in using a particular product of product category.

6. **Brainstorming.** Group creativity can be stimulated through brainstorming techniques developed by Alex Osborn. The usual brainstorming group consists of six to ten people. The problem should be specific. The sessions should last about an hour. The chairman starts with, "Remember, we want as many ideas as possible—the wilder the better—and remember, no evaluation." The ideas start flowing, one idea sparks another, and within an hour over a hundred or more new ideas may find their way into the type recorder. For the conference to be maximally effective.

PRODUCT MARKET STRATEGIES

A major product strategy input relatés to the degree, if any, of change in the basic characteristics of the product that may seem desirable at a particular time. These alternatives range from no change to an entirely new product, and the impact of each depends upon the degree of other marketing change taking place at the same time. It shows nine different combinations of the product market strategies that a company might consider using to improve its profitability. Notice that each product strategy is associated with some market strategy and that each has important implications for the other:

1. **No Product Change—No Market Change.** This is the least complex product-market strategy. There are two main versions : simplifying the product's design and altering the amount of integration in the product's manufacturing materials instead of buying them. Both seek to improve profitability mainly through cost reduction, and both involve selling essentially the same product to the same market.
2. **No Product Change—Improved Market.** This strategy aims to improve the product's market and profitability by increasing sales to present markets. This process of remerchandising, in other words, leaes basic features of the physical product unchanged but changes the accompanying services.

3. **No Product Change—New Market.** This product-market strategy is especially significant for companies with products already in, or about to enter, the market maturity stage of the life cycle. During this stage, industry sales tend to reach a plateau and then gradually fall off. But some companies explore the possibility of rejuvenating the product's sales and profit growth rates through finding new markets. In searching for new market segments for a product approaching saturation in its present market, management should consider both possible new users and new uses.
4. **Product Change—No Market Change.** The three versions of this strategy are product line simplification and product discontinuance, new models (really new or improved products), and planned obsolescene (designing a new modification that makes the consumer want to replace the old model, such as an annual model change). Strategies involving product line simplification and product discontinuance envision profit increases through cost reductions. Those involving either new models or planned obsolescence seek profit increases through growth in sales volume.
5. **Produt Change—Improved Market.** The two main types of the strategy are product customization (tailoring product specifications very closely to buyer needs), and product systems (combining a series of separated operations into a system as in the automatic washing machine). Both aim to improve profitability through increasing sales volume.
6. **Product Change—New Market.** This strategy seeks increased profitability through additional sales volume generated by changing certain features of the product and selling it to a new market segment, so companies often must change certain product features to match them better with the individualized needs of new target market segments.

Trading up and trading down are the main forms of this strategy.

7. **New Product—Improved Market.** This strategy aims to increase profitability through adding sales volume gained from new products sold to the same market segments. Often the new products are extensions of the present product line, for example, the ready-to-eat cereal added to a line of regular cereals or the addition of new flavours to an old product line, as was done by Ovaltine. Sometimes the new product are members of related product lines sold to the same market segments as present products, for example, the pet food added by a marketer of breakfast cereals.

8. **New Product—No Market Change.** This strategy seeks increased profitability through selling a new product to the same market segment, the new product replacing an older product sold for the same general purpose. Thus, product replacement strategy aims at retaining the level of sales now coming from a particular market segment where an older product's sales are being endangered by competitor's new products serving the same uses. Examples of new products that replaced old ones are numerous. A few of them are automobiles, which replaced carriages, diesel carriages, diesel locomotives, which replaced steam locomotives, jet planes, which replaced piston-driven aircraft, the transistor, which replaced the vacuum tube, and the ballpoint pen, which largely replaced the fountain pen. For companies having products in the market maturity stage, new products should be waiting in the wings, ready for market introduction at the proper time.

9. **New Product—New Market.** This strategy to increase profitability through greater sales volumes obtained from selling new products in new markets. Thus, it involves product mix diversification—selling unrelated product lines to entirely different markets. Companies adopt this strategy

for reasons such as an unexpected research breakthrough or discoveries of profitable opportunities to develop products for new markets.

VARIOUS STEPS TAKEN IN PRODUCT DEVELOPMENT PROCESS

The experience of many firms shows that the process of developing a new product contains of six steps that can be fairly well described as follows:

(1) Exploration. This is the search stage in which ideas for new products are sought. In this stage of product development, careful attention is paid to developing products that meet company objective. The explanation for a new product may be done through *(a)* consumer's requests, *(b)* letters to produces, *(c)* competitive products, *(d)* market research, *(e)* capacities of plant *(f)* policies of state and *(g)* objectives of customers etc.

(2) Screening. Screening cosists of a preliminary evaluation, to determine whether the ideas has possibilities and should be further pursued, or should be dropped. In this phase, questions such as the following should be asked about product:

(a) What is the approximate market for new product?

(b) Can this product be sold by the existing sales forces, agents or dealers?

(c) Are any serious difficulties foreseen in producing?

(d) Are there any important patterns, licensing agreements, or other legal restrictions which affect the manufacture of product?

(e) Will there be any serious difficulty in obtaining raw material etc.

(f) How much money will be needed for the production and distribution of this item?

(g) Can financing be obtained and at a reasonable cost?

(h) What is the estimated cost of production, selling price, and gross margin?

(3) **Specification.** If the proposed product passes the screening test, it is expanded into a realistic recommendation. In this step, a more through analysis is made of the marketability of the product, the features that consumers may desire, and competitor's probable actions. Finally a scheduled and budged are established for prototypes or models.

(4) **Development.** This step consists of transforming an idea for a product, into an actuality. Prototypes of the new product are built so that they can be shown and demonstrated.

(5) **Testing.** This is a critical stage where the worth of the original product idea and the judgement about its feasibility are proved or disproved. Sample product are market tested, and user reactions are analyzed. When a final agreement is reached on the exact specifications for the product, the design is "forzen", that is no additional design changes are made. The product is then ready to be produced.

(6) **Commercialisation.** This is the final step in the series and is the one with which we are most familiar. Commercialization consists of all the actions involved in fullscale production of the product, advertising and selling the product, and pledging that the company with its resources will stand behind and guarantee the new product.

FACTORS RESPONSIBLE FOR THE FAILURE OF A NEW PRODUCT

The development of a new product is always not successful. There may be following reasons responsible for the failure of product:

(i) **Weakness in Distribution.** The distribution of the product is one of the major marketing problems. It is this marketing function, which enables the product to reach the proper markets at proper time and at a proper price. Distribution management is considered to be one of the important ones where management decisions requires farsightedness and vision.

(ii) Insufficient Marketing Effort. It is wrong to assume that a manufacturer just ends his efforts the moment a product is ready for sale. Advertising and proper promotional activities also form a part of his job to make the product known to consumers. Proper selection of the channels of distribution and the methods of physical distribution also help in proper and efficient marketing of products.

(iii) Inadequate Sales Force. Selling is done by personal or impersonal methods. Impersonal methods include advertisement and similar promotional activities. Personal methods, on the other hand, are more intimate and more efficient promotional activities should be backed by adequate sales forces to introduce the product properly in the market. If salesmen are not trained or do not possess salesmen qualities, the product will not succeed.

(iv) Competition. Severe competition leads products to struggle hard in the market. There are various methods to overcome severe competitions including price cuts (mark down prices) and various kinds of discounts etc. Consumer products are most affected by severe competition. However, it should be noted that it is not the low prices alone that will help a product to compete and succeed in the market. Basically offering high quality products excelling the existing ones is the basic determinant in deciding the success of a product in the market. There is a wide spread recognition that it is ultimately the quality of a product which will enable the product to withstand competition.

(v) Poor Timing. The fundamental principle to be followed in product planning is to find out the exact time at which the product is to be introduced in the market. Usually when and how are the two questions a manufacturer is often finding difficult to answer. A close analysis of the market conditions and consumer behaviour and attitudes is essential to find an answer to the two problems.

(vi) **Higher Costs.** Higher final costs than anticipated at the time of product planning is another reason for product failure. It might be partly due to wrong pricing policies adopted by the firm. The cost estimates also often go wrong when the products are finally introduced into the market.

(vii) **Product Defect.** This arises out of technical flaws in the process of production. This is a fundamental reason for product failure. Low quality of products, poor design or packing may lead to product failure. This can be done away by the proper product testing.

(viii) **Indequate Market Analysis.** Biased information or improper analysis of the market will yield only wrong data. Acting on such data leads to product failure.

All these problems could be solved by the timely action of the management. Blain Cooke opines that today three products or more of new products fail. According to him, "the new products which fail are not in literal marketing sense products at all—they are merely interesting but worthless artifacts of the product process".

CONSUMER ADOPTION PROCESS

Once a product is introduced in the market, the major challenge rests with the marketing function. The product so introduced is to be 'adopted' *i.e.*, purchased and diffused *i.e.*, percolated through out the markets. Any new idea or brand catches on through a gradual process which starts with some adopting it easily and other doing so only after the so-called 'opinion' leaders' have satisfied themselves and set and example. The faster it happens the better it is for the firm. Addition is the decision of an individual to use the product; while diffusion is the collective spread of individual adoption decisions the rough out a market. Thus, adoption process is concerned with the individual whereas the diffusion process is concerned with the aggregate behavior.

The fundamental reason for studying the diffusion and adoption process is the increase in the level of understanding of how? when? and why? new products are accepted or rejected. Naturally a more comprehensive understanding of this rocess will enhance the success of future new product introductions.

Stages in Consumer Adoption Process

The adoption process is belived to follow a five stage sequential process beginning with actual awareness of a product's existence and ending with adoption or comitment to the product. From the point in time when an individual first hears of an innovation to the point in time when adoption occurs has been recognised as consisting of five logical stage names awareness—interest—evaluation—trial and adoption.

1. **Awareness Stage.** Here the individual is exposed to the innovation but lacks complete information about it. That is, the individual is aware of the innovation but is not yet motivated to seek further information. He knows of product existence.

2. **Interest Stage.** The individual becomes interested in the new idea and seeks additional information about it. The innovation is favoured in a general way but is not yet judged in terms of its utility to a specific situation. He seeks further information.

3. **Evaluation Stage.** The individual applies his mental faculty to the innovation to compare present and anticipated situation and then decides to whether or not try it. It is to do with careful weighing as to whether or not to try it.

4. **Trial Stage.** The individual uses the innovation on a small-scale in order to determine its utility in his own situation. That is, he tries it once or twice to confirm its utility.

5. **Adoption Stage.** The individual decides to continue the full use of the innovation. That is the purchases and repurchases.

It is worth emphasizing here that any innovation may be rejected at any stage of adoption process. Even rejection can take place after adoption which is called as discontinuance. Further, a consumer may move through several of these stages simultaneously as it happens in case of impulse buying.

However, understanding of the sequence of these stages of adoption and types of communication most effective in each stage will enable the firm to develop a promotional campaign consistent with behaviour of consumer particularly in case of a firm attempting to market a new product, Initially more mass media should be employed to relay product awareness and information on product utility. As time assess, the appeal should be moulder to include more personal appeal, as consumer is keen on evaluating, trying and adopting the new product. The strategy employed, of course, must give some consideration to the nature of the new product. The new product characteristics affect the adoption process. Factors such as the relative advantage, compatability, complexity, divisibility and communicability, normally determine the ease with which consumers accept a new product.

Adopter Categories

Companies are finally interested in the level and rate of diffusion because, the ultimate level of diffusion is a limit on the total sales of the company, while the rate of diffusion affects how quickly the company covers its costs and begins to make a profit. The notion of diffusion suggests that some people adopt a new product well before others. That is, people vary in they degree of innovativeness. One means of classifying people according to their innvativeness is based on the normal distribution curve as developed by Mr. E Rogers and Mr. Shoemaker in 1971. Using the mean and standard deviations, it is possible to categories the adopters into five main classes as given in the figure on next page. These are; innovators—early adoptors—early majority—late majority and laggards.

1. **Innovators.** These represent the first 2.5 per cent of the total adoptors. They are young risk runners, better educated,

more cosmopolitan, but less integrated with local groups. They are the forerunners and important to the victory of new product so introduced.

2. **Early Adoptors.** These represent the next 13.5 per cent of the total adoptors. These adopt in the per groups act as taste-makers or opinion leaders in their local group. These are wealthier and better educated and have greater technical knowledge of the innovation. As they are integrated with the community they exert influence. Others turn to them for their advice the moment they come in contact with these persons.

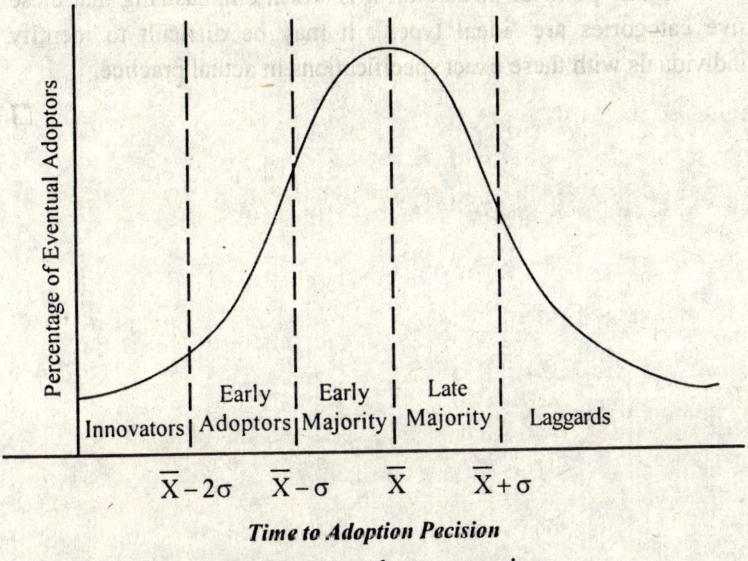

Fig. Consumer adoptor categories

3. **Early Majority.** This group accounts for the next 34 per cent of the total adoptors. These are average people in terms of income, education, age and occupations. These tend to be more cautious before adopting normally waiting until its benefit and other features have been clearly demonstrated well before adoption.

4. **Late Majority.** This group represents the next 34 per cent of the total adoptors. These are more conservative, less educated and older with limited purchasing power. The reason for their adoption is that majority of the people have adopted or the product is within their purchasing power now.

5. **Laggards.** This last chunk accounts for remaining 16 per cent of the total adoptors. This group considers adopting as the last resort as there is no alternative. The features of this group are not available because, very less is known about this group.

At this point of discussion it is worth emphasizing that these five categories are 'ideal types'. It may be difficult to identify individuals with these exact specifications in actual practice.

❐

7

Pricing Decisions

Pricing is perhaps the most crucial aspect of marketing management since it has significant economic and social implications. Price is the source of revenue for a businessmen whereas it is an expense item for the consumer. The businessmen want to get the highest possible price for the products he sells whereas the consumer wishes to pay the least possible price for his purchases. Since prices affect all of us, directly or indirectly, they are a standard topic of discussion at various places including house, offices, buses, schools, colleges, markets and streets. This is particularly so because prices in general are changing quite often and the inflationary conditions severely hurt many segments of society. The man in the street complains about rising prices of such essential items as grains, sugar, vegetables, clothes etc., and even the rent for the house he has to live in. On the other hand, farmers argue that the prices for their farm products are too low to support their families. Business persons declare that they cannot hold down the prices of their finished products as they are incurring increasing cost for the raw materials. The politicians in general and the Government in particular express a lot of concern and agony over the prices both at public meetings and partlimanetary debates. Everyone in society—the housewife, the farmer, the minister, the businessmen, the consumer and so on—seems to wail against hight prices, yet none is able to do much for controlling them. Perhaps we believe that we are helpless creatures in this world or we do not know what to do.

Price may be defined as the exchange value of a commodity or service. Thus, the value of any item-consumer product, industrial product, or service—is what it can be exchanged for in the market place. The worth of any commodity or service is what some one is prepared to pay for it in the market. In the primitive barter economy when commerce made its beginning, the exchange value of one commodity was expressed in terms of another commodity. For example, one horse might be worth twenty baskets of wheat or two apples might be worth two leaves of bread. With the advancement of societies, money came into existence as a medium of exchange. This method of expressing the value of goods in terms of money is called the "Price System". Thus, in a modern money-using economy, price refers to the exchange value of a good or service in terms of money.

PRICING OBJECTIVES

As another areas of business activity, every firm must have certain objectives in the sphere of pricing too. Objectives povide direction for future action. Pricing objectives are a crucial part of the overall organisation objectives. The goals of the firm and the marketing organisation form the basis for determining pricing objectives, which should be clearly defined before implementing pricing policies and procedures. Pricing goal is, thus, a means to achieve certain primary objectives of the firm. For example, a firm may have as its primary objective the goal of becoming the most dominant supplier in the national market. Its marketing goal, then, may be to penetrate in all States and make the maximum sales. The related pricing objective would be sales maximization which, in turn, might lead to the adoption of low price policy with highest cash and trade discounts in the industry. Similarly, a company may try to maximise its profits by pricing a new technological innovation very high.

I. Volume Objectives

Another explanation of pricing behaviour is the sales maximisation concept. This means that the management sets a level of lowest acceptable profit and then tries to maximize sales within the limits of this level. A low price is often a good strategy to increase the sale and strengthen the competitive position of the firm in the long run. The firm will continue to expand its sales so long as its total profits do not fall below the minimum level acceptable to management.

A second volume objective in the market share is the percentage of total market sales controlled by a certain firm or product. Securing a high percentage of market share is frequently a major objective of many firms, especially when the market has a potential for growth. The high market share in a growing market means increasingly more sales, larger revenue, mass production and lesser cost of production per unit through economies of scale.

II. Profitability Objectives

Profitability objectives include target return and profit maximisation goals. Profit maximisation has been considered to be the most important objectives of business firms by the classical economic thinkers. The entire micro-economics is based upon the assumption that buyers and sellers take rational decisions. The rational behaviour is defined as an attempt to maximise gains and minimise losses. In operative terms, it means that the basic objective of all individual firms is profit maximisation. As has been stated earlier, profit is equal to revenue minus cost and revenue is determined by the selling price and the quantity sold. Thus, price is an important factor in achieving profit goals. Many firms continue to increase their price for maximising their profits so long as it does not result in a disproportionate decrease in the number of units sold. In other words, the point of profit maximisation is where the marginal cost and marginal revenue are equal. Since it is difficult to achieve this delicate balance in practice, hardly a few firms are able to accomplish profit maximisation goals. Larger number of firms prefer to achieve some feasible objectives, one of which is the target return on investment.

Many firms follow a particular return on their investment figure as one of their major pricing objectives. This concept has recently become more important because of the public criticism of profit maximisation objective. Target return objectives may be set either for short-run or long-run operations of the firm. The return on investment is calculated by dividing net profits by the investment money used to obtain the net profit figure. Under this pricing objective, management usually stipulates a return on investment figure below which it does not want to go. This may be, for instance, 15%. Very often this minimum acceptable return is the cost of assets which a firm has acquired for running the business and earning a particular level of profits. Thus, if a firm has borrowed Rs. 8,00,000 from some financial institution @ 10% interest charge, it would certainly want that the profits from this Rs. 8 lakh investment must exceed 10% because at least this amount will be needed to pay the interst expenses. This type of pricing objectives serve as useful guidelines for evaluating organisation activity. As one writer has put it. For management consciously accepting less than maximum profits, the target rate can provide a measure of the amount of restraint. For firms making very low profits, the target rate can serve as a standard for judging improvement.

III. Other Objectives

Other objectives, though not directly related to profitability or volume objectives, are very important in the pricing decisions of many firms. These include (a) social and ethical condination, (b) status quo objectives, and (c) prestige or image goals.

(a) Social and ethical consideration may be determining factors in some pricing situations. For example, the prices of certain products or services may be fixed on the basis of customer's ability to pay. A few medical doctors, specially in the semi-urban areas, do not charge the same fees from all patients; the charges vary according to the income level of the patient. Such a practice is based on social and ethical evaluation of different people.

(b) Status quo objectives refer to the maintenance of stable prices. The idea is to minimise competitive pricing action by different firms so that they may concentrate their efforts in other areas of marketing, such as product design or promotion. In practice, a particular price is set by some leading firm and everyone else in industry follows the leader. Of course, such a pricing strategy is undesirable from the social point of view and it may lead to charging higher prices from customers than what would be possible in the competitive situation.

(c) Image goals are another type of pricing objectives. Some firms set their product's price in such a manner that it builds a good deal of image for them. Setting a high price, for example, may be considered as a reflection of better quality. Others may prefer a 'low price' strategy for image building among their customers.

The business firms may formulate their pricing policy or strategy on the basis of he broad pricing objectives discussed above. In other words, a price policy or strategy is meant for acheiving some of these objectives.

INFLUENCE OF OTHER MARKETING MIX ELEMENTS ON PRICE

The final price must take into account the brand's quality and advertising relative to competition. Farris and Reibstein examined the relationship between relative price, relative quality, and relative advertising for 227 consumer businesses and found the following results:

(A) The positive relationship between high prices and high advertising held most strongly in the later stages of the product life cycle for market leaders, and for low-cost products.

(B) Brands with high relative quality and high relative advertising obtained the highest prices. Conversely, brands with the quality and low advertising charged the lowest prices.

(C) Brands with average relative quality but high relative advertising budgets were able to charge premium prices. Consumers apparently were willing to pay higher prices for known products than for unknown products.

Company Pricing Policies

The contemplated price must be consistent with company pricing policies. Many companies set up a pricing department to develop pricing policies and establish or approve pricing decisions.

Their aim is to insure that the sales people quote price rate are reasonable to customers and profitable to the company.

Impact of Price on Other Parties

Management must also consider the reactions of other parties to the contemplated price. How will the distributors and dealers feel about in? Will the company salesforce be willing to sell at that price or complain that the price is too high? How will competitors react to this price? Will suppliers raise their prices when they see the company's price Will the government intervene and prevent this price from being charged? In the last case, marketers need to know the laws affecting price and make sure that their pricing policies are defensible.

NEED OF PRICING DECISION OF A PRODUCT

The need of princing decision of a product is accounted for the following reasons:

1. **Prices are Very Important from Society's Point of View.** Every society must ensure the optimum use of its resources, both material and labour. Price allocates these resources to different productive units on the basis of their efficiency. Since every resources has price, more resources are attracted to the profitable industries which offer relatively higher prices. Similarly, those industries which do not maintain high prices are not able to attract much resources.
2. **Price is a Very Important Element in Determining Both the Revenue and Profit of the Enterprise.** Profit is equal to revenue minus costs. Revenue is equal to the price multiplied by sales volume. The sales volume is, thus, influenced by the price level. In general, the higher the price charged for a product, the lower would be its sales volume and vice versa. In other words, the price affects the sales volume of the business firm which, in turn, determines its revenue. Since revenue is an important factor in determining the profit of an enterprise, the price has an influence on the profits too. Besides, price has an impact on the competitive strength of a firm.

3. **Prices also Help the Business System in Allocating its Scarce Resources Economically.** A firm employs various factors of production including land, labour and capital. The extent of the use of each of these factors depends on the relative prices they receive. For example, if the wage rates are high, the firm may go for labour saving machinery. Similarly, high interest rates may induce management to make lesser capital expenditure in future. Price of production inputs influence the cost of production which, in turn, determines the profits of the firm.

4. **In a Free Market System, Price Mechanism has Considerable Impact Upon the Competitive Strength of Different Firms.** Obviously, more consumers will be attracted to the seller charging lesser price for a given product. Each firm would try to outsell others through price reduction resulting in competitive conditions in the market. In this way also price helps in maximising social welfare.

5. **Price are Important both for Consumers and Sellers.** They determine the supply and demand for various products in the market. Price is an important element in meeting consumer needs. All commodities have some degree of utility, or want satisfying power. But the individual consumer cannot purchase every product he desires he has limited amount of money at his disposal. Therefore, he faces the problem of allocating his limited resources among various alternative uses. The price mechanism helps him to make these allocation decisions. For example, a person might prefer a new colour television to a sofa but if the price of the television is too high the consumer might reconsider his preference order and allocate his limited funds for the pruchase of sofa.

In short, prices play quite an important role in our daily lives. To quote Keith and Gubellini "The price of goods and service affects, both directly and indirectly, the producer, the distributor and the consumer. The volume of production within the economy is influenced greatly by price. Price helps determine how people will spend their incomes, since the price of goods often influences the decision to buy. Prices fix costs and the level of the profit. For the consumer, price control the standard of living since the relation between. wages and prices is a measure of the purchasing power of the buying public".

PROBLEM INVOLVING IN PRICING NEW PRODUCT

Pricing a new product is an art. It is one of the most important and puzzling marketing problems faced by a firm. Pricing is important in two ways as far as new product is concerned:

(a) It affects the quantity of the product to be sold.

(b) It determines the amount of the revenue of a firm.

New products when introduced appeal to many as novel items. But this distinctiveness created by novelty is only temporary. The price factors which may be ignored initially would become important when the product becomes an ordinary one because of being constantly used. Furthermore competitors may also appear in the market. Therefore, the new products are hard to be priced especially with a right price. Incorrect pricing will definitely lead to product failure. For setting a price on a new product three guidelines are to be adopted:

(i) Markeintg the product accepted.

(ii) Maintaining the market.

(iii) Retaining the profit.

There are two options available for pricing a new product—

(i) Skimming, and *(ii)* Penetration pricing.

If a product is entirely new in the market skimming method could be used. A strategy of high prices coupled with large promotional expenditure in the initial stages has proved successful in a number of cases. Skimming pricing is recommended on account of the following reasons:

(i) Initial sales would be less.

(ii) Helps to take the cream of the market through high prices.

(iii) People may like to own a new product even at a higher cost.

(iv) Helps to develop demand as the price is gradually reduced.

(v) High sales volume on account of higher price.

However, it should be noted that high initial price may also prevent quick sales.

The second option is to adopt penetration pricing. A comparative analysis of these two pricing systems reveal that both these methods are not free from errors. The difference between these two methods could be illustrated through the following example: When an electric clock was first introduced consumers were reluctant to buy it because it was relatively low priced when compared to quality spring wound clock. Consumers apparently felt that a quality clock could not be sold so cheap. The clocks were withdrawn from the market and reintroduced subsquenlty at a higher price that sounded attractive; after that they sold clock successfully.

In the case of new products pricing has to be made with little knowledge of demand cost and competition. The new product has also to bear the cost of promotion or creating a market. The initial cost therefore will be definitely greater. The cost incurred in constructing a proper channel of distribution may also be accounted for in pricing.

Management should consider using penetration pricing under any or all of four different conditions: *(1)* when the new product's demand is highly price elastic, even early in the market pioneering stage; *(2)* when the marketer can realize substantial manufacturing and marketing economics if it obtains a large sales volume (such economics, of course, bring down average total costs); *(3)* when the marketer expects strong competition soon after introducing the product, that is when it expects the product's market pioneering stage not to last long; and *(4)* when there is little or no elite maket segment made up of buyers who will probably buy regardless of price.

The innovating marketer's single most important consideration in choosing between price skimming and penetration pricing is the relative ease and speed with which competitors can lauch their own versions of the new product. For revolutionary new products with large potential markets, penetration pricing is the most appropriate strategy. This is because the existence of a large potential market is certain to attract large competitors soon after introduction of the innovation.

PRICING POLICIES IN PRACTICE

Pricing policies constitute the general frame work within which pricing decisions should be made in order to achieve the pricing objectives. They provide guidelines within which pricing strategy is formualted and implemented. The following statements will clarify the meaning of pricing policy.

(a) Prices should be adopted and individualized to fit the diverse competitive situations encountered by different products.

(b) A predetermined and systematic method of pricing new products should be provided.

(c) Prices should be set to promote the long-term welfare of the enterprise, *e.g.*, to discourage competition in the market.

(d) Prices should aim at maximising profits for the entire product line.

A systematic approach to pricing the products of a firm requires that decision of individual pricing situations be generalised and codified into policies covering all the pricing policies. Pricing policies should be tailored to meet the various competitive sitautions. This implies that a firm can follow different pricing policies with regard to different markets or different customers. For instance, full cost pricing may be followed to sell the products to a big buyer like Government, particularly when the plant capacity is lying idle.

It is very difficult to ascertain precisely the pricing policies and practices followed by a business enterprise because all the policies are not in an explicit form. For instance, a company may follow the practice of charging lower prices to prevent competition in the market, but this may not be admitted publically. Similarly there are many other pricing policies and practices which are not laid down expressedly, but may be known by studying the behaviour of business enterprises. The major pricing policies which are followed by the business enterprise are as follows:

1. Keep-out Pricing

As the name suggests, it is a pre-emptive pricing policy which aims at discouraging the other firms in the market to offer substitutes. Keep out pricing should be followed for only one product of a firm. It is very risky venture particularly,when the product is offered to the public at a price which is less than the actual cost of production and distribution. This policy can be followed by big firms with huge resources at their command. But once the price at a low level is fixed, it may not be possible to increase it because of the fear of other firms introducing the substitutes.

2. Skimming-the-cream Pricing

Under this pricing policy, higher prices are charged during the initial stages of the introduction of a new product. The manufacturer fixes higher price of his product in order to recover his initial investment quickly. This policy has been quite successful in many cases because of the following reasons:

(i) Demand is likely to be more inelastic with respect to price in the early stages than it is when the product is fully grown. Promotional elaslticity is, on the other hand, quite higher, particularly for the products with high unit price.

(ii) Introducing a new product with a high price is an efficient device for dividing the market into segments that differ in price elasticity of demand. The initial high prices serves to skim the cream of the market that is relatively insensitive to price. Price may be reduced subsequently to attract successively more elastic segments of the market.

(iii) A manufacturer may charge higher prices in order to restrict the demand to the level which he can easily meet. He may also use this strategy to avoid the loss resulting from the competition when the entery to that line is quite easy.

(iv) High initial price finances the cost of raising a product family. The manufacturer may charge high prices and plough back the excessive profits into the business for further expansion.

3. Penetration Pricing

Under this pricing policy, prices are fixed below the competitive level to obtain a larger share of the market and to devlop popularity of the brand. Unlike skimming prices policy, it facilitates higher volume of sales even during the initial stage of a product's life cycle. This method of pricing is usually found at the retail level of distribution. Many retailers offer discount to attract more and more customers. They operate on the principle of low markup and higher volume.

Penetrating pricing may also be used at the time of introduction of a new product to prevent the entry of new firms by keeping the profit margin very low. This policy helps in developing the brand preference of the people and is useful in marketing the products which are expected to have a steady long-term market.

4. Leader Pricing

A firm may cut prices temporarily on a few items in order to attract customers. In other words, 'loss leaders' are used to promote higher sales of different products offered by the firm. Leader items are generally well-known *i.e.*, are highly advertised and purchased frequently. The term 'loss leaders' is used because a few popular items are offered at a prices below normally expected prices. In fact, this term is a misnomer. The term 'profit leaders' would be more descriptive of the goal of the policy. The rationale of the policy is that customers will come to the store to buy the advertised items and then stay to buy other regularly priced merchandise. The net result will be increased total sales volume and profits.

5. Psychological Pricing

Under this policy, prices are fixed in such a way that they have some kind of psychological influence on the buyers. Customary pricing and price lining are the examples of psychological pricing. Another form of psychological pricing is Odd Pricing *i.e.*, prices are set at odd amount such as Rs. 19, Rs. 49, Rs. 99 etc. For example, a customer may pay happily Rs. 99.95 for a pair of shoes and may not like to buy the same pair if it is priced at Rs. 100. Old pricing is widely used by the publishers of paperbacks.

6. Price Lining

Price lining is used extensively by the retailers. The retailers usually offer a good, better and best assortment of merchandise at different price levels. For example, a retailer of ready-made shirts may sell shirts at three prices: Rs. 60, Rs. 90 and Rs. 120. The first price stands for the economy choice, the second for the medium quality and the third for the super-fine quality. Price lining simplifies pricing decisions in the future as retail prices are already set. This helps the retailer to plan his purchase to suit his price lining. It also simplifies buying decisions by the customers.

7. One Price Versus Variable Price Policy

In case of one-price policy, the seller charges the same price to similar types of customers who purchase similar quantities of the product under essentially the same terms of sale. The price may vary according to the quantity of purchase. However, price charged for different quantities to different customers are the same. For example, a seller may sell his product @ R. 10.000 per unit if less than one dozen units are purchased and @ Rs. 9.000 per unit if one dozen or more units are purchased. On the other hand, a seller may follow a single price under which the price per unit of a product remains the same regardless of the number of units being purchased.

8. Resale Price Maintenance

Resale price maintenance (RPM) is he policy under which a manufacturer fixes the price of his product below which his product would not be sold to the consumers or distributors. "Resale price maintenance refers to that price policy under which the manufacturer of a branded product in open competition establishes the price, or the minimum price at which such product shall be resold to the consumers."

Resale price maintenance is possible in case of branded products only. A manufacturer of a popular brand of a product may enter into an agreement with the distributors of his product under which resale is fixed by the manufacturer and the distributors will not sell the product below that price. The resale price maintenance practice is generally followed by the manufacturers of consumer products such as electric appliances, drugs, cigarettes, liquor and sports goods. The basic purpose of this policy is to protect the interest of the manufacturer and to create a good image in the market of the manufacturer and his product.

9. Discrimination Pricing or Charging what the Traffic will Bear

Some business enterprises follow the policy of charging different prices from different customers according to their ability to pay. This policy is very popular with the service enterprises like law and medicine. Business enterprises marketing tangible products also use the policy of price discrimination successfully if they are able to divide the market in various segments on the basis of the customer's capacity to pay. These days it is not possible to sell the same product at different prices in different market segements because of improved means of transportation and wider communication between the market segments. The manufacturers generally try to differentiate the product through improved packing and after-sale service. Thus, they charge different prices for the same product by slightly differentiating the features of the product. Price discrimination is successful if the elasticity of demand in one segment of the market is lower than in another.

10. Follow the Leader Pricing

This pricing policy is generally used under oligopolistic competiton where there are a small number of sellers and any one of them operates on such a scale that an increase or dicrease in his turnover will appreciably affect the market price. The commodity produced by the sellers may be standardised or differentiated; the size of each seller's output in relation to the total supply is the major test of oligopolistic pricing. Each seller considers the probable effect of variation in his output upon the price and adjusts his production accordingly. He also considers the probable reaction of his competitors to variations in his pricing. Small firms cannot influence the market significantly. They charge the prices which are charged by the major producers. In such a situation, undercutting of prices is dangerous because of changed reaction by the other producers. Over charging is not possible in such a situation because it is very difficult to sell the product at a price higher than one charged by other producers. Thus every firm tries to avoid price competition in its own self-interest and in the interest of the industry. However, it is free to capture a large share of the market through sales promotion, advertising and other promotional activities.

11. Compeititive Pricing

The management of a firm may decide to fix the price at the competitive level during certain situations. This method is most likely to be used when the market is highly competitive and the product is not differentiated significantly from the competitive products. This situation resembles the perfect competition under which prices are determined by the forces of demand and supply. There is no product differentiation, buyers and sellers are well-informed about the market price and market conditions, and the seller has no control over the market price. In such a situation, every firm will follow the price which is in tune with the market conditions. The market based price method is also used when a prevailing or a 'customary price level' exists. For instance, there are many soft drinks in the market which are sold to the consumers at one rupee only. This price is prevailing for a number of year even though the general price index has increased so much. In such a case, no seller dares to disturb the customary price. Every manufacturer tries to adjust his cost to the customary price by reducing the quality or quantity of the product. If a manufacturer raises the price above the customary level, there will be a sharp drop in the revenue because of severe fall in the demand.

12. Cost Oriented Pricing

A great number of firms set their price largely or even wholly on the basis of their costs. Typically, all costs are included, including a usually arbitrary allocation of overhead made on the basis of expected operating levels:

(a) Mark up Pricing. The most common examples of cost-oriented pricing are markup pricing and cost plus pricing. They are similar in that the price is determined by adding some fixed percentage to the unit cost. Markup pricing is most commonly found in the retail trades (groceries, furniture, clothing etc.) where the retailer adds pre-determined but different markups to various goods he carries. Cost-plus pricing most often used to describe the pricing of jobs that are non-routine and difficult to "cost" in advance, such as construction. Mark ups vary considerably among different goods. Some common mark ups on the retails price in department stores are 20 per cent for tobacco goods, 28 per cent for camera, 34 percent for books. Many hypotheses have been advanced to explain the variations in mark ups within selected product groups. Lee F. Pzeston conducted a detailed study to examine how much of the mark up dispersion within common grocery-product groups could be explained by their commonly used sales of thumb:

(i) Markups should vary inversely with unit costs.

(ii) Markups should vary inversely with turnover.

(iii) Markups should be higher and prices level on reseller's (private) brands than on manufacturer's brands.

(b) Target Pricing. In target pricing the firm tries to determine the price that would give it a specified rate of return on its total costs at an estimated standard volume. This pricing methods has been closely associated with the pricing policies of the public utilities, which have a large investment and are constrained by regulatory commission in view of their monopoly position to seek a fair rate of return on their costs.

The pricing procedure used in target pricing can be illustrated in terms of the breakeven chart in the fig. Management's first task is to estimate its total costs at various levels of output.

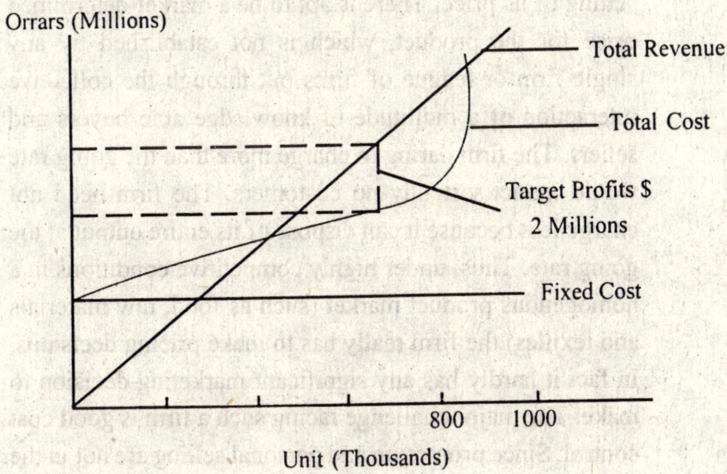

13. Competition-Oriented-Pricing

When a company sets prices chiefly on the basis of what its competitors are charging, its pricing policy can be described as competition oriented. The competition oriented-pricing firm may seek to keep its prices lower or higher than competition by a certain percentage. The distinguishing characteristics is that it does not seek to maintain a rigid relation between its price and its own costs or demand. Its own costs or demand may change, but the firm maintains its price because competitors maintain their prices. Conversely, the same firm will change its prices when competitors change theirs, even if its own costs or demand have not changed.

(a) **Going-Rate-Pricing.** Where costs are difficult to measure, it is felt that the going price represents the collective wisdom of the industry concerning the price that would yield a fair return. It is also felt that confirming to a going price would be least descriptive of industry harmony. The difficulty of knowing how buyers and competitors would react to price differentials is still another reason for this pricing.

The firm selling a homogenous product in a highly competitive market has actually very little choice about the setting of its price. There is apt to be a market-determined price for the product, which is not established by any single firm or league of firms but through the collective interaction of a multitude of knowledge able buyers and sellers. The firm daring to charge more than the going rate would attract virtually no customers. The firm need not charge less because it can dispose of its entire output at the going rate. Thus, under highly competitive conditions in a homogenous product market (such as food, raw materials and textiles) the firm really has to make pricing decisions. In fact it hardly has any significant marketing decision to make. The major challenge facing such a firm is good cost control. Since promotion and personal selling are not in the picture the major marketing costs arise in physical distribution and here is where cost efficiency may be critical.

(b) Sealed-bid Pricing. Competitive-oriented pricing also dominates in those situations where firms compare for jobs on the basis of bids, such as original equipment manufacture and defence contract work. The bid is the firm's offer price and it is a prime example of pricing based on expectations of how competitors will price rather than on a rigid relation based on the firm's own costs or demand. The objective of the firm in the bidding situation is to get the contract and this means that it hopes to set its price lower than that set by any of the other bidding firms.

On the one hand the firm cannot quote a price below marginal cost without worsening its position. On the other hand, as it raises its price above marginal cost, it increases its potential profit but reduces its chance of getting the contract.

PRICING DECISIONS

Pricing decisions are the most important decisions to be taken by business and industrial enterprises. These decisions determine the market share and competitive situation of an enterprise. These decisions also determine total revenue and net profit of the enterprise. In addition to this, advertisement and sales promotion programmes are also affected by pricing decision. Therefore, a decision of determining price for a product must be taken only after considering all the relevant features.

Pricing decision means a decision of determining price of a product. Such price must be determined after considering many factors altogether, such as—cost of production, cost of transportion, cost of distribution, cost of advertisement and sales promotion, demand of the product, situation of supply of the product, situation of competition in the market, purchasing power of consumers and the the object of enterprise etc. The term pricing decision has been defined as under:

Converse, Huegy and Mitchell, "Decision concerning price to be followed for a period of time may be called Price Decision."

Thus, pricing decisions are related with a certain period of time because necessary changes must be made in these decisions according to the need of time and circumstances. The price of a product must be determined in the manner that it may offer a reasonable amount of profit to the manufacturer, a reasonable amount of remuneration to the middlemen and maximum satisfaction to the consumers.

OBJECTIVES OF PRICING DECISIONS

Objectives of pricing decisions may be described as under:

(1) Proper Return on Investment. Main object of every business and industrial enterprise is to earn a proper return on its capital. Therefore, an important object to be considered while determining the price of a product is that it may yield proper return on the investment of enterprise.

(2) **Maximum Profit through Maximum Sales.** A main object of every enterprise is to earn maximum possible profits by making maximum possible sales. Therefore, the price of a product must be determined in the manner that it may increase the demand of the products so that maximum sales may be made and maximum profits may be earned.

(3) **Price Stability.** Though the price of a product is never stable. It has to be changed keeping in view the changing marketing conditions. Still the price of a product should be determined in the manner that minimum fluctuations should take place in it. Stable prices win the faith of consumers and get good share in the market.

(4) **Certain Margin of Profit.** Though the prices of products have to be changed because of many reasons, margin of profit of the enterprise on one hand and wins the favour of middlemen on the other.

(5) **Competition.** Competition is perhaps that most important object to be considered while determining the price of a product. Every enterprise wants to determine a price which may get success in the market and which may compete similar products of competitors.

(6) **According to Paying Capacity of Consumers.** Every product is sold to the consumers. Every consumer has a certain purchasing power. If the purchasing power of consumers is not considered at the time of determining price of a product, it would mean an invitation to the failure of the product and the enterprise itself. Therefore, the price of a product must be determined keeping in view the paying capacity of the consumers for whom the product is made.

(7) **Long-term Success of the Enterprise.** Every business and industrial enterprise has to maintain its standing in the market for a long period. Pricing decisions of the enterprise play an important role in determining such standing of the enterprise. The price of the products of an enterprise must

be determined in the manner that they may contribute in capturing more and more share in the market. If, for any reason, it is not possible for the enterprise to increase its share in the market, the prices should contribute in maintaining present share.

(8) **Uneconomic Objectives.** Pricing decisions of an enterprise have some uneconomic objectives also, such as—*(i)* Social welfare; *(ii)* To bring industrial stability; *(iii)* To contribute in the industrial development; *(iv)* To increase, Gross National Product (GNP) and Net National Product (NNP); *(v)* To achieve the object of expansion of the enterprise.

CONTENTS OF PRICE DECISION

Main contents of a Price Decision are as under:

(1) **Determination of Objectives of Price Policy.** A marketing manager must determine the objectives of price policy of his enterprise. These objectives must be very clear and well defined because all the further decisions are taken in the light of these objectives.

(2) **Determination of Factors Affecting Price Decision.** There are many factors which affect price decision of an enterprise. These factors may differ from enterprise to enterprise and from time to time. Some of the important factors affecting price decision of an enterprise are—*(i)* Cost of raw-materials; *(ii)* Cost of production; *(iii)* Administration overheads; *(iv)* Cost of marketing; *(v)* Profit margin; *(vi)* Competitive situation; *(vii)* Paying capacity of consumers; and *(viii)* Government policy etc.

(3) **Determination of Pricing Policy and Formulae.** After the determination of objectives of pricing policy and the factors affecting price decision, pricing policy and formulae are determined according to the needs and circumstances of the enterprise.

(4) **Development of Long-term Consolidated Pricing Policy.** After determining a certain pricing policy and formulae for

the enterpise, consolidated pricing policy for long-term must be developed for the enterprise from time to time in the light of this consolidated long-term pricing policy.

FACTORS AFFECTING THE PRICING DECISION

Pricing Decisions of an enterprise are affected by many factors. Some of the important factors affecting pricing decisions of an enterprise are as follows:

(1) **Objectives of the Enterprise.** Objectives of the enterprise affect pricing decisions of the enterprise to a significant extent. There may be many objects of the business and industrial enterpise. Some important objects of a business and industrial enterprise may be—*(i)* To earn proper return on investment; *(ii)* To earn maximum profits through maximum sales; *(iii)* To bring price stability; *(iv)* To bring stability in the margin of profit; *(v)* To face the competition; *(vi)* To increase market share or to maintain it; *(vii)* To determine the prices of products according to the paying capacity of consumers; *(viii)* Long-term welfare of the enterprise.

(2) **Cost Factors.** Cost factors are the most important factors affecting pricing decision. Cost factors include the following—*(i)* Cost of raw-materials; *(ii)* Manufacturing cost; *(iii)* Administrative overheads; *(iv)* Cost of transportation; *(v)* Cost of storage; *(vi)* Cost of advertisement; *(vii)* Cost of distribution; and *(viii)* Cost of selling etc.

(3) **Characteristics of the Product.** Characteristics of a product also determine the pricing decision of an enterprise. Important characteristics of the product affecting a pricing decision are—*(i)* Nature of product; *(ii)* Stage of product in its life-cycle; *(iii)* Availability of substitutes to the product; *(iv)* Possibilities of the postponement of demand of product; and *(v)* Product diversification etc.

(4) **Price Elasticity of Demand.** Price elasticity of the demand of a product affects pricing decision of its enterprise. If the demand of product is inelastic, higher price may be fixed for such product. If, on the other hand, the demand of a product is highly elastic.

(5) **Channels of Distribution of the Product.** If a product passes through many channels of distribution from producer to consumers, the price of such product will be higher, because every channel of distribution has to be paid some remuneration. If, on the other hand, the number of channels of distribution for a product is limited, the price of such product can be low because less remuneration will have to be paid to its channels of distribution.

(6) **Characteristics of the Consumers.** Characteristics of consumers for whom the product is generally kept low. The price of a product purchased by the consumers of high income grade extent. the price of industrial products is generally kept low. The price of a product purchased by the consumers of high income grade may be fixed higher.

(7) **Pricing Policies of Competitors.** Pricing policies of competitiors of a product also play an important role in the determination of price of the product. If the price determined by the competitors for their product is low, the enterprise will also have to determine its price low.

(8) **Trade Conditions and Customs.** Prevailing conditions and customs in marketing a particular product also affect pricing decisions of an enterprise. For example, guarantee of free service for a certain period has been a common practice for consumer products of technical nature, such as—Fans, T.V., Refrigerator, Camera, Watch, and Type-recorder etc. Therefore, the price of such products must be determined keeping in view the estimated cost of repair of these products for such period.

(9) **Economic Environment.** Economic environment of the country also affects pricing decisions of an enterporise. If,

there is economic slump, the prices of products must be kept low in other to maintain their demand.

(10) Other Factors. Some other factors also affect pricing decisions of an enterprise. These factors may be— *(i)* Government policy; *(ii)* Dominance of labour unions; and *(iii)* Reactions of consumers etc.

PRICING AND PRODUCT LIFE CYCLE

At the introductory stage of a new product, relatively high price per unit is fixed with correspondingly high per-unit margins. This is being a product is generally meant for those customers who have a strong need and ability to pay a relatively high price.

At the growth stage, prices are fixed fairly high the these begin to decline as the market reaches maturity stage, and becomes highly competitive.

In the decline stage, the remaining buyers are usually highly conscious and therefore price-cutting is generally resorted to.

Cost enters into pricing decisions by its influence on the supply side of the demand supply relationship. Over the long run, selling price must cover costs or the firm will drop the product. Therefore in the long run costs govern supply. In the short run, under unusual circumstances, the supply of a product may continue even though price is insufficient even to cover the cost of manufacture. But as a rule "... cost at any given time represents a resistance point to the lowering of price. In time, if reductions in cost do not keep price with reductions in selling price, the supply of the given commodity will be reduced. In the long run, those who wish to be supplied with the commodity must pay a price that will cover cost, including a reasonable margin of profit, if the supply to be kept healthy."

The prices may be set or fixed in one of the three ways:

(a) Prices may be set by competitive market conditions.

(b) Prices may be based on a balance between market demand and cost of production and marketing *i.e.*, marginal cost pricing.

(c) Prices may be based on total costs plus a desired profit.

In order to understand pricing based upon costs, it is necessary to understand the cost concept, which includes terms like fixed cost, variable costs, incremental costs, average unit cost, etc.

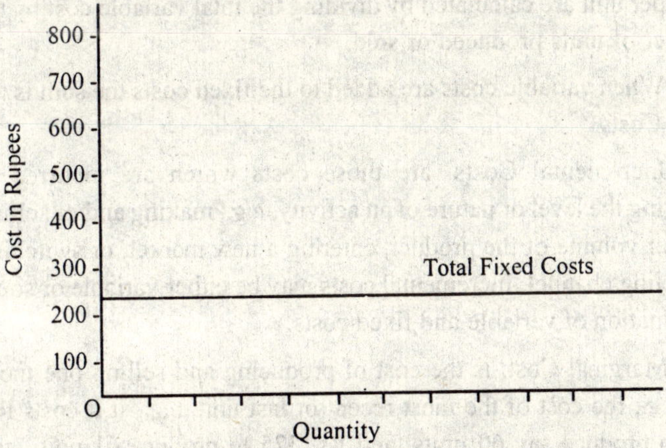

FIXED COST

Fixed Costs often called "overhead costs", are cost which remain constant, *i.e.*, do not vary with the number of units produced. It includes salaries, rent, light, derpeciation, local property taxes, interest, etc. These costs continue even if production ceases completely.

Variable Costs, on the other hand, are cost which vary automatically with the output produced or sold, and includes such

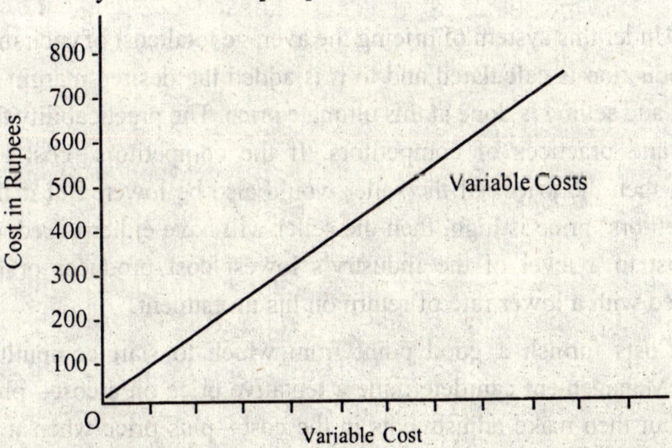

cost at those of raw materials, labour paid, sales man's commissions, cost of packaging, packing, warehousing and shipping. Variable costs per unit are calculated by dividing the total variable cost by the number of units produced or sold.

When variable costs are added to the fixed costs the sum is the Total Costs.

Incremental Costs, are those costs which are incurred in changing the level or nature of an activity, *e.g.*, making and/or selling a larger volume of the product, entering a new market, or switching marketing channel. Incremental costs may be either variable or some combination of variable and fixed costs.

Marginal Cost, is the cost of producing and selling one more unit, *i.e.*, the cost of the most recent or last unit, *e.g.*, if it costs Rs. 300 to produce say 60 units, and Rs. 325 to produce 61 units, the marginal cost is Rs. 325—Rs. 300 = Rs. 25.

The classification of costs as either fixed or variable depends on the time period involved; advertising and selling costs, *e.g.*, may be fixed if a period upto one year is being considered; but varible if longer period is being cosidered. Thus fixed costs are independent of volume in the period concerned, whereas variable cost we directly related to volume in that period.

Cost Plus A Desired Profit

Under this system of pricing the average total cost of each unit of production is calculated and to it is added the desired margin of profit, and selling is done at this ultimate price. The practicability the costs and practices of competitors. If the competitors' cost are lower, then the prices of the seller would also be lower. But it the competitors' price is high, then the seller will have either to reduce his cost to a level of the industry's lowest cost producer or be satisfied with a lower rate of return on his investment.

Costs furnish a good point from which to start computing price. Management can determine a tentative price on a cost—plus basis but then make adjustments in the cost—plus price when it is able to measure demand factors. When used by itself, cost—plus is a weak and unrealistic method of pricing because it completely ignores the influences of competition and market demand.

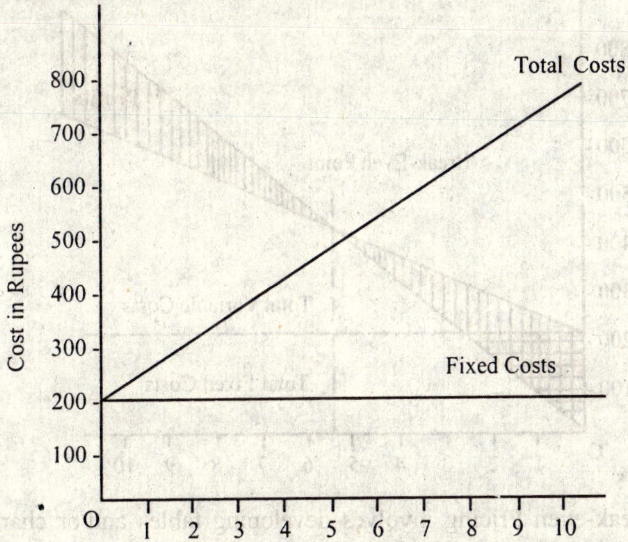

Cost-plus pricing is mostly used by retailing and wholesaling middle-men. Suppose a retailer gives Rs. 100 for a particular product with the instructions that it should be delivered at his shop. He then adds to the acquisition cost an amount (mark up) which he estimates is necessary to cover his expenses and leave him a reasonable profit. He may add the same percentage mark-up to all his product. This is an average mark-up which is large enough to cover the costs and profit for his entire business.

Marginal or Incremental Cost Pricing

Under this method, price is so set that it covers only the marginal costs, and not the total costs. When new product is introduced, such method is usually adopted. By this method, labour may be kept employed even during slack seasons. However, this method cannot be followed for long as the fixed costs have also to be taken into consideration. If certain products are priced on this basis, and others on cost plus basis, then some customers would be required to pay higher prices while others would get the product at the cost of the last unit. This discrimination may drive some customers towards competitors.

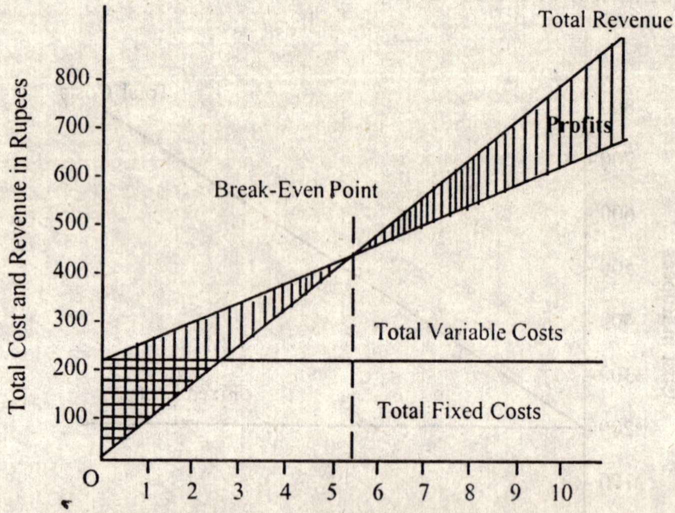

Break-even Pricing involves developing tables and/or charts which will help a company determine at what level of output the revenues will equal the cost, assuming a certain selling price. Sales at levels above the break-even point will result in a profit on each unit, and further above the break-even point, a firm goes, the higher will be the total and units profit. Output below the break even point will result in a loss to the seller. The point where the total revenue line and the total costs line interest is known as to the break-even point. At this point neither profit nor loss is earned or loss sustained.

Pricing Relative to Competition

Every company adheres to some policy regarding the prices of its products relative to those of competitors. If price is the main basis of competition, each company will price its products the same as competitors. If there is non-price competition, pricing will still be done taking into consideration the competitor's prices:

(i) **Pricing Above Competition.** The seller may set higher than average prices for his product to convey an impression that his products are above average quality. The buyer may pay this price on the belief that it is of higher quality. Manufacturers sometimes keep more than average price to give some margin of profit to the middlemen in return for the latter's making aggressive sale promotion. "For a consumer product to compete successfully at a price above the market, it must either be so strongly differentiated that consumers believe it is superior to competitive brands, or middleman most enthusiastically and heavily promote it.

(ii) Pricing Under Competition. Many firms may price their product under the market. Sometimes a firm has low costs because its product is of lower quality, and, therefore, price of products is usually kept low than those of the competitors. At other times, lower price may be substituted for promotional efforts used by its competitors. In both these cases, firms following this policy must either have very low costs, or be willing to accept a very low profit per unit in the hope of radically increasing sales volume.

In using cost for any business decision, the guiding principle should be "different costs for different purposes", *i.e.*, use those concepts that are appropriate for the purpose at hand. No single cost concept is applicable in all business decisions or even in all pricing decisions, one must tailor the cost concept to the purpose for which it is intended.

PROBLEMS IN SETTING PRICE OBJECTIVES

The following are the problems in the way of setting price objectives:

1. The Problem of Multiple Parties. The theoretical pricing model assumes that the only significance group to consider the pricing of a product is the firm's customers. But in reality, several parties have to be considered simultaneously:

(a) Suppliers. The company's suppliers of materials funds and labour also must be considered. Many suppliers interpret that product's price as indicating the level of the firm's revenues (and profits), from the product. Labour unions will act as if a high price, or price increase, constitutes grounds for higher wages. Thus the firm may have to consider various supplier group in setting a price.

(b) **Intermediate Customers.** The firm must think through its pricing not only for its ultimate customers but for its intermediate customers as well. Some companies in fact set a price for distributors and allow them to set whatever final price they wish. This is done where it is thought that each distributor is in the best position to determine the price suited to local conditions and to set it high enough to provide sufficient selling incentive. The disadvantage is that manufacturers relinquishes control over the final price.

(c) **Rivals.** The price set by the manufacturer influence the rate of entry of new rivals and the pricing policies of existing rivals. The traditional demand curve is too summary a way to represent the dynamic reactions and counter reactions occasioned by a pricing policy.

(d) **Other Company Executives.** Price is a concern of different parties with the company. The sales manager wants a low price so that less salesmen can "talk price" to customer. Controller likes to see a price leading to an early payment. The price makes an important difference in copy and media tactics to the advertising manager. The production scheduling manager is interested because the price will affect the rate of sales. There and other executives in the organisation can be expected to have strong views on where to set the price.

(e) **Government.** Another price-interested party is the government. Public utilities must justify their rates before regulatory commissions. The steel industry must move cautiously with price increases because of the government's interest in price stability. At various times, pricing in the meat, drug and heavy equipment industries has been subjected to govt. pressure. And various state and local governmental units pass legislation and rulings affecting the prices that can be set by sellers.

2. The Problem of Estimating Demand and Cost Function. In the case of a new product, there is no experience upon which to base these estimates. Unless data are available on a similar, established product, estimate are likely to take the form of soft facts and guesses rather than hard facts. Data on established products are usually not much more satisfactory.

Since the demand and cost equation are estimated with an unknown degree of error, the criterion of maximizing process may have to be replaced with the criterion of maximizing expected profits or the criterion of maximizing the minimum possible gain. If any situation of risk and uncertainty, the pricing executive will want to see how sensitive the theoretically calculated price is to revisions in the estimated data.

3. The Problem of Marketing Mix Interaction. The theoretical pricing model also assumes that other marketing variables are held at some constant levels while the effect of price on sales is being examined. This is evident in the usual treatment of the demand function as a relationship only between quantity demanded (Q) and Price (P). But he begs the whole question of how optimal value can be set on advertising, personal selling, product quality and other marketing variables before price is set.

DISCOUNTS AND REBATES DURING PRICING DECISIONS

Discount and rebates are special concessions in price which many firms offer to their middlemen and also to the users. Discount and allowances are granted to a customer for the acitivity of value which he performs. These are granted to encourage the buyers mainly during the stipulated period and purely at the discretion of the sellers. The most common discounts allowed are Quantity discount, Trade discount, cash discount, seasonal discount and Price level discount.

Quantity Discant

Quantity Discounts are debentures offered from list prices by a seller in order to encourage a customer to buy in larger amounts or to concentrate his purchases with this seller. Such discount may be non-cumulative discount or cumulative discount. The former is offered on an indiviudal order of one or more products. Wilson pen may be sold at Rs. 1.50 each or 3 for Rs. 4.00. The latter is based on total volume purchased over a period of time. These are patronage discounts because the more business a buyer gives to a seller, the greater is the discount. Either type of these discounts can be used for selling related or unrelated products which are purchased by a single buyer. The slow moving item may be sold with more popular item, if some attractive discount is offered. Such discounts also bring the advantages of large-scale economies to the seller.

Cash Discount

It is a deduction from price granted to the buyer by wholesalers or manufacturers as a means to observe punctuality in payments whether the payment may be of a bill which is not yet due or it may be a cash payment. The discount is calculated on the net amount due after first deducting trade and quantity discounts from initial price. Functions of cash discounts as described by Prendergast are.

"For the seller, the cash discount affords a ready means of judging the credit standing of his customers and also for eliminating the credit risk on a considerable part of his accounts. It also enables him to concentrate his attention on the poorer credit risks which do not take the discount and, hence, tends to ensure the efficiency of his credit work at the same time curtailing the total amount of such credit work and reducing the cost of the credit department. In consequence, it should tend to decrease the total amount of loss due to bad debts. More rapid turnover of capital and more accurate planning of financial needs is also accomplished."

"From the point of the banking and credit system, the use of the cash discount results in having the buyer as far as possible obtain his funds directly from the bank instead of having recourse directly to the seller through buying on time and taking the net terms. The bank then measures the credit of the buyer directly and not the seller. The latter only measures the credit of the poorer accounts, which do not take the discount and him-self borrows from the bank in turn in order to obtain funds with which to carry these accounts. He thus in fact guarantees such accounts to the banking system. He then has either a contingent liability on the receivables he has discounted or a direct liability for his own borrowings, whereas with a buyer who takes the cash discount he assumes no responsibility whatsoever."

The privilege of cash discount is sometimes abused. Firstly, taking unearned discounts or in other words of taking the discount after the expiration of the discount period. Secondly, the abuse of cash discount arises when buyers who know themselves to be excellent customers and who buy comparatively large quantities insist upon special discounts for cash. "This state of affairs is due partly to the method employed by some stores of penalizing departments whose buyer fails to secure a specified minimum discount. If the buyer fails to receive the required discounts, his department is charged with the difference between the discount obtained and the discount required. Similarly the department is credited with the discounts which are secured in excess of the required figures. This practice is known as 'loading' and is regarded by enterprises which use it as a means of making sure that all buyers secure the largest possible discount. Another argument in its favour is that it enables executives to judge the abilities of various buyers on a uniform basis. Because of this practice hard and unusual terms are demanded of sellers, with the result that the cash discount systems greatly harmed and sentiments are thereby credited for its abolition.

Trade Discount

It is allowed by manufacturers or producers to wholesalers and retailers are in the nature of deductions from the list or quotations appearing in the catalogue of the firm. Rate of discount to be allowed is not fixed. For example, a manufacturer may quote a retail price of Rs. 300 with trade discount of 30% and 10%. The retailer pays Rs. 210 (Rs. 300 less 30%), and the wholesaler pays the manufacturer Rs. 189 (210 less 10%). He is expected to keep 10% to cover the cost of wholesaling functions and pass on 40% to the retailers. Sometimes very high discounts are offered whereas well-established firms allow lower discounts. It is not always easy to distinguish between trade discounts and quantity discounts. The latter is allowed because of large single purchases or because of large purchases over a period of time. However, a single customer may receive both kinds of discounts and as Clark says, "It is impossible to determine where one ends and the other begins" Trade discounts are useful in suggesting to the retailer the prices at which the manufacturers or wholesalers think that merchandise should be resold to the consumer, such discounts are some-times used to deceive the buyer. This happens when the retailer agrees to order something for the customer which is temporarily out of stock but which is listed in the catalogue. The dealer puts forward the catalogue and the price list to the purchaser and agrees to allow a certain percentage if an order is placed, and if the customer agrees to take and pay cash for the product whenever available.

Seasonal Discount

It is the deduction allowed in case of products which have only seasonal demand. Manufacturers of electric fans, coolers or refrigerators, may allow a discount of say. 5, 10, or 20% if an order is placed during the slack season. This type of order placing enables the manufacturer to level out his production schedule and make better use of his facilities.

Promotional Allowances are deductions allowed to buyers for undertaking promotional services. Promotional aids and materials for display may also be supplied to the buyer free of charge.

❐

8

Marketing Communication Decisions

MARKETING COMMUNICATION MIX

One can take a broad or a narrow view of the tools in the marketing communications mix. The broad view says that each of the four Ps belongs in the marketing communications mix. The product's styling, the colour and shape of the packaging, and the price all communicate something. Once the company decides on a target market position, all the marketing-mix tools should reinforce this position.

The narrow view says the marketing communications mix consists of the subset of marketing tools that are primarily "communicational" in nature. They are the tools normally classified under promotion, one of the four Ps. They are called promotools, and include various forms of advertising, packaging, sales presentations and demonstrations, point-of-purchase displays, sales aids (catalogues, literature, firms), incentive tools (contests, trading stamps, premiums, free samples, coupons), and publicity programs.

Each of these promotools has specific potentialities and complexities that could justify managerial specialisation. Yet a company, even a very large one, typically does not have a specialist in each area but only in those areas where the importance and usage frequency of the tool warrant specialisation. Historically, companies first made a separate function out or personal selling, later out of advertising, still later out of sales promotion, and ultimately out of publicity. These four major tools are defined as follows:

(i) ***Advertising.*** Any paid form of non-operational presentation and promotion of ideas, goods, or services by an identified sponsor.

(ii) ***Personal Selling.*** Oral presentation in a conversation with one or more prospective purchasers for the purpose of making sales.

(iii) ***Sales Promotion.*** Short-term incentives to encourage purchase of sale of a product or service.

(iv) ***Publicity.*** Non operational stimulation of demand for a product, service, or business unit by planting commercially significant news about it in a published medium or obtaining favourable presentation of it upon radio, television, or stage that is not paid for by the sponsor. Here we will discuss the special qualities of each promotional component.

(i) Advertising. Advertising comes in many forms and has many uses. It involves such varied media as magazines and newspapers, radio and television, outdoor displays (such as posters, signs, skywriting),' direct mail, novelties (matchboxes, blotters, calendars), cards (car, bus), catalogs, directories, and circularise. It can be carries out for such diverse purposes, as long-term buildup of a particular brand (brand advertising), information dissemination about a sale, service, or event (classified advertising), announcement of a special sale (sales advertising), and so on.

Because of the many forms and uses of advertising, it is hard to advance all-embracing generalisations about its distinctive qualities as a component of the marketing communications mix. Yet the following qualities can be noted:

(a) ***Public Presentation.*** Advertising, unlike personal selling, is a highly public mode of communication. Its public nature confers a kind of legitimacy to the product and also suggests a standardised offering. Because many persons receive the same message, buyers know that their motives for purchasing the product will be plurality understood.

(b) ***Pervasiveness.*** Advertising is a pervasive medium that permits the seller to repeat a message many times. It also allows the buyer to receive and compare the messages of various competitors. Large-scale advertising by a seller says something positive about the seller's size, popularity, and success.

(c) ***Amplified Expressiveness.*** Advertising provides opportunities for dramatising the company and its products through the artful use of print, sound, and colour. Sometimes the tool's very success at expressiveness may, however, dilute or distract from the message.

(d) ***Impersonality.*** Advertising, in spite of being public, pervasive, and expressive, cannot be as compelling as a company sales representative. The audience does not feel obligated to pay attention or respond. Advertising is only able to carry on a monologue not a dialogue, with the audience.

(ii) Personal Selling. Personal selling also takes several forms, such as sales calls by a field representative (field selling), assistance by a sales clerk retail selling), and a golf invitation from one company president to another (executive selling). It can be used for many purposes, such as creating product awareness, arousing interest, developing product preference, negotiating prices and other terms, closing a sale, and providing post transactional reinforcement. Personal selling has certain distinctive qualities:

(a) ***Personal Confrontation.*** Personal selling involves an alive, immediate, and interactive relationship between two or more persons. Each party is able to observe at close hand the characteristics and needs of the other and make immediate adjustments. Each party has the potentiality to help or hard the other by showing interest or lack of it, and this can make the encounter stressful.

(b) ***Cultivation.*** Personal selling permits all kinds of relationships to spring up, ranging from a matter-of-fact selling

relationship to a deep personal friendship. In most cases, the sales representation must use art to woo the buyer. The sales representative at time will be tempted to put on pressure or to dissemble to get an order, but normally will keep the customer's long-run interests at heart.

(c) ***Response.*** Personal selling, in contrast with advertising, makes the buyer follower some obligation for having listed to the sales talk or using up the sales representative's time. The buyer has a greater need to attend and respond, even if the response is a polite "thank you".

(iii) Sales Promotion. Sales-promotion is the catcall for various promotools that are not formally classifiable as advertising, personal selling, or publicity. These tools may be sub-classified into items for consumer promotion (*e.g.*, samples, coupons, money-refund offers, prices-off, premiums, contests trading stamps, demonstrations), trade orienting (*e.g.*, buying advances, free goods, merchandise allowances, cooperative advertising, push money, dealer sales contests), and sales-force promotion (*e.g.*, bonuses, contests, sales realise).

Although sales promotion tools are a motely collection, they have two distinctive qualities:

(a) ***Product Demeaning.*** Some of these tools suggest that the seller is anxious for the sales. If they are used too frequently or carelessly, they may lead buyers to wonder whether the brand is desirable or reasonably priced.

(b) ***Insistent Presence.*** Many sales promotion tools have an attention-getting, sometimes urgent, quality that can break through habits of buyer interact toward a particular product. They tell the buyers of a chance that they won't have again to get something special. This appeals to a broad spectrum of buyers, although particularly to the economy minded, with the disadvantage that this type of buyer tends to be less loyal to any particular brand in the tong run.

(iv) Publicity. A company and its products can come to the attention of the public through being newsworthy. The seller pays nothing for the news coverage. The, results of free publicity can sometimes be spectacular. Consider the case of the diet drink Metrical:

(a) ***Off Guard.*** Publicity can reach many potential buyers who otherwise avoid salesmen and advertisements. This is because the message is packaged in a way that gets to the buyers as news rather than as a sales—directed communication.

(b) ***Dramatisation.*** Publicity has, like advertising, a potential for dramatising a company or product.

(c) High Credibility. News stories and features seem to most readers to be authentic, media-originated reports. They have a higher degree of creditability than if they came across as sponsored by a seller.

A MODEL OF THE COMMUNICATIONS PROCESS

We are now ready to examine how the process of communications works, Years ago; Lasswell suggested that communications involve five major questions: who... says what... in what channel to whom with what effect. These can be rephrased into saying that communication consist of a sender transmitting a message through media to a receiver who responds. Communications specialists spend their time doing source analysis, message analysis, media analysis, audience analysis, and response analysis.

The model consists of eight major communications elements. Two of them (in rectangles) represent the major partics in a communication-sender and receiver, Two others (in diamonds) represent the major communications tools-message and media. The remaining four (in ovals) represent major communication functions—encoding, decoding, response, and feedback. Each of these is defined below.

(i) ***Sender.*** The party sending the message to another party (also called the source or communicator).

(ii) ***Encoding.*** The process off-putting thought into symbolic form.

(iii) ***Message.*** The set of symbols that the sender transmits.

(iv) ***Media.*** The paths through which the message moves from sender to receiver.

(v) ***Decoding.*** The process by which the receiver assigns meaning to the symbols transmitted by the sender.

(vi) ***Receiver.*** The party receiving the message sent by another party (also called the audience or destination).

(vii) ***Response.*** The set reactions that the receiver has after being exposed to the message.

(viii) ***Feedback.*** The part of the receiver's response that the receiver communicates back to the sender.

The model indicates the factors in effective communications. Enders must know what audiences they want to reach and what responses they want. They must be skilful in encoding messages that take into account how the target audience tends to decode messages. They must transmit the message over efficient media that reach the target audience. They must develop feedback channels so that they can monitor whether the audience got the intended message.

This might suggest that skilful communicators can exercise great powers of persuasion over their audiences, a view propounded in The Hidden Persuaders and other books criticising marketing communicators. However, the same model shows this is not the case. The audience is far from manipulable. The model shows an active rather than passive audience. The audience, because of decoding, does not necessarily receive all of the message or receive it in the intended way. Furthermore, the audience can show a wide variety of responses after decoding or interpreting the message. Finally, the audience may initiate or control the feedback to the sender, thus also playing the role of communicator. The audience, far from being passive, is an active party in the marketing dialogue.

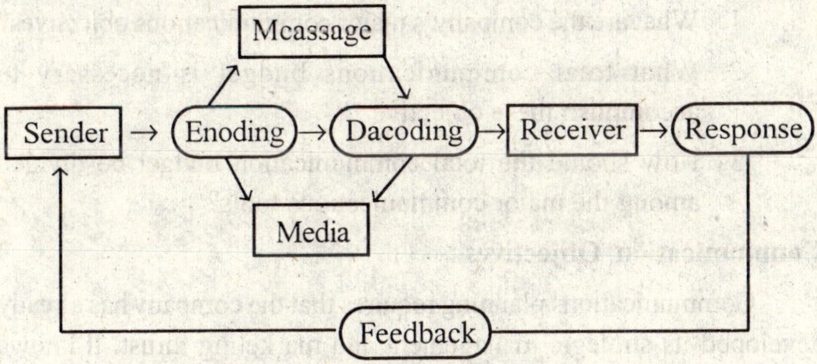

Fig. The Communication Model

The model permits the drawing together of many interesting findings about the communications process that have a bearing on effective marketing communications planning. We will discuss the elements not in the order of the message flow (from communicator to audience) but mainly in terms of the planning flow (from target audience backward to the communicator). The marketing communicator must make decisions on the following elements:

1. Who is the target audience? (Receiver)
2. What response should be sought? (Response and decoding)
3. What message should be developed? (Message and encoding)
4. What media should be used? (Media)
5. What source attributes should accompany the message? (Sender)
6. What feedback should be collected? (Feedback)

THE MARKETING COMMUNICATIONS PLANNING PROCESS

Having examined how the process of communications works and the various factors that influence communications defectiveness, we can appreciate the challenging task facing management. Management must make three major decisions in the communications arena:

1. What are the company's major communications objectives?
2. What total communications budget is necessary to accomplish these objective..?
3. How should the total communication budget be divided among the major communications tools?

Communication Objectives

Communications planning requires that the company has already developed its strategic management and marketing thrust. It knows the business that it is in, the product/markets and market segments that is wants to reach, the product positions that it is aiming for, the resources and strengths that it has, and the basic marketing mix that it will use. It has analysed the target markets with respect to awareness, knowledge, attitude, and buying behaviour towards the company's and the competitors' products.

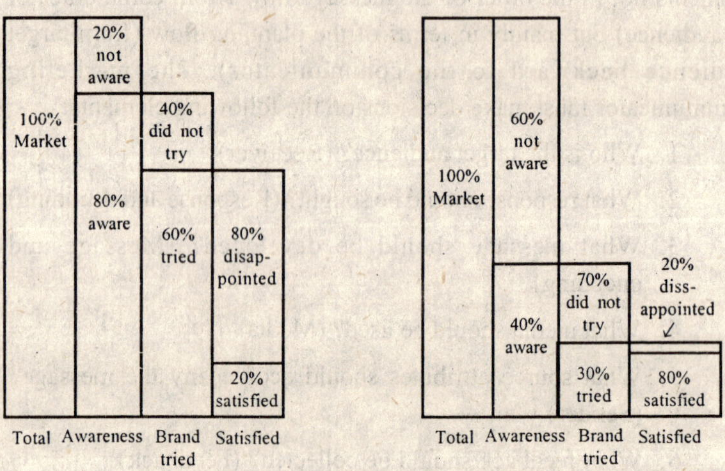

Fig. Current Consumer States for Two Brands

Communications objectives can be derived from analysing how the target market is currently distributed over various states of readiness to buy the product. Consider a company that is preparing to set marketing communication objectives for two of its brands, A and B. Far each brand the company has conducted marketing research to ascertain how many persons are in the market and the percentage distribution of these persons in three classes: awareness, brand trial, and satisfaction. The results are shown in above figure. As for brand A, 80 percent of the total market is aware of the brand, 60 percent have tried it and 20 percent of those who tried it are satisfied. On the other hand, only 40 percent of the total market are aware of brand B, only 30 percent have tried it, and 80 percent of those who have tried it are satisfied. Clearly, these two profiles have very different implications far advertising objectives and strategy. The market is highly aware of brand A, but a substantial partial of those who have tried it are disappointed. This indicates that the advertising exposure schedule and creative message are effective in creating awareness but the product fails to live up to the claims. Brand B has the apposite problem. The advertising has produced only 40 percent awareness, and only 12 percent of the market have tried the product. But of those who have tried brand B, satisfaction round in the order of 80 percent. In this case the entire advertising program, including the media, the message, and the level of expenditure may be much too weak to take advantages of the satisfaction-generating power of the brand.

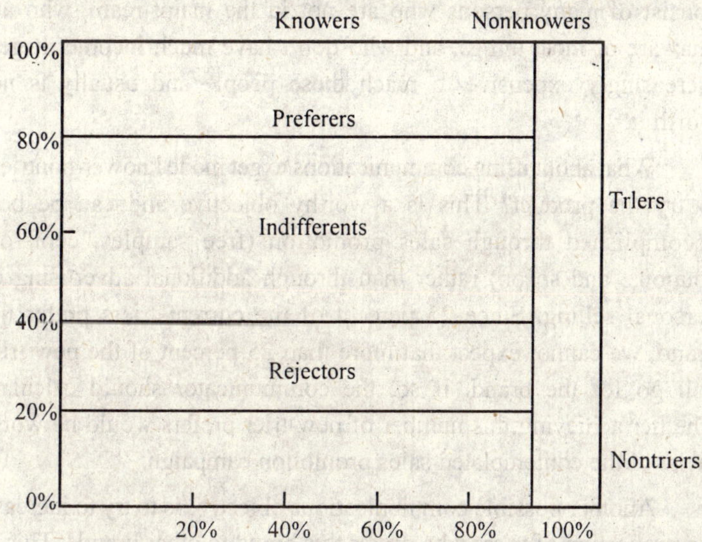

Fig. A Market Map Showing Percentage of Brand Knowers and Triers

Ottesen has suggested an alternative device called a market map for determining communication objectives (see following figure). The horizontal dimension shows the current percentage of the market that has knowledge of the brand. This percentage increases through the life cycle of the rand, and is the illustration stands at 90 percent, indicating a mature brand. The vertical dimension shows the percentage of the market that has tried the brand. In this case, 80 percent of those who know the brand have tried it, another indication that the brand has been around for a while. There is a further breakdown of the knowers-triers into those who prefer (25 percent); are indifferent (50 percent), and have rejected (25 percent) the breakdown can imagine (not shown) a similar breakdown of knower-nontriers into those who have a positive, indifferent, and negative attitude toward the brand.

The task is to set communications objectives for this brand. Since 90 percent of the target market already know the brand, it would not make sense to devote a Large effort to building awareness in the remaining 10 percent. Ninety percent is a fairly high awareness level in the population. The 10 percent who do not know this brand consist of many persons who are not in the mainstream, who are unaware of most things, and who don't have much income. It gets increasingly expensive to reach these people and usually is not worth it.

What about using communications to get mode knower-nontriers to try the product? This is a worthy objective and can be best accomplished through sales promotion (free samples, cents-off coupons, and so on) rather than through additional advertising or personal selling. Since 25 percent of the current triers prefer the brand, we cannot expect that more than 25 percent of the new trier will go for the brand. If so, the communicator should calculate whether achieving this number of new-trier prefers would be worth theist of the contemplated sales promotion campaign.

Another possible communications objective is to try to increase the proportion of triers who prefer this brand to other brands. This is a difficult task since consumer attitude is largely a function of how the consumer experiences the value of the offer—*e.g.*, performance and price rather than the communications appeal. If the company wants to increase preference, that is better accomplished through product improvement and lower prices.

Looking at the three trier attitude groups, the following conclusions can be drawn. Communication to those who already prefer the brand is usually not very productive unless there is high consumer forgetfulness or a higher level of competitors' expenditure aimed at preferers. Communication directed to the rejectors is probably wasted because the rejectors are not likely to pay attention to the advertising and probably would not retry the brand. Communication directed to the indifferents will probably be effective in attracting a proportion of their purchases, especially if the advertising has some point to make to this audience.

The main conclusion is that the communications objectives depend very much on the state of the market. When it brand is new, there are few knowers and triers, and communication can be very effective in increasing their number. When the broad is in the mature stage of its life cycle, it makes sense to try to convert nontrieers into triers through sales promotion and to fight for a normal share of the indifferent triers; it makes less sense to try to increase the percentage of knowrs, or reinforce preferers, or try to get rejectors to retry the brand.

Total Communications Budget

The communications budget should be set at the level necessary to accomplish the communications objectives. The budget can be established by using "objectives-and-tasks" thinking; that is, deciding on the tasks that have to be performed to accomplish the communication objectives and then estimating their costs. Here is an example:

1. We want to convince 100,000 people to try our brand.
2. This means getting our message into the attention set of 1,000,000 people since only 1 in 10 will try the product after hearing about it.

3. We will need 8,000,000 exposure because only 1 in 8 exposures gains attention.
4. The average cost-per-thousand exposures to the type of audiènce we want is \$6. Therefore we can buy 8,000,000 exposures for a total budget of around \$48,000 (= \$6 8,000,000/1,000).

In this way, managed is able to estimate a total budget to accomplish a specific communication task.

Communications Mix

Most companies set their total communications budget first and them divide it among the alternative communications tools. The most striking fact about the various communications tools is that they can be interchanged with each other and with other marketing mix elements. It is possible to achieve a given sales level by increasing advertising expenditures, personal selling, or sales promotion. It is also possible to achieve the same sales level by product improvement, lower prices, or additional customer revises. This substitutability explains why marketing departments are increasingly trying to achieve administrative coordination overall of the tools of communication and marketing.

In allocating the communications budget to the various tools, companies should pay attention to the following four factors: *(i)* the type of product consumer versus industrial, *(ii)* the communications task to be accomplished, *(iii)* the stage of the product life cycle, and *(iv)* the economic outlook.

Type of Product—consumer Versus Industrial

Historically, there has been a considerable difference in the communication mixes used by consumer and industrial marketers. Advertising is widely felt to be the most important promotool in consumer marketing, and personal selling the most important promotool in industrial marketing. Sales promotion is considered to equal, though smaller, importance in both markets. And publicity is considered to have even smaller, but equal, importance in both markets.

This view leads some marketers to act as if advertising is unimportant in industrial marketing and as if personal selling is unimportant in consumer marketing. Such conclusions are erroneous and can be refused both in terms of common sense and by some recent studies.

While sales calls will normally have more impact than advertising industrial marketing situations, especially where the product is complex, advertising can perform several useful functions:

(i) Awareness Building. Prospects who are not aware of the company or product may refuse to see the sales representative. Furthermore, the sales representative may have to use up a lot of time describing the company and its products.

(ii) Comprehension Building. If the product embodies new features, some of the burden of explaining them can be effectively carried on by advertising.

(iii) Efficient Reminding. If prospects know about the product but are not ready to buy, advertisements reminding them of the product would be much more economical than sales calls.

(iv) Lead Generation. Adertisements carrying return coupons are an effective way to generate leads for sales representatives.

(v) Legitimation. Sales representatives can use tear sheets of the company's advertisements to legitimatise their company and products.

(vi) Reassurance. Advertising can remind customer how to use the product and reassure them about their purchase.

RESPONSIBILITY FOR MARKETING COMMUNICATION PLANNING

Members of the marketing organisation have strong and varied feelings about the proper proportions of the company's communications budget to spend on the different promotools. The sales manager finds it hard to understand how the company could get more value by spending $80,000 to buy a single exposure of a thirty-second television commercial than by hiring three or four additional sales repsentatives for a whole year. The public relations manager feels that the company can gain by transferring some of the advertising budget to publicity.

Historically, companies left these decisions to different people. No one was given the responsibility for thinking through the of the various promotional tools and coordinating the company's communication mix. Today companies are moving toward the concept of integrated communications. This concept calls for:

(i) Developing a corporate position, such as marketing communications director, who has overall responsibility for the company's persuasive communications efforts.

(ii) Working out a philosophy of the role and the extent to which the different promotools are to be used.

(iii) Keeping track of all promotion a investments by product, promotool, stage of product life cycle, and observed effect, as a basis for improving subsequent effective use of each tool.

(iv) Coordinating the promotional activities and their timing when major campaigns take place.

Integrated management of promotional activities promises more consistency in the company's meaning to its buyers and publics. It places a responsibility in someone's hand—where none existed before—to constructively unify and manage the company's image as it comes through the thousand activities the company carries on. It leads to the determination of a total marketing communications strategy aimed at showing how the company can help customers solve their problems.

❒

9

Rural and Social Marketing

CHANNEL MANAGEMENT MANAGED IN RURAL CONTEXT

(1) The Existing Market Structure. It has been estimated that the India rural market is composed of 22,000 primary rural markets and 20 lakh retail sales outlets of which nearly one lakh are fair price shops of the Public Distribution System (PDS). One retail shop serves on an average 60 to 70 families in the rural areas. The structure involves stock points in feeder towns to service these retail outlets at the village level. The stock points belong to either the manufacturer or the marketer/distributor for the area. In either case, the stock point in the feeder town in the key to rural distribution.

(2) The Private Village Shops. For a large variety of consumer products; the private shops are the main channel in the rural markets; they are also the cheapest and the most convenient channel to aligh with. As such, we shall examine in some detail how the private village
381 shops are utilised by the business firms in their rural distribution effort.

It is quite natural that firms seeking an effective presence in the rural market, willingly embrace the private village shops as the major component of their distribution outfit. And on their part, the village shops function as an effective bridge between the scattered rural consumers and the urban based producers.

Organising one's channel out of these private shops, however, required assiduous efforts on the part of the firm. It has to select its outlets from out of existing shopkeepers or select a few freshers and appoint them as the outlets. The choices are usually confined to the following categories:

(a) Existing traditional private shops

(b) Money lenders willing to branch off to trade

(c) Land owners willing to branch off to trade

(d) Educated unemployed persons.

The firm has to select personnel from among the above groups depending on the product line and other relevant factors and then train them and develop them into competent dealers.

(3) The Available Channel Choices. Today, the channel types that are available in the rural markets are as follows:

(a) The private shops

(b) The cooperative societies

(c) The Fair Price Shops (FPS), (cooperatives of private), of the PDS

(d) The village shandy or weekly market.

Out of the above, the cooperative societies are mainly concerned with the distribution of rural inputs and the FPS with the distribution of essential commodities consumed by the common man. The role of these institutional agencies in reaching the interior markets of India, has been dealt with a length on Distribution Channels. The 'village shandy' is a widely used channel of the rural market. But its role in marketing branded products is somewhat limited.

(4) Satellite Distribution. A concept that has come to be known as 'satellite distribution' can be tried in developing a distribution channel in the rural market. Under this system, to start with, the firm appoints stockists in feeder towns. They take care of financing of goods, warehousing of goods and sub-distribution of goods in the area covered by the feeder town. The firm also appoints a number of retailers in and around the feeder towns and attaches them to the stockists. The firm supplies the goods to the stockists either on cash or on credit or on consignment basis. The stockists take care of the sub-distribution job on the terms and conditions determined by the firm.

PROBLEMS

(1) Multiple Tiers, Higher Costs and Administrative Problems. In the first place, the distribution chain in the rural context requires a larger number of tiers, compared with the urban context. The long distances to be covered from the product points and the scattered locations of the consuming households cause this situation. At the minimum, the distribution chain in the rural context needs the village level shopkeeper, the mundi level distribution and the wholesaler/stockist in the town. And on top of them, it involves the manufacturers' own warehouses/branch office operations at selected centres in the marketing territory. Such multiple tiers and scattered outfits push up costs and make channel management a major problem area.

(2) Inadequate Bank Facilities. Distribution in rural markets is also handicapped due to lack of adequate banking and credit facilities. Rural outlets need banking support for three important purposes.

(a) To facilitate remittances to principals and to get fast replenishment of stocks.

(b) To receive supplies 'through bank' (retiring documents with the bank).

(c) To facilities are inadequate in the rural areas, the rural dealers and handicapped in all these aspects. It is estimated that there is only one bank branch for every fifty villages.

(3) Inadequate Credit Facilities from Banks. Inadequate of institutional/bank credit is another constraint. The rural outlets are unable to carry adequate stocks due to lack of credit facilities. They are unable to extend credit to their customers. And the vicious circle of lack of credit facilities leading to inadequate stocking and loss of business, finally resulting in poor viability of outlets, gets perpetuated.

(4) Poor Viability of the Retail Outlets. Moreover, sales outlets in the rural market at the retail level suffer from poor viability.

A familiar paradox in rural distribution is that the manufacturer incurs additional expenses on distribution and still the retail outlets find that the business is unremunerative to them. The scattered nature of the market and the multiplicity of tiers in the chain use up the additional funds the manufacturer is prepared to part with. And no additional remuneration accrues to any of the groups. Moreover, the business volume is not adequate enough to sustain the profitability of all the groups and the retail tier is the worst sufferer.

(5) Non Availability of Dealers. In addition, there is the problem of availability of dealers. Many firms find that availability of suitable dealers is limited. Even if the firm is willing to start from scratch and try out rank newcomers, the choice of candidates is really limited.

(6) Scope for manufacturer's Own Outlets United: Greater Dependence on Dealers Inescapable. The scope for manufacturers' direct outlets such as showrooms or depots is quite limited in the rural market unlike in the urban context. It becomes expensive as well as unmanageable. Dependence of the firm on intermediaries is very much enhanced in the rural context as direct outlets are often ruled out. But controlling such a vast network of intermediaries is a difficult task. Control is mostly indirect. And because of these factors the firm has to be more careful while selecting the channel members in the rural context.

CHARACTERISTICS FEATURES OF RURAL PRODUCTION

Agriculture is the basic industry. It satisfies the demand for foodstuff on one side and unnecessary raw materials for industrial production on the other. Rural marketing faces different problems. The cultivator has no assurance of the prices he could obtain in the market. The characteristics features of rural products are as follows:

(i) **Small-Scale Production.** Commercialisation of agriculture is still a new concept to Indian agriculturists. Indian farmers own very small plots of land and very often the production just sufficient to cover the family needs. On account of small holdings, the production also tends to be small. The marketable surplus with an average agriculturist is, therefore, meagre.

(ii) **Perishable Nature of Products.** Unlike manufactured products the rural goods are perishable in nature. This demand speedy marketing activities which are very often prevented by transport facilities. The storing facilities in villages are so primitive and crude that they are not capable of preserving the goods over a long period.

(iii) **No Concerted Conscious Marketing Activities.** Agriculturists in India have not yet fully appreciated the value of a joint or combined action for the purpose of bargaining on equal terms with the buyers of rural goods. The cultivators concentrate on production only ignoring the marketing aspects.

(iv) **Unorganised Nature of Markets.** The markets for rural products are generally unorganised and manufactured by numerous middlemen. These middlemen use their upper hand in the buying process. In the opinion of the Central Rural Marketing Department, "Wheat cultivator gets only Re. 0.23 out of each rupee paid by the consumer".

(v) **Malpractices in the Market.** Because of the lack of standardisation unguarded products are marketed. The absence of accepted grades makes it possible to indulge in malpractices. Prices are decided by intermediaries and not buy the producer.

(vi) **Inelasticity of Demand.** Since most products are necessaries, price changes do not bring about any great changes in demand. This creates problems during the harvest season when the adundant supply creates a glut in the market causing a fall in price. It is because of this that recently the Food Corporation of India has started procuring excess supply (marketable surplus) and keeping a buffer stock.

DIFFERENCE BETWEEN MANUFACTURED PRODUCTS AND RURAL PRODUCTS

1. The manufacturer on the one hand will have to be engaged in continuous production and on the other must be able to utilise his production capacity to the fullest extent possible. He is cost conscious. He can concentrate equally on production and marketing activities. The agriculturist is purely a producer and nothing else.

2. A manufacturer wants to wield an unfettered control over the sale of his products to the middlemen. This is not so in the case of the rural producer where intermediaries like arthtiyas, village shopkeepers (Mahajans), Beoparis and Dalals have entrenched themselves firmly in the marketing scene. These middlemen have earned notoriety of many malpractices including the use of incorrect weights.

3. Manufactured goods are mostly produced on a large scale and are item broken up into smaller lots of each successive stage in marketing. Whereas rural produce is collected in small quantities which ultimately swell the mighty stream of marketing.

4. Manufactured goods can be easily controlled both qualitatively and quantitatively and can also be fixed in advance in almost inaccurate terms. Both these aspects are beyond the control of an agriculturist and the entire production is based on natural conditions such as climate, rainfall, soil, etc.

5. Manufactured goods are subject to effective demand for creational activities. Such activities are completely absent in the case of rural marketing.

6. Manufacturers can identify themselves completely with their products. There are many manufactured products that are bought not only on the real quality of the product but also on the basis of reputation of the producers. This is totally impossible in the case of rural produce. Once they are assembled the dealers identity alone could be examined by the buyers.

SPECIAL PROBLEMS IN PHYSICAL DISTRIBUTION IN THE RURAL CONTEXT

The special problems in physical distribution in the rural context arise in the following areas:

(i) Transportation

(ii) Warehousing

(iii) Communication

(iv) Transportation problems

(i) Transportation Problems. Transportation infrastructure *i.e.* quite poor in rural India. Several parts of rural India are not accessible to the marketing man.

Absence of a proper and adequate network of rural roads is the first constraint. Nearly 50 percent of the 5,76,000 villages in the country are not connected by roads at all. The government had planned to connect at least those villages with a population of 1500 and above with all weather roads by 1989-90. Even this limited objective has not been accomplished. Today, many parts in rural India have only kacha roads. And even these kacha roads become unserviceable during the monsoons, leaving the rural interiors totally unconnected.

In adequacy of suitable carriers is the second constraint. The mechanised transport and a human drawn transport. The constraints in roads and the constraints in carriers together act as a major inhibitor on any company that seek to provide a new marketing thrust in the villages of the country. It is evident that without proper accessibility, delivery of products and services is extremely difficult.

(ii) Warehousing Problems. Business firms find it quite difficult to get suitable godowns in many parts of rural India. And there is no public warehousing agency in the interiors of rural India. The Central Warehousing Corporation (CWC and the State Warehousing Corporations (SWC which constitute the top tier in public warehousing in India, do not extend their network of warehouses to the rural parts. In short, in practical terms, a firm has to operate in the rural market without the facility of institutionalised warehousing.

It would be a welcome development if a Rural Warehousing Corporation is established in the country, offering public warehousing services in the rural parts.

(iii) Communication Problems. Posts and telegraph and telephones are the main components of communication infrastructure. It is common knowledge that these facilities are quite inadequate in the rural parts of out country. Since communication is the first requirement of marketing, lack of proper communication infrastructure posses certain special difficulties, especially in physical distribution.

Cost-Service Dilemma Gets More Acute

The effect of all these problems is certainly felt by any business firm venturing into the rural market. They affect adversely the service aspects as well as the cost aspect. Maintaining the required service level in the delivery of the products to the dealers and the consumers becomes very difficult. At the same time, physical distribution costs get excluded, compared with urban marketing situation. While cost-service dilemma is a basic problem in physical distribution in all markets, the dilemma attains acute proportions in the rural context.

In the section on the profile of the rural market, we had drawn attention to the scattered location of the rural consumers. Eighty percent of the total rural consumer is accounted by the 'less than 1000 people' category of villages. The scattered nature of the market and its distance from the urban based production centres, combined with the constraints in transportation, warehousing and communication, make delivery of products and services in rural markets a particularly difficult task. Longer lead between the production centre and the consumption centres, larger pipeline stocks and larger inventory in warehouses are the natural outcome of the constraints. It means higher transportation costs, higher inventory carrying costs and higher transit and storage losses. Consequently, the total distribution cost per unit in respect of any product is considerably higher in the rural market, compared to the urban market. In fact, experiences of some major companies operating in the rural market show that the cost of distribution in rural areas is nearly two and a half times that of urban.

VARIOUS TYPES OF SALESFORCE STRUCTURE

1. Territorial Structured Salesforce. In the simplest sales organisation, each sales representative is assigned an exclusive territory in which to represent the company's full line. This sales structure has a number of advantages. First, it results in a clear definition of the salesperson's responsibilities. As the only salesperson working the territory, he or she bears the credit or blame for areas sales to the extent that personal selling effort makes a difference. Second, territorial responsibility increases the sales representative's incentive to cultivate local business and personal ties. These ties contribute to the sales representative's selling effectiveness and personal life. Third, travel expenses are relatively small, since each sales representative travels within a small geographical area.

Territorial sales organisation is often supported by many levels of sales management positions. For example:

Each higher-level sales manager takes on increasing marketing and administrative work in relation to the time available for selling. In fact, sales managers are paid for their management skills rather than their selling skills. The new sales trainee, in looking ahead, can expect to become a sales representative and then a district manager and, depending on his or her ability and mutation, may move to higher levels of sales or general management.

In designing territories, the company seeks certain territorial characteristics. The territories are easy to administer; their sales potential is easy to estimate; they reduce total travel time; and they provide a sufficient and equitable workload and sales potential for each sales representative. These characteristics are achieved through deciding on territory size and shape.

> ***Territory Size.*** Territories can be designed to provide either equal sales potential or equal workload. Each principle offers advantages at the cost of some dilemmas. Territories of equal potential provide each sales representative with

the same income opportunities and provide the company with a means to evaluate performance. Persistent differences in sales yield by territory are assumed to reflect differences in ability or effort of individual sales representatives salespersons are encouraged to work to their top capacity.

But because customer density varies by territory, territories with equal potential can vary widely in size. The potential for selling drill presses in Chicago is larger than in several western states. A sales representative as sighed to Chicago can cover the same sales potential with must less effort than the sales representative who sells in the Far West. The sales representative assigned to the larger and sparser territory is going to end up with either fewer sales and less income for equal effort or equal sales through extraordinary effort. One solution is to pay the western sales representatives more compensation for the extra effort. But this reduces the profits on sales in the western territories. Another solution is to acknowledge that territories differ in attractiveness and assign the better or more senior sales representatives to the better territories.

Alternatively, territories could be designed to equalise the sales workload. Each sales representative can then cover his or her territory adequately. This principle, however, results in some variation in territory adequately. This principle, however, results income variation in territory sales potential. That does not concern a salesforce on straight salary. But where sales representatives are compensated partly on their sales, territories will vary in the re attractiveness even though their workloads are equal. A lower compensation rate can be paid to sales representatives in the territories with the higher sales potential, or the territories with the better potential can go to the higher performers.

Territory Shape. Territories are formed by combining smaller units, such as countries or states, until they add up to a territory of a given sales potential or workload. Territorial design must take into account the location of natural barriers, the compatibility of adjacent areas, the adequacy of transportation, and so forth. Many companies prefer a certain territory shape because the shape can influence the cost and ease of coverage and the sales representatives job satisfaction. Most common are circular, cloverleaf, and wedge-shaped territories.

2. Product-Structured Sales Force. The importance of sales representatives knowing their products, together with the development of product divisions and product management, has lead many companies to structure their salesforces along product lines. Product specialisation is particularly warranted where the products are technically complex, highly unrelated or very numerous. For example, Kodak uses different salesforces for its firm products and its industrial products. The firm products salesforce deals with simple products that are intensively distributed, while the industrial-products salesforce deals with complex products that require technical understanding. As might be expected, the firm salesforce is paid a salary, while the industrial salesforce works on a salary and commission plan.

The mere existence of different company products, however, is not a sufficient argument for specialising the salesforce by product. Such specialisation might not be the best course if the company's separate product lines are bought by the same customers. For example, Baxter has several product divisions, each with its own salesforce. It is conceivable that several Baxter sales representatives might visit the same hospital on the same day. Much cost could be saved by sending only one Baxter salesperson to represent Baxter's whole product line to that hospital.

3. Market-Structured Salesforce. Companies often specialise their salesforces along industry or customer lines. Separate salesforces can be set up for different industries and even different customers.

For example, IBM set up a sales office for finance and brokerage customers in New York, another for GM in Detroit, and still another for Ford in nearby Dearborn.

The most obvious advantage of market specialisation is that each salesforce can become knowledgeable about specific customer needs. At one time; General Electric's sales representatives specialised in products (fan motors, switches, and so forth), but it later changed to specialisation in industries, such as the air-conditioning industry and auto industry, because that is how customers saw the purchase of fan motors, switches, and so forth. A market-specialised salesforce can sometimes reduce total salesforce costs. A pump manufacturer at one time used highly trained sales engineers to sell in both original-equipment manufacturers (who needed to deal with technical representatives) and jobber (who did not need to deal with technical representatives). Later, the company split its salesforce and staffed the jobber salesforce with lower-paid, less-technical sales personnel. The major disadvantage of market-structured salesforces arises when the various types of customers are scattered throughout the country. This require extensive travel by each salesforce.

4. Complex Salesforce Structures. When a company sells a wide variety of products to many types of customers over a broad geographical area, it often combines several principles of salesforce structure. Sales representatives can be specialised by territory-product, territory-market, product-market, and so on. A sales representative might than report to one or more line managers and staff managers

SALES FORCE IN RURAL MARKETS

As a general rule, rural marketing involves a greater amount of personal selling effort compared to urban marketing. Personal selling also brings in greater returns in the rural context. While the basic traits of personal selling consisting of empathy, enthusiasm, communication-skill and knowledge of selling techniques are required in equal measure by urban and rural salesmen, the latter require certain additional capabilities in order to match the peculiar conditions of the rural market.

In this section we shall briefly discuss the unique demands that the rural markets place on the salesman and the special problems that arise in managing the salesforce in the rural context.

Rural Marketing Calls for Certain Unique Traits on the Part of the Salesmen

(i) Willingness to be Located in Rural Areas. First of all, only those who are genuinely happy in living and working in the villages can become good rural salesmen. The rural areas are definitely lacking in modern amenities compared with the urban areas. There is accordingly a reluctance on the part of many salesmen to getting located in rural centres. To circumvent this problem, some firms locate their salesmen in towns and allow them to cover the rural areas assigned to them from these towns. Experience has shown that such an arrangement does not produce optimum results. Experience has also shown that successful rural marketing firms are prepared to locate their rural salesmen right in the midst of the rural market to be covered. Lipton India for example, has located one of its salesmen in Khategaom, an interior place in Dewas district in Madhya Pradesh. It takes three full hours by bus from Indore to reach the location. Similarly, it has located a salesman at Anthiyoor in Tamil Nadu, which can be reached only with a 2½ hours journey by bus from Coimbatore and l/2 an hour walk through paddy field. The company proudly cites this practice as one main source of its 'bazar power' .

(ii) Cultural Congruence. Location is just the starting point. The salesmen must have proper acquaintance with the cultural pattern of rural life in the given rural territory. Since the cultural patterns of rural communities differ from one another, a cultural background that is in consonance with the culture of the given rural community is a specific requisite of success for the rural salesmen. Urban market is contrast, involves a convergence of cultures into a common pattern.

Rural salesmen must also be able to perceive clearly the unique problems of the rural customers and be able to guide them in the choice of products. They should not hook them into bating whatever products they have in their catalogues. On the contrary, they must help them to eliminate items that are outside their specific requirements and those that are beyond their reach.

(iii) Attitude Factors. Attitude is of particular significance too rural salesmen. And ability to listen patiently is an important aspect of attitude in the rural sales context. The rural salesmen have to be patient listeners, as their customer is an extremely traditional and cautious person. Perseverance is another aspect. It will not be possible for the rural salesmen to chancy the sale quickly. They may have to spend a log of time with the customer and make several visits to him to gain a favourable response from him.

(iv) Good Knowledge of the Local Language. Another special requirement is that the rural salesman should be well versed with the local language. Whereas his urban counterpart can successfully manage with? English and a working knowledge of the local language, the rural salesman needs a strong background of the local language. In fact, he has to go one step further; he must be well versed in the specific lingo and idiom of the local area/community, for, in rural India, within each major language group, the colloquial expressions and speaking manners vary considerably from locality to locality.

(v) More Intensive Training. The rural salesmen are often required to handle a much larger number of product lines compared with their urban counterparts and to that extent their job becomes more difficult compared with the job of the urban salesmen. In urban cremating, the salesmen are able to generate economic size of business through a limited number of product lines. As such, their employers do not have to load them with too many items. The rural salesmen on the contrary, usually find it difficult to generate economic volume of business if their dealings are restricted to a few product lines. They are compelled to handle a large variety of items. Quite often, the items differ widely from one another. In other words, the rural salesmen are required to become a 'jack of all trades'. They are also required to devote more time for getting trained, as they have to take the training for handling a variety of products.

Again, as a general rule, the rural salesmen are required to travel more compared with their urban counterparts. Whereas the urban salesmen move in highly concentrated incompliant market segments, the rural salesmen have to cover larger territories and scattered customers. His workload and strain could therefore be more.

(vi) Greater Creativity. Rural selling is also relatively a more creative task. Many products are even now very new in many rural parts. The rural salesmen cannot sit back and say that it will take several years for a particular product to penetrate the rural market. On the other hand, he must endeavour to introduce them in the rural areas through creative selling, using the consumption pioneers and opinion leaders. Rural marketing also presupposes the delivery of a higher standard of living to the rural masses and is essentially developmental marketing. The rural salesman has to keep in view the development ingredient in his task. He is not mere order taker. He is a carrier of a developmental message to the less privileged village community.

CONTROLLING THE SALES FORCE

Control over the activities of the salesman is needed for running the sales office efficiently and this is possible only when the office maintains up-to-date records and schemes. These are available from the salesman in the form of order forms, reports of calls, expense details and other reports. However, any delaying receiving the call reports of expense sheets may be tolerated but discipline and punctuality are necessary in office. Control over the sales force is maintained. There are certain cases where the sales manager feels no difficulty but the problem crops up when the salesmen does something which is beyond his authority and in respect of making delivery, promises, making concession, and allowing discounts or special periods for settlement of accounts. Some of the work is usually delegated to the assistant by the sales manager and he comes to know of the trouble only when it has developed sufficiently. Therefore, to avoid such situations contact with the assistant and the salesman becomes necessary. The failure to maintain contact frequently leads to the failure of the sales manager himself.

This contact is maintained in many ways such as through periodical letters bulletins, the telephonic calls, weekiy conferences, periodical conventions, visiting salesmen on their territories. Each one of these methods may be used to build up the organisation into a much solid and enthusiastic enterprise.

Aspects of Control. There are three main aspects of control of salesmen:

(i) Activities of the salesmen are to be so directed that they fit into the general marketing plan of the firm. This means that sales manager's duty is to see that salesmen's efforts are concentrated in effective execution to the sales plan. With this end in view sales territories are allocated to individual salesmen and their routes planned. They are told to how much efforts should be put in to sell a particular line of products, to sell to new customers and to retain old customers.

(ii) Salesmen's results are to be analysed with view to *(a)* ensure achievement of pre-determined standard of efficiency in their performance, and *(b)* determine the ratio of selling expenses to sales. This aspect involves finding out Whether each salesman is doing what is expected of him. This is done by comparing sales achieved by him with sales quota allocated to him. Analysis of his sales record would be helpful in detecting errors and failings as well.

(iii) Actual supervision and guidance to individual salesmen when necessary. This aspect comprises taking necessary steps to discover the cause of errors and failings and measures to rectify such errors. For this purpose salesman's actual working may be observed and he may be helped in improving his selling technique by instructions and example.

Control over the salesmen may be exercised either by personal contact (through regional, divisional, district or branch managers); or by correspondence; or through reports-daily, weekly, or even monthly.

The sales management involves control of subordinates. It does not mean bossing over them. The sales manager should therefore, in order to have cordial relations with the salesman must:

(a) Never try to show his authority

(b) Never throw his weight about

(c) Never boast of orders he may have obtained in the past

(d) Never boast of his achievement.

He should be modest to all at all times. Let his actions speak for him. In cases where the salesmen have to he reprimanded, because of their mistakes, even this should be done in a kindly manner and in privacy.

He should always be careful to check up his appearance, always be punctual and watch his language and should be smiling and dynamic. He should build up his salesman and he will eventually build up a good team.

The success of salesmen's team depends largely on what the sales manager is willing to do for them. Therefore, he should—

(a) Win their Admiration for the way they work

(b) Win their Respect by his own integrity

(c) Win their Loyalty by his unselfishness.

Effective supervision and control of salesman presupposes the following:

(a) The sales manager should know what exactly does he expect a salesman to do.

(b) Salesmen should be given idea of what he is expected to do.

(c) Sales manager should know that the salesman is doing what he is expected to do.

(d) Salesman should be made to know that the sales manager knows what he does.

(e) Salesman should know that sales manager appreciates what he does.

The first condition is met by establishing sales quotas for individual salesmen; the second is achieved during training period; the third through reports and fourth and fifth through reports and records and personal talks across the table with the individual salesman.

MANAGING THE RURAL SALESFORCE

In tune with the special requirements which the rural salesforce has to meet, the task of salesforce management in the rural context carries certain added dimensions compared with the task in the urban context. In selecting the salesmen, in giving them orientation, in motivating them and in developing them, the sales manager has to keep in view the unique requirements of rural selling. For example, in the matter of orientation of the newly recruited salesmen, the sales manager may have to devote a longer time in the moral marketing context. And mere classroom training will not meet fully the requirements of orientation of rural salesmen. The salesmen need intensive on the job coaching in selected village markets and they need to be educated about the rural marketing environment in addition to being trained in salesmanship and selling techniques.

The sales manager must also help his salesmen to be creative in their choice of techniques and media for marketing communication, since the traditional techniques and media do not work that well in the rural markets. For example, while the urban salesmen can be supported by mass media advertising, the rural salesmen may have to be given the support of puppet shows to be enacted at the time of a temple festival. Alternatively, they may have to be trained to take the support of the gramsevak.

In short, salesforce management in the rural context becomes an exacting job, especially when the firm has big stakes in rural marketing and when it operates on a nationwide basis. For example, Hindustan Lever's rural salesmen have to cover 70,000 rural locations. Lipton India has in, its fold 1,260 salesmen covering more than 4,000 markets and monitoring 6,60,000 dealers. Obviously, administering such a large and scattered salesforce, supervising them, supporting them in sales calls an coaching them on the job, attending to their official and personal problems, and above all, motivating them for better results, is a task that throws up exacting demands on the sales manager in charge of rural salesforce.

CHANNEL MANAGEMENT IN RURAL MARKETS

Organising an effective distribution channel is the second major task in rural marketing. This task too is be set with many unique problems.

I. The Problems

In the first place, in the rural context, the distribution chain requires a larger number of tiers, compared with the urban context. The physical distances to be covered for reaching the market and the scattered location of the households in the market cause this situation. At the minimum, the rural chain needs the village level shop-keeper, the mundi level distributor and the wholesaler/stockist in the town. And on top of them, it involves the manufacturers' own warehouses/ branch office operations at selected centres in the marketing territory.

(i) Multiple Tiers and Scattered Outfit Pushes up Costs and Makes Administration More Complex. The implications of this reality are two-fold: *(a)* the cost of operating a dealer network in the rural market is quite high and *(b)* the management problems relating to the channel are quite complex.

(ii) Scope for Manufacturers' Own Outlets, Limited. Secondly, the scope for manufacturers' direct outlets such as showrooms or depots is quite limited in the rural market. It becomes expensive as well as unmanageable.

(iii) Greater Dependence on Intermediaries. Thirdly, dependence of the firm on the intermediaries is very much enhanced in the rural context compared to the urban. At the same tie the firms control over them is lessened compared to the urban context. The dependence on the intermediaries is more as direct outlets are often ruled out. Since the rural context involves multiplicity of distribution tiers and since the networks are scattered, the manufacturer is unable to exercise a strong direct control over the channel members, especially those in the forward links of the long chain. At best his control is indirect. And the greater dependence on the intermediaries and the inability to exercise a strong direct control over them compels the manufacturer to be more careful while selecting the channel members. Afterwards, he has to assign them a high degree of responsibility in distribution.

(iv) Poor Viability of the Outlets at the Retail Level. Fourthly, a good number of sales outlets in the rural market suffer from poor viability. In fact, it has become a familiar paradox in rural distribution that the manufacturer incurs additional expenses on distribution and at the same time, the links in the distribution chain find that the business is unremunerative to them. The scattered nature of the market and the multiplicity of tiers in the chain use up the additional expenses, without resulting in any additional remuneration to any of the groups. And the business volume is inadequate to sustain the profitability of all these groups. The retail tier is the worst sufferer.

(v) Dealers are Just Not Available. Fifthly, there is the problem of availability of dealers. Many firms find that available dealers are not suitable for their purpose. Even if the firm is willing to start from scratch and try out newcomers, candidates of the right type are not turning up for consideration. Often, the choices are quite limited.

(vi) Inadequate Banking and Credit Facilities. Distribution in rural markets is also handicapped due to lack of adequate banking and credit facilities. As a matter of fact, rural outlets need banking support for three important purposes:

(a) To enable remittance and to get replenishment of stocks

(b) To enable supplies 'through bank'

(c) To help credit transactions in general and to obtain credit support from the banks.

The intermediaries as well as the firm are handicapped in each of these aspects due to the inadequacy of banking facilities. Even after the expansion in rural banking facilities in recent years, there is only one branch for every fifty villages.

Inadequacy of credit facility is the other equally important constraint. The retailers are unable to carry adequate stocks in the absence of adequate credit fadity. Nor are they able to offer credit to the customers. And the vicious circle of inadequate credit facility leading to inadequate stocking and the latter leading to low volume of business and poor viability of the sales outlets, gets perpetuated.

Analysis shows that many companies hesitate to venture into rural markets largely because of the channel problems. From the cost angle, they find it very expensive, almost uneconomic to maintain outlets in rural areas, especially in the interior markets. They find that cost of selling, cost of transportation, cost of sub-distribution and cost of servicing the outlets are all quite high. They also find that managing the rural outlets is a difficult task.

TYPES OF RURAL MARKETS

Three kinds of rural markets are found in practice: *(a)* Local markets, *(b)* Regional or district markets, and *(c)* Terminal markets.

(a) Local Markets. They are also called "assembling markets" because the main function of such a market is to assemble products from various individual sources. They are mostly located within the area of production and hence are sometimes referred to as village markets or primary markets. The produce from individual farmers is collected and made into economical lots. In primary markets grading and packaging are undertaken. A large number of intermediaries are found in these markets.

Arhatiyas — Commission agents, assemblers, brokers and financiers.

Beoparis — Assemblers.

Mahajans — Financiers, large-scale assemblers.

Palledars They undertake transporting and receive palledari (fright).

Dallals — Brokers.

Tolas — Weight men.

Paikars — Village merchants.

The government controls the organisation of cooperatives and the introduction of regulated markets have imposed some kinds of control over the methods and practices followed in these markets.

(b) Regional or District Markets. These markets often constitute intermediate step of concentration between local assembly point and central terminal markets. These are essentially wholesale markets and located in populated centres large quantities are handled in these markets. These Markets perform three functions: concentration equalisation and dispersion. These markets are economically important and act as equalisers of demand and supply to maintain stability in prices. It is in these market that price making, final grading, and packaging activities are undertake. There are a few kinds of middlemen in addition to those mentioned above.

Gabbers. They buy in huge quantities and like wholesalers bear marketing risks. For all purposes they are wholesalers.

Retailers. They buy products in comparatively smaller quantities exclusively meant for dispersion to ultimate consumers through terminal markets. In regional markets where future and forward transactions are permitted, some other dealers are also found such as speculators, hedgers and floor traders. .

(c) Terminal Markets. These markets represent the final stage in the concentration of the supply of the commodity. Very often they are places from where dispersion to industrial users or to ultimate consumers take place. Various marketing functions such as grading, financing warehousing, etc. are undertaken at full length in these markets.

MARKET SEGMENTATION IN RURAL MARKETS

In addition to the major problem areas explained above, other aspects like Jharket segmentation, product management etc. also require a unique handling in rural markets. Let us first discuss market segmentation.

Market segmentation is as important in rural marketing as it is in urban marketing. As a matter of fact, in view of the high cost involved in tapping the rural markets, segmentation becomes all the more important in the rural context. It would be unwise for any firm to assume that the rural market is one homogeneous market and can be served with the same product-price-promotion combination. The firm should carry out a through and data based market segmentation, select the relevant segments as its target market, and develop distinctive positioning strategies and distinctive marketing mix for the chosen segment(s). Fortunately, the rural market lends itself will for segmentation. In fact, it can be segmented in a number of ways, using different bases.

1. Geographic Segmentation. In the first place, the rural market can be segmented geographically and different bases can be used for this segmentation.

(i) ***Climate.*** Climate can be the first of these bases; regions endowed with favourable climate are usually more prosperous compared with climatically handicapped regions.

(ii) ***Level of Irrigation.*** Level of irrigation can be another base. Irrigated areas and dry land response different marketing environments. And within irrigated areas, single crop, double crop and triple crop areas indicate varying levels of prosperity.

(iii) ***Rural Productivity.*** Rurally prosperity and rural production and productivity can be yet another base. Rural prosperity after all, is not uniform in all rural parts of India. Certain areas have developed at a rapid rate, while certain other areas have remained undeveloped. This fact can be used for a geographical segmentation. Rural productivity will generally be a better characteristics to rely upon that rural production. And per capita productivity will be a more reliable base than per hectare productivity. Level of advancement attained in agriculture in overall terms, can also be a basin this approach, parameters like adoption level of high yielding varieties, adoption level of fertiliser use, standard of rural practices, will have to be reckoned in addition to the level of rural production and productivity.

(iv) ***Nearness to Feeder Towns.*** Yet another form of geographic segmentation can be tried, using 'nearness to a feeder town' as the base. Studies have revealed that rural consumer who are located in the immediate hinterland of a feeder

town visit the feeder town at least once a month to sell their produce and/or to buy their requirements. Studies have also revealed that in exposure and buying habits, those who are located in the hinterland of a feeder town are different from those living in the deep rural areas. It may be therefore, possible to segment the rural market into consumers who are located closer to a feeder to town and consumers who are located away from the feeder towns. Evidently, different approaches of marketing can be adopted to serve the two different segments.

Similarly, nearness to an industrial project centre also can be used as a relevant consideration for segmentation. There is a cross flow of population between centres and rural hinterland. As such, the project centres act as conduits for the flow of products and ideas. This fact can be used for segmentation.

2. Demographic Segmentation. Demographically, there are many possibilities of segmenting the rural market.

(i) ***Population Spread.*** Population spread can be one base. 36 percent of rural population live in seven percent of the villages in the country and remaining 64 percent live in 93 percent of the villages. Evidently the description of 'rural' does not have the same meaning in respect of the two segments. The rural market can be segmented on the basis of these size classes. The size classes can also be changed so as to make them more relevant to the situation.

(ii) ***Agewise Segment.*** Segmentation using age as the base has a good scope in rural marketing. For example, from the age wise distribution of the rural population discussed in table under the rural market profile, it can be seen that about 26 percent of the rural population falls within the 5-15 years age group. This means that there is a population of more than 15 crore in this age group in the rural market. These facts have some relevance to the marketing man. This can serve as a base for segmentation. Surveys have revealed that a major share of the rural purchase is done by

the younger generation. Partly due to their greater literacy and exposure and partly due to their changing values and styles, the younger groups dominate the consumer goods purchases in the rural market. This group can be cultivated as a specific segment through a specific strategy; they can be used for the introduction of new products.

Table

Age Wise Distribution of Rural Population

Age group		*Share of total population* 1971	1986
0-4	years	15.8	10.6
5-15	years	25.6	22.7
15-59	years	53.4	60.5
60 and above		5.2	6.2
Total		100.0	100.0

(iii) Literacy. Literacy can be another base for the demographic segmentation. Though rural India in general is characterised by low literacy, there are wide variations in this regard from area to area and state to state. For example, while the rural literacy rate in Kerala is 60 percent, that of Bihar is only 12 percent.

(iv) Income. Income can be yet another base. In fact, income win be a particularly useful base of segmenting the rural market, since income distribution in the market is quite uneven. It will be unwise to assume that all people in the villages will be in a position to consume a particular product even if it is relatively low priced. It will be equally unwise to paint the whole of the rural market with the same brush and brand it as a market with low purchasing power'. Thirteen percent of the land-owning farmers account for 57 percent of the total cultivated land. And 10 percent of the rural population account for as much as 37 percent of the total expenditure on consumer products.

The potential market for many periods is at the top end of the spectrum.

Then is another way of using income as a base of segmentation. The consumers can be divided into regular income segment and seasonal income segment. Today, all rural consumers are not characterised by seasonality of income. There is a sizeable salaried class in the rural area.

This class may have different buying habits compared with the rural class. They may buy certain products which are not usually bought by the other class.

(v) ***Overall Profile of the Villages.*** The overall profile of the village can also be used as a base for segmenting the rural market. Obviously, in the overall profile, all the different parameters mentioned earlier will get reflected. It is well known that the villages of India considerable differ in their overall profile from zone to zone and state to state. For example, a village in Rajasthan and a village in Kerala are thoroughly dissimilar. And the consumers in these villages will differ in their buying habits and their use level of different products. Thus, the ollerall profile can serve as a base for segmentation.

PRODUCT MANAGEMENT IN RURAL MARKETS

In product management, the most crucial decision in the rural context is whether the product that is sold in the urban market can be supplied to the rural market, as it is, or it must be adapted. The decision depends on the situation and the nature of the product. In some cases, the firm may have to find out what kind of product is required by the rural consumer and then try to make and supply the product that is required. Income other cases, the same product may be equally acceptable in both rural and urban areas. In yet other cases, the basic product can be the same but the colour, size and package may have to be specially designed for the rural target group. For example, in the paint business, Asian Paints understood the substantial difference between the urban buyer and the rural buyer in colour preferences. AP introduced paints with bright colours for the rural markets. AP also communicated it through thousands of retail outlets and through mass communication.

Packaging

As far as packaging is concerned, as a general rule, it can be stated that smaller packages are more popular in the rural areas. Many fadors may be contributing to this reality. On account of low purchasing power and limited funds for shopping, the rural consumer may prefer smaller packs; the cash outflow at a time would after all be small in such purchases. In many cases, they are also preferring smaller package so that they can make a beginning with a small pack and after trial and satisfaction they can make regular purchases.

Product Quality

Product quality is a matter where no compromise can be had in the rural context. As a matter of fact, quality products at reasonable prices is the plank on which rural marketing has to be carried out. And quality has to be stable. Stability in quality and stability in price together will ensure durable success in rural marketing. On the contrary, the rural customer's confidence will get shaken if immediately after he adopts a product, the basis on which the adopted it gets knocked out. In so far as package quality is concerned, studies reveal that the rural consumer does not mind foregoing packaging frills, provided it results in a lower price to him.

Branding

Branding also needs skilful handling in the rural markets. The rural consumers have already graduated from generic products to branded products. And the rural marketers would do well to introduced branded products in the rural market and build them up on a sustained basis. The brand is the surest means of conveying quality to the rural consumers and they need such a communication about quality. To them, buying an established and well spoken of brand is the sure way of reducing the risk. In other words, brand is the key to confidence building among the rural consumers. Besides quality, it conveys that the manufacturer is going to show sustained interest in those products and markets.

Nationally advertised brands are preferred by the rural consumers to local brands: Analysis shows that contrary to the commonly held view, the rural consumer has a strong preference to the nationally advertised and promoted brands over the local regional brands. The popularity of the national brands in the advertised and promoted brands over the local regional brands. The popularity of the national brands in the rural markets in respect of diverse product categories ranging from kerosene chula to shampoo, substantiates the rural consumers' preference for national brands over local brands.

Rural Marketing Means Development Marketing

The rural market of India is fascinating and challenging at the same time. It offers large scope on account of its sheer size. And it is growing steadily. Even a gradual growth pushes up the sales of a product substantially, in view of the huge base. It is attractive from yet another angle. Whereas the urban market is highly competitive, the rural market is relatively quiet In fact, for certain products, it is totally a virgin market.

The market pioneers can certainly have their rewards from the market. Simultaneously, the market also posses several problems and hurdles. The firms have to squarely encounter them and put in a great deal of effort, if they have to bet a sizeable share of the market. They must 1 recognise that rural marketing is out and out developmental marketing.

It is often said that markets are made, not found. This is especially I true of the rural market of India. It is a market meant for the truly creative marketer.

SOCIAL MARKETING

We have so far been concerned mainly with describing current and ideal practice in marketing management in a profit-oriented organization. However, this should be viewed merely as an example, a special case, of marketing management, which is applicable to any human organization. All human organizations do have marketing problems. When applied to non-profit organizations, we call it "social marketing."

Marketing was defined at the beginning of this book in terms of communication processes. As such, it can be seen as a part of all human organizations. Largely because of this commonality, a wide variety of non-profit organizations is becoming interested in applying marketing principles. At a recent meeting of the International Music Council (UNESCO), for example, a question raised was, "How can one induce the potentially enormous listening and viewing public to take an interest in the better things of music?" In describing this international event the reporter stated, "The word 'marketing' applied to serious music, recurred frequently throughout the sessions."

It is well of be in mind, however, that an implicit aspect of the definition of marketing is freedom of choice by the client. Like all marketing, social marketing implies changing behaviour (in the marketer's favour) or preventing behavior change (to favour a competing alternative). Force of a public or illegal private nature is a way of changing human behavior, but it is inconsistent with marketing. The course of action in changing behavior by marketing is to identify the buyers' needs ancient to provide him with an alternative that fits his needs better. Your response may be, "Any stupe can do that!" It is difficult for an organization's objectives.

Another implicit aspect of marketing is that a transaction is involved. In a transaction, each party gives up something in return for something. Probably with few, if any, exceptions, accepting something involves a cost in some form, even if no more than opportunity cost of time. To the extent the need being served is not important, the client will exhibit fewer of the characteristics of choosing, such as looking for information.

The difference between profit and social marketing does not appear to be marketing techniques and concepts but the underlying assumptions that guide their implementation. We have not yet had the experience with social marketing to know what these underlying assumptions are and to know whether they are different. We will examine three aspects: basic marketing concepts, organization, and the "new marketing technology."

The basic marketing concepts in social marketing of positioning, product class, segmentation, target markets, marketing strategy, marketing mix, marketing plan, and organizational strategy (the social counterpart of corporate strategy) would seem to be relevant to any organization. When applied, these concepts can provide a fairly systematic way of organizing and thinking about a marketing plan.

Organizational problems in social marketing would also seem to be similar. Questions of efficiency inevitably arise. Incongruities among goals, impersonal attitudes and evaluative criteria must surely be present to weaken the organization's effectiveness. Coordinating different parts of the organization is as difficult as with any corporation. The choice of an integration or differentiation principle of organizing must be made. Control may be more difficult because of less emphasis on the money calculus.

The new marketing technology in social marketing, as represented by the theory of consumer behavior and structural models, is just-as-applicable, at least in some cases. They are being used in family planning in Kenya, for example. True enough, when the client receives an intangible item he probably has greater difficulty conceptualizing it than he would a tangible product. This, however, is true of any service marketed by either a non-profit or profit organization.

We are confident that it would be a valuable experience for marketers to concern themselves with social marketing projects. It would increase the generality of marketing concepts and offer new ideas. Such attempts should be approached with some caution, however. The track record of those engaged in marketing is not a scintillating one. First, as we have attempted to show in the latter chapters of the book, they have not been terribly effective in relating marketing concepts to the more general corporate-policy kinds of problems. We suspect that many diversification mistakes have been substantially failures in the marketing aspects.

Second, they have been unsuccessful in introducing sophisticated market research techniques into company practice. From the marketing literature one would be led to believe that these in large measure constitute the body of marketing knowledge.

❐

10

Marketing Organisation and Control

Organisation is the "process of determining what must be done if a given aim is to be achieved; dividing the necessary activities into segments small enough to be performed by one person; and providing means of coordination, so that there is no wasted effort and the members of the organisation do not get in each other's way". However, from the managerial stand-point, organisation may be regarded "as the establishment of authority relationships, with provisions for structural co-ordination both vertically and horizontally between positions to which have been assigned specialised tasks required for the achievement of enterprise objectives". These sets of relationships existing amongst members of the organisation performing different functions is referred to as organisation structure. The different activities performed by different members brought together under the leadership of one person by a conscious managerial exercise is designated as department.

Based on the above premise, organising for marketing may be defined as determining the breadth of activities comprising the marketing function, grouping them into sub-functions, establishing authority relationships, and providing for an appropriate mechanism for integrating these activities aimed at achieving marketing objectives. The set of relationships amongst marketing personnel may be referred to as marketing organisation structure and grouping of their activities under the leadership of a marketing manager may be designated as marketing department.

The organisational relationships amongst people manning the marketing department may be broadly classified into two types, namely, formal and informal. Formal relationship is one which is consciously brought about between two individuals working in the organisation. It is a planned relationship and emerges out of the structured lines of communication. Informal relationship, on the other hand, is an unplanned and unintended relationship. It is not consciously brought about but develops when people working in the organisation cut across the formal lines of communication to communicate informally with people placed at other levels and establish a personal relationship not intended and planned in the formal organisation structure. The relationship, therefore, remains structureless. It emerges out of the behaviour of members of the formal organisation at the personal level who know each other well enough to exchange relevant information in organisational pursuits.

In the marketing department, all persons manning different positions and performing different functions have both formal and informal inter-relationships. However, intermediaries composing the company's distribution channel do not have any formal organisational relationship as they do not form part of the marketing organisation in terms of its definition. Nonetheless, the current managerial thinking in the area of marketing favours integration of intermediaries in the organisational structure without any formal relationship.

In the marketing department, the formal relationship, may be classified into four types, namely, line, direct or vertical, lateral or horizontal, functional and staff.

The line, direct or vertical relationship emerges with the flow of authority from its source downward to the lowest level. It exists between a senior, say marketing manager, and his subordinate, say, sales executive, wherein the senior gives valid orders to the subordinate so as to stimulate action.

The lateral or horizontal relationship may exist among individuals at the same level of responsibility. It is called horizontal because the structural lines establishing it happen to be horizontal.

The functional relationship between two individuals is based on functional specialisation and expertise. It emerges when one renders to the other some specialised service, for instance, the personnel department helps marketing departemnt in the recruitment of salesmen.

The staff relationship emerges when a manager extends his personality by appointing an assistant. It is termed 'staff because the assistant deals only with the manager whose personality he extends and has no direct relationship whatsoever with anybody else in the organisation. He advises and helps his superior in the performance of his managerial duties.

NEED FOR A MARKETING ORGANISATION

Notwithstanding the willingness of individuals to undertake marketing responsibilities and establish organisational relationships, they need to be brought together to form an organisation. The need for a marketing organisation in a company arises on account of the following reasons:

1. Lack of spontaneity on the part of these individuals to undertake specific responsibilities, and inability of these individuals to come together and establish mutual relationships by themselves cause the need for organisation. These people need to be brought together, woven into relationships, and assigned responsibilities and positions.
2. The need may also arise out of the necessity to impart a sense of orderliness and purpose to the activities of these individuals.
3. The reason may also be traced to the nature of the organisational job that these willing individuals are called upon to perform. Marketing function requires these indviduals to deal more with intangibles, like ideas, innovations and behavioural aspects with reference to consumers, competitors, intermediaries. Unless they are properly organised it is difficult to productively channelise them and bring order and system in the working.

4. The personality characteristics of and personal purposes of these individuals are often at variance with the job demands and organisational goals. These variances do not get reconciled by themselves; it requires deliberate organisational action.

GOALS OF THE MARKETING ORGANIZATION

The modern view is that an organization is a group of people brought together to participate in a common effort to accomplish certain goals. The basic goals of a company, they indicate to a large extent what the company wants to be, since they tend to override and permeate the rest of its administration. Certain goals has particularly important implications for the marketing organization. The seven goals listed here may have considerable impact on the marketing organization in a firm:

1. **Desired Financial Results.** Traditionally, business are intended to be economic institutions. Generally, the organizers anticipate that a company's operations will generate profits. Once operations are under way, profits must be forthcoming on a sufficiently regular basis to permit the company's continued survival. The company's profit goal is of great importance to the marketing organization. It affects both the amount of sales volume targeted and the level of cost allowed. Also important is the time allowed for reaching a target profit goal, as this affects management's willingness or unwillingness to trade current profit for potentially greater future profits.

2. **Disposition toward Change.** A company's attitude toward change largely determines the types of employees who are attracted to it and the scheme by which they are welded into an organizational framework. Clearly, firms operating under the marketing concept have opted in favour of emphasizing change rather than stability. They recogzine the need for making continual adjustments in operations and organizational structure when adapting to changing market requirements and competitive conditions.

3. **Desired Place in the Industry.** A company defines its desired place in the industry along several dimensions : size of operation, major function (manufacturing, wholesaling, retailing, etc.), quality and price levels for its products, and specialization or diversification of its acitvities. Different decisions on these matters are reflected in different marketing organizations. For instance, a company that strives to have the largest market share in the industry requires a larger and more sophisticated marketing organization than does one that aims to have the highest quality products.

4. **Competitive Posture.** A company's posture with respect to its competition has direct implications for the marketing organization, such as whether or not it will incorporate features permitting aggressive selling and advertising. A firm choosing to take leadership in a competitive market requires a stronger marketing organization than does a "follower" firm.

5. **Desired Customer Service Image.** There is a world of difference between a company seeking long-run customer satisfaction and one emphasizing quick "one-time" sales. This fact of a company's image is important to all departments producing, selling, and servicing the product line.

6. **Social Philosophy.** The basic goals controlling a company's relationship with the community and governmental units affect the operations of all departments and, most certainly, the marketing department. Thus, a firm with strong concern for the environment emphasizes different elements in its marketing organization than does one with only short-term profit goals.

7. **Relationship with Suppliers.** The nature of a company's desired relationships with its suppliers has indirect but important implications for the marketing organization, since

these relationships affect product quality, availability of repair and replacement parts, pricing practices, and the like.

PRINCIPLES OF MARKETING ORGANISATION

In developing a consumer-oriented marketing organisation structure, management should follow some of the basic principles. These are also the tests against which an organisation sturcture can be evaluated in terms of its ability to implement the marketing concept. These principles include the following:

1. **Division of Work and Functional Definition.** The activities of the marketing department would be so divided and grouped that they contribute most effectively to the attainment of the marketing objectives. Grouping of similar activities has a synergic effect in the departmental working. Also, the content of every position and the department within it should be clearly defined in terms of activities expected, authority delegation, and authority relationships involved within it on the one hand and between it and other positions on the other.
2. **Organisational Orientation.** The first and foremost principle in structuring the marketing organisation is its market orientation. Usually, organisational structures are developed from the top. But the marketing organisation structure should be built from below and according to the needs of the market. It should be structured on the premise that it is an instrument of solving consumer problems. For example, if consumers have problems in using and maintaining product (s) owing to its complexity, the whole marketing organisation should be based on the product right from the salesmen to the top level. The crux of the matter is that the structuring should reflect arrangements to sovle consumer problems in which are embedded profit possibilities.
3. **Information Flows.** The next important principle that should govern organisational structuring is that the

information should become from specific to general as it flows upwards the line and from general to specific as it flows downwards the line. Besides, the pattern of information should be compatible with the type of decisions taken at different decision points in the organisation. The information capsule, therefore, should feed adequate and needed information.

4. **Line and Staff Relationships.** As a corollary of the preceding principles, the next principle or organisational structuring is the clear definition of the line and staff relationships among people working in the organisation. A clear enunciation of the line and staff relationship, for example, between selling and marketing research, would help foster working harmony between the two. The marketing research men would know the limitations of their position which involves assisting, advising, and informing the selling personnel about the market behaviour. This principle may be effectively applied by formulating appropriate position descriptions which may spell out such relationships.
5. **Authority Principles.** Authority principles refer to those rules which govern the inter-personal relationship with authority as the reference point among people working in any organisation. In a way these are universal principles and, therefore, applicable to a marketing organisation. Some of the important and relevant authority principles which should govern organisational structuring include the following:

   (i) Scalar Principle. The authority must rest somewhere in the organisation, for example, the marketing manager, and from where a clear line must emerge leading to every subordinate position.

   (ii) Principle of Responsibility. The responsibility of the subordinate to his superior for authority received by delegation is absolute, and no superior can escape responsibility for the authorised activities of his subordinates.

(iii) ***Principle of Parity of Authority and Responsibility.*** The authority delegated to a subordinate should be commensurate with the responsibility entrusted so that it may be discharged properly. The application of this principle in marketing, however, creates some difficulties because of the nature of marketing job. For example, the Sales Manager has the responsibility to sell and achieve a certain predetermined target but he has no authority over the activities of persons managing marketing research, product planning, and pricing which considerably impinge on his job and effectiveness. Such difficulty is overcome by encouraging sales manager's interaction with these persons either through formal media of co-ordination or informal lines of communication.

(iv) ***Principle of Unity of Command.*** A subordinate should receive command for action from only one superior, these should not be dual subordination entailing receipt of command from two superiors. For example, a salesman should not receive orders for action from both the product manager and the pricing manager. Dual subordination leads to low employee morale and ineffectiveness.

(v) ***Authority Level Principle.*** At some level in the department authority should exist for making relevant decisions; only those decisions should be referred upward in the hierarchy which cannot be made at a given level. This requires determination of appropriate decision points in the organisation.

6. **Informal Relations.** While structuring the organisation, marketing management should also provide room for the growth of informal relations called 'grapevine' or network of alliances or spheres of influence among the people

working in the department. It helps passage of information at different organisational echelons relevant from the decision-making viewpoint and which otherwise cannot be made available through formal lines of communication. It also helps in building goodwill and team spirit essential for effective marketing. When informal relations abound and gradually get inbuilt, management should always think of formalising them in some way in so far as these augment the efficiency and effectiveness of management. Till it is done care should always be exercised to see that informal relations do not vitiate the formal structure.

7. **Span of Control Principle.** Also referred to as the span of management, the principle of span of control refers to the rule that there is a limit to the number of subordinates that should report to a manager. Described differently it entails that a manager should not control an unduly large number of subordinates to be controlled because it depends on a number of factors like training, level of subordinates, delegation of authority, clarity of plans and policies, the degree to which objective standards can be and are being applied, effectiveness of communication techniques used, nature of duties—routine or varied—and the complexities of the decisions being made.

8. **Principle of Balance.** This principle holds that the various parts of the organisation should be in balance and no function should receive a disproportionate emphasis. Also, there should be balance between short span of control and short chain of command, between centralisation and decentralisation and between line and staff relationships.

9. **Flexibility and Continuity.** The organisational structure should ensure flexibility and continuity. Flexibility refers to the capacity of an organisation to respond to environmental changes. Continuty refers to the perpetuation of the organisation itself. Flexibility in an organisation is indicated in procedures which are easy to understand, follow, and

change; in managerial proneness to plan and accept change; and in not too firm departmental lines which may breed inability to meet environmental challenges. Continuity in an organisation is indicated by the number of positions open for people to occupy with the passage of time and building up of experience. It provides for people to rise in the organisational echelons, and also provides for their (people's) organisational growth. The principle entails provision for structural innovations in the organisation to keep it attuned to market dynamism.

BASIS TO BUILT MARKETING ORGANISATION

The organisational structure of a marketing department establishes the authority relationship among marketing personnel and species who is responsible for making certain decisions and performing certain activities.

A large compnay operating under the marketing concept must have some formal organisational structure. "Companies may have the will and the desire to serve the customer, but all too often they are indequately organised to do so. Proper organisation must result in a total integration and coordination of all the factors that can influence the final sales." In other words there must be total integration and coordination of all corporate functions (marketing, research and development, manufacturing, financial etc.) into a single operating system directed toward achieving company goals and at the same time, effectively serving the market and the changing wants and desires". Peter Druker observes, "organisation is not an end in itself, but a means to the end of business performance and business results. Organisation structure is an indispensable means and a wrong structure will seriously impair business performance and may even destroy it. The structure must be so designed as to make it possible to attain the business objectives even five, ten, and fifteen years hence."

Organizing a marketing unit involves dividing the work into specific activities and delegating responsibility and authority to perform these activities to persons in various positions, such as sales manager, research manager and advertising manager. This internal structure provides the vehicle for directing marketing activities.

The organization of the marketing unit may be on the basis of the functions, products, regions, types of customers, or a combination of these. Which of these types will be adopted will depend upon the company objectives, managements philosophy of organization, manufacturer's views of marketing, the importance of different marketing tools, the types and numbers of products, the character of competition, the characteristics and needs of customers in the target market etc.

I. Functional Organisation. Under this type, the work of marketing department is divided according to functions, such as product development, marketing research, sales promotion, advertising, distribution and customer relations. The personnel incharge of these departments report directly to the top level marketing executive. This type is based upon the principle that "more varied skills are needed to handle different marketing functions effectively than to manage different products or regions or customers." This type is the simplest and most commonly used in small business house with centralized marketing operations. It may also be used in a larger centralized company in which products and types of customers are not many or diverse.

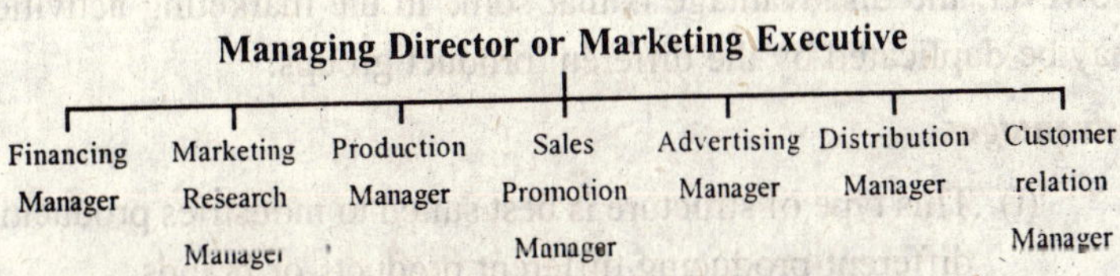

Function Oriented Organisation Structure

Advantages

(i) As because the marketing function is divided into various subfunctions and each subfunction is performed by and undersupervision of an efficient manager, various activities are carried on efficiently.

(ii) There is elasticity in the the organisation. The sub-activities may further be divided with the increase in size of the organisation.

Disadvantages

(i) This type of organisation is suitable only for small enterprises. As the firm grows in size, this types of structure will lose its importance.

(ii) Sub-division of marketing function is also a difficult task. Some activities are of such a nature that they cannot be associated with one type of subfunction or the other. The result is that each activities are performed by more than one departments and this duplication of work creates the problem of responsibility.

II. Product Organization. Under this type, a business that produces different products organizes its marketing unit according to product group or brands. The product manager, in charge, takes full responsibility for marketing the product. He takes and executes decisions on matters like advertising and sales promotion, in consultation with the advertising, sales promotion, marketing research and publications manager. This type gives a firm the flexibility to develop special marketing mixes for different products. For example, it can hire specialists in the marketing of specific types of productions. However, the disadvantage is that some in the marketing activities may be duplicated by the different product groups.

Advantages

(i) This type of structure is best suited to industries producing different producing different products or brands.

(ii) Every department can be controlled efficiently by the department incharge.

(iii) The performance of different departments may be evaluated and compared.

(iv) It stresses on specialisation and helps in increasing the efficiency of the personnel.

Difficulties of the Prdouct Structure

(i) The product manager is sometimes confused with as to be familiar with different jobs. His own background may be too limited to enable him to take the total marketing approach.

(ii) Conflicts may even develop with other line of activities.

(iii) It is suitable only for medium sized industries producing different products or different brand of a product.

III. Market Oriented Marketing Organization. This type of structure is used by big companies who serve large number of customers spread over very lare territory. The structure is based on regional basis duties and specific areas are assigned to different persons. The total area may be divided into four basic regions or in more division for the sales points of view.

Each region is subdivided under the Sales Supervisor. Their numbers depend upon the characteristics and requirements of the particular region. Each supervisor is given the number of salesmen who are under his direct control. In this way the market is fragmented into sales territories which may be a district, division or region. This type of structure has the greatest advantage that the regional manager and his staff become experts for the allotted regions as regards the customers. They become careful of the competitions that mark that area and so they act accordingly.

Advantages

(a) This types of structure is suitable for big concerns having their sales-net throughout the country.

(b) There is much elasticity under this structure. As the size of business grows, more territorial sub-divisions may be had. it facilitates better control.

(c) It enjoys all the advantages of functional type organisation.

(d) The organisation regularly is in touch with the customers. It comes to know the changing habits, fashion and needs of the customers of every region and therefore can maket necessary change in its product within a short span of time.

(f) Responsibility can be fixed easily for any lapse.

Disadvantages

(a) it is not fit for small organisations, as it is much expensive.

(b) Each territorial division has its separate entity for marketing the product in that area. The organisational policies for each region are different into account the nature of customers of the area. It is therefore, very difficult to formulate or follow an integrated policy for all the regions.

IV. Organizing by Types of Customers. Under this type, the organization is done on the basis of the types of customers such as large retail stores, wholesalers and institutions. In this type, the marketing manager for each customer group reports to the marketing executive. The marketing manager for each group is responsible for most marketing activities for that specific group. Usually, the managers of various marketing functions help to direct the activities required for marketing products to a specific customers group. This type or organization is suitable for a firm that has several group of customers whose needs and problems are different.

Advantages

(a) Under this type of organisation, full attention can be paid to each class of customers and their problems can be well understood by the organisation.

(b) The organisation comes is contact with the customers regularly. It then becomes easier to the organisation to estimate their demands and satisfy them.

Disadvantages

Although customer satisfaction is the main aim of the structure but, it is suitable in those organisations only where the nature of customers is different.

V. Using Combined Bases for Organizing. Under this, the function and product type of structure is combined with the territorial type. Such type of organisations usually have functional managers of sales, marketing services, and marketing information; product managers of food, chemicals, pharmaceuticals, toileteries, etc and the market managers of consumer, agricultural and industrial products.

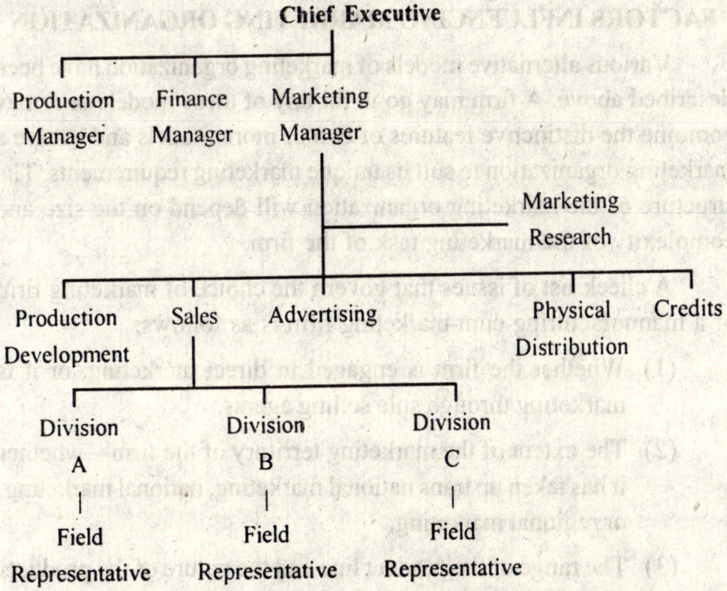

Combined form of Organisation

Suitability of the Organisation Structure

We have discussed above the four basic concepts of marketing organisation structure and the combined form of organisation structure. Which one is suitable to a concern, through depends very much on the nature of the business and of its customers, yet we may conclude that:

(a) The customer oriented organisation structure is suited best to the organisations having different types of customers and where different marketing policies are followed for different class of customers.

(b) The product or the market type organisation structure is suitable for a big concern having its sales-net throughout the country because due attention is paid under these two structures on each product and in all the territories.

(c) The functional type organisation structure is suitable for small enterprises which products only one type of product.

FACTORS INFLUENCING MARKETING ORGANIZATION

Various alternative models of marketing organization have been described above. A firm may go in for any of these models or it may combine the distinctive features of two or more models and evolve a marketing organization to suit its unique marketing requirements. The structure of the marketing organization will depend on the size and complexity of the marketing task of the firm.

A check list of issues that govern the choice of marketing firm or a mannufacturing-cum-marketing firm is as follows:

(1) Whether the firm is engaged in direct marketing, or it is marketing through sole selling agents.

(2) The extent of the marketing territory of the firm—whether it has taken up trans national marketing, national marketing, or regional marketing.

(3) The range of the product line and the nature of the products of the firm

(4) The extent of customer service the firm opts to provide

(5) The size of the physical distribution job—transportation, field warehousing, etc., that the firm may have to undertake.

After deciding the organization model based on the above mentioned issues, further decisions concerning the span of control, inter relationships of departments, delegation, the staff strength needed at each level, etc., have to be made.

It is evident that there is no such thing as the typical marketing organization. It will vary from firm to firm, depending on the requirements already explained.

While structuring and developing a marketing organization, a proper work relationship between the line functions and the staff functions have to be ensured. In any organization line and staff conflicts may occur. The source of friction and the consequent inefficiency can be eliminated only by proper and meaningful integration of the two. The test of all good organization is whether there is an effective and co-operative relationship between the various divisions/ departments.

The levels in the organization and the span of control of each executive position must be carefully planned and built in. The modern trend in organization structuring is to avoid too many levels. If there are too many levels, the information flow gets delayed, and results in ineffective communication, dilution of responsibility and poor control.

The organization should also provide for the correct co-ordination among the various departments. Co-ordination should become a built in factor in the marketing organization.

The marketing organization has to provide for effective co-ordination among the various marketing departments of the firm like production, finance, personnel, corporate planning, etc., on the other.

Developing clear job specification in respect of each executive position in the marketing organization is an integral part of organization creation. Clear job specification helps remove ambiguities about functions and provides role clarity. It also reduces friction within the organization. Job specifications describe the basic function of the position, to whom the incumbent will report, his tasks/responsibilities, the authority delegated to him and the financial powers assigned to him.

We give below a brief description of the tasks which the chief marketing executive of any large sized firm has to undertake:

(1) The chief marketing executive will be broadly responsibile for setting marketing objectives.

(2) Marketing planning and development of marketing strategics.

(3) Developing marketing budgets

(4) Determining policies, relating to products, pricing, distribution and promotion

(5) Manpower planning for the marketing division integration of all marketing activities

(6) Integration of the marketing function with other functions of the firm.

It is evident that the day-to-day administration of the marketing activities is not the major responsibility of the chief marketing executive. His main role is in planning, execution and control of the marketing programmes and marketing activities. He heads the marketing organization and sets and pace of growth of the firm. Again, his concern should be more with men than with materials. He has to be a successful team leader and an efficient motivator. He also has to ensure that his men and the systems he has introduced are together in a position to take advantage of the marketing opportunities that come in the way of his firm. He must also be prepared to attempt reshuffling of the marketing organization, if the changing marketing environment warrants such a change.

SIZE OF MARKETING ORGANISATION

Some of the important factors described below largely determine the size of the marketing organisation in a company:

A. **Distribution Channel.** The size of the marketing organisation in a company depends on the type of distribution channel selected by it. When a company opts for an indirect channel it sells through intermediaries and dispenses with its own sales force. But when it opts for a direct channel it employs its own sales force. The size of the organisation would be larger when it sells direct relative to one when it sells indirect. For example, in "the cotton textile companies selling through sole selling agents (now disallowed), the size of the marketing department has found to be smaller because the selling responsibility is completely undertaken by them.

B. **Market.** The size of the market and its distance from the manufacturing site also determine the size of the marketing organisation. When the market is widely dispersed and manufacturing activity is centralised, then the need for human resources to manage the different marketing activities would be greater, making the organisation larger in size unless the marketing tasks are assigned to external agencies like intermediaries, advertisies, etc.

C. **Product-line.** When the product-line of a company is diversified it requires more human resources to handle it both at the headquarters and in the field. The high degree of product divergence futher aggravates the need for human resources. As such, the size of the marketing department would be larger when the product-line is diversified and there is high degree of product divergence.

D. **Functional Breadth.** The functional breadth of marketing refers to the number of functions integrated under the marketing organisation. Larger the number of functions integrated, larger may be the size of the marketing unless some functions are assigned to external agencies. Usually a company integrates those functions under marketing which its management finds relevant to carry out the marketing task. However, it also depends on the managerial orientation of the company.

ORGANISATIONAL PURSUITS

Broadly speaking, the pursuit of a marketing organisation in any company is to sub-serve the enterprise purposes—the purposes for whose achievement the whole business enterprise is geared. However, in terms of specifies two basic objectives may be identified, namely attaining profitable sale and delivering consumer staisfying value satisfactions. It is for achieving these objectives that all human activity in the marketing department is geared, all idea generation and innovation are promoted, and all intra-and extra departmental operations are integrated. Nonetheless, marketing operations are also organised to achieve other limited purposes, for example, attaining percentage market share, entering a market segment, launching a new product, strengthening the field team to meet competition, etc. The achievement of these limited purposes spanning over a known time horizon influence the determination of tasks, and their grouping and assignment to people. It also involves establishing new relationships and modifying the old ones.

Besides the ones discussed above, given here are a new more important organisational pursuits:

1. **To Ensure Functional Performance.** Marketing being a component of the functional-mix of business, it is the primary pursuit of every marketing department to ensure that it functions—and functions well. It means that all individuals assigned with specific marketing responsibilities discharge them to the best of their abilities. It also means that different marketing functions get activated at the schedule time and in the specified manner so that all functions synchronise and impart maximum total impact on the market.
2. **To Define Relationships.** One of the important organisational pursuits in relation to marketing is to clearly spell out both the vertical and the horizontal relationships amongst people. A clear definition of these relationships goes a long way in preventing conflicts arising out of the violation of lines of authority. It ensures proper direction of the marketing effort and secures subordinates confirmation to these directions.
3. **To Achieve Co-ordination or Balance.** Organisational co-ordination or balance refers to synchronisation in a pre-determined manner of all marketing functions in terms of time and content. It may be achieved by scheduling and activisation through some system. It also refers to co-ordination between the personal purposes of individuals and the organisational goals. Co-ordination may be indicated in terms of job satisfaction and high morale, and may be achieved by goal congruence induced through appropriate motivational inputs and revision of organisational goals.
4. **To Promote Ideas and Innovations.** A marketing organisation should be a living organisation. It should promote new ideas and organisations. It is possible when persons manning the department are not tied down by the sheet formalism of authority lines. They should be allowed to interact amongst themselves with relative ease to generate new ideas and crystalise them. This purpose is all the more

relevant to the marketing department because the success or failure or marketing activities hinges on its ability to innovate and to offer to consumers some distinct value satisfactions in different and unconventional ways.

5. **To Optimise Use of Managerial Time and Effort.** One of the important organisational pursuits is to optimise the use of managerial time and effort. This can be ensured by relieving executives from the non-essential tasks and thereby allowing them to concentrate on essential tasks. This becomes possible when managers manage by exception.

ORGANISATIONAL PROBLEMS

To a very large extent an organisational design based on the principles described above ensures smooth departmental working. Notwithstanding, marketing management faces some typical problems which need attention and resolution. These problems may be broadly classified into two classes—one class of problems are rooted in implementing the marketing concept and the other class of problems are rooted in organisational relationships. These are described below:

(I) Problems Rooted in Implementing the Marketing Concept

One set of organisational problems in marketing arises when management attempts to implement the marketing concept and restructure the organisation. These problems are of particular relevance in India because many companies are slowly and streadily imbibing this concept. Some of these problems include the following:

(a) **Increased Functional Breadth and Charge of Empire Building**. The implementation of the marketing concept entails shifting of certain functions like marketing research, product planning, and pricing, etc. from their traditional slots to the new marketing department. Their integration under the marketing departments creates problems at the corporate level. The heads of those departments from which these functions are shifted feel a sense of loss and accuse the marketing manager of "building an empire". They go slow and ineffective and attribute it to this loss. It also breeds organisational jealousy, inter-personal problems and conflict among departmental heads. The major problem areas include marketing, manufacturing and finance.

(b) **Promotion from Within.** The implementationn of the marketing concept entails creation of a new position of marketing manager. This position becomes the bone of contention in the organisation. The sales manager, hitherto incharge of the company's entire selling operations—the chief line executive, naturally stakes his claim. But it may not be always possible for management to promote him to this new job. It may be so because selling develops a typical push attitude not always suitable for the marketing manager's position which requires a person to be sensitive to market and consumers problems. The conditioned reflexes of the sales manager may not make him a suitable incumbent for the new job.

When the sales manager is not promoted to the new job it creates organisational problems. In such a situation either the sales manager leaves the organisation or resigns to his 'demotion', gets frustrated, and thus adversely infacts the whole organisation. If the leaves, the problems is to find a suitable new incumbent and aslo to sustain the morale of other subordinates working in the sales department. But if he stays on, the problem is to manage him, make him endure and overcome the status loss, and motivate him to still contribute to the company.

(II) Problems in Organisational Relationships

Besides the problems described above, a marketing organisation also faces problems which grow out of organisational relationship. In fact, these problems are universal in the sense that these may be found to exist in all types of departments. A large number of these may relate to violation or avoidance of the authority principles. But some of them are indeed typical and emerge on account of growth. These problems are described below:

(a) **Problem of Delegation.** As the organisation grows, the span of control also widens. It makes managers to devote disproportionate time and energy to the operational aspects of their jobs, and the planning and co-ordination tasks unduly suffer. This necessitates delegation of managerial authority to subordinates. Delegation of authority means transfer of authority to subordinates by superior without escaping responsibility for the job performance. When delegation of authority comes in the natural way there is no problem. But problem arises when the marketing manager or other exectutive refuses to delegate, has no confidence in the ability of subordinates to assume authority, and considers his skills indispensable for the job, or alternatively, when subordinates are not willing, lack training or are incapable of assuming authority. The need for delegation in marketing is relatively more pronounced because the marketing executive must have sufficient time to think, plan and formulate strategies so as to innovate, be different, and counter-balance competitive manoeuvres.

(b) **Promoting Innovation and Creativity.** Another problem is to ensure that the organisation continues to create and innovate. But creativity and innovation usually disturb order; they are prone to flourish in the violation and avoidance of rules, procedures, and formal lines of communication, than in their observance and adherence. The managerial problem is to strike a balance between the two. The problem is to promote innovation and creativity and also save the organisation from the dangers of disorder.

(c) **Centralisation-decentralisation Dichotomy.** As the organisation grows and expands, it gets functionalised and based on product, geography and customer. In such a situation the problem arises as how much authority should be transferred at the lower levels and how much should be retained at the top and in respect of which functions. In the organisation charts given in the preceding pages, we see that certain staff functions are retained at the top whereas others are not. The problem regarding degree and areas of centralisation and decentralisation of authority is a great problem and is repugnant to the marketing concept because it requires that as for as possible decisions should be taken nearer the markets. But then excessive decentralisation too create problems of co-ordination and control. The problem is to strike a balance between the two. For this purpose usually staff activities are centralised and line activities decnetralised.

TECHNIQUES AND STEPS OF MARKETING CONTROL

Marketing control is a crucial part of the marketing job. It is the tool for ensuring that the marketing programmes and activities of the firm always get directed towards the marketing objective of the firm. Marketing control provides the means of testing whether the desired goals and results are actually being achieved or not. It is an ongoing monitoring of the marketing activity in all its aspects. Inherent in the process is the assumption that the desired results are known beforehand. And knowledge of the desired results in advance, involves planning. In this sense, planning and control are closely interrelated. In fact, "Planning-Happening—Evaluating-Controlling" are the four inter-related phases of the marketing job.

Marketing control involves gathering information on marketing performance and comparing the achieved performance against planned or budgeted performance, using predetermined stardard and yardsticks. It provides feed back; it regulates; and it exercises a restraining influence or a redirecting influence. It ensures that the marketing activities does not derail or go off the track; it act as a radar system for marketing, recording and segnalling the ups and downs and deviations in the marketing performance; it also provides the required clues for the timely correction of deviations. In a dynamic environment, marketing programmes cannot be implemented effectively without continuous controlling and corrective adjustments. Marketing control takes care of this requirement. It paves the way for the maximisation of profitability and the maximisation of productivity of all the marketing activities.

1. Budgetary Control. Budgetary control is yet another mrketing control device. It is applied to every function of the business including marketing. Budgeting in the area of marketing is usually an elaborate exercise, involving sales forcasting, sales budget, sales expense budgeting and profit planning.

Budgetary control, essentially involves preparation of control statements at specified intervals of time, showing the budgeted figures, the achieved figures and the variances. Review and remedial action is the other part of budgetary control. In marketing, sales volume, sales expenses and profits are the main aspects to be controlled through the budgetary control device.

Budgetary control presupposes awareness of costs and profits associated with each product/territory/customer group. It involves the correct or near-correct allocation of the total marketing effort in financial terms to each individual product, individual marketing function and individual marketing territory. The analysis should also be : By product, by territory, by function.

Analysis done on the above basis would reveal areas of variances and fluctuations. If the variances are wide, the concerned marketing activity must be carefully monitored and controlled in the remaining period.

2. Ratio Analysis. In addition to the budget-actual-variance analysis described above and the standard costing comparison described earlier, most firms use ratio analysis also as a control device in markcting as well as other areas. As far as marketing is concerned, ratio analysis seeks to measure the effectiveness and profitability of the various marketing fucntions and activities by the use of certain ratios. Whereas budgetary control reveals absolute figures, ratio analysis focuses attention on relative figures. Some of the important ratios used in marketing control are:

A. Return on investment (ROI). It is the ratio of net profit to capital employed.

B. Return on net worth (RONW). It is the ratio of net profit to net worth.

C. Net profit to sales ratio

D. Sales to capital employed ratio

E. Gross profit to sales ratio

F. Turnover to working capital ratio

G. Inventory to turnover ratio

H. Turnover to distribution expenses ratio

I. Turnover to promotion expenses ratio

J. Turnover to bad debts ratio.

3. Market Share Analysis. Market share analysis is another useful marketing control tool. However, if it is not handled properly and interpreted correctly, it can throw up highly misleading information. It becomes an effective control tool only when it meets the following pre-conditions—it is accurately measured; it is measured both at macro and micro levels; the comparisons to targeted and actual market shares are also made both at macro and micro levels; the comparisons are made over reasonably long spells of time.

Before a firm attempts a market share-based evaluation and control it must have clarity on whether it is consiously seeking a definite share of the market. It is implied in any market share evaluation that the marketing performance will be assessed based on the market share. It is also implied that a definite minimum share of the market is the real aim of the firm. Otherwise, the evaluation becomes a purely theoretical exercise and loses its control potential.

Market share analysis can be utilised for evaluating the performance of a firm; for setting targets for the firm and for developing long-term sales forecasts of the firm.

Market share has to be measured on rational grounds. Comparisons may be made with the most efficient firms in the industry, or the industry leader, or a group of growing firms. Comparisons can also be made against industry-average performance.

Whatever be the criteria of comparison, the general economic conditions which have a bearing on the industry's performance have to be given the weightage. Quite often, the market share of a firm may go up substantially without any effort on the part of its marketing department. The increase may be due to environmental factors. Unless these dimensions are understood in the proper perspective, market share analysis will give the wrong interpretation. So it is essential to use market share analysis in an intelligent and objective manner. It is also essential to understand one's product/market boundaries correctly to make market share analysis purposeful. Share can be worked out at product subcategory level, product category level, national level and regional level. Each measurement has its own use and implications.

4. Credit Control. Business firms are often forced to extend credit to increase sales. In some business, the entire sales takes place on credit, cash sales being negligible. In certain businesses, hire purchase and instalment payments are the normal practices. Even in those cases where the sales to consumers are on a cash basis, credit is extended to the distribution channels. It is assential for any business firm to evolve a clear policy on credit and exercise proper control on it.

5. Marketing Information for Marketing Control. Timely and relevant marketing information facilitates the timely identification of variances between targets and achievements in respect of sales volume, market coverage and market share. It also throws light on market standing, advertising and personal selling effectiveness and channel and physical distribution effectiveness.

While using marketing information for marketing control, it is however essential that in the first place, control data, planning data and general purpose statistics are properly distinguished for the one another out of the various marketing information outputs. Only then can marketing information be used as an effective control too. The following are samples of marketing information, useful for control purposes.

(a) Information on marketing goals

(b) Information on actual marketing performance

(c) Information on emerging opportunities

(d) Information on impending threats.

At times, essential control information is left out and the available information is inadequate for control; at times, the information lacks clarity or, there is a mix up of vital information and trivial information; in some other cases the information is not related properly—it is disjointed; in some cases the information is not timely for effective control. The firm should avoid these pitfalls if MIS has to become the support for control.

By instituting proper procedures for the information flow and by pinpointing the specific role of MIS in the matter of control, the problems described above can be overcome. The firm must appreciate that the control system is essentially an information system or, more precisely, a cybernetics system, consisting of information flows and mechanisms for corrective action.

6. Contribution Margin Analysis. We often come across instances where a particular product or customer does not bring in any net profit to the firm, but still makes a valuable contribution by carrying a significant part of the overheads. It is unwise to summarily drop such products or customers on the ground that they do not bring in any net profit. At the same time, they cannot be carried blindly. The firm should know whether these products and customers absorb at least a part of the firm's overheads and if so, to what extent. The financial technique that comes to the rescue of the marketing in this respect is called contribution margin analysis. It is partly a pricing technique and partly a marketing control technique.

To find out the contribution margin of a particular product, the cost incurred as a direct result of the particular product must be found first. In other words, those costs which could have been avoided if the particular product had been discontinued, must be found. Such cost are the escapable costs. The other costs are non-escapable cost or joint costs. Joint costs must be allocated to those products that are profitable and therefore in a position to absorb these costs. It must be examined whether the unprofitable product is in a position to absorb at least the escapable costs and produce a slight surplus. By this analysis, we can find out if a particular product is at least bringing in a little more revenue than the escapable costs, even though it may not be contributing to profits. In other words, the products, though unable to bear its share of the joint costs in full measure, is able to meet the escapable costs in full measure and partly the joint costs. But for this product carrying the joint costs, at least partially, these costs would have been added to the overheads of the other products, thereby making them less profitable. The firm should make such a contribution analysis and then decide whether the 'not so profitable products and customers' should be dropped or continued.

7. Marketing Costs Analysis. Marketing cost analysis is another important tool or technique of marketing control. In recent years, business firms all over the world have experienced steep escalations in their marketing and distribution costs. They have found, to their dismay, that increased sales do not necessarily bring them increased porofits. Containing marketing and distribution costs has become an imperative for optimising profits.

The marketing chief of any firm has to give maximum attention to marketing cost control. And if he has to effectively control the marketing costs, he has to comprehend the components of the marketing costs and the methods available for their control. He must have an effective system to track down. He must also analyse them systematically. For, without systematic analysis of the marketing costs, it will not be possible to control these costs, and without such costs control, marketing control is meaningless. Today, in most firms, marketing cost analysis has become a prominent marketing control technique.

8. Marketing Audit. Marketing audit is a continuous, systematic and objective study of the total marketing efficiency of the firm. It critically evaluate the marketing policies and marketing activities of the firm, the measures the extent and direction of its growth. Marketing audit is concerned with the long-term business interests and challenges of the firm rather than short-term achievements.

No firm can ever take the stand that everything is fine with its marketing. It is essential for the firm to assess whether the marketing policies, programmes, systems and methods established in the past are now valid and would be effective for the future. Marketing audit ensures such assessments.

The strength of marketing audit lies in the fact that while other control techniques aim at a piece meal evaluation of various marketing functions, marketing audit aims at a total evaluation of the entire marketing system and process. It leads to specific plans for improving the marketing efficiency of the firm. It also measures and evaluates the effectiveness of all other marketing control techniques employed by a firm. In this sense, marketing audit can be described as control to controls.

Several fundamental aspects of business are investigated through marketing audit. To tackle these aspects, marketing audit raises some basic questions and seeks to answer them correctly. Some of these questions are:

(i) What business are we in? Do we understand our business correctly?

(ii) What business are we heading for?

(iii) What is the business we should be doing tomorrow?

(iv) What changes do we need in our current direction of growth?

(v) What is our marketing strategy and plan? Are they the right ones? Will they ensure the achievement of the objectives of our business.

(vi) What are the emerging trends in competition and the general business environment?

(vii) Do the marketing activities lend themselves to measurement? Are they reviewed and measured periodically?

We may recall here that these are some of the questions raised and answered at the marketing strategy formulation stage. Marketing audit thus seeks to review even basic assumptions of strategy. From the nature of these questions, it becomes evident that marketing audit as a control technique is different from budgetary control, ratio analysis, etc. While the latter are essentially financial and quantitative techniques, marketing audit has a much wider scope. For the mojor part, marketing audit is qualitative and strategic in character.

9. Marketing Control Through MBO. Management by Objectives, or MBO, is a popular and effective management techniques. MBO can be used as a control techniques in the area of marketing management; it is an area where measurable objectives can be set; the characteristics of the marketing function readily make marketing a fertile ground for the application of MBO. The technique consists of three main steps : (i) fixing of objectives in each of the important areas of business; (ii) measuring performance against such pre-determined objectives, and (iii) managing the business keeping these objectives in focus.

MBO is relevant to marketing control in two ways. Firstly, through MBO, the top management of the firm can use control procedures to monitor the achievement of marketing objectives. Secondly, marketing programmes are the right ones, that the programmes are being implemented in the right way and that the programmes actually take them to the objective they have agreed upon.

Once marketing objectives are set carefully, MBO in marketing is easy, Another equally important step is the ıdentification of Key Results Areas (KRAs). The two in fact are interrelated. The correct sequence is that KRAs are specified first and the objectives are set in each of them. The KRAs of marketing may differ from industry to industry, company to company and manager to manager within a compnay. They may even differ somewhat from year to year.

Marketing control is an integral part of management control. Control, after all, is not peculiar to marketing; it is a part and parcel of the total job.

Before we examine the components of an effective marketing control syste, it would be useful to have a proper understanding of management control systems in general and the place of marketing controls within them.

In designing a management control system the following steps are involved:—

1. Start with the predetermiend objectives.
2. Set clear measures of performance.
3. Measure performance.
4. Decide the parameters of control.
5. Define the level at which different controls are to be active.
6. Develop a monitoring system that would provide the feedback to different levels.
7. Choose the tools and techniques of control.
8. Observe, analyse, interpret and evaluate the variances.
9. Develop a mechanism that can correct existing activity so as to achieve the predetermined norm/objectives.

TYPES OF MARKETING COSTS

Marketing cost in modern large-sized firms are of a kaleidoscopic variety. These are many components to the marketing costs and they vary in their significance, size, measurability and controllability.

Marketing cost can be broadly categorised as follows:

(a) Physical distribution costs.

(b) Inventory cost or cost of holding stocks.

(c) Channel cost or cost of remunerating and administering the distribution channel.

(d) Selling/sales administration costs.

(e) Promotional costs.

(f) Cost of credit sales.

(g) Cost of marketing information and marketing research.

Generally, marketing costs are more difficult to measure and control, as compared to other costs, such as material costs and manufacturing costs. Within the various components of marketing costs, some are relatively more amenable to measurement and control than others.

The first step in marketing cost anslysis is to gather the cost details by the various marketing functions and analyse the function-wise cost. For doing, this, in the first instance, the various marketing activities have to be grouped into a few major and clearly identified marketing functions. The marketing expenditure must be broken up into parts—each part clearly identified and related to the respective functions. The costs incurred by each of the major marketing functions must be then measured against the budgeted figures and the standard costs for that function. Again, the cost incurred by the function should be compared with the results accomplished, *e.g.* sales volume achieved, gross margins achieved and net realisations made.

After analysing the costs function-wise, the firm should analyse the costs by each marketing entity—each product, each territory, etc. For this purpose, there must be an accounting system which facilitates the assignment of financial expenses to various products, markets and customers.

❐

11

Merchandising

Merchandising is the term used by marketing men to denote all those sales promotion activities which aim to generate the customer's interest in the product or service other than conventional press and television advertising or the use of Public Relations. The purpose of merchandising is to bring product and customer into the closest possible proximity in order that the attributes of the merchandise may become fully apparent and in so doing, sell themselves.

PRINCIPLES OF MERCHANDISING

It is no exaggeration to say that merchandising is the basis of the modern concept of marketing. Yet its principles are as old as trading itself. The pedlar who travelled from village to village in Norman times, presented his wares by inviting his clientele to see, touch, hear or smell the goods he had to offer. The market stallholder, through the centuries, has practised the art of merchandising by encouraging his public to examine closely his merchandise, to pick up items and test them: knives for sharpness and strength of blade; silks for fineness and delicacy, cloths for weight and firmness of weave.

In our more sophisticated age, we have seen the same principles of merchandising exploited with success by such stores as Woolworths and Marks and Spencer, pathfinders of the self-selection method of retailing which has become paramount today. Merchandising techniques have been developed as an aid to the retailing of practically every class of product. Much of the success of marketing now depends upon one's ability to find novel ways of getting one's goods into the hands of potential users.

The greatly extended use of merchandising techniques has been caused not only by the implementation of marketing theories. There has been an important practical consideration which has coerced both manufacturer and distributor to adopt new methods of presentation. During the past twenty years there has been a steady rise in the cost of labour in retail distribution coupled with increased difficulty in attracting a sufficient number of men and women to work in retail shops and stores. The quality of the labour force of the distributive trades has diminished whist its cost has escalated. As a result, personal salesmanship in retailing is fast disappearing in many trades. Thus, means other than the persuasive ability of the shop assistant must be found to sell goods to the public. The result has been the rapid development of merchandising as a means of reducing the shopkeeper's dependence upon the selling skill of his staff to a minimum.

The modern self-service store was born of merchandising out of labour shortage. Supermarkets can be operated almost entirely without skilled labour. Staff is needed only to replenish the display racks with merchandise drawn from the storeroom; cashiers, aided by adding machines, check the goods purchased and collect the money. No personal selling of any kind is required.

There are still many retail trades, of course, in which personal selling is paramount. Whether this will change in the future one can only conjecture. It seems likely, however, that the experience of self-selection methods which is currently being learned in the foodstuffs, hardware and pharmaceutical fields will ultimately be applied to an increasing number of other trades.

FACTORS IN MERCHANDISING

There are certain factors which have become apparent from the accumulated experience of self-service retailing which are of particular importance for all marketing personnel. The first of these is the undoubted fact that goods sell by sight and touch. The old notion, that customers should be abjured not to touch the merchandise unless they intend to buy, is an anachronism. The customer must not only see the product, he must be encouraged to handle it.

Secondly, the positioning of goods within the retail outlet plays an important part in selling them. It is probably not surprising that items placed at eye-level sell faster than those placed either above or below the level at which the majority of customers are likely to look. What may be less apparent, is the fact that a large display of one item of merchandise will promote greater sales than a large selection of different products. Further more, the artistically constructed pyramid which the customer dare not touch for fear of knocking it over produces less sales than a jumbled display which invites handling and examination.

In a personal-selling shop, the assistants can suggest additional items of purchase to the customer to create extra sales. The self-service store does not have this facility. In order to draw the attention of shoppers to special offers or slow-moving merchandise, it is necessary to get them to circulate. One of the ways this can be done is to scatter the display of 'demand goods'—those which are bought regularly—all over the shop, thus compelling the customer to move about and visit each part of the store. If one alters the position of these displays frequently this mobility will be maintained, otherwise regular shoppers quickly learn where to find their essential items of purchase and defeat the merchandiser's attempts to make them look at every shelf and be conscious of the slower-selling goods he hopes to promote.

Another important factor in self-service retailing, is that the whole shop should be treated as one for the purposes of merchandising. This is a breakaway from the traditional idea of departmentalism. It aids the juxtapositioning of goods to create related sales—eggs and bacon or fruit and cream as menu ideas—bearing in mind that research shows that the majority of purchasing decisions are made after, and not before, the customer enters the shop.

These are merely the rudiments of the merchandising of consumer goods. They are important to the Marketing Manager because, by understanding them, he will anticipate and grasp more readily the opportunities which merchandising techniques may offer him for the promotion of his own products. More sophisticated methods are to be seen in the development of 'package deals', such as the supply of deep-freeze refrigerators together with a contract to deliver to the user a regular supply of frozen meat, vegetables and dairy produce. The 'free-trial offer' of the mail order trader, in which he permits his prospective customer to have the use of an appliance, a book or a set of gramophone records, for seven days and return them if he is not satisfied, is a good example of a more advanced form of merchandising, which provides the consumer with unfettered experience of the virtues of the product before he buys it. Car distributors encourage potential customers to have a free ride in the model of their choice before making up their minds whether or not to purchase. Similarly, many manufacturers of food products, upon introducing a new brand., invite shoppers to taste a sample before buying the package.

Most distributors of domestic appliances are happy to arrange demonstrations in customers' homes. Some of the most imaginative examples of merchandising are, in fact, designed to introduce the product in the home. Part-time agents are employed to promote a variety of merchandise by means of organized coffee parties, at which groups of housewives are invited to drink coffee at a friend's home and witness a free demonstration of the product. They are able to seek information, discuss its attributes and, by a process of mutual conviction, be assured of its merits and desirability.

PLANNING PROMOTIONS

In view of the significant role which merchandising will play in the marketing of his product, the Marketing Manager should consider the types of promotion he proposes to use and to for-mulate a plan of campaign on the following lines:

1. Objectives. The aims and objects of the company's merchandising activities for the next twelve-month period should be set out in detail. These may include:

(a) The launching of a new product.

(b) The launching of an existing product into a new market or market segment.

(c) Increasing the existing product's market share.

2. Methods. The merchandising methods to be employed to achieve these aims will depend upon the nature, both of the product and the market. One or more of the following may be suitable:

(a) Free demonstrations

(b) Special displays

(c) Price reductions

(d) Deal-ins or trade promotions.

(e) Deal-outs or consumer promotions.

Under this heading also one should define the product or products, the geographical areas and the class of customers it is intended to feature in the promotions.

3. Training. The salesmen will have to be briefed on all promotional arrangements and may require some special training in order that they may play their part to the full. Some iarge firms, particularly those producing grocery and pharmaceutical products, employ specialist merchandising staff who operate alongside and in addition to the salesmen. The merits of this system are the saving of the time of the sales force, saving in the cost and inconvenience of having to train salesmen to undertake merchandising work and the assurance that the merchandising effort is being undertaken by men experienced and qualified in this specialized aspect of marketing. On the other hand, there is the hazard of confusion which can result from divided responsibilities and the inconvenience which may be caused to distributors who have to deal with more than one representative from the same supplier.

4. Cost. Merchandising activities can be expensive and can erode profits quickly unless kept under tight financial control. The cost of every promotion should be budgeted in advance and related to the increase in revenue which it is designed to achieve.

5. Co-ordination. Successful merchandising depends upon proper co-ordination of the activities of all departments in the company which are likely to be involved in special promotions. The Marketing Manager should ensure that Production, Despatch, Advertising, Public Relations and the Sales Department are kept fully informed and co-operate with the merchandising personnel to obtain the maximum results from promotional activity.

6. Programming. Good organization is vital to merchandising. Arrangements have to be made, well in advance, not only with other departments within the company, but with such outside agencies as printers, manufacturers of merchandise for premium offers, distributors of coupons, samples or sales literature as well as with retailers. A programme of dates for each stage of the merchandising campaign should be prepared and circulated to all concerned.

It is fairly standard practice, in the field of packaged groceries, soaps, detergents and toothpaste, for promotions-or 'deals'to be in two parts. The first part, called, the deal-in, usually consists of an offer made by the manufacturer to the retailer of a price reduction for a specified period. This offer is conditional upon the retailer accepting an agreed minimum supply of the product. In the second part, known as the deal-out, a special attraction is offered to the consumer. This can take several forms. It may be the offer of some desirable item such as a kitchen utensil or a toy or gadget which the housewife can purchase at a reduced price upon presentation of two wrappers or labels of the product. Alternatively, it may be entry into a competition, with the chance of winning a holiday for two, a car, or a considerable cash prize. The offer may, perhaps, be merely the opportunity to buy the product at a reduced price such as 'lp off.'

TRADE PROMOTIONS

The purpose of a trade promotion is to induce the retailer to acquire an increased stock of the product. If this can be achieved then certain advantages must automatically accrue. The trader who holds a large stock of one's brand is compelled to make a special effort to sell it. He will take an active part in the manufacturer's deal-out campaign to attract increased sales of the product to the consumer. This propensity on the part of the retailer to push the sale of one's product is of especial importance where brand preference on the part of the buying public is weak. The shopkeeper can often bring influence to bear upon the consumer's choice of product either by giving it prominent display in the fastest-selling position in his store or, in the case of personal service shops, by instructing his staff to introduce it to customers. The pressure of a heavy stockholding can produce advantageous results for the manufacturer, particularly where the retailer has been stocked with a new product, or an improvement to an existing product, and where a fast build-up of consumer sales is vital.

One of the side-effects of a successful deal in is that, having been induced to purchase a large consignment of one's own product, the retailer with limited capital does not have the resources available to maintain a high stock of competitive brands. In some markets, where competition is particularly fierce, it can be almost as important to deny the opportunity for sales to your competitors as it is to achieve sales for yourself.

There are three main methods employed by manufacturers to encourage retailers to accept a bulk supply of their particular brands. The first is the provision of either a percentage discount or a straight cash allowance for each case of the product ordered during the period of the promotion. This discount is given for every case of the product which the retailer orders, not merely on the excess quantity he accepts over and above his normal ordering quantity.

An alternative method is to increase the case content, that is to say, if the normal case size contains a dozen items of the product, during the period of the promotion cases containing, say, fifteen items, will be supplied at the normal price applicable to twelve items.

The third method, one which often appeals more to the proprietors of small independent shops, is the offer of a gift in kind for the placing of an order of a given size. From the view point of the manufacturer, there can be merit in this approach, because he can usually buy a quantity of gifts at a discount and the cost to him of a promotion of this nature will often work out cheaper than the provision of a cash allowance.

Apart from the tactical advantage to be gained from filling up the retailer's shelves and storerooms with one's product and thus denying sales to competitors, the deal-in offers the manufacturer a further benefit. It provides a means of transferring rapidly his own stocks and freeing his capital for other forms of investment or to create additional liquidity should the need arise.

CONSUMER PROMOTIONS

The deal in will, of course, achieve greater long-term benefits for the success of the product if it is accompanied by a deal out or consumer promotion, designed to help the shopkeeper to sell quickly these additional stocks which he has acquired on good terms.

There are five frequently employed techniques for consumer promotions:

(1) The use of coupons.

(2) The use of self-liquidating offers.

(3) The supply of bargain packs.

(4) The provision of samples.

(5) The offer of 'give-aways'.

Coupon Promotions

In this type of promotion, the product manufacturer supplies to the consumer, by hand or by post, a coupon which offers him a price reduction of a stated amount against the purchase of the product, provided this is made within a specified time: The consumer 'redeems' the coupon by presenting it to the hop-keeper at the time he makes his purchase. The retailer obtains from the manufacturer repayment of the value of the coupon together with a small handling charge.

Coupon promotion schemes provide an incentive to the consumer to buy one's product. They are also an additional incentive to the retailer to stock it in order that he may enjoy the business to be obtained from consumers wishing to 'redeem' their coupons.

It is not surprising that the higher the coupon value the higher the redemption rate will be There are, however, certain problems. Where a brand is already established in the market, many people will be 'redeeming' coupons who would have bought the product in any case. Each sale to a regular user, therefore, will be made at a lower price than would have occur-red if the promotion had not taken place. Another difficulty is that known as *malredemption* when the shopkeeper accepts the coupon in part payment for goods other than the product for which it is intended. There are no easy answers to these problems and the Marketing Manager who embarks upon a coupon scheme must accept them as part of the cost of the promotion.

Self-Liquidating Offers

A self-liquidating offer is one in which the product manufacturer, having purchased in quantity a particular article, advertises it to the consumer at virtually cost price plus a number of labels from his product. The benefit to the consumer is that he is able to buy the article concerned at a very low price because he has the advantage of the manufacturer's bulk purchase. The manufacturer and the retailer benefit from the extra sales of the product which result from the consumer's additional purchases to obtain the necessary labels. The offer is termed self-liquidating because the consumer's purchase of the article reimburses the manufacturer for his original outlay.

Bargain Packs

This method consists merely of an offer of the product, usually in a special pack or wrapper, at a reduced price for a limited period of time. The consumer is invited, for example, to 'save 2p' by 'buying while the offer lasts'. The manufacturer hopes to win new customers to his brand who will be tempted, by the opportunity to save money, to try the product. Retailers, anxious to attract additional sales during the period of the offer, are likely to give the product extra prominence and to undertake special displays. The problem which arises, once again, is that advantage will be taken of the offer by many regular customers who would have bought the product anyway.

Sampling

The offer of a free sample has undoubted appeal for many people and some product manufacturers run promotion schemes by giving away either a full pack or a sample of their product in the expectation that, once tried and found acceptable by the housewife, it is likely to be purchased regularly in the future. This is not, however, a method which recommends itself to a brand leader or a producer whose product already holds an appreciable market share, because too great a loss of revenue can result from the use of free samples by users who would normally have bought the product. For a manufacturer new to a market, however, there is considerable merit in the sampling method. Not only does the new brand obtain wide distribution and testing by consumers; during the period of the promotion a drop in the sale of competitive brands is likely to occur.

'Give-aways'

The provision of 'give-aways' such as plastic flowers, small toys or novelties with each item of the product which is sold is yet another method of motivating the consumer to buy one's brand in preference to that of competitors.

There are considerable advantages to be gained from the use of promotions. It has been established that an increase in sales of up to one thousand per cent can be achieved during the period of a well-considered and well-run campaign. There are, however, disadvantages. After all the extra effort and outlay-on special printing, the provision of additional display material, the distribution of coupons and samples-has been costed, it is often found that there has been no lasting increase in sales. Consumers who have been attracted to buy the product during the promotion period, rapidly revert, once the campaign is over, to their former buying habits. Indeed, the very profusion of coupon schemes, self-liquidating offers and bargain packs provided by competing manufacturers has the effect of weakening the brand loyalty upon the promotion of which they spend vast sums of money in advertising. Increasingly, there is a tendency for promotional schemes to become defensive, for one manufacturer to believe that he must answer an other promotion with one of his own. It should be remembered, however, that trade and consumer deals are but one weapon in the Marketing Manager's armoury. Their value should be neither under-estimated nor over-stressed. Promotions are an adjunct to, not a substitute for, good marketing policy.

❐

12

Distribution Channels and Physical Distribution Decisions

However, for the purpose of this text, distribution or marketing channel may be defined as "a pathway composed of intermediaries, also called middlemen, who performs such functions as needed to ensure smooth and sequential flow of goods and services from the manufacturing ends to the consuming ends in order to achieve marketing objectives of a company". From this definition the following elements of distribution channel may be deduced:

A. **Patheway.** Distribution channel is a pathway through which products and services flow from manufacturers to consumers.

B. **Flow.** This flow of goods and services is sequential and usually undirectional.

C. **Composition.** It is composed of intermediaries, also called middlemen, who participate in the flow voluntarily.

D. **Functions.** The intermediaries perform such functions which facilitate transfer of ownership and possession of goods and services from marketers to consumers.

Nothing prevents a producer from meeting his customers directly and effecting states. If a seller does not use this privilege, he is to borrow the services of different middlemen to pass on the production to the actual users. The following are certain functions which are generally and more often performed by different channels of distribution or by middlemen:

1. **Routinisation of Decision.** Channels of distribution routines the sale of the producer. Once the route reaching the goods is fixed, the problem for selling the product is automatically solved. It reduces the cost of distribution as well.
2. **Pricing.** In pricing a product the producer should invite the suggestions from the middlemen who are very close to the ultimate users and know what they can pay for the product. Pricing may be different for different markets or products depending upon the channel of distribution.
3. **Stabilising the Prices.** The middlemen help to stabilise the prices. By stocking goods, constant flow of goods to the market is assured. They make the goods available at a place where they are wanting and at proper time. Thus middlemen create place, time and possession utilities to the products and maintain the prices.
4. **Promotional Activities.** Middlemen also perform various promotional activities like advertising, personal selling and sales promotion. Sometimes wholesaler does it alone for the producer. Retailer also performs such activities by displaying the product in his window which attract the customers.
5. **Financing the Producer.** Middlemen "collect huge orders and purchase products in bulk from the manufacturers in cash. This enables the producers to undertake large-scale production and adopting better techniques of production because they have no problem for finance. Sometimes manufactures and producers appoint stock agents and distributors and collect deposits from them as security. Finance problem in this way is solved by the channels of distribution.
6. **Aid in Communication.** The middlemen are connecting link between the producers and the buyers. Middlemen have complete knowledge of consumers' behaviour and the market and they communicate the necessary information

to the producer so that they may produce according to the needs of the consumers.

7. **Matching Demand and Supply.** The chief function of intermediaries is to assemble the goods from many producers in such a manner that a customer could effect purchases with ease. According to Wrote Alderson, "the goal of marketing is the matching of segments of supply and demand." The matching process is undertaken by performing the following functions:
   (i) ***Contractual.*** Finding out buyers and sellers.
   (ii) ***Merchandising.*** Producing goods that will satisfy market requirements.
   (iii) ***Pricing.*** Process of attaching value to the product in monetary terms.
   (iv) ***Propaganda.*** Sales promotion activities.
   (v) ***Physical Distribution.*** Disribution activities.
   (vi) ***Termination.*** Settlement of contract, *i.e.*, paying the value and receiving the goods.
8. **Help in Production Function.** The producer can concentrate on the production function leaving the marketing problem to middlemen who specialise in the profession. Their services can best be utilised for selling the product. The finance, required or organisation marketing could profitably be used in production where the rate of return would be greater.
9. **Other Functions.** *(i)* They help forecasting the demand; *(ii)* They are source for information at the time of market research.

TYPES OF MARKETING CHANNELS

Marketing channels vary considerably, from the simple types a spark plug manufacturer uses to sell the entire output to an automobile manufacturer or an investment bank uses to sell financing services to a company, to the long and complex channels employed in moving from nonperishables to market. Marketing channels consist of different kinds of building blocks producers, consumers, industrial users; wholesalers; and retailers. Thus, the possible number of different channels is large, Figure A shows the hierachical relationships of channel building blocks in some marketing channels. If agent middlemen are present in a marketing channel, they are generally situated further back in the channel than wholesalers and/or retailers. There are various types of marketing or distribution channels:

I. Manufacturer to Consumer or User. The shortest marketing channel has two levels: the producer and either industrial users or ultimate consumers. The producer—industrial user channel is the most common way to market industrial goods, because *(A)* many industrial products have compact markets made up of a small number of potential users. *(B)* some industrial products have markets conncentrated in one or a small number of geographic cluster; *(C)* some industrial products require special servicing and/or installation needs be provided by the manufacturer; *(D)* other industrial products are so highly technical that manufacturers deal directly with prospective users and, in many cases *(E)* industrial users insist on buying directly from the producer and buy in quantitative large enough to make these sales economically feasible for the producers.

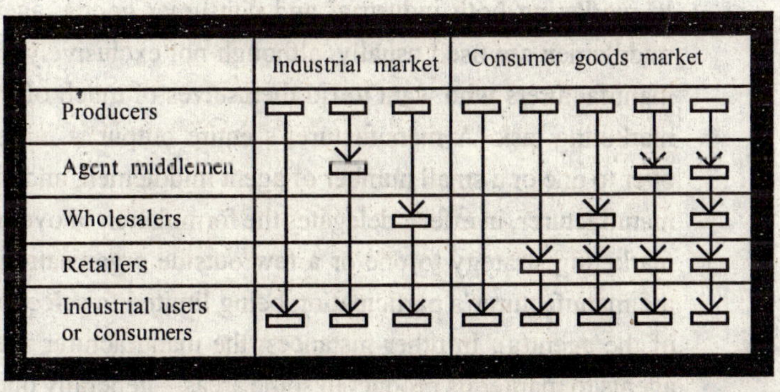

Figure A. Markting Channels Commonly Used in Distribution of Industrial and Consumer Goods

The producer—ultimate consumer channel is not nearly as common. But some farmers sell directly to consumers at roadside stands and in public markets. Some small business, such as bakéries and dairies, and some larger businesses, such as tire manufacturers and cosmetic makers, sell directly to consumers, either through their own retail outlets or even via house-to-house selling. A few manufacturers, in such lines as shoes and shirts, sell directly to consumers through mail-order departments. However, not many consumer goods manufacturers rely wholey or even mainly on direct-to-consumer marketing the main reasons being that ultimate consumers are numerous and widely scattered, and they generally buy in small quantities.

2. **Manufacturer Through Agent Middleman to Consumer or User.** Some producers use agent middlemen as intermediaries between themselves and the next level of distribution. Agent middlemen, generally at the wholesale level, see much use in agricultural marketing, partly because most farmers are too small to handle their own distribution efficiently and partly because the main growing areas are separated geographically from major markets.

   In marketing both industrial and consumer goods, agent middlemen are used usually, although not exclusively, by manufacturers who want to rid themselves of much of the marketing task. A manufacturer's entire output is turned over to one or a small number of agent middlemen, and the manufacturer, in effect, delegates the formulation of overall marketing strategy to one or a few outside organisations, the manufacturer's participation being limited to selection of the agent(s). In other instances, the manufacturer uses agents to market its product in some areas—generally ones with limited sales potentials—and either uses its own sales force or merchant middlemen in other market areas.

Agent middlemen negotiate the transfer of legal title to the producer's merchandise with instutitions active on the next distribution level. In marketing consumer goods, they negotiate with either merchant wholesalers or retailers or both, or the agent arranges for further negotiations by other agent middlemen situated further along the marketing channel and nearer the ultimate consumer. For products sold through a limited number of retail outlets, such as furniture, the agent negotiates with retailers. For products sold through numerous retail outlets, such as most grocery items, the agent negotiates with merchant wholesalers, who, in turn, sell to retailers. However, in marketing grocery prodcuts, agents also deal directly with large-volume retails grocery chains and retail co-operatives. In marketing industrial goods, agents negotiate directly with industrial users; but for lines such as small hand tools, it is common for agents to negotiate with merchant wholesalers, such as industrial distributors or mill supply houses, which, in turn, sell to industrial users.

3. **Manufacturer—Retailer—Ultimate Consumer.** This is one of the most common marketing channels for consumer products. Manufacturers using it have some compelling reason for avoiding wholesale middlemen: *(A)* the products may be perishable, either physically or fashionwise—hence, speed in distribution is essential (movement through another middleman step increases the elpased time in moving the product to the final buyer;) *(B)* the retailer customers may be predominantly large organisations (such as chains, department stores and mail-order houses) that refuse to buy through wholesalers because the formers' buying power equals or exceeds that of most wholesalers; *(C)* the locations of the retailers may be concentrated in a few market areas, making it convenient and economical to sell them direct; *(D)* the available wholesalers may be unable or unwilling to provide the necessary promotional support; or *(E)* the manufacturer may simply desire direct contract

with retailers to have closer contacts with ultimate consumers.

Manufacturers who distribute their products directly to retailers must finance the inventories that merchant wholesalers would otherwise carry. Furthermore, they need either a product line wide enough to permit their sales representatives to write large orders or a narrower line that retailers order in large quantities.

One important reason for distributing directly to retailers is the manufacturers' desire to use franchising. A franchise is a continuing relationship between a manufacturer (or an expert in the performance of some service) and a retailer in which, for a consideration, the manufacturer supplies the retailer with manufacturing and marketing techniques, a brand image, and other know-how. This method of operation, which has long existed in such fields as petroleum marketing, has increased enormously in importance. The franchiser-franchisee relationship requires continuing close contact so that the franchisor can provide advice, supervision, and help when needed. The manufacturer-retailer—ultimate consumer marketing channel meets this requirement.

4. **Manufacturer—Merchant Wholesaler—Retailer—Ultimate Consumer.** The manufacturer—merchant wholesaler—retailer—ultimate consumer channel is often called the traditional or orthodox channel. A manufacturer finds it suitable under some or all of these conditions; *(A)* it has a narrow product line; *(B)* it is unable to finance distribution directly to retailers or can put the funds to more productive use elsewhere; *(C)* retail outlets are numerous and widely dispersed; *(D)* wholesalers are able to willing to provide strong promotional support or the product does not require such support; *(E)* the products are staples, not subject to physical or fashion deterioration; or *(F)* the manufacturer's advertising to ultimate consumers

exerts a strong pull in causing retailers to stock the product. Manufacturer using this channel but desiring closer contact with retailers often employ "missionary" selling personnel who; while calling on retailers, refer orders to local wholesalers for filling and delivery.

5. **Manufacturer—Merchant Wholsaler—Industrial User.** The manufacturer-merchant wholesaler-industrial user marketing channel is used by many producers of industrial item such as small tools and other standard pieces of equipment. These are products of small unit value bought by numerous and diverse industrial establishments. Merchant wholesalers serving the industrial market, although their operations resemble those of consumer goods wholesalers, sell directly to industrial user and are known as industrial supply houses, mill supply houses, industrial hardware distributors, or equipment distributors.

MIDDLEMEN

Middlmen are the persons who provide a link between the manufacturer and the consumer. They facilitate the purchase and sale of goods and services and also perform the marketing functions. They charge for their services and to that extent they are responsible for the increase in the cost of the product to the ultimate consumer user. Despite this, the middlemen constitute an important link of the channels of distribution. They help the manufacturers in selling their products and help the consumers in getting the want satisfying products.

Middlemen may broadly be classified into two categories, namely, merchantile agent middlemen and merchant middlemen.

I. Merchantile Agents

Merchantile agents are also agent middlemen and functional middlemen. They do not handle the goods in the capacity of owners, but they render important service for the exchange of goods. They assist in the buying and selling of goods by taking part in negotiating purchase and sale of goods. Since they do not own the products, they do not earn profits. They take their remuneration for the services rendered in the form of commission or brokerage. Mercantile agents are of the following types:

(a) **Commission Agents.** A commission agent acts on behalf of some other person known as principal for all agreed commission. He undertakes to sell the goods in the name and on the sole risk of the principal. Such as agent may also be employed for the purchase of goods on behalf of the principal. A selling commission agent takes possession of the goods, makes necessary storage arrangements and passes title to the goods to the buyers and gets commission at a fixed percentage on sales. When an agent is authorised to sell the goods on credit and he assumes the risk of collecting the bad debts he is known as a del credere agent. He gets some additional commission for bearing the risk of bad debts.

(b) **Factor.** A factor is a merchantile agent who keeps the goods of others for sale. He can sell goods in his own name, pledge goods in his possession and do all such acts as can be done by the principal. He receives commission at a fixed percentage on sales from his principal. He has a general lien on the goods of the principal for the amount due to him as an agent.

(c) **Auctioneer.** An auctioneer is a mercantile agent who sells the goods on behalf of his principal by undertaking auction of goods. Like commission agent, he takes possession of the goods, displays them to the intending purchasers and receivers offers for sale or bids from the intending purchasers. He sells the goods to the highest bidder and transfers the ownership of goods to him. He receives a certain percentage on the sale proceed of goods as his commission for the services rendered to the principal.

(d) **Broker.** A broker is a mercantile agent who negotiates purchase or sale of goods on behalf of other parties. He is called the selling agent if he is engaged by the seller and the buying agent if he is engaged by the buyer. Brokers obtain neither the possession nor the ownership of goods, but only serve to bring the buyers and sellers together. They receive their remuneration in the form of brokerage which is a certain percentage of the value of the tansaction involved. Brokers specialise in bringing the buyer and sellers in close contact to facilitate trading in commodities.

II. Merchant Middlemen

Merchant middlemen, also known as merchants, are the dealers in goods and services who purchase and sell in the own name for a margin of profit. They assume title of ownership to the goods in all cases though physical possession of the goods may not take place in all cases. They undertake marketing risk and perform many marketing functions. Merchant middlemen may be classified into two categries, viz, wholesalers and retailers.

(A) Wholesalers. The term 'wholesalers' applies to all merchant middlemen who purchase and sell in large quantities. A wholesaler provides an imporant link between the manufacturer or producer and the retailer. He takes title to the goods he handles and assumes marketing risk in the process of distribution of goods. He purchases in bulk and sells in small lots to the retailers or industrial users and is generally away from the ultimate consumer. However, some wholesalers also sell directly to the consumers. Wholesalers may be classified into three broad categories:

(i) ***Pure Wholesaler.*** A pure wholesaler is a merchant who concentrates entirely on buying and selling in large lots and does not engage in manufacturing or retailing operations. He is also known as distributor or wholesaler proper. He purchases goods from one manufacturer or a number of manufacturers in large quantities and sells to the retailers in small lots. He geneally maintains warehouses for storing the goods and also arranges for transportation for the transfer of the goods to the retailer. A pure wholesaler who purchases raw materials from a number of producers for the purpose of selling to the manufacturers is known as a

'mill supply wholesaler'. Some wholesalers specialise in a particular line of product.

(b) ***Manufacturer Wholesaler.*** A manufacturer wholesaler undertakes the manufacturer of goods along with distribution to retailers. He may also distribute the goods of the other manufacturers. The purpose of combining these two functions is to reduce the overhead expenses per unit of product handled.

(c) ***Retailer Wholesaler.*** A retailer wholesaler combines with his business of wholesale the functions of retail trade. He purchases goods from the manufacturers in large quantities and sells them to retailers and ultimate consumers through his retail outlets.

Functions of Wholesalers

The wholesalers perform the following important functions of marketing in the process of distribution of goods and services.

1. **Dispersing.** The wholesalers' job does not end with the selling of goods to the retailers.
2. **Risk taking.** Wholesalers assume a large number of risk in the process of distribution of goods. These risk may occur on account of change in prices and demand, spoilage of goods and bad debts. Thus, they undertake many marketing risks which would have been undertaken by the manufacturers and retailers.
3. **Financing.** Wholesalers provide financial accommodation to both the manufacturers and the retailer. They generally purchase goods on cash basis from the manufacturers and sometimes also give advance to the manufacturers. Thus, the manufacturer need not wait till their products are sold. The wholesalers help the retailers by selling the goods on credit.
4. **Grading and packaging.** Wholesalers grade the goods according to certain standards which they have purchased from different manufacturers. Some wholesalers also give

brand names to the graded products to convince the consumers or industrial users about the quality of the products they deal in. They also undertake the packaging of goods in conventient lots.

5. **Transportation.** Wholesalers make transportation arrangements from the premises of manufacturers to their godowns to the retail stores. They often maintain their own fleet of vehicles for this purpose.

6. **Storage.** Wholesalers keep the goods assembled by them in their warehouse in order to be able to supply them to retailers whenever they require. They relieve the manufacturers and retailers from the botheration of making storage arrangements.

7. **Buying and assembling.** The wholesalers make an estimate of the demand for the goods and purchase and assemble different varieties of goods form different manufacturers spread throughout the country. They also undertake the import of goods from different countries.

(B) Retailers. "Retailing includes all activities directly relating to the sale of goods or services to the ultimate consumer for personal, non-business use." Retailing or retail trade involves all such activities which are related to direct sale of goods to the ultimate consumers. Retail trade is usually done by the retailers. A retailer may be defined as a dealer in goods and services who purchases from manufacturers and wholesalers and sells to the ultimate consumers. The term 'retailing' does not cover sale by producers of industrial goods, and industrial supply houses or by retailers to industrial buyers for conduct of their business. It is also important to point out that retailing may be done by any other institution in addition to retail stores. A manufacturer or a wholesaler selling the products directly to the ultimate consumers for non-business use is engaged in retailing.

A retailer is an important link in the channel of distribution. He purchases and collects various kinds of goods from numerous sources and sells them to the consumers in small lots. He is in direct touch with the ultimate consumers. Retailers are generally located near the thickly populated residential areas. Retail stores are mostly organised in proprietorship or partnershp basis and their capital invesment is small as compared to wholesaling and manufacturing enterprises.

Functions of Retailers

Retail stores or retailers have strategic importance as a channel of distribution. They perform the following functions:

(a) Retailers edcuate the customers by informing them about availability and diverse uses of new products.

(b) Retailers perform transportation function by carrying the goods from the wholesalers and handing it over to the ultimate consumers. Sometimes, they also provide free home delivery of products to the customers. Retailers sell the goods on credit to the customers and thus increase their short-term purchasing power. In this process they undertake the risk of bad debts.

(c) Retailers keep a large number of products of different varieties in stock to sell them to the customers whenever they required. Thus, they create time ultimately.

(d) Retailers purchase and assemble goods from a large number of wholesalers and manufacturers to meet the neds of the ultimate consumers.

(e) Retailers act as the agents of customers. They communicate the needs or demands of their customers to the wholesalers and manufacturers. Thus, they help the customers in getting the want satisfying products and help the manufacturers in purchasing the products which are desired by the customers.

Retailers provide invaluable services to the consumers, wholesalers manufacturers. They help the consumers in getting the products of their choice at the time when they need them. The customers are allowed to purchase in very small quantities. Thus they are saved from the trouble of buying goods in bulk and storing them. Retailers help the wholesalers and manufacturers in selling their products to the ultimate consumers. They are saved from the botheration of selling in small lots to a large number of consumers. The retailers also help them in making products which are required by the customers by providing them the necessary marketing information.

Retailing institutions may broadly be classified, on the basis of their scale of operations, into small-scale retailers and large-scale retailers. Small-scale retailers include mobile retailers and fixed shopkeepers who operate with small amount of capital. The mobile retailers do not operate from fixed business premises, but move from place to place for selling their products to consumers. They are also known as 'itinerant retailer'. They include hawkers, peddlars, market traders and pavement sellers. On the other hand, small-scale fixed retail shops are located near residential areas. Such retailers generally deal in all types of consumer goods. They may also take the help of their family members or may employ salesmen to sell their products to the customers. They keep personal contacts with their customers and also provide them free home delivery services.

Large-scale retailing has assumed great importance these days. Many types of large-scale retail stores have come into existence to meet the needs of urban population. These include departmental stores, multiple shop or chain stores, mail order businesss houses, co-operative stores and super markets.

ROLE OF MIDDLEMEN

Those who are for the continuance of middlemen put forth the following arguments in support of their claim:

(i) Middlemen perform some of the important functions of marketing like assembling, dispersion, warehousing, transport, risk assuming etc.

(ii) They enable the producers and manufacturers to concentrate on their own problems. In this manner, they bring about a division of labour in the business world. Specialisation is the keynote of such dividsion of labour. As Clark puts it, "There seems to be ample scope for the division of the marketing processes among specialised classes of dealers."

On the other hand, those who advocate the elimination of middlemen generally criticise them on the following grounds:

1. The intermediaries who interpose themselves between the manufactures and the consumers add considerably to the cost of marketing and thus raise the price. Their profit comes partly from the profit of the producer and partly from the price that the consumer has to pay. The fact that middlemen take away as much as 37 P. to 53 P. of every rupee that is paid by the consumer as the price of various commodities, itself indicates that the middlemen constitute a heavy burden on the consumers and the producers. One of the reasons for it possibly is that there are too many middlemen engaged in directing the flow of goods from producers to consumers. Another reason, of course, is their effort to appropriate as much as possible out of the price paid by the customers.
2. Most of the middlemen are either market intermediaries or mere transfer agents. "Their places of business are more or less of the nature of superfluous roadside stations where goods are unnecessarily halted on their journey from the manufacturer to the consumers. These detentions hamper the unrestricted flow of goods to the consumers. If, therefore, they are eliminated from the system of distribution goods can be placed in the hands of the consumers more quickly and even more efficiently.
3. None of the industrial risks is shouldered by the middlemen. Strikes and disturbances in industry, risks arising out of depression, losses and difficulties of various kinds experienced by the manufacturers, all of them affect the consumers and manufacturers almost invariably. But the middlemen remain perfectly uneffected. Far from sharing the risk of above-mentioned kinds with the manufacturer, the middlemen use such occasions to exploit the situation and add to their own profits. Quite often, we hear of middlemen sitting tight over stocks and covering them or

manipulating prices or even indulging in balck-marketing when the rest of the community is passing through a crucial emergency.

The public sentiment is increasingly turning against middlemen. This trend is well evidenced by some successful attempt on the part of the manufacturers to estabish direct contacts with consumers through multiple shops and mail order houses. It will be noted that the wholesaler is more a target of criticism than the retailer. Attempts at elimination of middlemen have generally resulted in pushing out the wholesalers rather than the retailers.

It cannot be denied that middlemen do perform some of the most important functions of marketing. These functions are absolutely essential for any system of distribution, particularly under a capitalistic economy. But this does not necessarily mean that middlemen are indispensable for a distributive system, for they, after all, are not the only agencies in the business world which can perform these functions. If, therefore, the functions of marketing can be performed efficiently with fewer middlemen or without middlemen, it will only strength the system of distribution. This will call for a complete rationalisation and reorganization of the marketing organization. These steps will be aimed at the elimination not of the middlemen functions but of those individual middlemen without whom goods flow through straight channels into the hands of consumers. Attempt at reducing the number of middlemen already resulted in the development of chain stores, departmental stores, mail order system. One noticeable tendency in the domain of distribution is the integration of marketing functions with the other functions of business enterprise. Many large concerns have started developing their own sales organisations to look into many of their interests which were previously ignored by the wholesalers. Thus, in conclusion, it may be pointed out that although "middlemen functions" are indispensable, individual middlemen in unduly large numbers only hamper the free and unrestircted flow of goods much in the same way as accumulation of silt and sand in river. The number of middlemen definitely calls for a reduction, for there seems to be too many of them. Rationalization on the lines outlined above will perhaps provide the answer.

FACTORS IN SELECTING A SUITABLE DISTRIBUTION CHANNELS

A rational decision regarding the choice of the appropriate channel(s) of distribution can be taken only after all the relevant factors are taken into consideration. The procedure for the purpose will depend upon the nature of the product. Specifically, the procedure for established products will be different from that followed for new products. Also the factors or critieria on which a decison is made may be quantitative and qualitative. Here we shall concern ourselves first with the critieria for the choice of channels by existing products. Of course, the goals underlying the critieria are; *(a)* maximum geographical coverage of the market, *(b)* maximum promotional efforts, and *(c)* minimum cost.

The choice of a suitable channel of distribution which can be utilised for canalising the flow of existing products from the producer to the ultimate consumers is generally governed by the following factors:

I. The Type of Product. The peculiarities of the product influence and determine the number of middlemen through whose hands the product will pass before it gets into the hands of the consumers.

- ***(a) Seasonal Character.*** If a commodity is in seasonal demand there may be no need for middlemen.
- ***(b) Unit Value.*** Generally, products of lower unit value and high turnover are distributed extensively through indirect channels, *e.g.*, hosiery goods, cosmetics, etc.
- ***(c) Bulk or Weight.*** Where the movement of goods involves heavy freight and poses problems of transportation, limited channels may be employed. Selling may be mostly direct in the such cases.
- ***(d) Perishability.*** As a rule, fewer middlemen are required for selling perishable goods and commodities. Most of the bakery products and food products, generally pass through

only one middlemen—the retailer—and may in many cases be sold directly by the producer.

(e) ***Servicing Required.*** Products like automobiles and sewing machines which require servicing, expensive handling equipment, or instructions before use also pass through the hands of a few middlemen. Fashion goods generally require direct selling since their special features have to be explained to the consumers effectively. Retailers may not do this very well.

II. Consumers or Market Consideration. The consumers influence the choice of the distributive channels in the following ways:

(a) ***Number.*** If the number of consumers is small, as in the case of bulky and expensive machinery, the manufacturer can employ his own sales force to sell directly to the consumers. If, however, there is a large number of consumers interested in a product the producer has to make use of service of wholesalers and cannot afford to employed sales staff for direct selling or even deal with the host of retailers. Cigarettes and other consumer goods belong to this category.

(b) ***Geographical Location.*** If most of the consumers using a particular product (say, bread) live in the same city or locality as the producer, the producer can sell his products through his own salesmen. On the other hand, if the consumers are large in number and scattered over a wide area, the producer, will have to depend upon wholesale and retail channels for the sale of this products.

(c) ***Order Size.*** The size of orders received and the volume of goods supplied to individual firms will influence the channels used to reach them. A food products manufacturer will sell directly to large grocery chains because the total volume of business makes this channel economically feasible.

(d) ***Consumer or Industrial Market.*** The purpose for which the products purchased by consumers also influences the choice of channels of distribution. If a product is used for industrial purpose, direct purchase from the manufacturer adopt direct selling.

III. Size and Structure of Manufacturing. The larger the producer, the more profitable it may be for him to establish direct contact with consumers through his own sales force. A small producer, on the other hand, finds it more profitabe to rely on indirect channels making use of wholesalers and retailers. Also if the manufacturing is widely dispersed geographically, in relation to the demand, the greater will bc the necessity of using indirect channels, particularly wholesalers. This is so because the wholesalers will have to collect products from a wide area. Further the width or the range of the product-line also determines the broad pattern of distribution that a firm will adopt. If a manufacturer deals in a wide range of products, he will tend to serve the retailer directly eliminating the wholesaler because it is more convenient for the retailer to purchase from as few a sources as possible. Besides, it may mean some saving in the personal selling cost per unit as the salesman will be able to handle large sales volume for the same salary.

IV. Consumer Buying Habits. The channel policies are affected by the buying habits of consumers and industrial users, the amount of effort the consumer is willing to expend, the desire for credit, the desire for after-sales service, etc.

V. Company Considerations. The character of the firm making the choice of channels of distribution will also affect the channel policies of firms. Some of the important factors in this regard are:

(a) ***Reputation.*** Firms with established goodwill can usually make choice of middlemen and enter into advantageous agreements with them.

(b) ***Financial Resources.*** A financially strong firm will have a tendency to set up its own channels rather than depend upon middlemen.

(c) ***Exprience and Competence of Management.*** Where the management lacks marketing know-how, it prefers to depend upon indirect selling through middlemen.

(d) ***Desire for Control of Channel.*** A manufacturer may establish a short channel just because he wants to control the distribution. Moving closer to the final customer affords the manufacturer greater opportunity to gather current market information and control the freshness of the product and its retail price.

VI. Structure of Retailing. The structure of retail trade in a product has also an important bearing on the choice of channels. One important aspect of this factor is the number of stores selling mainly the product in question. Generally, if there are many such stores, the manufacturer will like to make use of the available retail channels instead of selling direct to the consumers. Also, retailers will be used for marketing a product if the retail stores provide convenience of shopping to the potential consumers.

In short, the important considerations relating to the structure of retailing are:

(a) Service provides by retailers.

(b) Availability of desired retailers.

(c) Attitude of middlemen toward manufacturer's policies.

(d) Sales volume possibilities.

VII. The Customer Channels. In cases where an established network of channels exist, the manufacturer may make use of such customary channels. For example, if washing soap is being marketed through grocers, a manufacturer may find that selling it through general merchants does not add substantially to the sales volume. However, the firm must be on the look out for new channels and should explore them and experiment with them.

VIII. Selectivity For Distribution. An important decision in regard to the choice of channels is the one relating to the number of middlemen to be used. Three alternate policies are available to the manufacturer: *(a)* extensive distribution, *(b)* selective distribution, and *(c)* exclusive distribution.

(a) Extensive distribution means that the manufacturer is willing to make use of any and all distributive outlets prepared to handle his product. A good example is provided by cigarettes. In following this policy, the manufacturer may use an independent wholesaler through whom he can reach all the retail outlets, or he may sell direct to the large retailers and reach the rest of the market through wholesalers.

(b) Selective distribution means that the manufacturer will select from among the available outlets rather than use all of the outlets. The purpose of this policy is to provide the channels chosen with enough sales to keep them selling the manufacturer's product in a satisfactory way. This may increase the sales at reduced distribution costs and bring forth better cooperation from the dealers. The manufacturer may be able to achieve a good measure of control over disribution through this policy. On the other hand, it may happen that this market coverage is weak in that potential customers are not able to find his product because it is being marketed through selected channels.

(c) Exclusive distribution implies the grant of sole selling rights for a product in a certain territory to a middlemen under a contractual agreement. Generally, the middlemen acting as the sole distributor for a territory does not handle competing products. The benefits and drawbacks of this policy are extension of those arising from selective distribution.

IX. The Profit Criterion. After the qualitative criteria indicated above have been applied and a broad choice regarding the type and number of channels made, the next step will be the use of the quantitative criterion in the from of estimates of profit. This means that estimates of demand, revenue and costs for each channel should be prepared and compared to make the final choice regarding the channels of distribution. The sale volume potential differs considerably channels by channel and the cost tend to move in direct relationship to the directness to the channel. As we move progressively from a direct manufacturer to user channel to the most indirect channel through one or more independent wholesalers, the costs of distribution tend to become progressively lower. At the same time the manufacturer's control over his product also gets reduced thus limiting the sales that might be achieved. The net gain from a comparison between these variables will be the criterion for the choice of a channel.

In case of a product being put on the market for the first time, it is important to ensure that the potential buyer learns from some source that the product exists and that it will satisfy certain specifc needs of his. If it is an important product, the buyer will seek considerable information (whether from the advertisement or from the middlemen) before deciding to go in for it. This may be said of items like refrigerators, room-coolers, air-conditioners, etc. If, however, it is a relatively unimportant thing, the potential buyer may not want much information and may be inclined to make a purchase just as soon as the product is made available. The choice of a channel or a set of channels will be dictated by the kind of product that is being introduced.

The seller of a new consumer product can generally choose from among a number of alternatives. A wholesaler may not promote the product aggressively but he does usually have useful connections with retailers and charges a lower margin of profit. If the manufacturer can create a response for the product through advertising the wholesaler will be a good choice. A speciality shop may promote the product with force but will generally demand higher profit margin. Direct sales could also be made to the retailer. This will call for a large sales force. As a further alternative missionary salesmen may be employed to call on the retailer and the product may be marketed through wholesalers. This may mean more cost but it will ensure better dealer co-operation.

In practice, a beginning may be made with a channel that ensures aggressive promotion of the product even though the cost in the form of margin is high. As the product becomes accepted in the market, the manufacturer can switch over to the channels that mean less cost (say, wholesalers). Of course, in making this switch-over, utmost care should be taken to avoid ill-will on the part of the original channel as it may be required again to promote another new product.

While selecting a particular dealer for the sale of his products, a manufacturer must consider the following points:

(i) Ability to arrange for repair and maintenance of the product, if need be.

(ii) The other goods or products dealt in by the dealer—whether they are allied products or competitive ones.

(iii) Ability to cover the territory or areas over which goods have to be sold.

(iv) Capacity to secure business.

(v) Ability to maintain sufficient stock of the product.

(vi) Dealer's knowledge about the product characteristics and its market.

(vii) Credit standing of the dealer.

(viii) The ability and the willingness of the dealer to handle the product.

FACTORS INFLUENCING THE CHOICE OF CHANNELS OF DISTRIBUTION

There may be many channels of distribution for a product and a manufacturer has to select any one or more of these channels. Selection of a particular channel is a decision upon which the success of all the marketing efforts of an enterprise depends. Therefore a particular channel must be selected ony after a careful study and consideration of all the relevant factors. Factors affecting the selection of channels of distribution can be divided into five parts:

(I) Factors Related to the Manufacturer

Following are the factors related to the manufacturer which affect the selection of a channel of distribution:

(1) ***Financial Resources.*** The very first factor affecting the selection of a channel of distribution is the availability of financial resources with a manufacturer. If the manufacturer has sufficient financial resources, he may decide to sell his products direct to the consumers. If, on the other hand, a manufacturer does not have sufficient financial resources, he must decide to distribute his products with the help of middlemen.

(2) ***Goodwill.*** Selection of a particular channel of distribution depends upon the goodwill of manufacturer also. If a manufacturer enjoys high reputation in the market and his products are popular among consumers, he can select any channel of distribution according to his desire because every middlemen wants to sell the products of such manufacturer. If a manufacturer does not enjoy such reputation, he should take the advantage of goodwill of middlemen and he should select the channel of distribution which enjoys high reputation.

(3) ***Marketing Experience and Managerial Ability.*** Marketing of goods is an art. If the enterprise has sufficient marketing experience and managerial ability, the decision may be taken for distributing products direct to the consumers. If the enterprise lacks marketing experience and managerial ability, the enterprise must decide to distribute its products with the help of middlemen.

(4) ***Size of the Enterprise.*** If the size of an enterpise is large and it has sufficient financial resources, marketing experience and managerial ability, it may select any channel of distribution. It may also decide to distribute its products to the consumers directly. Otherwise, the manufacturer will have to depend upon the experience and ability of middlemen.

(5) ***Desire to Control.*** If the manufacturer wants to have complete control over all the marketing activities, he should select a short channel of distribution or he should distribute

his goods direct to the consumers. If, on the other hand, the manufacturer has no such desire, he may decide a long channel of distribution.

(II) Factors Related to the Product

Following are the factors related to the product which affects the selection of channel of distribution:

(1) ***Perishability of Product.*** If the product is of perishable nature, it must be distributed within shortest possible time and therefore, shortest channel of distribution must be selected. If the product can be stored for sometimes, longer channel of distribution may also serve the purpose.

(2) ***Price Per Unit.*** It has been the experience that the channel of distribution for distributing the goods of low price unit is generally long and that for the goods of high price unit is generally short.

(3) ***Ordered Products.*** If a manufacturer manufactures goods according to orders only, he usually decides to distribute these products direct to his consumers. If a manufacturer produces goods according to standards, he may decide for distributing these goods through a long channel.

(4) ***Weight.*** It also has been the experience that the goods of high weight are generally distributed direct by the manufacturers. On the other hand, the goods of light weight are distributed through a long channel of distribution.

(5) ***Technical Nature of Product.*** If the product is of technical nature, it becomes necessary for the manufacturer to provide after-sale-services to the consumers. In case of such products, it becomes necessary that these products must be supplied direct by the manufacturer or through shortest possible channel of distribution.

(III) Factors Related to the Market

Following are the factors related to the market which affect the selection of a particular channel of distribution:

(1) ***Number of Consumers.*** If the number of consumers of a product is very large, it must be distributed through a long channel of distribution so that it may be made available in all the segments of the market at all the times. If, on the other hand, number of consumers of a product is limited, it must be distributed through short channel of distribution.

(2) ***Regional Concentration.*** If the consumers of a product are scattered all over the country, it will not be possible for the manufacturer to distribute such product directly. Therefore, it becomes necessary that such a product must be distributed through a long channel of distribution. If, on the other hand, the consumers of a product are scattered over a particular region, it can be supplied by the manufacturer himself or it can be distributed through a short channel of distribution.

(3) ***Policies of Competitors.*** Marketing policies of competitors also affect the decision of an enterprise regarding the selection of a particular channel of distribution. If most of the competitors are distributing their products through middlemen, the enterprise should also decide to do so. If the competitors are supplying their goods directly to the consumers, the enterprise may also decide to do so.

(4) ***Size of Orders.*** If a product is bought by the consumers in large quantity, the manufacturer may decide to distribute it direct to the consumers. If, a product is bought by the consumers in small quantity, the manufacturer will have to arrange to supply the product at all the places and at all the times. Thus, such a product is distributed through a long channel of distribution.

(5) ***Nature of Market.*** A very important consideration affecting the secltion of a particular channel of distribution is the nature of market for the product. If the product is industrial, it can be distributed directly by the manufacturers to the industrial users. On the other hand, consumer goods are generally supplied to the consumers through middlemen.

(IV) Factors Related to the Middlemen

Following are the factors related to the middlemen which affect the selection of a particular channel of distribution:

(1) ***Availability of Desired Middlemen.*** If desired middlemen having enough experience and capability are available in the market, the manufacturer may determine to distribute his products through such middlemen. If, on the other hand, desired middlemen are not available for a particular product, the manufacturer will have to supply it directly.

(2) ***Sales Possibilities.*** If it is expected that the sales of a product can be increased through middlemen, the manufacturer may take the help of these middlemen for the distribution. If the increase in sales is not expected through middlemen, the manufacturer may decide to distribute his products directly.

(3) ***Services Provided by Middlemen.*** A manufacturer should select a channel of distribution which may meet his requirements. Thus a channel must be selected for the services provided by middlemen.

(4) ***Cost Consideration.*** If the cost of distribution of a product through a channel of distribution is within the range of enterprise, a decision may be taken to adopt it, otherwise, it is better to distribute the goods directly.

(5) ***Marketing Policies and Strategy.*** Sometimes, a manufacturer adopts a channel of distribution for distributing his products because of his marketing policies and strategies to do so. Main reason of such decision may be to get the advantage of goodwill of middlemen.

(V) Factors Related to the Environment

Some environmental factors also affect the selection of channels distribution for a product. Such as,—in the market condition of slump, a channel of distribution must be selected with a view to provide goods and services to the consumers at lower rate. In addition to this, some legal restrictions also affect the selection of a channel of distribution. The channel selected by the enterprise must also meet social expectations.

SELECTION OF A PARTICULAR CHANNEL

Success of a product in a market depends to a great extent upon the channel through which it is being distributed. The decision of selection of a particualr channel of distribution is a difficult task because there are many alterantive channels available for the distribution of a product and every channel has its own merits and demerits. No channel is free from limitations and no channel be regarded as most suitable channel for every product. A channel may be very effective can be regarded as most suitable channel for every product. A channel may be very effective and very successful for distributing a particular product but the same channel may fail in achieving its objects in case of another product. Therefore, it is very important and sensitive decision to select a particular channel for the distribution of a product.

A manufacturer must carefully consider all the relevant factors, before aking a final decision in this regard. Financial resources, managerial ability, marketing experience, characteristics of product, situation of competition, policies of competitors, buying behaviour of consumers, social expectations and government policies are the most important factors to be considered by a manufacturer in this regard. After this, he must study respective merits and demerits of all the channels of distribution available for a particular product. Final decision in this regard must be based on such study. The process of selection of a particular channel of distribution for a particular product does not end with the selection of a desired channel. Analytical study of the performance of the channel must also be made in order to evaluate the effectiveness of the channel. If it is felt at any stage that the channel is unable in achieving desired results, the decisions may be taken to change it.

CHANNEL MANAGEMENT DECISIONS

Main difference between the channel as a team and any other type of organisation is that the channel is composed of business firms rather than individuals. The main five elements of the channel are arranged into the simple model presented in the figure below.

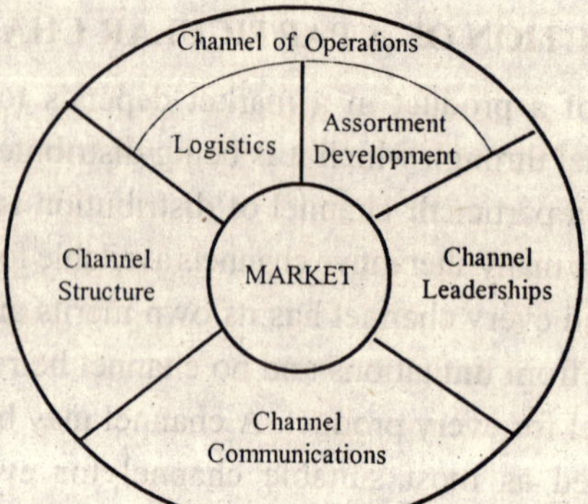

Fig. Elements of the Channel Team

Source. Walter, C. Glenn, "Marketing Channels",

The market is placed in the centre and four internal factors of channel team efforts are placed around the market. This arrangement demonstrates their equal importance and emphasises their interaction with each other and with the market.

Channel operations are important to reach the desired markets. Channels perform the two operations of assortment development and logistics. Assortment development is the practice of combining different types of products with specific services throughout the channel. Logistics is the movement of products to market.

Channel Leadership

Channel leadership is necessary to focus channel members on the objective and to provide the decision making necessary to perform operations. The channel leader is responsible for effective decision making, stimulating, motivating and coordinating members of the marketing channels.

Channel Communications

It is the basis for all interactions within the channel and between channel members and outsiders. Without proper communication it becomes difficult for the leader to convey the clear message and control members. Internal information flow includes order directives, memorandums, information, etc., and passes between members.

Channel Structure

The manner in which channel members are organised, their status, and their roles with the team. The members who constitute the channel structure can be broadly divided into agents and merchants. The main difference between the merchants and agents is that the former take the title to goods while latter do not take title.

Classification of Distribution Channels

The channels of distribution which are also known as trade channels are classified mainly into conventional (non-integrated) and non-conventional (integrated) with further ramifications as shown in the figure given below:

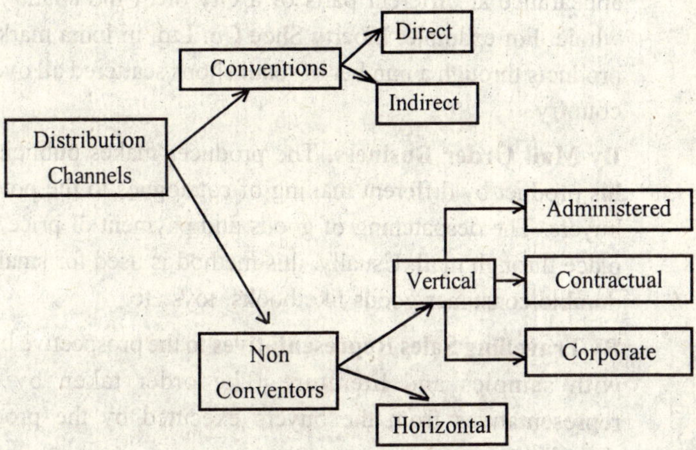

Fig. Types of Distribution Channels

Conventional Channels

A distribution channel may have a number of stages and a number of intermediaries between the producer and buyer. Among the converntional distribution channels, two types of choice are available *i.e.*, direct and indirect channel.

Direct Channel

The producer can sell directly to the customers without the help of intermediaries. Some of the important examples where direct distribution channel is used are as follows:

* Through opening retail shops
* Through mail order business
* Through travelling salesmen
* Through the marketing of industrial products.

Direct channel takes the shortest route to the consumer. Costly goods like computer and costly automobiles, industrial and heavy machinery are directly sold to the consumers.

By Opening Retail Shops. A producer of consumer goods of daily necessity opens a number of retail shops with similar appearance at different parts of a city or of the country as a whole. For example. Liberty Shoe Co. Ltd. in India market its products through a number of retail shops scattered all over the country.

By Mail Order Business. The producer makes publicity for his product by different mailing of catalogues to the potential buyers. The despatching of goods and payment of price takes place through mail. Usually, this method is used for small and durable consumer goods like books, toys etc.

By Travelling Sales Representatives to the prospective buyers with samples and literature. The order taken by sales representatives from the buyers executed by the producer directly.

By Marketing of Industrial Products. Usually sending of sales representatives procedure is followed for marketing industrial goods like raw material, machines, machine parts, tools, machine oil etc.

However, due to heavy investment and managerial responsibility in the activities of disposal of goods and payment realisation, most of the producers do not prefer to adopt direct distribution method.

Indirect Channel

Indirect channel means distribution of goods through middlemen or intermediates. The whole process of indirect channel of distribution looks like a chain as follows:

Producer to Retailer to Consumer. Channel is preferred where the purchasers of goods are big retailers like department stores, chain stores, super markets, consumer co-operative stores etc. Some of the Indian companies like D.C.M. and Bata Shoe Company use this channel by establishing their own retail stores. This channel is also suitable in the case of perishable products.

Producer to wholesaler to consumer channel is preferred in distributing industrial goods which further used for production.

The term industrial distributor is commonly utilised in the industrial market to refer to those wholesalers who take title to the goods they handle. The wholesalers are involved in the marketing of small accessory equipment and operating supplies, such as building supplies, office supplies and small hand tools. These two channels discussed are the indirect shortest channels and are known as one level channel.

Producer to wholesaler to Retailer to consumer is also referred to as the traditional or orthodox' marketing channel. This is the most commonly used channel in case of consumer goods particularly where the demand is elastic and a number of similar products are available. That is, it is the method used by literally thousands of small manufacturers that produce limited lines of products and by small retailers. Small companies with limited financial resources utilise wholesalers as immediate sources of funds and as a means to reach the hundreds of retailers who will stock their products. This channel is known as two level channel.

Producer to Agent Middlemen to Wholesalers to Retailer to Consumer is the longest indirect channel where products are produced by a larger number of small companies, a unique middlemen-the agent-performs the basic function of bringing buyer & seller together. This channel is used by those firms who cannot afford to develop a sales force of their own. A firm with diversified product mix may find it more appropriate to adopt a variety of distribution channels. Agents are used in such industries as canning and frozen food packing.

In these industries, many producers supply a large number of geographically scattered wholesalers. The agent wholesaling middlemen, often called a manufacturer's representative, also serve as an independent sales force in contacting the wholesale buyers. Usually, the manufacturer pass on the risk of marketing the goods to the selling agents and he concentrates only on production.

RETAILERS

The word 'Retail' is derived from a French word with the prefix re and the verb tailer meaning "to cut again". Evidently, retail trade is one that cuts off smaller portions from large lumps of goods. It is a process through which goods are transported to final consumer. In other words, retailing consists of the activities involved in selling directly to the ultimate consumer for personal, non-business use. It embraces the direct-to-customer sales activities of the producer, whether through his own stores by house-to-house canvassing or by mail order business." It is immaterial who does the selling, but to be classified as retailing selling activities must be direct to the ultimate consumer. While most retailing is done through retail stores, it may be done by any institution. Manufacturers engage in retailing when they make direct-to-consumer sales of their products through their own stores (as Bata and Corona Shoe Companies., D.C.M. stores, Mafatlals and Bombay Dyeing) by door-to-door canvass, or mail order or even on telephone. Even a wholesaler engages in retailing when he sells directly to an ultimate consumer, although his main business may still be wholesaling.

A retailer is a merchant, or occasionally an agent, or a business enterprise, whose main business is selling directly to ultimate consumers for non-business use. He performs many marketing activities such as buying, selling, grading, risk taking, and developing information about customers' wants. They are marketers and customers of producers and wholesalers. A retailer may sell infrequently to industrial users, but these are wholsale transactions, not retail sales. If over one half of the amount of volume of business comes from sales to ultimate consumers, *i.e.*, sales at retail, he is classed as a retailer. Retailing occurs in all marketing channels for consumer products.

IMPORTANCE OF RETAILING

The retailer is an intermediary in the marketing channel because he is both marketer and customer, who sells to the last man to consume. He is a specialist who maintains contact with the consumer and the producer; and is an important connecting link in a gigantic mechanism of marketing. Though producers may sell directly to consumers such method of distributing goods to ultimate user is inconvenient, expensive and time consuming as compared to the job performed by a specialist in the line. Therefore, frequently the manufacturers depend on the retailers to sell their products to the ultimate consumers. The retailer, who is able to provide appropriate amenities without an excessive advance in prices of goods is rewarded by larger or more loyal patronage.

The general service which a retailer provides are:

(1) The retailer anticipates the wants of the consumers and then supplies them the right kind of goods at a reasonable price. His job is to make the consumers' buying as easy and convenient as possible, *i.e.*, he acts as a consumers' agent.

(2) He performs the service of bulk-breaking, *i.e.*, dividing large quantities into small units, such as individual cans, bottles, boxes, wrappers, packages, appropriate for consumer use.

(3) He also assumes risks by guaranteeing the goods he sells to the consumers.

(4) He also offers free delivery of goods, credit on open accounts, free alteration, liberal exchange facilities, instructions in the use of goods, revolving credit plans, and long term instalment programmes.

(5) He offers a large assortment of merchandise of suitable size, colour, design, style and seasonal items-ranging from domestic utensils, household requisites to speciality goods.

(6) He creates time and place utility by storing the products in off season and by transporting these goods to the places where they can be readily available as and when needed by the consumer.

(7) He adds to the convenience and case of consumer purchasing by offering convenient shopping locations, market informations, personal salesmen, and other services as free parking privileges, children's nurseries, cooking and sewing classes, style shows, unformed doormen, lessons on product use and a multitude of other facilities may be offered and found sufficiently desired to result in increased patronage.

(8) He acts as a specialist in selling. He offers physical facilities and man-power so that producers and wholesalers can meet the consumers at their doors.

(9) He helps the producers in distributing their products by using advertising display and personal selling.

(10) He provides useful inforamtion to the producers about the like and dislikes of the consumers, their wants and needs and their buying behaviour.

(11) The level of retail sales is one of the most useful barometers of the nation's economic health. *e.g.*, when sales of cycles pick up, sales of steel and components also increase, as does employment and thus increasing purchasing power. But when sale godown, manufactuers cut back production, unemployment increases, and retail sales also goes down.

Facilitating Services

In order to carry out functions involving transfer of ownership and physical supply effectively, retailers perform a number of facilitating functions, *i.e.*, functions relating to standardisation and grading, financing risk taking and market information.

A retailer of fresh fruits and vegetables has to standardise and grade these to make these acceptable to customers. They establish standards, inspect goods they receive, and sort them in various classifications. Quite often they purchase in large quantities and then divide them and repack them before selling when the retailers sells goods on credit he performs financing function. From the moment he sells and collects the last penny from the customer, when goods are sold on credit, he is said to be performing a financing function.

Another function performed by retailers is that of risk taking. During the entire time a retailer holds title to particular goods, he must inevitably bear a wide variety of risks. Not only the goods may be destroyed through fire or flood, but also there is often the danger of theft, deterioration, or spoilage. Furthermore, such merchants are also faced with the threat that consumers will not accept their product or will purchase them only at unprofitable prices. He also undertakes risk in handling of fashion goods and other items for which consumer demand varies greatly from time to time.

Since the retailer knows about the wishes of his customers the price, quality and the kind of merchandise available in the market as well as the existing and anticipate style trends, he keeps in stock the goods usually required by customers.

CLASSIFICATION OF RETAILERS

Retailers may be classified in more than one way such as on the following basis:

1. **Size.** That is according to their sales volumes during a particular period, say a year. Retailing may be both a small scale and a large scale operation; and it may be integrated and non-integrated.
2. **Geographic Location.** The stores classified according to these criteria tell about consumer buying habits. The retailers may be found in rural trading centre, large cities, outlying suburbs, or along the main streets of a town.
3. **Product-line handled.** That is according to the goods dealt with. They may be classified: *(a)* General merchandise

stores (such as department stores, dry goods stores, variety stores, and general stores) dealing in furniture, home furnishings, appliances, household goods, groceries, drugs, convenience goods and shopping goods; *(b)* single-line stores, dealing in assorted group of products (such as grocery stores, furniture stores, medical stores, building material stores, hardware stores, sporting goods stores, cloth stores and book stores); they may also carry two related lines, such as men's and women's clothing; *(c)* Limited-line or speciality stores, which carry a limited variety of products such as shopping or convenience goods—apparel, shoes, gifts and decorative accessories selling stores.

4. **Form of Ownership.** On this basis we have independent stores and corporate chain stores; less important are leased department, company stores, consumer co-operatives, etc.
5. **Method of Operation.** On this basis retailers may be of two types; *(a)* full-service retailers, where the sale is generally made at the counter, especially of high-fashion goods or where a salesman's demonstration, explanation or fitting is needed. Such retailers are super markets, and discount retailers *(b)* non-store retailing, where buyers and sellers meet and transact their business at the buyer's home or at some other non-store location, known as door-to-door or house-to-house selling. Major forms of non store retailing are mail order selling, automatic vending and personal selling on a door-to-door basis.

ESSENTIAL REQUIREMENTS OF RETAILERS

The essential requirements of a retailer are:

(1) **Selection of Goods.** Retailers are more in touch with the consumers as compared to the wholesalers, and therefore, it is necessary for the retailers to be more careful in judging the future needs of the market. Sometimes such stocks are maintained the use of which has already become obsolete. The retailers must be up-to-date in their selection of the

goods to be stocked by them. More heavy stock would not attract customers, but a moderate customer to their well-equipped shops. The 'dead stock' is the bug-bear of business and that unsold and unsaleable stock has brought ruin to many business men should never be overlooked.

(2) **Knowledge of Merchandise.** Individuality has so much developed amongst the masses that a great variety of goods has considerably increased and is still increasing. The retailer should, therefore, be more up-to-date in this respect and must have a practical knowledge of the merchandise which will satisfy this new demand. His work is, thus, more complicated and he should take enough care while appointing salesmen, selecting shop assistants, etc., who would be called upon to deal with the customers.

(3) **Bying and Selling.** The success of a retail business is more dependent on the buying of merchandise in the right market, at the right price, and at the right time. Such retailers who are new in the line, are sometimes heard to say to their customers that they cannot sell at the price charged by some other shopkeepers on account of their buying the goods at a higher price, without taking into consideration the fact that this is of no concern to their customers who will not consent to pay a higher price for their article merely for its being purchased at a dearer market. Retailers must compete in price and quality and should charge their customers at a definite rate of profit which ought to be the lowest possible in the circumstances and which should not be more than what is charged by others.

(4) **Cash and Credit Purchases.** A good many retailers at important trade centres buy beyond the capacity of their capital and become inextricably entangled in debt to their creditor, wholesalers, who naturally sell for price which is more than normal because they grant credit. The retailer, therefore, finds himself in a helpless position when he is

called upon to compete with those who purchase for cash. Buying on credit may, of course, be allowed to a limited extent but over-buying should always be avoided and retailers should not trade too much beyond the limits of their available capital. Financial consideration, as a rule, should dictate the maximum stock that can be safely kept. On the other hand, a well-selected variety of stock should always be held by a retail shop unless it is a multiple shop, as loss is frequently suffered on account of inadequate stock, for this means not only lost sales but loss of customers, who being disappointed to have their wants supplied transfer their purchases elsewhere.

(5) **Price, Quality and Cypher System.** Higgling and hesitancy should be avoided and a competitive fixed price should always be asked for with uprightness. The price charged ought to be such that the customers will not generally be in a position to purchase the same article in the market at a cheaper price. The competitive price and quality of the goods sold are two most important factors which are the keynotes of success in business and their supreme necessity cannot be too much exaggerated. Retailers should know that it is better to have a quick turnover of stock at a lower margin of profit.

(6) **Display of Goods.** Sometimes goods are so disorderly arranged that the goods required, though available on the spot, cannot be produced on the requisition by the consumer. The goods should, therefore, be not only properly arranged but should also be properly displayed to draw the attention of the customers. Window dressing which costs little but is very effective in retail trade as it makes an emotional appeal to the shopping public at the start, frequently results in solid business. "In the newer window-dressing," said Mr. George Edger, "the three cardinal principles are: *(i)* to show reasonable thing, *(ii)* to show it as simply as possible, and *(iii)* to show it so that the eye

can determine every detail put into the window. In such window-dressing instead of crowding the window, the trade aims at a display which represents the prevailing note of the season."

(7) **Situation.** Locality of the shop is a great factor to attract customers. The best locality is the place where there already exist other shops of the same nature, because for shopping purposes customers generally visit the place where a market for their requirements has grown up and where they can select the articles of their need from more than one shop. While opening shops this essential matter of selection of site in a desirable locality should not be overlooked. No particular place can be pointed out for the retailer to reach his goal. Success can be achieved by combining the various qualifications essential for a businessman with other necessary factors. Personal aptitude, knowledge, enthusiasm and apprenticeship, combined with the possession of saleable goods and adequate stock generally make for success.

Mr. Nystrom has summed up the chief requirements of the retailers thus:

In order to attract customers retailers should have:

(i) accessibility to consumers;

(ii) a satisfactory trading place;

(iii) suitable stocks of merchandise offering an opportunity for cosnumer choice;

(iv) service offered and rendered to customers;

(v) personal relation of store employees towards customers including not only promptness of attention but also courtesy, interest, friendliness and honesty;

(vi) reasonable price;

(vii) window display and counter display (which are the most effective forms of advertising);

(viii) sales promotion including all methods and devices for giving the public information about the goods and services offered;

(ix) the demand of customers should be aroused by means of suitable advertising so that they may be persuaded to pay a visit to the shop;

(x) trained salesmen who are the backbone of the success of the retail house;

(xi) staff employed should be polite, courteous and attentive to customers; and

(xii) clearance sales, which are usually organised at the end of a season to attract customers in large numbers.

WHOLESALER

Physical distribution of goods and services produced or dealt in by all enterprises is an important function of marketing management. It includes all the activities to be performed by an enterprise in the process of distributing goods and services from the place of production to the place of consumption. Thre are various channels of distribution for a product. An important channel commonly used, particularly for the distribution of consumers goods, is under:

Manufacturer→Wholesalers→Retailers→Consumers

Wholesaler is an important chain of the channel of distribution because it is an agent between a manufacturer and retailers. A wholesaler purchases the goods from manufacturer in bulk quantity and re-sells it to retailers in small quantity. The term 'Wholesaler' has been defined as under:

Mason & Rath, "A person or firm that buys merchandise and re-sells it either to retailers for subsequent re-sale to the consumer or to business firm for industrial and business use is called a wholesaler."

Marris E. Hurley, "Wholesalers and marketing middlemen who occupy position midway between retailer and the producer or manufacturer."

American Marketing Association, "Wholesalers sell to other merchants and or industrial, institutional and commerical users but they do not sell in significant amounts to ultimate consumers."

On the basis of above definition, it can be concluded that a wholesaler is the first link in the chain of middlemen. A wholesaler purchases goods from manufacturers and sells to the retailers. He buys goods in large quantities and sells them to retailers in small quantities for re-sale to the industrial and commerical consumers. He does not sell the goods directly to the consumers. A wholesaler may be a sole trader, or a partnership firm or a company.

Characteristics of Wholesalers

Some of the important characteristics of wholesalers are as under:

1. A wholesaler buys the goods direct from the manufacturer.
2. A wholesaler purchases the goods generally in large quantities.
3. A wholesaler purchases the goods generally for cash.
4. Wholesalers have a team of agents who help them in selling the products to the retailers. Wholesalers provide the goods to the retailers generally at their trading places.
5. Wholesalers sometimes make grading of the goods under their own name or brand.
6. Wholesalers generally deal in a single product or limited products (generally in the products of a single product line.)
7. Wholesalers generally deals in the products of a single manufacturer as some limited manufacturers.
8. Wholesalers maintain warehouses and godowns at different places in the city or in different cities of the country.
9. The location of godown or office and display of goods is not of much importance to the wholesalers.

CLASSIFICATION OF WHOLESALER

Wholesalers can broadly be classified on the following basis—*(I)* On the basis of functions, *(II)* On the basis of areas served, *(III)* On the basis of services rendered. The deatils in this regard are as follows:

(I) Classification of Wholesalers on the Basis of Functions

On the basis of functions, wholesalers can be divided into three parts as follows:

(1) ***Manufacturer Wholesalers.*** Manufacturer Wholesalers are the persons engaged in manufacturing activities as well as in distribution activities. The manufacturers who sell their goods to the retails are known as manufacturer wholesalers. They may also make large-scale purchasing from other manufacturers so that the demand of retailers may be met. Main object to act as a manufacturer wholesaler is to play double role in marketing. It increases their profits.

(2) ***Retailer Wholesalers.*** Retailer wholesalers are the wholesalers who purchase goods directly from manufacturers, and sell them to the consumers. Thus, the manufacturers who retail their goods direct to the consumers through their own shops, are also called retailer wholesalers. In this manner, retailer wholesalers also play double role in marketing. It also helps them in minimising the costs, and increasing the sales and profits.

(3) ***Pure Wholesalers.*** Pure wholesalers are the wholesalers who carry the business of purchasing and selling the goods in large quantities only. Such wholesalers do not enagage themselves in the activities of production or retailing. Such wholesalers maintain their warehouses or godowns in different parts of the city or in different cities of the country. They collect goods from different manufacturers and supply these goods to the retailers. Such wholesalers are known as Distributors also.

Pure wholesalers can be further divided into three parts as follows:

(i) Mill Supply Wholesalers. Mill supply wholesalers are the wholesalers, who supply goods to the mills or manufacturers. Such wholesalers deal in raw-material, capital goods, equipments and other supplies. They purchase these materials and equipments from a large number of manufacturers in large quantities and supply to the industrial users. Such wholesalers generally sell their goods throughout a state or country through their agents.

(ii) Single Line Wholesalers. Single line wholesalers are the wholesalers who deal in a particular product line only. They purchase and sell different product items from different manufacturers of their line. In this manner, they maintain large varieties of goods of their line and sell them to the retailers.

(iii) Complete Line Wholesalers. Complete line wholesalers are the wholesalers who deal in complete line of goods required by a particular industry or a trade. Such wholesalers concentrate upon the needs and requirements of a particular trade only and they deal in all the necessities of such trade. For example, hospital supply wholesalers can supply all the requirements of hospitals.

(II) Classfication of Wholesalers on the Basis of Area Served

On the basis of area served, wholesalers can be divided into threc parts as follows:

(1) Local Wholesalers. Local wholesalers are the wholesalers who purchase goods from a number of manufacturers and re-sell these goods in a particular area or city only. Such wholesalers generally deal in the goods according to the requirements of retailers of their area. As these wholesalers are very close to the retailers, retailers feel it very convenient to purchase their requirements from such wholesalers.

(2) ***Regional Wholesalers.*** Regional wholesalers are the wholesalers who purchase goods in large quantities from different manufacturers and sell them to the retailers of a particular region. This region may be a state or some particular districts of state or a particular district. This type of wholesalers is very common these days.

(3) ***National Wholesalers.*** National wholesalers are the wholesalers, who purchase goods from different manufacturers and distribute these goods to the retailers all over the country. Such wholesalers supply goods to the local or regional wholesalers also.

(III) Classification of Wholesalers on the Basis of Services Rendered

On the basis of services rendered, wholesalers can be divided into five parts as follows:

(1) ***Jobbers.*** Jobbers are the wholesalers who purchase goods from different manufacturers and store these goods in their own godowns and sell them to the retailers. These wholesalers perform the activities of purchasing and selling only. They do not engage themselves in production activities. Such wholesalers are also known as Pure Wholesalers.

(2) ***Processors.*** Processors are the wholesalers who purchase goods from different manufacturers for grading and processing. They classify the goods into different grades and sell these goods according to their grades, generally in small packets. Sometimes, they sell these goods under their own brand name.

(3) ***Industrial Distributions.*** Such wholesalers act as wholesalers or distributors for a single manufacturers. These wholesalers collect goods from a single manufacturer only and sell these goods to the retailers in their authorised area.

(4) ***Exporters.*** Such wholesalers purchase goods from different manufacturers of their country and sell these goods in

foreign countries. They may sell these goods in the same from or after processing.

(5) ***Importers.*** Such wholesalers purchase goods from foreign manufacturers and sell these goods to the manufacturers or wholesalers or retailers of their country. These wholesalers may sell the goods in the same form or after processing.

FUNCTION OF WHOLESALER

Wholesalers occupy a predominant position in the channels of distribution. This is more so in a widespread economy, where the wholesaling function is of vital importance. They assemble merchandise from many sources, warehouse it, and regroup the goods for convenient buying by retailers. Most modern wholesale merchants provide information and advisory services to retailers, and they are often in a position to provide local market information to manufacturers as well. Their most important service, of course, is that of making it possible for the manufacturer to sell to thosands of small retailers to whom the merchandise cannot be sold direct from the factory. This is more so because of their lack of resources and storage space to purchase in large quantities to make such direct purchase economically feasible. On the basis of functions they perform, wholesalers could be grouped as follows:

1. **Limited Function Wholesalers.** They are basically merchant wholesalers but do not provide full services, and often provide only the minimum services among the limited functions.
2. **General Merchandise Wholesalers.** Such a wholesaler never restricts the varieties of products to be handled. He may even handle unrelated product lines. For eample, a wholesaler may stock food items together with hardware. These kinds of middlemen are fast disappearing from the city areas since all fields are gradually getting specialised.
3. **General Line Wholsalers.** Contrary to the above kinds of wholesalers, they deal in closely related items, for example, a wholesaler dealing in various types of cosmetics.

In industrial goods marketing, these wholesalers are known as "industrial distributors." This kind of wholesalers is found in hardware and automobile spare parts business.

4. **Speciality Wholsalers.** As the name suggests this kind of wholesalers has introduced specialisation in the wholsale trade. Such a wholasaler deals only in one merchandise. But within that limited line he might offer the whole range and also specialise in concentrating of the products of a single or a special group of manufacturers. This will enable him to get all support from manuacturers including the sales promotional supports.

5. **Functional Wholesalers.** This kind of wholsalers actually falls under the category of Agent middlemen. They do not take title to merchandise nor do they see the goods they sell. Their main function is to facilitate selling, although there are some buying functional middlemen. They are classified into:

   (a) ***Brokers.*** This group operates to bring the buyer and the seller together. Brokers are especially important in the food, textile, real estate and in secondhand machinery markets. Primarily, brokers sell information—information of products available for sale or purchase.

   (b) ***Drop-shipment Wholesalers.*** Though by nature they are also wholesalers, they do not handle the good they sell. They simply collect orders from retailers and pass them on the manufacturers who deliver the goods direct to the retailers. Such wholesalers are found in industrial marketing. They perform most of the wholesaling functions, with the exception of storage and handling.

   (c) ***Commission Merchants.*** They are mostly found in the agricultural marketing field and handle the selling function for large numbers of producers. Like the broker, a commission merchant finds markets for the products. But unlike the broker, he generally handles

the goods he sells but does not own them. Consequent on the emergency of co-operative marketing in the agricultural sector in recent years, the importance of these merchants has declined.

(d) ***Manufacturers' Agents.*** These agents work for several non-competing manufacturers and act as sales representatives for them in a territory. Their man job is to call on and sell to wholesalers and industrial buyers. As a rule, the manufacturer's agent does not handle goods. He sends the orders to the manufacturer, who, in turn, delivers the products direct to buyers.

(e) ***Selling Agents.*** Like the manufacturers' agents, selling agents sell for the manufacturers but usually handle the entire output of such manufacturers. They take over the entire marketing job for a commission. The selling agent is prominent in the texitle and drugs and pharmaceutical industries, where many small producers have to sell products fast and at the lowest possible cost.

(f) ***Converters.*** They operate both as manufacturers and wholsalers. But their production operation would be simple, concentrating more on selling. This is found in textile industry, where the raw cotton is bought and after dyeing, printing, etc., finished cloth is sold. These kinds of wholesalers are rarely found in India.

(g) ***Assemblers.*** Their specialisation is in the agricultural field. Some are agent middlemen and some are merchant middlemen, and in most cases they combine both the types. Their main job is assembling goods from various places.

SERVICES OF WHOLESALERS

Whoesalers are vital link between manufacturers and retailers. They purchase the goods from different manufacturers and sell these goods to the retailers. Thus, wholesalers render very important services both to the manufacturers and retailers. Some of the important services rendered by manufacturers are divided into three parts: *(I)* Services to the manufacturers, *(II)* Services to the retailers. *(III)* Service to the consumers. The details in this regard are as follows:

(I) Services to the Manufacturers

The wholesalers render following services to the manufacturers:

(1) **Facilities of Distribution.** Wholesalers take over the liability of manufacturers to distribute the goods produced by them. Thus, they relieve manufacturers from this liability.

(2) **Helpful in Concetrating upon Production.** As most of the liabilities of manufacturers are taken over by wholesalers, manufacturers can concetrate upon production. They have not to bother about distribution.

(3) **Helpful in Large-scale Producton.** Wholesalers help in increasing the sales of goods. They purchase the goods from manufacturers in large quantities. It enables the manufacturers to produce at large-scale. Large-sale production help the manufacturers in reducing the cost of production considerably.

(4) **Helpful in Expanding the Market.** Wholesalers distribute the goods produced by the manufacturers in different segments of the market. They try to sell these goods in new market also. It is the wholesaler who makes the goods produced by a manufacturer available in all parts of the country. Thus wholesalers help in expanding the market for products.

(5) **Benefit of Advertisement.** Generally, the wholesalers advertise on their own expenses. It helps manufacturers in increasing the sales of their products, it re-doubles the effect of advertisement.

(6) **Helpful in Standardisation and Grading.** Some of the wholesalers sort out the products into different grades.

These grades are developed on the basis of common characteristics or quality or nature of products. It helps manufacturers to adopt the policy of standardisation and grading.

(7) **Helpful in Price Determination.** As wholealers are in close touch with the retailers they can be of great help in determining the price of products.

(8) **Facility of Raw-materials.** Wholesalers provide the facility of raw-materials also to the manufacturers. Different type of raw-materials are collected by wholesalers from different manufacturers and sold to the manufacturers of consumer goods.

(9) **Financial Help.** Wholesalers provide financial help also to the manufacturers because they purchase goods in large quantities and generally on cash payment. Some wholesalers make advance payment also while placing their orders.

(10) **Facility of Storage.** Wholesalers take over the liability of manufacturers of storing goods also. They store the goods manufactured by manufacturers in their own godowns and thus, the manufacturers are relieved from the liability of storing the products.

(II) Services to the Retailers

Wholesalers provide some very important and useful services to the retailers. These services may be explained as under:

(1) **Financial Assistance.** Financial resources of retailers are generally limited. Wholesalers provide valuable financial assistance to them by selling the goods to them on credit. It helps the retailers in maintaining rotation of their working capital.

(2) **Benefit of Advertisement.** Wholesalers generally advertise for the products dealt with by them. Such advertisement is very helpful to the retailers because they get direct benefit from it. It increases their sales and profits.

(3) **Valuable Consultation.** Wholesalers advise retailers on their marketing problems for time to time. Advice of wholesalers is very useful for the retailers in solving their marketing problems and in increasing their sales.

(4) **Helpful in Making Selection.** A wholesaler generally maintains large variety of a product. It helps retailers in making the selection of variety.

(5) **Helpful in Purchasing the Goods According to Needs.** As the goods are purchased by wholesalers in large quantities and sold to the retailers in small quantities, the retailers get the facility of purchasing the goods in the quantity of their need.

(6) **Stability in Prices.** Wholesalers purchase the goods in large quantities and sell them to the retailers in small quantities. Thus, the risk of fluctuations in price is borne by the wholesalers themselves. This helps retailers in stabilising their prices.

(7) **Facility of Packaging.** The goods are packed generally by the wholesalers. They pack the goods in different sizes according to the specifications suggested by retailers. It helps retailers in selling these goods to the consumers in different size or quantities.

(8) **Facilitiy of Sorting, Grading and Standardisation.** The activities of sorting, grading and standardisaton are performed by the wholesalers. It relieves the retailers from this liability.

(9) **Facility of Transportation.** Generally,the wholesalers provide goods to the retailers at their shops. It relieves the retailers from the liability of transportation.

(10) **Benefits of Specialisation.** Generally, the wholesalers deal with the product of a particular product line or a particular producer. It this manner, the wholesalers are generally the specialists of their line. Retailers get the advantage of their ability, efficiency and experience.

(III) Services to the Consumers

Though the wholesalers are not in direct touch with the consumers, yet they offer some valuable services to the consumers. Some of the services provided by wholesalers to the consumer are as under:

(i) Wholesalers provide neccessary information to the consumers about new products introduced in the market. They do so by their advertisement programmes.

(ii) Wholesalers distribute the goods to the retailers according to the needs, wants and requirements of consumers.

(iii) Wholesalers maintain large variety of a product. Therefore, the wholesalers help in increasing the variety to be maintained by retailers and thus, the consumers get full range of a product.

(iv) Wholesalers undertake market research also. This is also beneficial to the consumers.

(v) Wholesalers maintain equilibrium in the demand and supply of products.

(vi) Wholesalers help in stabilising the prices of products in the market.

(vii) Wholesalers help the manufacturers in production. It provides the goods to the consumers at most reasonable prices.

ELEMENTS OF PHYSICAL DISTRIBUTION

Physical distribution can be defined as those activities involved with the storage and movement of products from the producer to the consumers. Physical distribution creates 'time' and 'place' utility, which maximizes the value of products by delivering them when and where they are wanted. The basic elements that make up physical distribution are as follows:

1. **Communication.** This includes the inforamtion system which should link producers, intermediaries, and customers. Computers, memory systems, display equipment and other

communication technology facilitate the flow of information among other members in the channel.

2. **Transportation.** It is an essential element of physical distribution. It involves integrating the advantages of each transportation method by adopting containers and physical handling procedures to permit transfers among different types of carriers. For example, to place containers in railway flat cars and then load the containers on motor vehicles is called "piggyback," and if containers are off loaded to water carriers, it is called "flashback." Exchange of containers between air and truck carriers are referred to as "Air Truck" or "birdyback."

   The marketing manager has to decide to *(i)* What mode or combination of modes of transportation (rail, truck, pipe line, water-ways or air) should be used to transport products to warehouses and from there to customers? *(ii)* Should the transport equipment be owned or leased? *(iii)* How can transportation cost be reduced and the desired levels of customer service still maintained.

3. **Order Processing.** Order processing and inventory control are related to each other. It comprises in undertaking the processes that are needed to make certain orders processed quickly, accurately, and efficiently. The marketing manager has to decide about these along with such issues as what is the most efficient way to bill customers: how can the paper work be minimised? And how can be the physical function of assembling orders more efficient?

4. **Inventory Planning & Control.** Inventory refers to the stock of products a firm has on hand and ready for sale to customers. It is manufactured goods to the manufacturer who hopes these can be sold to middlemen or industrial users. It is goods ready for the retailers or wholesaler which can be resold. For example, a hotel's inventory is the number of rooms it has available. An airline is the

number of seats (for people) or pallets (for freight) it has available.

Marketing managers undertake an inventory planning to develop assortments of products for the target market and also try to control the costs involved in obtaining and maintaining inventory. Marketing managers generally take three dicisions while conducting inventory management, *viz.*, *(i)* How can the track be kept, on a day-to-day basis of location, amount and the condition of the inventory? *(ii)* How can inventory information best be channeled to production managers or buyers for resale to help them schedule their activities *(iii)* What inventory information can other departments in the organisation use to help them perform their functions efficiently.

5. **Organisational Structure.** The person incharge of the physical distribution should coordinate all activities into an effective system to provide the desired customer service in the most efficient manner. Examples of organisational consideration are: *(i)* How can the five elements of physical distribution best be co-ordinated so that a team effect results? *(ii)* How can compartmentalisation thinking be avoided? *(iii)* If a central head is established to direct all physical distribution activities, to whom should he report? The Head of the Marketing? The Chief Executive Officer?

6. **Materials Handling** involves moving products in and out of a stock. It consists of routine tasks that can be performed through mechanisation and standardisation. Efficiency is increased through use of eletronic data processing to control conveyor systems, order picking and other traffic flaws. Under this, the marketing manager generally decides such issues as: *(i)* how can the product change be minimised in ware-houses, in distribution centres, and while the goods are in transit *(ii)* What kinds of equipments are needed to help more goods inside warehouses and to

transportation modes in the most efficient manner and with the least damage? *(iii)* How can it be made certain that prodcuts are shipped in the most efficient manner? *(iv)* Can containerization (use of sealed containers for sizing) and palletization (use of pallets for handling materials) be used more effectively?

Significance of Physical Distribution

1. It represents a large shape in the national wealth in the form of facilities-railroad, trucks, highways, aircrafts, ships, docking facilities, pipelines, and storage facilities and equipment.
2. It facilitates geographic specialisation. Each area produces goods that its natural resources, climate or pool of manpower resources enable it to produce more efficiently.
3. It creates utilities of time and place, by making availble a product when it is needed at the place where it is needed.
4. It accounts for a major portion of marketing costs. According to one estimate, physical distribution costs require as much as 60% of the total marketing cost and range according to industries, from 10 per cent to 30 per cent of sales revenues—for machinery these were 9.8%. wood products 16.1% paper and allied products 16.7%. Chemicals, petroleum and rubber 23.1% and primary and fabricated meals 26.5%.
5. It determines standard of living. This is so because distribution of products properly make them available to a large number of people, at a relatively lower cost.

Objectives of Physical Distribution

The principal broad objective is to move products to other channel members and to consumers in the efficient way that is consistent with the level of service that customers require. In other words, efficiency and satisfactory service are key goals of physical distribution, although there might be some conflict with each other. Other objectives are:

(a) To provide better customer service. By improving the physical distribution system, the firm's promotional efforts are strengthened.

(b) To increase sales, by making certain that basic products in regular demand are always available, and having contingency plans for quick order processing of items.

(c) To reduce cost, by intelligently managing the physical distribution system and determining the optimum number and location of warehouses, improving materials handling, increasing stock turnover, and using sealed containers to ship products.

MARKET CONSIDERATIONS IN PHYSICAL DISTRIBUTION

The marketing manager should take the following considerations in mind while making decisions about physical distribution:

(1) The changes in customers or technology, can be met by combing orders and developing more central control over the physical movement of products.

(2) The requirements of an organization's marketing strategy. The requirement for reducing cost to meet customer satisfaction can be fulfilled by looking to speedy delivery, reliability of product and the availability of service.

(3) Adjustment to changing environment circumstances, such as delivering the goods at the very door of the customers or using coupons that may be exchanged for the product at the supermarkets.

(4) Analysis of the characteristics of the target market, and then designing a system to provide products at an acceptable price.

Determination of Channel Length

Channel of distribution may be classified into two categories, short and long.

A short channel is one where few middlemen are involved in the marketing of the product: In such a channel, the product moves from a producer directly to consumer.

On the other hand, a long channel is one where the product moves from a product to agent to another agent, to a merchant wholesale, to a retailer, and, finally to the consumer.

The marketing management has to decide the length of the channel of distribution, keeping in view certain factors, although there may be some exceptions of these—such as common sense and a solid knowledge of ones market, product, competition, and own strength. The factors are:

1. **Market Concentration.** Short channel is to be used in a high-density market area than in a low density market area, for in the former case, more calls per day can be made by the salesmen so that their expenses could be covered in a better way. On the other hand, if customers are scattered over a wide area, long channels would be more desirable.
2. **Order Size.** When the value of the orders received is low, long channel need be utilized. Processing many small orders at the company's plant is usually a costly way to distribute goods. Other middlemen, accustomed to buying in large quantities and then breaking bulk, is cheaper for the company.
3. **Technical Product.** The greater the technical aspects of the product, the more likely that short channels are to be used. Where technical knowledge or technical sales services is needed, the number of middlemen, between the manufacturer and customer, should be as few as possible.
4. **Size of the Product Line.** The broader the product line, the shorter the channel should be. The producers of a simple product find it difficult to sell directly to the customer. Salesmen may not be able to sell a large enough quantity on each call to cover the expense of the call.

5. **Unit Value.** The larger the unit value of a product the shorter the channel.

6. **Gross Margin.** The higher the gross margin, the greater is the opportunity for using a short channel. Products that can be priced so as to support the costs of selling direct from manufacturer to customer can support shorter channels.

7. **Financial Resources.** When the manufacturers have lesser financial resources, they generally use long channels.

8. **Resale Price Maintenance.** Shorter channels are usually preferred where the producer wants to maintain control over the pricing of the product. In dealing with price, advertising, or distribution, a manufacturer can better control how, when, where and to whom his product will be sold, if he maintains close surveillance of his product.

9. **Convenience Goods.** Long channels are desirable for goods which are frequently purchased; but where goods to be sold are speciality or shopping goods, short channels are preferred:

10. **Location.** Where the location of the firm is near the customers, short channel is to be used so that better results could be got.

❐

13
Advertisement Management

Advertising is only one of the tools of marketing, playing a greater or lesser role than product policy, pricing, packaging, distribution, personal selling, or sales promotion, dependent upon the goods or services offered. Its function is to inform and enhance the value of the thing avertised.

How it Works

While most effective advertising to some degree encompasses both, advertising is usually strategically designed to accomplish one of two objectives: *(1)* inform or *(2)* persuade.

Informational. Informational advertising is used to introduce new products, services, or ideas, announce events or sales, or to remind people of existing products or services.

Persuasion. Persuasion advertising is used to convince the target audience to prefer the product or service advertised over alternatives. The approach may be rational, offering a logical reason based upon an evaluative scale that supports the superiority of the product or service offered. It may also either emotional or humorous.

Advertising Accountability

There is, of course, no room for dishonesty in advertising, and advertisers should be prepared fully to document any statements of fact they make about their product or service. Critics of advertising usually concede the importance of informational advertising, but attack persuasion strategy on the grounds that it talks people into buying things they don't want or need or that it misrepresents the benefits one actually received.

To gain an understanding of the value of persuasion advertising, one must recognize that human needs are often conceptual in nature, not materialistic. Quoting Theodore Levity: "The human audience demands" symbolic interpretation in everything it sees and knows. Without symbolism life would be even more confusing and anxiety-ridden than it is with it.

...The product is not what the engineer explicitly says it is, but what the consumer implicitly demands that it shall be. Thus, the consumer consumes not things but expected benefits—not cosmetics, but the satisfactions of the allurements they promise; not quarter-inch drills, but quarter-inch holes: etc."

Thus, rather than misrepresenting products or services, persuasion advertising should enable the consumer to perceive products and services as fulfilling various needs he might otherwise over look.

Client/Agency Relationships

Compensation. For the most part, clients compensate their advertising agencies on an illogical basis. Although the agency reports to the client and must gain client approval of all its recommendations, and is very often held responsible for the sales performance, the agency is paid for its services by the media. Furthermore, this compensation fluctuates with the media budget-typically 15% of space and time billings—which mayor may not have anything to do with the agency's performance.

The agency fee system is a more logical answer to this obviously unstable 15% media-commissioned system. The fee is a negotiated contract, usually based upon the historical compensation that the agency has expected, and is related to the tasks to be accomplished. Working under the fee system, the agency is free objectively to analyze a given marketing problem without biasing its judgment in favor of increased advertising spending.

How to Work with Your Agency. Effective advertising is a unique combination of business science and art form. The agency will perform most effectively when the business aspects are highly disciplined by the client and the creative execution is left to the agency. This means that your agency should demonstrate a thorough knowledge of your business. The client, on the other hand, must make this happen by freely discussing both short and long-range marketing plans and sharing all sales data regarding performances and projections.

The agency is then held responsible for a written statement of what the advertising should accomplish and how it will be done. This document is usually called the Creative Strategy and should contain the objective of the advertising, the Target Audience, the Buying Incentive (or "Reason Why") and the Totality of the advertising.

When this statement has been agreed to by the client and agency, all creative submissions should be evaluated only by the criteria of the written statement. Creative judgments should be left to the agency. In a similar manager the agency should prepare written strategies for media and sales promotion. If an advertiser needs only some marketing advice and a few ads and commercials, he can get high-caliber work at a reduced cost. However, most large advertisers will continue to require the range of services offered by large agencies.

In addition, the international advertiser will most often find his needs best served by the large international agency that can coordinate worldwide marketing efforts through a network of offices and local agency affiliations.

Development of Advertiser In-House Capabilities

Over the years, a number of advertisers, motivated by cost consciousness, developed in house capabilities to perform services traditionally handled by advertising agencies-media, research, and creative. An extreme form of this development is the so-called "house agency."

This trend originally gained impetus from cost-cutting needs, as well as from the adoption of the brand-management system.

However, disaffection with the idea stemmed from the difficulty of attracting outstanding creative talent from the more stimulating agency environment.

The in-house agency phenomenon is still extant, but analysis by the 4-A's (American Association of Advertising Agencies) show that the trend has peaked. Only the largest advertisers with the volume to support the additional overhead (*e.g.*, Lever) can afford to bring the entire advertising function in-house.

Consumerism

"Consumerism" will certainly continue to affect the future of advertising. While Consumer-Research and other organizations representing consumer interests have been active for many years, the current highly publicized phase began with the publication of Ralph Nader's book. "Unsafe At Any Speed." The timing was right. People's needs for products and services were becoming stated. Now they could afford to become critical.

In terms of its impact on advertising, consumerism has given rise to, or has strengthened, existing watchdog agencies, particularly the Food and Drug Administration and the Federal Trade Commission. Product labeling and product advertising claims re being questioned not merely on a factual basis, but also in terms of product presentation.

Another aspect of the impact of consumerism on advertising is the considerable concern over the quantity and quality of advertising directed at children, since children are assumed to be less able to discriminate between advertising claims of competitive-products.

Advertising Research

The function of advertising research is first to provide maximum input to the creative people, and then to reduce the number of alternative strategies which inevitably develop as the creative process unfolds.

Development of Creative Strategy. In the first stage, research can provide basic intelligence about motivations and needs. The research techniques used include qualitative analysis of competitive advertising, focus-group and individual depth interviews among consumers representative of the users of the product category, and thorough research of existing secondary source material.

Once alternative creative strategies have been developed, research aids in isolating the one strategy likely to have the greatest leverage with the consumer. The techniques typically include individual or group interviews, concept tests with or without advertising roughs, etc.

Pretesting Individual Advertisement. The objective is to determine the strongest execution of a given creative strategy. For print advertisements, this is frequently accomplished through the placement of the test ad(s) in a portfolio of control advertisements, or in a dummy magazine. A sample of consumers is exposed to the portfolio or magazine, and subsequently questioned on a variety of criteria.

For television commercials, pretesting can be accomplished by substituting test commercials for regularly scheduled commercials in a number of markets, and then conducting telephone interviews with a sample of viewers of the respective television programs. Alternative techniques include the screening of test commercials with sample groups in theaters, in mobile vans or storefronts located in shopping centers, or by screening the commercials on portable motive projectors in respondents' homes.

Frequently, tests conducted in shopping centers include the added refinement of distributing "cents off" coupons to the consumers exposed to the various test commercials. Subsequent coupon redemptions provide a behavioral measure of the relative effectiveness of the commercial tested.

Media

In recent years, media planning and media buying have become increasingly important and complex. During the past decade audience data have proliferated-specifically magazines and televisions. The major services, American Research Bureau (ARB) and Nielsen for TV, and Simmons and Brand Rating Index (BRI) primarily for magazines, have made it possible more clearly to pinpoint demographic target audiences and product users through media selection.

Thanks to computerization, it is now possible to retrieve these data and analyze them to select media. The computer has been used not only for the purpose of data retrieval, but also for simulation techniques (setting up a model that simulates the universe) and optimization in media selection (the combination of media elements that best satisfy the objectives). Because the costs of media are increasing, planning is critical to ensure a minimum of wasted advertising effort.

There are five major media, all of which have experienced major changes during recent years:

Television. Television trends are:

(1) TV is a nature medium, with penetration of 98%. The per centage of homes owning color TV sets has now increased until it is almost 83% of TV homes. The total number of TV stations exceed 750.

(2) Greatest growth is expected in cable. There are over 4,000 cable systems now serving 14 million homes (19% of all TV homes). By 1990, cable penetration is expected to be 45%.

(3) New technology like communication satellites that feed programming from distant points has already spurred the development of satellite networks and alternative program suppliers in competition with the currently existing three networks.

(4) TV is moving to a more personalized medium with growing acceptance in the future of programming supplied on video cassettes and video discs. Pay cable may erode network TV viewing levels by 1990 by an estimated 10%.

(5) Despite pressure of increased costs to use TV, the basic advertising unit continues to be a 3D-second commercial. No trend is discerned in the use of shorter length commercials because of fear of erosion of effectiveness.

Magazines. Magazine trends are:

(1) Magazines increase cover prices to consumers and continue escalating space rates to advertisers because of inflationary costs of paper, printing, and subscription mailing.

(2) Increased availability of small-circulation specialized consumer magazines to reach and segment upscale selective audiences. These consumer magazines fall within three categories:

(a) Avocational Magazines, Ski, Golf, Popular Photography.

(b) General Editorial, Harper's, Atlantic, Saturday Review, Reader's Digest.

(c) Metropolitan: New York, Chicago, LA.

In addition to the above of course are the traditional specialized trade and professional publications.

(3) Advertising flexibility in terms of shorter closing, regional and demographic flexibility to continue as magazines offer greater availability of standard size 7-in by 10-in page.

(4) Trend toward reducing charges for bleed as more magazines move toward computerized printing using of set and gravure reproduction on lighter paper.

(5) Cost experimentation with alternate distribution methods, *e.g.* newspaper carriers, to help keep advertising costs down and in line with other media efficiencies. Greater reliance on newsstand and supermarket distribution.

Newspapers. Basic trends in the newspaper industry are:

(1) Daily newspaper circulation during the past ten years has grown at a much slower rate than the general population.

(2) Non-dailies (*i.e.* weekly suburban and shoppers) have increased circulation at a faster pace than metro dailies.

(3) Ability to utilize color via Rap (Run of Press), Spot Color, HiFi, Spectacular, is growing, but fastest growing segment of the newspaper medium is the pre-printed insert which now totals about 30 billion.

(4) Newspapers are providing more opportunity to provide greater reader selectivity through special editorial sections on living, food, sports, etc., greater reliance on features,

and emphasis on state and local news. Geographic flexibility *via* availability of zone editions.

(5) Newspapers, in an effort to increase national advertiser usage, are now offering continuity rates and standardized fixed size ads to avoid increased production costs of material requireds by different newspaper formats.

Radio. Trends in radio are:

(1) Radio has become a highly personalized medium because of the emergence of the portable transistor radio.

(2) Radio has shifted from the all-family/all-entertainment medium to all casual listening" background medium.

(3) Eight thousand radio stations have become highly selective in appealing to different consumer demographic audiences by programming varied music offerings from disco, rock to classical music preferences, and all news.

(4) FM radio has exploded into a mass audience medium with listening levels now exceeding AM.

(5) Technological developments on the horizon for radio include satellite transmission (RKO radio network), stereophonic (AM), and quadrophonic sound (FM)

Media Buying Services

Media buying services buy broadcast time for an advertiser or an agency's client(s) and receive remuneration in the form of an agreed-upon fee, or the difference between an advertiser's planned expenditures versus actual expenditures by the buying service in satisfying a client's advertising support levels. The services degree of success is dependent upon a number of factors:

(1) The ability of their personnel to negotiate for broadcast time.

(2) The inability of agency media departments to get the most for their money.

(3) The emergence of small agencies, specializing in creative output, that are unwilling to assume the financial overhead required by an in-house media staff.

The buying service phenomenon, like that of the in-house agency, has crested. Agencies have increased their buying capability and controls. The greater sophistication of advertiser and more agency accountability have enabled agencies to help sell their media expertise to advertisers. Additionally, financial failures such as those by Media Corporation of America and Air Time have served to remind advertisers of the fiscal responsibility of agencies and the risk of double liability.

"Creative" *vs.* "Selling" Messages

With the proliferation of products (and ad messages), it became apparent that success in the market depended heavily on the ingenuity of the creative minds in advertising agencies. Headline are written, visuals are drawn. The result is a rough layout of an ad. How to evaluate it? Is it interesting? Believable? Readable? Understandable? Factual? Does it meet the marketing strategy?

The communications tools available to creative departments are many. and varied humor, emotion, demonstration, testimonial, emulation, animation, live action, color, sound, photography, illustration (even smell coming up). All must be considered.

As ad budgets expanded during the last half of the 1960s, a certain creative carelessness" crept into advertising. Television advertising, in particular, was carried to excess. The advertiser's product was often left behind as commercials became mini-movies in which the most important criterion was "Is it entertaining?" rather than "Is it selling?" Some commercials tried to become 60 second Hollywood musical extravagances. Other commercials tried, to establish their creative reputations by using incredibly expensive production techniques or talent.

The recession that ushered in the 1970s changed this situation dramatically. Budgets were cut. Creative staffs were pared down to a professional hard core. And media cost efficiencies all but doomed the 60-second TV commercials as the 30-second length became the popular buy.

Advertising: Results

Every advertising message has different results among its receivers. Each ad plays many different roles, simultaneously contributing to many of the firm's goals. Exhibit I depicts a way of thinking about the roles of advertising as a means of attaining certain desired ends in a business enterprise. In this example, top management's principal end is to increase profits by reducing costs or increasing sales. Here we shall concentrate on "increase sales."

Marketing Means

Marketing has fouraltemative means for reaching its end: the "Four Ps of Marketing" product, price, and promotion. Our concern is with the fourth P.

The marketing means of improving promotion automatically become an end for the sales manager, the sales promotion manager, and the advertising manager. Translated into their own areas of responsibility, the three ends are *(1)* improve personal selling, *(2)* improve sales promotional and *(3)* improve advertising. Five strategy areas are available to improve advertising: *(1)* copy *(2)* medial *(3)* budget *(4)* size *Vs.* frequency and *(5)* timing.

Copy as used here refers to all of the physical elements in the finished advertisements—not only the words in headline text and script but also layout artwork photographic and film techniques animations and sound effects. Media strategy variables are the alternative offerings of magazines newspapers broadcast stations or networks outdoor, and car-card representatives and direct mail services. Budget strategy may be varied in absolute amounts or by share of product-class or industry advertising expenditures. Within a given media mix at a given cost the advertiser must decide such size-frequency strategy questions as: Shall he use ten daytime sixty-second TV commercials per week or fewer more expensive commercials in prime evening time? Double spreads every other issue *vs.* a full page in each issue? Timing or continuity strategy determines the period within a year during which the advertising shall be exposed.

Goals for Advertising

It is impossible to assign to advertising specific communications tasks that are separate from marketing goals. Thus, rather than having its own goals advertising has a continuing responsibility to learn more about the ability of advertising to serve as a means of attaining higher-order company goals, For example can advertising be used to increase distribution? Will a consumer contest increase market share? Is it possible to change the coverage or frequently of the media schedule to increase incremental profit? For every product or brand there are literally hundreds of unanswered questions such as these.

A complete marketing plan calls for an integrated marketing attach with advertising personal selling and sales promotion all striving for the same goals (*e.g.*, more distribution more displays more shelf facings) as a means for marketing management to attain its end of increased sales.

Marketplace Outcomes

One of the ways of varying promotion strategy is to vary advertising strategy. The resulting marketplace outputs may be conveniently classified under the following "response" headings:

(1) Advertising Memory, (2) Brand Image, (3) Marketing Environment, (4) Sales, and (5) Profit.

Advertising Memory Response. The most frequently measured result of advertising is the memory of the advertisement itself. This may be measured by the recognition method in which the ad itself is used to stimulate memory of it, or measurement may be by the limited exposure tachistoscopic technique or the aided recall method.

Brand Image Response. The differing mental pictures of the company, brand, product, or service form a continuum running from awareness through beliefs to intention. A prospective customer can have brand awareness of high or low saliency. High saliency is though to be indicated by the response to a question of the type,

"What brand to you think of when mention 'cigarettes'?" This response, or top-of-mind awareness, is a composite effect of all previous message received about the brand, plus the experience of use, if any.

Beliefs may be expressed as specific product attributes stated by respondents or classified by the interviewer's assessment of the amount of information possessed by respondents. Beliefs can also be expressed as semantic differentials along a peasant-unpleasant scale. Intention may be defined as a "predisposition to act" to buy or recommend a product.

Marketing Environment Response. It is in the changing of the surrounding conditions or influences that lead to sales, that advertising can often make its greatest contribution. Sales miracles can occasionally happen when a product is offered for a different end use (as occurred dramatically when Listerine advertising was switched from offering the product as a household antiseptic, to advertising it as a mouthwash to prevent "halitosis.)" Similarly, pricing, packaging and display strategies, and the advertising of special offers can often cause larger units of sale, with a consequent increase in consumption rate. Advertising can affect timing of purchase. Consumer desire for the newest model or current fashion is a powerful environmental effect. Upgrading is an important response to advertising, e.g., buying the new car with accessories that have been made essential. Other environmental responses afflicted by advertising are increased distribution, increased product display and dealer promotion, and increased store traffic. (Examples of the last-named are sweepstakes which only require visiting a dealer to qualify for a chance to win a prize, and contests which call for getting entry blanks at the point of sale.) Inquiries developed through advertising are important sales leads.

Sales Response. Variations in total sales volume and in sales share are widely used measures of marketing success. Two specific sales effects of particular interest are variations in trial purchases and repeat purchases. The former should be a focal point for advertising management's attention. Repeat purchases are primarily the result of satisfactory product experience, although the reminder effect of advertising does influence rebuying.

Profit Response. The profit contribution of advertising expenditures is, of course, the most difficult to measure of all market-place outcomes. The most appropriate measure is some form of incremental profit caused by advertising, *i.e.*, the difference in the firm's total profits with and without the advertising cost. This is difficult to do, but not always impossible.

Field Measurement of Advertising Results

Any method of measuring advertising results would necessarily include: *(1)* at least one finished or rough advertisement, *(2)* a sample or samples drawn from the target market population, *(3)* a means of exposing the advertisement to the samples, and *(4)* a survery of the samples so that their responses to the advertisement can be inferred.

Pre-advertising surveys can be either in the laboratory or in the field. For example, in one type of syndicated TV theater, the questions are asked while the audience is in the theater; in another, the questions are asked by telephoning to the respondents hoses the nexting-especially that of the manufacturer is entrusted to an advertising agency.

History

In the 1800s there were fewer than a dozen advertisers who spent as much as Rs. 1,00,000 a year. The largest magazine was the Anand Bazar Patrika with a circulation of 3200, and the leading advertisers were sellers of patent medicines. There was at that time no advertising agent (he was principally a space broker). In some four generations we have seen the development of America's mass markets, the development of a multitude of media, and the development of today's advertising agencies which in 1992 handled about Rs. 150 crores of annual advertising volume.

In those early days, publishers found that their white space was not particularly salable. Prospective advertisers were inclined to say, "I might buy some space, but what would I say?" The need for another service-planning of a comprehensive campaign, writing copy, creating layouts, etc. became apparent. However, publishers found that they could not successfully prepare advertising for competing manufacturers. Two soap manufacturers, for example, found it impracticable to go to one publisher and each rely on him to prepare an effective competitive campaign. Similarly manufactures discovered that they could not prepare their own advertising most efficiently. This required specialized talent, an outside objective viewpoint to appraise sales opportunities, and experience with many advertising problems on which to base decisions.

As a result, around 1880 the advertising service agency began to evolve, and it developed rapidly during the next 20 years. By 1900, the service agency was offering expert and specialized services both in planning the advertising program and in executing it. Its services had reached the professional stage. Creative activities were stressed, and the role of the agency had become that of increasing the effectiveness of the client's advertising. Today there are some 10,000 advertising agencies.

Approaches and Techniques

The agency must justify itself in dollars and cents: It must produce for the client a more profitable return on his advertising expenditure, usually in the form of sales, than he can secure through any other means—spending the money on other dynamic activities, handling the advertising himself, or delegating it to a competing advertising agency. The primary function of the advertising agency is to convert the white space of print media and the blank time of broadcast media into advertising influence to help sellers find customers for their goods and services.

Nearly all of the advertising of products and services seen and heard on television and radio, in magazines, on outdoor posters and painted bulletins, on car cards, and in newspapers (except the display advertising of retail stores, most classified advertising, and much direct mail) is created and placed in these advertising media by advertising agencies.

What Advertising Agencies Are

An advertising agency can be described as:

(1) An independent business organization

(2) composed of creative and business people

(3) providing a comprehensive advertising plan

(4) who develop, prepare, and place advertising in advertising media

(5) for sellers seeking to find customers for their goods and services.

It is emphasized that an advertising agency is an independent business organization independently owned and not owned by advertisers or media or suppliers which brings to the clients' problems an outside objective point of view made more valuable by experience with other clients' sales problems in other fields. It is independent of the clients so as to be always an advocate of advertising (seeking to apply advertising to help clients grow and prosper); it is independent of media and suppliers so as to be unbiased in serving its clients (the sellers of goods and services).

An advertising agency is composed of creative and business people—the writers and artists/ showmen and market analysts, media analysts, merchandising and research people, advertising specialists of all sorts. But with all this/ they are business people, running an independent business, financially responsible, applying their creative skills to the business of helping to make their clients' advertising succeed. These people develop, prepare, and place advertising in advertising media, seeking in every way they can to apply advertising to advance their-clients' business. Every thing that goes before and everything that comes after the advertisement is preparation of advertising follow up to help make it succeed. The agency does this/ not for itself, but for sellers' goods and services. To prepare and place advertising-successful advertising for the advertiser is the primary purpose of the advertising agency.

What Advertising Agencies Do

The work that advertising agencies do is described in the "Agency Service Standards" of the American Association of Advertising Agencies. These Service Standards, a delineation of fundamentals of successful agency operation, enable advertisers and media to know what to demand and agencies to know what may be expected of them in dealing with the problems of advertising. Agency service, according to the "Agency Service Standards," consists of interpreting to the public or to that part of it which it is desired to reach, the advantages of a product or service. This interpretation is based upon:

(1) A study of the client's product or service in order to determine the advantages and disadvantages inherent in the product itself, and in its relation to competition.

(2) An analysis of the present and potential market for which the product or service is adapted:

(a) As to location

(b) As to extent of possible sale

(c) As to season

(d) As to trade and economic conditions

(e) As to nature and amount of competition

(3) A knowledge of the factors of distribution and sales and their methods of operation.

(4) A knowledge of all the available media and means which can profitably be used to carry the interpretation of the product or service to consumer, wholesaler, dealer, contractor, or other factor. This knowledge covers:

(a) Character

(b) Influence

(c) Crculation

Quality

Location

(d) Physical requirements

(e) Costs

Acting on the study, analysis, and knowledge as explained in the preceding paragraphs, recommendations are made and the following procedure ensures:

(5) Formulation of a definite plan and presentation of this plan to the client.

(6) Execution of this plan:

(a) Writing, designing, illustrating of advertisements, or other appropriate forms of the message.

(b) Contracting for the space, time, or other means of advertising.

(c) The proper incorporation of the message in mechanical form and forwarding it with proper instructions for the fulfillment of the contract.

(d) Checking and verifying of insertions, display, or other means used.

(e) The auditing and billing for the service, space, and preparation.

(7) Cooperation with the client's sales work, to insure the greatest effect from advertising.

These are the elements of agency service, whether all of the functions above are shared by a few persons or each function is carried on separately by a specialized department. Into this pattern fit account executives who contact the client, art directors, copywriters, space and time buyers, researchers, production people, and others who work in advertising agencies.

Additional Agency Service

In addition to the advertising services described above, there is a willingness among many agencies today to assist the client with his other activities of distribution. Thus they do special work for the manufacturer in such fields as package designing, sales research, sales training, preparation of sales and service literature, designing of merchandising displays, public relations and publicity. But always the agency must justify such work by doing it more satisfactorily than can either the manufacturer himself or a competing expert.

The agency must be prepared to handle advertising in any medium for a client, even though he has never used it, if the agency deems the medium best for the client's purposes. It must be prepared to serve a client whenever and wherever his advertising should run—as for example, advertisers having seasonal peaks. The agency must therefore have adequate personnel with specialists in many fields. The expense of the "readiness to serve" is an important factor in agency costs. In general, the advertising agency is a hazardous business.

Sources of Agency Compensation

Nearly all major media—newspapers, magazines, television, radio, business publications, outdoor plant owners, and transit advertising companies—allow commissions to advertising agencies, which the media recognize individually.

Larger advertising agencies receive, on the average, about 75% of their income in the form of commissions allowed by advertising media, 25% from the agencies' own per centage charges on purchases (which they specify and/or supervise for their clients) and fees of various kinds for special services. Among medium sized agencies the corresponding figures are 70% and 30%, and among smaller agencies 50% and 50%. Agency service charges and fees are arrived at individually by agreement between each agency and client.

The principle of media allowing commissions to agencies is the sparkplug incentive for agencies. It makes advertising agencies dynamic. More than anything else, it is a great incentive principle, and the principle has benefited all business. The agency business has attracted a high type of businessman, a particularly enterprising type, one who is willing to take the risk that his agency will not get paid at all if the creative work is not used.

Because the agency is rewarded in proportion to the use made of its creative work, the agency owner is encouraged to hire the best creative people he can find. He is not led to stint on staff or to take too much of profits for himself. This means that the finest possible creative organization is put behind the service and development of advertising. It is the main reason why American advertising. It is the main reason why American advertisers have available to them some of the most skilled advertising agencies in the world. In uncounted instances, advertising agencies have enabled small companies to prosper and grow into large ones.

ADVERTISING MEDIA

Broadcasting

Broadcasting is the newest method of selling goods and services through advertising. Commercial radio began in the early 1920s and commercial television has been with us just over three decades. Yet in this short period of time, radio and television have established themselves as a dynamic tool of merchandising which reaches vast audiences of potential customers. More importantly, to a greater degree than any prior medium of communication, they have become a part of the lives and habits of the American people.

Organization of the Industry

The radio industry consists of almost 300 commercial AM stations and nearly 12 FM stations. From the advertiser's point of view this means that there is a local radio station in nearly every city and town of over 5,000 population and a good many in smaller towns than this. Radio is thus ideally suited for advertising which seeks to get to the grass roots on local basis. There are almost 450 million radios in working order and nearly every home has one or more sets. Most automobiles are equipped with radios. The development of portable transistor receivers means that radios may be taken to the beach, camping, and on picnics. In short, radio reaches everywhere.

The television industry consists of over 200 commercial television stations and three nationwide television networks. (Regional networks are also available to the advertiser in both radio and television). There are about 145 million television sets in use. Though the television industry is less than 35 years old 60% of all the households in the United States have one or more television sets.

In both radio and television, local stations are affiliated with networks under business contracts. The stations guarantee that they will carry a certain amount of network programming at certain hours, for which the network will compensate them. Thus, it is possible for the networks to offer a national advertiser a simultaneous network hookup which will carry its message throughout the entire United States. Stations provide their own programming if they are independent or during those hours when they are not carrying network programs. These programs may be locally developed or they may be purchased from outside sources. Thus the local station, whether affiliated or independent, can offer advertising time on a local basis.

How Broadcast Advertising is Sold. Broadcasting advertising can be defined as the use of commercial broadcast facilities, AM radio, FM radio, and television, by advertisers to promote and sell their services and products to the consumer. Commercial broad casting is thus an advertising medium like newspapers and magazines, but with a substantial difference. Unlike these media, which make a charge to the customer, broadcasting's only source of revenue is the advertise or sponsor.

The single most important characteristic of broadcast advertising is its flexibility. That is, the ability of an advertiser to purchase any amount of advertising and to distribute that advertising geographically in a manner which best suits his purposes. The advertiser can purchase announcements which vary in length from ten to sixty seconds, and they can be purchased in any quantity from one to several hundred or more. Such announcements may falt between programs or may be a part of a program in which other advertisers also participate. The client company may also sponsor an entire program and associate itself with it. Announcements or programs can be purchased in any combination of geographic areas up to and including national coverage. The advertising campaign can run at various times and can reach audiences of varying composition.

There are three basic methods of purchasing such advertising:

(1) Network Advertising. A network consists of a large number of stations geographically dispersed to provide national coverage and generally connected by microwave, satellite, or coaxial cable so that they simultaneously carry programs to a nationwide audience. Normally these programs are produced and transmitted from The production centres in New York. Holywood, and Washington. The network produces the program itself or purchases it from an outside program, source. An advertiser who Durchases a program, a portion of a program, or announcements pays the network, and the network in turn pays its affiliated stations for carrying these programs, at a specific rate which has been agreed upon in the business contract between them. The network thus undertakes the cost of production, distribution, and station compensation. Those sponsors who desire simultaneous national impact for their campaigns may purchase network advertising.

Years ago networks sold largely full program sponsorships. In an effort to accommodate the smaller advertiser, networks have devised various types of advertising such a participating shows in which several sponsors join. This makes it possible for the advertiser with the smaller budget to make good use of network advertising.

(2) National Spot Advertising. A promotion campaign can be planned to use "spot" radio or television. Advertising can be purchased on a station-by-station basis which enables an advertiser to tailor a campaign to specific needs by varying the markets and the stations used, frequency of exposure, the time periods and duration of the campaign. Spot advertising is often used by regional advertisers because it can be closely tailored to a limited distribution pattern. His also frequently used by national advertisers who have various reasons for wanting to advertise their product heavily in a particular area or particular combination of markets. Through spot advertising and advertiser can move in arid out of markets as his sales strategy dictates. In purchasing spot advertising the advertiser can use various programs which have been developed by the local station. Also available are various combinations of announcements.

Most stations retain a national spot representative. These organizations have offices in cities where most of the national spot buying is done, and they represent groups of stations, serving at their out-of-town sales for national advertising.

(3) Local Advertising. Advertising may, of course, also be purchased from a single local station. All stations have a variety of programs which are suitable for local advertisers who may purchase an entire program, a participation in a program, or announcements between programs. The writing of this business is handled by the local salesmen employed by the station. The local advertiser often relies on the station to develop commercials, which may include writing, artwork, and recording. Local advertising is designed especially for local business such as car dealers, drug stores, movie exhibitors, supermarkets, banks, department stores, etc.

Advertising Costs

As in most advertising, costs are determined by the size of the audience reached by the commercial message. In broadcasting, this audience varies substantially by time of day, the appeal of a particular program, and the popularity of a particular station. Thus, in radio and television the cost of advertising varies substantially, based upon these factors. For example, television reaches its largest audiences in the evening time period, and these time periods therefore carry the highest rates. This applies to network programs and to the cost of local announcements which are available between network programs. Radio typically reaches its greatest audience in the driving times of early morning and evening, and radio rates are thus highest during those time periods.

Most stations give discounts to advertisers on volume purchases. An advertiser who purchases a "package" of ten or twenty announcements per week will pay less for each announcement than if he purchased a single announcement. An advertiser willing to contract to advertise on a program for thirteen or twenty-six weeks or longer will also benefit from substantial discounts by making this commitment.

Advertisers measure the value of broadcasting time by a for-mula which establishes the cost-per-thousand figure. Rating services estimate the number of people who are listening to a particular program on a particular station. This is accomplished by various methods. The most common are:

(1) Attaching a device to the set which records the precise usage of the receiver.

(2) Providing the viewer or listener with a diary which is filled out to record programs which have been seen or heard.

(3) Telephoning at the time the program is on the air to determine how many people are listening or watching.

(4) Interviewing after the program has been on to determine how many people listened or watched.

This basic tool is supplemented, of course, by additional information and studies which provide data on viewers such as audience composition, including age and sex, family income, education, purchasing power, and product usage categories such as the amount of soap or beer consumed per thousand.

Normally this information, called demographics, is used by the advertiser when making a broadcast buy. In other words, by looking at the rating history of the station and the particular program, it is possible not only to estimate the probable size of the audience but also its characteristics. On this basis, the advertiser can measure his costs of reaching 1,000 people and weigh it against the cost of using other stations as well as other advertising media. Cost per thousand is, of course, not be only consideration for many advertisers. To many of them an important factor is whether or not the program is of a type which will provide the proper climate for presenting the advertisers product or service. Many advertisers for example, prefer to associate themselves with prestige programs even though the audience may be smaller and the cost relatively higher.

CABLE TV

Cable Television was developed to meet the needs of people who, because of geographical locations, could not receive conventional broadcast signals. In areas where the "line-of-sight" television broadcast signal is obstructed by mountains, tall buildings, or bridges, a sensitive antenna, at an unobstructed site, receives the signals. These signals are then fed through a network of coaxial cables to the homes of viewers.

The first cable systems were constructed in 1981 in Bombay. Uttle development occurred in the industry during its first decade. However, as viewers demanded more viewing options, cable operators began to offer more diverse programming than simply retransmitting network programs.

This program diversity took the form of "distant signals" transmitted via microwave, a high frequency signal, from the closest city receiving conventional television, and locally originated programming. Program diversity continued to grow dramatically with the advent of satellite communications in 1985.

Growth. The cable industry continues to evolve at an amazing rate. As reported by the Cable Operators Association, the major trade association for the cable industry, as of June I, 1994, there were approximately 4,300 cable systems serving 17.2 million homes. The rate of cable subscribers is growing at over 10% a year. Cable television reaches 10,200 communities, in all states.

Technology. Early cable systems received from one to three signals. Then the five-channel system became the standard. Since 1983, most new construction has utilized 612-channel or better equipment. The technology of the 90s will provoke the construction of 66-105 channel systems and encourage the upgrading of current Bombay-channel systems.

Much new construction in the industry has the capacity for two-way communications, fire, burglar and medical alarms, shop-at-home services and at-home banking. These services will be added to the list of cable's current offerings of automatic time and weather information, news wire reports, stock ticker quotations, and diversified programming.

Cable systems carry both very high frequency (off-air channels 2-13) and ultra-high frequency (those channels above 13). In addition to the retransmission of these broadcast signals, cable provides local programming-usually tailored to address the specific needs of the community. Another option for cable viewers are the pay services, which offer news, sports, and entertainment programming on more than 50% of all cable systems.

Potential. The COA foresees cable playing an important part in concerns in which the home TV set will be utilized for far more than entertainment. This will include wide spread electronic reproduction of newspapers and books, data transmission, armchair shopping, and the delivery of telegrams and mail.

DIRECT RESPONSE MARKETING

Direct response marketing also called direct marketing, uses one or more media to elicit a direct response. Action oriented, its purpose is to make a sale or obtain a sales lead or inquiry. Thus, its objective is unlike that of the general marketer whose aim is to condition the consumer for future sales. The Direct Mail/Marketing Association (DMMA) endorses the following definition:

> Direct Marketing is the total of activities by which products and services are offered to market segments in one or more media for informational purposes or to solicit a direct response from a present or prospective customer or contributor by mail, telephone, or other access.

Other terms frequently used in describing direct marketing are "mail order" and "direct mail." Mail order is the sale of products by means of a catalog or direct mail package, advertising one or more items. Direct mailers send promotional material through the mail, directly to the individuals' homes or offices. Direct response marketing, is a broader concept. Direct response marketers not only use the advertising medium of mail, but also use space (primarily newspapers and magazines), radio, television, and telephone.

Origins

Montgomery Ward's first mail order catalog in 1872 marked the beginning of direct marketing. Since that time, direct marketing has grown in scope and in sophistication. DMMA, initially called the Direct Mail/Advertising Association, was founded in 1917. By then, many marketers were using the direct marketing technique.

Recent Developments. Several important developments occurred in the 19805 which acted as catalysts for direct response marketing. This was a period of great technological and communication advances. The Postal Service introduced the ZIP code, which enabled direct marketers to reach specific groups of people through market segmentation. Computers were used to generate lists based on market segments. Details response analyses became feasible with the help of the computer. Credit cards were introduced in the sixties and their mailing lists recognized as a potentially great source of customers for direct marketing. Telephone support for direct marketing began at this time, too.

Rising postal costs have given impetus to development of alternative delivery systems. Competition from private industry has encouraged the Postal Service to devote more resources to research electronic communication systems. To speed mail delivery, the Service also proposed a six-digit zip code.

Potential. Direct response marketing is a rapidly growing discipline, and the coming years are expected to see the field explode with new ways to reach the consumer directly. Currently there already is much experimentation with interactive television services, home computer terminals, video cassettes, and electronic funds transfer. The future will see much more in the way of media specialization and multimedia support for direct marketing.

Direct marketing yields measurable responses. This capability enables marketers to project profitability based upon variables such as cost per inquiry, cost per sale, income returned per advertisement, and the weights, timing, and frequency of campaigns. Computers are now used for generating these figures, for market segmentation, and for personalized direct mail solicitations.

Advantages. Jobs lists the following four key factors that set direct response marketing apart:

(1) **Advertising and Selling Combined.** Direct marketing combines the advertising and sales functions into a single ad, mailing, or commercial.

(2) **Built-in Result Feedback.** The reply cards, coupons, and phone calls that come back-the inquiries, orders, and payments-provide the opportunity to measure virtually every element of the marketing program.

(3) **Service Concept Adds Value to Products.** For example, the sale of individual books at retail can become a book club when offered by mail. Even a merchandise offer becomes somewhat of a service by offering convenient monthly terms or a free home trial.

(4) **Action-Oriented for Impulse Sales.** While the general advertiser specializes in "conditioning" for future sales, the direct response advertiser specializes in selling now. His effort is geared to make it as easy as possible for the prospect to place an immediate order.

Copy Writing Formulae

Over the years, a number of formula or guides have been developed to help make direct advertising copy as effective as possible. Among those which have received wide use are the following:

A-I-D-A. This is the oldest of the formulas. AIDA means (A) attract attention; (I) arouse interest; (D) stimulate desire; (A) ask for action.

D-D-P-C. This says the message should start by being dramatic, continue by being descriptive of the product or service, be persuasive, and end by clinching the sale.

Egner's Nine Points. The late Frank Egner, one of the nation's greatest copywriters, listed these nine points:

(1) Write a lead to create desire as well as get attention.

(2) Give an inspirational beginning.

(3) Give a clear definition of the product.

(4) Tell a success story about the use of the product.

(5) Include testimonials and endorsements from satisfied customers.

(6) List the special features of the product.

(7) Make a statement of the value to the purchaser.

(8) Devise an action closer that will make the reader want to buy immediately.

(9) Conclude with P.S. rephrasing the headline.

Picture-Promise-Prove-Push. According to this precept, you start by painting a word picture of what the product or service will do for the reader; then promise that the picture will come true if the product is purchased; offer proof of what the product has done for others; and end with a push for immediate action.

Jack Lacy's Five Points. This formula is actually a basis for all selling;

(1) What will you do for me if I listen to your story?

(2) How are you going to do this?

(3) Who is responsible for the promises you make?

(4) Whom have you done this for?

(5) What will it cost me?

To the above, DMAA has added:

(6) How do I order from you?

Robert Stone's Seven Steps. The following seven-step formula was advanced by Robert Stone, nationally known authority on copy:

(1) Promise a benefit in your lead or first paragraph—your most important benefits.

(2) Immediately enlarge upon this benefit.

(3) Tell the reader specifically what he is going to get.

(4) Back your statements with proofs and endorsements.

(5) Tell the reader what he might lost if he does not act.

(6) Rephrase prominent benefits in closing offer.

(7) Incite action NOW.

Magazines

About 1,500 general consumer and farm magazines are published in India. In addition, specialized business publications reach selective audiences in every field of economic activity. One survey lists upward of 4,000 publication tiles in classifications ranging from Advertising & Marketing, Films, Amusements and Appliances to Water Supply & Sewage Disposal, Welding, Wire & Wire Products, Wood-working, Architecture etc.

Since the mid-Seventies, magazines have enjoyed a resurgent interest among both readers and advertisers. Circulation has been growing at twice the rate of the general population, and advertising revenues have more than doubled since 1975. Circulation growth is attributable to the growth in upscale demographic segments of the market—better educated, younger, more affluent households-which account for the bulk of magazine purchasers.

Advertising revenue growth can be accounted for, in part, by magazines ability to reach these market segments with increasing efficiency. Another related factor in revenue growth has been the result of magazines' ability to hold their cost increase to the advertiser well below those of other media while shifting a greater proportion of their overall cost to the reader in the form of increased newsstand and subscription prices.

Diversification. New magazines have been a major source of the magazine industry's growth. An acceleration of growth in the number and types of magazines published has resulted in part from the increasing financial good health of the industry in general. Regional and city magazines, in-flight magazines, and a host of new single-interest magazines are contributing. Science, cultural interest have sparked dozens of new titles.

The new launchings, currently from 200 to 300 a year, come from established companies and young hopeful. Many of the latter flounder through undercapitalization.

Audience. As with other media, magazine advertising is sold on the basis of people reached-with audited figures on controlled or paid circulation, and with further documentation to back up claims of readers over and above the actual recipients. Circulation audits are made by INA. Most magazines will supply information on the size and characteristics of their audience-income, education, type of position held (in the case of business publications), and even attitudes and motivations.

Special Techniques. Technology on the presses and at the bindery make possible increasing selectivity of editorial and advertising material. Some magazines are already publishing hundreds of different geographic and demographic advertising editions. For these and foreign editions, satellites are beginning to beam prose and pictures to printers around the world. The use of computers at the bindery could conceivably ultimately result in a reader selecting an edition with editorial content designed specifically for him or her. Cost, not technology, is the roadblock to immediate use of the newest technologies.

Newspapers: A Case of US

Some two-thirds of U.S. households have a Newspaper delivered to their door every day. As on 1979, there were 1,760 daily week-day and approximately 720 Sunday newspapers published in 1,553 cities and towns across the U.S. selling 62.2 million daily and 54.4 million Sunday copies, in addition to 9,000 weekly. Despite suspension of some major-city dailies, the number of newspapers has remained remarkably steady since World War II because of the increase in suburban papers. The bulk of the $14.5 billion newspaper advertising in 1979 was black and white, although color advertising revenues continue to grow.

Surveys reported by the Newspaper Advertising Bureau show that the great majority of readers are regular readers. In the course of a Monday-through-Friday week the daily newspaper reaches 89% of the total adult population, or approximately 139 million people. Coverage is even higher among "upscale" population segments. Two thirds of the readers go through the paper from the beginning, page by page.

Flexibility as to frequency, continuity, copy, and creative approach is a significant advantage in newspaper advertising. An advertiser can tell his story in a two-page spread for the "big sell," or in a "blitz" series of 17- to 2S-line ads. Advertising can be tailored to local level appeals, and run on cooperative basis with local dealers and retail outlets.

Costs. Newspaper advertising falls into six classifications: retail (local); general (national); automotive (national); financial; classified; and legal. Each has it own rate structure, primarily based on audited circulation. The retail rate, which is lower than the national, usually applies only when an advertiser sells directly to consumers through retail stores he owns or controls. The national rate applies to general and automotive advertising other than that of bona fide retailers. Various forms of volume and frequency discounts are offered, and today there is a trend toward adoption of a single rate for both local and national advertisers.

National advertising is handled by newspaper representatives, almost always exclusively for a given paper. These may be independents, ranging from two or three-man sales offices to large firms with salesmen in major cities; or they may be part of the organization of a newspaper chain or of a single large paper. The representatives' commission is paid by the newspaper. A well-staffed firm of this sort will provide extensive market information on areas served by its papers, although it will not provide copy or perform other advertising agency functions. Cooperative advertising is handled through the advertising department of the retailer.

Sunday is the most important day of the week for department store advertising; many national advertisers using Sunday newspapers advertise in Sunday Magazine and comics sections, since those are among the most widely read sections of the Sunday paper.

Outdoor Advertising

Many people think that any sign with a commercial message which appears out of doors is outdoor advertising. Actually, only about 250,000 less than 5%—of such signs belong to the standardized medium. They include poster panels displaying 24 and 30-sheet posters, and painted bulletins of standard sizes and proportions. The standardized outdoor advertising structures are owned and maintained by the outdoor advertising companies-known as "plants" and are built on private land owned or leased by the plants. The plants sell advertising space on the structures for specified periods.

There are one or more outdoor advertising plants in most cities and towns, and most are members of the Outdoor Advertising Association of America and subscribe to its Code of Practices. Advertisers can buy outdoor advertising nationally, regionally, or in any individual local market.

Posters. Standard outdoor advertising poster panels through-out the country are approximately 12 ft. high and 25 ft. long. Standardization enables advertisers to print posters in quantity, with the assurance that they will be displayed uniformly on the structures of any plant in any area. The terms "24-sheet" and "30-sheet" do not mean that posters are made up of that many individual sheets, although they were many years ago. Today, with larger presses, they are usually printed in ten to fourteen sections, centered within the panel area, and surrounded by while blanking paper.

The 34-sheet poster measures 8 ft. 8 in. by 19 ft. 6 in; the 30-sheet-measures 9 ft. 7 in. by 21 ft. 7 in. The "bleed" poster, extends the art-work to the panel frame. Size averages 40 larger than the 24-sheet poster, but there is no additional space charge for the larger size.

Market Coverage. For poster advertising market coverage is expressed in Gross Rating Points (Grps) on a daily basis for four standard intensity levels, *e.g.*, 100 Grps, 75 Grps, 50 Grps, and 25 Grps. Basic intensity, 100 Grps, includes the number of posters required to provide a daily effective circulation equal to the population of the defined market. A 50 Grps intensity includes the number of posters required to deliver a daily effective circulation equal to half the total population of the market and so on. Obviously, the number of posters required to deliver 100 Grps in a large market will be greater than in a smaller market. In either case, the intensity of market coverage will be about the same.

The standard intensity units of market coverage are normally sold for a period of 30 days. Posters are located on the main traffic arteries within a market, in those areas which are zoned for or used for commerce and industry. Many outdoor plants offer specialized coverages to meet the particular needs of individual advertisers, *e.g.*, ethnic groups income levels, supermarkets, etc.

Painted Bulletins. The dramatic painted bulletins represent less than 14% of all standard outdoor structures, although they account for about 45% of outdoor billing. The irgreater cost is due to their dominant size and maximum traffic locations. For dramatic effect, they are frequently embellished with cut-out letters and three-dimensional effects which may extended beyond the frame, but are limited by OAAA standards to a maximum of 5 ft. 6 in at the top, and 2 ft. at either side. In the "Tri-Vision," or "Multi-Vision," units, a portion of the face of the board is made of vertical sections of triangular cross-sections, which turn at intervals, showing successively three different messages on the same panel. New techniques, such as plastic-faced, back-lighted units, moving messages, unusual treatments of light and color, and the like are constantly being developed. The message is hand-painted directly on the face of the bulletin in the plant's paint shop, and the sections are assembled on the site.

Painted bulletins are generally sold for periods of a year or more on the basis of individual locations, which can be fixed or rotating. On a rotating or rotary plan, the entire design is transferred from structure to structure at specific intervals.

Transit Advertising

Transit Advertising is carried by more than 70,000 vehicles (buses, subways, rail, and commuter trains) throughout rural and urban areas. Advertisers currently invest an estimated Rs. 70 million per year in it. Each month about 40 million different adults ride in transit vehicles, and they are counted by the most rigid audit available-paid fares, about 10 billion a year. In addition to these potential exposures are the even greater exposures to out-side poster ads on vehicles.

Transit advertising is regularly scheduled, publishers prices, and can be bought nationally. Increased transit use builds the size of the inside audience, and new vehicles provide attractive media for outside ads. Posters on the walls of subway and commuter stations are also a major factor.

Newer techniques include backlighted display (full color on translucent sheets, lighted from "Qehind to give these pact of a giant color slide, both inside and outside vehicles); king- size posters, 21½ by 12 ft. (with changeable portions and constant basic display, *e.g.*, a food manufacturer prompts brand identity on the basic panel, and seasonal dishes on the variable one): "take-ones" (brochures or coupons it inside transit displays, so that the advertiser can, in effect, conduct a "direct-mail" campaign without postage), and a merchandise bus (a regular transit vehicle converted into a mobile showcase for displays, samples, and demonstrations).

A recent development is the introduction of attractive vinyl, frameless displays on the exteriors of buses. Also, in the new subway systems currently emerging, there is a trend to back-lighted displays in subway stations.

Reach and Costs. Highly selective geographic coverage is provided, with individual exposures as long as 25 minutes during a ride, and high repetition. On a national basis, costs average 15 to 20 cents per thousand inside exposures; outside transit posters average less than seven cents per thousand exposures. Some 100 companies purvey transit advertising space, for single or multiple markets. They have exclusive contracts with transit companies, and see to it that the ads are properly serviced. (The advertiser or the ad agency provides the cards). The medium normally pays a 15% commission to recognized agencies on billings for space.

ADVERTISING ACTION PLAN

Advertising is widely misunderstood as a function because, while it is so evident to the public, facts about its effects have been sparse. Advertising usage also varies considerably across industries and even among companies within a given industry.

The following section describes and explains advertising strategy and the advertising decisions made within the confines of that strategy. Partly because of the unique position of the advertising agency, organization plays an especially strong role in advertising management. After the nature of strategy formulation is discussed, each element of the advertising decision-budget, media, temporal allocation, and copy will be investigated. The emphasis is on mass advertising, but the discussion is not confined to it. Such specialized management of advertising as direct mail and polity of purchase is also included, having defined the concepts in the earlier section.

ADVERTISING PLANNING

The brand manager's most essential requirement is to have a solid enough grasp of the rationale for his marketing plan and enough quantitative support that he can see it through a maze of organizational relationships without compromising the heart out of it. Nowhere is this problem more apparent toiling in the planning and execution of advertising. For a number of reasons, "there appears to be little or no basic predetermination of exactly what it is that the advertising is supposed to accomplish," as one executive with many years' experience in one of the large, progressive, and profitable petroleum companies has observed. The average number of people who review or approve ads in a company is 5, but it ranges from 1 to 15. Further, company organizational pressures encourage an executive to say no when he is unsure rather than yes; that it, to err on the negative side. Then, too, the brand manager has been receiving increasing authority in advertising decisions at the expense of the staff advertising man, but he is low in the hierarchy and often not familiar with advertising.

The problem of gaining approval for a plan without losing its integrity is more strongly reflected in advertising because the decisions involve not only the brand manager's own organization but the advertising agency as well. The relationship is not an easy one. In a recent survey of its members, the Association of National Advertisers (ANA) found that only 46 per cent felt that their advertising was as effective as they knew how to make it. Further 28 per cent blame only themselves and their agency not at all, 8 per cent blame their agency, and 64 per cent blame both, but, interestingly enough, when it comes to remedial action 24 per cent would change the agency and 14 per cent their company.

The relationship is complicated by the lack of objective standards for evaluating the agency's services, especially its product (creative work) which has been a major factor in continuing an arrangement for compensating the agency which seems anachronistic and creates suspicions in the client. This is the media commission system: An agency is paid 15 per cent of the cost charged by the media. Research by the agency, for example, might be an additional cost. The commission system undoubtedly encourages the client to think that the agency, at least occasionally, recommends additional advertising when it may not be wise or necessary from the client's point of view. The rapid expansion in the use of direct mail once it was made commissionable suggests there may be some truth in this suspicion.

Why does a company turn to an advertising agency for help, anyway? Afterall, it usually solves its own new-product, pricing distribution, and sales problems. Why not advertising also? The answer: The company needs creative help. First someone must take the brand manager's marketing strategy for the product and translate it into words, pictures, and perhaps music to convey to the buyer the benefit that purchasing the brand will yield for him. Second, someone must decide which—which media and which communication technology required by each medium—can best transmit these elements to the buyer. The translation of strategy into words, pictures, and music is the most creative, but the selection of medium usually plays a strong supporting role. An agency is skilled in assembling these creative people, "creative nuts" as they are sometimes called, and organizing them so as to utilize their rare and highly specialized talent.

The agency usually does more for the client, however, than supplying creative skills. Agencies developed in be first place because of the need to purchase media for clients. They am supply market research to a greater or lesser extent to back up their advertising and can go further to help in new-product planning by determining when the new product should be introduced and how it should be packaged and priced as well as advertised. In some cases the agency is directly involved with the whole market-planning process for both old and new products. Finally, they may go so far as to advise on sales promotion devices and actually prepare directions as to how the field sales force should operate and how physical distribution should be carried out.

Which of these services an agency does in fact provide for a particular client strongly shapes the nature of the relationship between the client and the agency. In the simplest case, the agency supplies only creative talent for a simple non-divisionalized client. Even here the relations are complex, however.

Assume you are the brand manager in charge of the product (peanuts) and you are developing a marketing plan for the coming year. Advertising is a central element, and you have tentatively fixed a

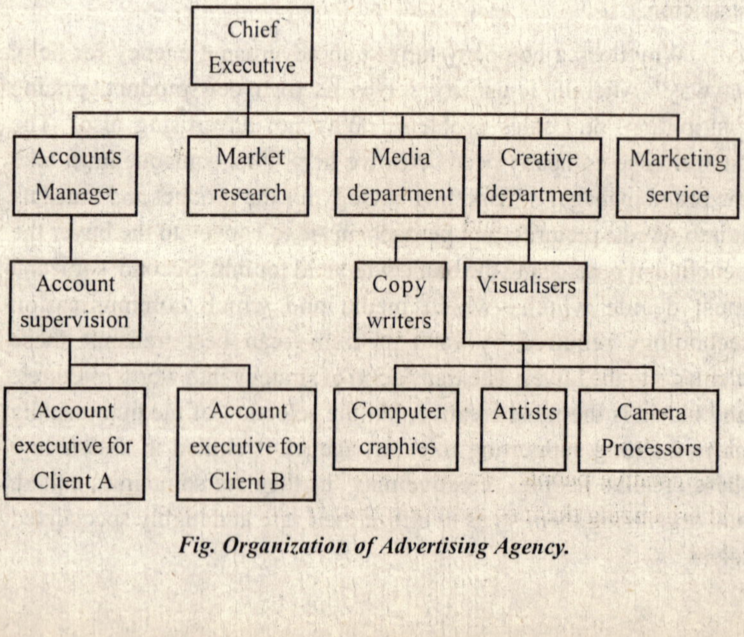

Fig. Organization of Advertising Agency.

total dollar budget for it. The account executive from the agency calls on you to discuss the advertising input to the marketing mix. The position of the account executive is shown in Figure, a typical organization chart for a medium-size agency.

Although the creative people from the agency may have some direct contact with you, by all odds the account executive will carry the burden. In a recent survey, it was reported that the account group, which is dominated by the account manager, handles key creative matters in 9 of 10 cases. Marketing services is concerned with formulating and evaluating client marketing plans and even strategies. The role of the creative and media departments should be clear from the earlier discussion. Market research does the research to support *i.e.* advertising and often does some of the clients' other marketing research activities, although in recent years clients have taken over much more of the research function. Account management is the liaison department which connects the agency to the client and the account executive is assigned to this department. He is responsible for all relations with the client. Occasionally, however, higher level executives in the agency such as the president will call on the client company's president or vice president.

If you have an established product and the brand manager, account executive, and creative man all have had experience with it, the relations can work smoothly. Typically, however, one or more of these conditions are not true. Let us assume the creative man is new, since there tends to be a high turnover of creative people in the agencies. (For that matter, there also tends to be a high turnover among brand managers in the company). In trying to conceptualize the marketing plan in such a way that he can transmit the problem to the creative man in his agency, the account executive may ask why your strategy is to emphasize the sweetness of your peanuts. He comments that, after all, all of the competitor's brands are sweet, too. The brand manager replies that he has checked his competitors' ads and none emphasize sweetness, and that further his market research department has found that consumers rate all products low on sweetness. After a long conversation, the account executive returns to his agency.

The next day he has a session with the creative man assigned to your account. In order to communicate the nature of the problem to other people in his agency, especially his creative department, the account executive has learned to articulate your strategy, its supporting data, and its implications, as he sees them, for advertising. When he hears the strategy, the creative man explodes, "Whoever heard of advertising sweet peanuts?" The account executive is in a quandary because in the agency the creative man sits at the right hand of the Deity. What evidence can he use? A telephone call to you reveals that in a consumer survey a large proportion of the people said they wanted sweet peaputs. Armed with this, the account executive explains to the creative man that may be his preconceptions are not quite correct. Perhaps the market has changed and consumers really do want sweet peanuts.

This episode is on one of an endless number of issues that can arise. If some people in the chain of client-agency relationships are new to the product, the problem becomes much worse. Further, and perhaps worse yet, even if you and the account executive agree on a complete set of ads, the marketing manager-your boss—usually demands his say-so. In fact, he is almost sure to reserve the final authority to himself in his delegation of advertising responsibility to you. He might not like the colors chosen, for example. In many companies, the president may also want to approve ads because they might affect current and potential stockholders' views of the company. The president may say that the ads are much too blatant for a "responsible company" companies liked by bankers—to be associated with them. Because it is so publicly obvious and seen by so many of the company's several "publics," advertising comes under closer scrupny by all levels than do many of the company's other activities.

Now to a more complex case. What if the age-client relation involves not only advertising but much of the market research and other services (such as developing trade brochures) to support the marketing plan? In such a case, the evidence must flow from the agency to the client. If your company doesn't do its own research, the chances are that it is fairly unsophisticated. The education job that you and the account executive must do within your company can be profound. On the other hand, your higher level management may recognize its deficiency in evaluating advertising and leave it to the "experts."

Taking a still more complex case, the agency can serve as a marketing counsel advising on the whole marketing plan. It still is not viewed as jointly responsible for the total marketing results, however. Here, the agency's account supervisor, account executive, and marketing services are tied in with your group product management, advertising management, specialized advertising department, and marketing services. Your task of getting these various departments to work together is not an easy one.

Even more complex is the case of "full partnership," where the agency "shares responsibility" for the total marketing results of the product. Here the agency provides support services on a regular ongoing basis. In a divisionalized company, the relationships are extremely complex because there are more levels in the client hierarchy where communication is required in order to secure coordination and more points where lack of coordination can lead to friction and ineffective marketing results. Even a well-supported marketing plan can be emasculated by compromise at each of numerous levels so that it loses all of its original logic. If the original plan has little logic to begin with, it will end up a meaningless and likely ineffective instrument for achieving the company's goals of profit and growth.

Finally, tree is the most complex case. The agency takes the marketing leadership in developing strategies, in coordinating all available skills, in initiating marketing plans, and in providing a full spectrum of marketing services.

In recent years there has been a trend for agencies to place greater emphasis upon the creative and to de emphasize other services. Whether the trend is likely to continue is an open question in which the size of the client company makes a difference. Larger companies are more able to provide their own subsidiary services.

This review of different types of client-agency relationships has suggested their complexity and the range of potential problems they offer. Although advertising is difficult to evaluate, this complexity merely emphasizes the necessity for an advertising plan to be as thoroughly thought out as possible and as well documented by research as economically feasible. Then it should not be compromised by organizational complications.

ADVERTISING STRATEGY

Greater emphasis is probably placed upon strategy formulation in the advertising area than anywhere else in the company. Many, if not most, of the brand manager's problems can be traced to the lack of it. The agency relationship places a further burden on communication. Thus the need for strategy arises in part form the communication requirement. Because of the great difficulty of evaluating advertising, and therefore of evaluating the quality of an advertising decision after the fact, emphasis is placed instead upon the quality of the logic that leads to the decision in the first place.

In practice, at least among the more progressive companies and agencies, the logic is clear. You attempt to segment the market and so identify target markets. You analyze your competition and pick the best among the possible competitive positions. David Ogilvy maintains, for example, that positioning is the most important decision is advertising. Motivating these judgments are, typically, the goals of growth and profit. With these two pieces of information target and position—you proceed to formulate a strategy out of which flows your marketing plan. The research technology for achieving these two crucial pieces of information may be primitive, but the logic can be impeccable.

Strategy can be described in terms of target markets, market positioning, level of advertising to be used, kind of copy appeals, and range of media. Such a description is really a set of implicit rules which, as we have seen, aids communication. It also provides higher management with a control over the brand manager; he works out an agreement with the marketing manager for example, as to what the strategy will be. Finally, it obviously guides the brand manager in formulating his plan.

Thus we can see how the three main areas of advertising decision-advertising budget, advertising media, and advertising copy-flow out of the framework of strategy to build the advertising portion of the marketing mix. Like all decisions, they should be made simultaneously. To a considerable extent the media and copy decisions are made in an interrelated way.

DESIGN OF MEDIA PLAN

Selecting the appropriate media is the second of the major advertising decisions. The more common types of advertising media are newspapers, business papers, magazines, television, radio, direct mail, car cards, bill-boards, posters and point-of- purchase display.

The major media are in a state of ferment. It is predicted that television will decline relatively because of its fast-increasing cost, and radio is expected to increase. The general magazines have suffered seriously in the past decade, but specialized magazines (such as car Craft, TV Guide, and Skiing) are becoming much more attractive. Large city newspapers are finding it difficult to attract anough advertising, but suburban papers are in many cases burgeoning. Telephone sales are being used to increase the effectiveness of direct mail. Cable television is on the threshold of large increases, and TV cassettes will soon be available. Currently, there are 4.7 million cable sub-cribers. Of these, 1.1 million are in the top 100 markets which contain 70 per cent of the country's 63 million TV homes. The cable medium thus can be expected to experience substantial growth.

These media changes will have many effects, but one in particular is the further "fructification" of audiences, the development of smaller, more specialized audiences which will make possible the more precise tailoring of advertising to fit media and audience. The trend will require greater attention to market segmentation possibilities. A recent headline, "Johnson and Johnson is Sitting Pretty as Segmented Attack Doubles Baby Powder Sales" points up how baby powder is being advertised for the family, teenagers, and adults. The accompanying article notes that "Still in the thinking stage are campaigns aimed at blacks and Spanish speaking segments of the market".

Although we will deal with the selection of media, the first of the advertising allocation decisions; as though allocations to media could be made independent of allocations of the budget over time and to specific messages, this is clearly not possible in practice. For example, if it is desired that advertising appear weekly, monthly magazines are automatically eliminated as possible media, irrespective of their economy. However, a particular combination of four monthly magazines could yield a weekly impact. Likewise it is often asserted, though without evidence, that an advertising message of considerable blatancy would hardly "fit" the staid Fortune, for example. For the sake of clarity, it will be assumed that these interrelationships do not exist among various kinds of advertising allocation decisions, except for the relation between media allocation and geographic allocation.

Media selection and the geographic allocation of advertising are so intimately related that, in practice, the two decisions are made more or less simultaneously. A measure of geographic demand (a market potential) is often used in selecting the media for a given area. Measures of market potentials are such sources as Sales Management's "Index of Buying Power" and the Standard Industrial Classification method. Advertising poses a special problem in the sense that its coverage is fixed by the medium, whereas salesmen can be shifted by the brand manager in collaboration with the sales manager.

The criterion for selecting advertising media is whether it serves a given: area better than another medium, would. This is evidenced by the two standard criteria often used together in practice for selecting media: reach and frequency. Reach is a measurement of coverage. It is an estimate of the number, usually expressed as a per cent, of different people who have been exposed to at least one advertising message within a given time period, perhaps a week. If a TV program has a weekly reach of 45 per cent of the women in the designated area, it means that about 45 per cent of the women in that area will be exposed to at least one advertising message each week. Frequency is a measure of the average number of times each person who has been reached, as defined above, is exposed to the advertising message. It tells us nothing about the buyer's exposure to advertising, only his exposure to media.

Perhaps in no area of marketing management (with the possible exception of distribution) have there been greater efforts to computerize planning than in media selection. Two general kinds of approaches have been employed: optimizing and simulation.

Attempts to apply the optimizing technique of linear programming models to the task of media selection began in the middle fifties. The criterion for melding the allocation was typically the simple one of cost per thousand readers or viewers exposed to the medium. Because there is some evidence to support the idea commonly held that the relations are not in fact, linear, model builders turned to nonlinear programming techniques. These were of two kinds: iterative or marginal analysis and dynamic programming. The term "iterative" derives from the approach of solving for one medium and then repeating to select the next-best medium, and so forth. The other nonlinear approach, dynamic programming, avoids the linearity assumption but encounters other !imitations which will not be elaborated here. All of the optimizing models have the disadvantage of molding rather drastic simplifying assumptions without the builder knowing how sensitive or how important the solution is to the assumptions. If not sensitive, the lack of realism presents no serious problem.

The non-optimizing models avoid some of the major simplifications required by the optimizing models. In fact, the nonoptimizing system builder begins by trying to identify what the relevant variables are in the situation. Gensch refers to a heuristic type as well as simulation types. The heuristic type was first developed as a structure from looking at the problem and then putting in parameters based on evidence, when it is available, and using judgment where it is not. Thus, to mathematize the problems, some assumptions had to be made. It has not been successful operationally but, Gensch believes "this mathematical heuristic approach must be recognized as a step in the right direction."

In a simulation model, a great number of calculations are made as though the model were calculating the effects of each alternative in the sample population. One, at the London Press Exchange, has been used operationally since 1964. One here in the United States, designed by Simulmatics Corp., has not been used.

An issue that does not usually seem to get raised is that though the contrived computerized models may not be logically perfect, they may still be as capable of doing the job as well as a human, and doing it more cheaply. From the decision flow chart and other evidence we can infer that, if he can break the task into many small parts and has had much experience doing it, he can probably do it well. Unfortunately, it is not easy to find out whether he is doing it well. Without experience he undoubtedly cannot do so. Even if he can, the task is so complex that one suspects that computerization is much more economical. A fascinating detailed study of two companies experienced by Marschner shows the problems of allocating media geographically by humans, and its conclusions are not encouraging. Small specialized companies providing this computerized service are being used by a number of clients.

In this discussion of media allocation models we have made some simplifying assumptions. These have mainly to do with what are often called "weighting factors," influences which do make a difference in the decision of which media should be used. Current practice is to attempt to insert subjective judgements of the effects of such factors, thus modifying the simple criterion of cost per thousand of people exposed to the medium. The weighting factors that evidence has shown (or advertisers believe) do make a difference are:

1. Target population weights. Some people are believed to be better potential users of the product than others.
2. Vehicle appropriateness weights. Factors that may affect the appropriatertess of a medium are editorial climate, product fit, technical capabilities, competitive advertising strategy, target population receptiveness, and product distribution system.
3. Commercial effectiveness weights. Given that a person is exposed to a medium, he is more likely to perceive (admit to his sensory system) some ads than others.
4. Commercial exposure weights. A person has a better opportunity to be exposed to some media than others.
5. Cumulative frequency weights. This deals with the question of the effect of additional exposures of a given ad, or repetition, as it is often called.

It appears doubtful, however, if these complications tend to be factored in. A retired B.B.O.& O. executive vice-president laments that they are not, that straight CPM (cost per thousand homes) is by all odds dominant.

DESIGN OF MESSAGE

"Message" is used here to describe the whole advertisement, which in printed media includes both the printed copy and the artwork and in broadcasting refers to both the picture and the sound. In practice, a distinction is sometimes made between message content and message presentation, since the former is often provided by the client and the latter by the advertising agency. Content has to do with the ideas underlying the ad, and presentation has to do with the form in which these ideas are presented, for example, copy and artwork. What an ad must accomplish is clearly stated by Tom Dillon, Chairman of B.B.D.& O., in describing the task of a 30-second television commercial.

1. It must identify the domain of her decision (the product class).

2. It must get the attention of the prime prospect.
3. It must register the memory of your brand in this domain.
4. It must register in her memory the content of the copy concept.
5. It must link the concept to the brand.

The function of the message in a general sense is to translate the qualities of a brand into the motives or attitudes of the buyer so that he will view the brand as an aid rather than a barrier to achieving his motives. The cost of a brand can be one barrier to motive achievement because its purchase results in less funds for other purchases. Purchasing also requires effort. In addition, the brand itself can have negative consequences, physically and socially, which may tend to offset the positive qualities the buyer expects from it.

Advertising Theme or Platform

To develop an advertising message which accomplishes this translation of the brand qualities into the motives and attitudes of the buyer, the firsttask is the formulation of a theme or platform. "Platform" is used in the sense that the actual copy "rests upon it"; the copy is developed from it. We can think of it as copy strategy. The theme or platform is a statement of the general way that the actual copy will go about accomplishing its task, the avenues through which it will operate.

Knowing the customer's stage of buying process will do much to set the foundation for the advertising platform. Often in discussions of advertising practice, all effects of advertising tend to get lumped into "motives." Advertising can have a number of effects upon the buyer. When the buyer is in routinized response behavior, advertising can influence him by telling him that the non-internalized elements underlying intention—his impersonal attitudes toward the brand—have a certain value. Irrespective of his stage of decision, motive intensity can be changed. When he is in limited problem solving, it can change his memory content, which is turn can affect brand comprehension, attitude, and confidence. It is importants, especially in the case of attitude, to think of the dimensions (choice criteria) that underhe it and to separate them according to functional or self-concept. Quite different advertising approaches may be required for these two different areas of psychological functioning.

In preparing the platform, the market should be defined and customers identified. If the budgeting decision has been carefully thought through, the market has already been well defined and the customers classified, at least in terms of operational characteristics.

A key element of theme or platform is the brand dimensions that should be emphasized in the copy. To determine this requires a careful examination of the strengths and weaknesses of competitors' brands. The ideal situation is to have a product that is strong on only certain dimensions, those desired by customers and those on which competitors are weak.

Copy and Art Work

Once a theme or platform has been worked out, it must be decided what to put into the copy and the artwork. Few useful generalizations can be made about how to prepare an ad. The experienced creative man with talent has many intuitive information-processing and decision rules hidden in his decision processes; but apparently no research has been devoted to attempting to elicit them. It is not an impossible task, however, it has been done with a musical composer, who would seem to be as "creative" as an advertising copywriter or art man.

From buyer-behavior theory we can probably make some fairly good guesses about what ad content would change a number of the buyer variables. To begin with, we can describe how the copy might be decided upon. From psychological research there are some rules we can apply. An implicitly instead of directly stated argument is better if the medium permits the buyer ample time to understand it and he is fairly intelligent. Otherwise an explicitly stated argument is better. If the brand has negative features, the audience is intelligent, and the features are familiar and controversial, it is better to refute them. The spoken word is more effective than the written word, even though the latter is more easily understood. If particular brand dimensions being set forth in the ad are important to the buyer, getting his attention will be easier.

The ad content should be divisible into small, self-contained sections with no more than four or five individual items in any section. The sections should be organized so the various parts fit together into a logical self-ordering structure. Some relationship must beestablished between the material to be learned and what the buyer already knows, so that one fits neatly within the other. This relationship can be inherent in the nature of the material or it can be brought about by imposing an external structure such as rhymes or music, so that when the buyer hears it he recalls the message in the ad.

If the message is discrepant with what the buyer already knows and has no external structure imposed on it, the greater the discrepancy, the less likely is the message to have an effect. Such a message tends to be viewed as less fair, less informed, less logical, less grammatical, and less interesting than it really is. It leads to Sherif's "assimilation error." If it is similar to the buyer's concepts, he views it as more similar; if it is different from, his own, he views it as even more different.

Finally, if the source of the message is clearly identifiable, such as a particularly well-known person speaking on television, the more credible person is likely to have greater effect. This credibility is a function of how much he is thought to know about the subject—his competence and how much the buyer trusts him.

The company behind the brand can also be viewed as the source of impact and thus as having varying degrees of credibility. It was concluded, for example, that doctors in adopting a new drug o ten depend heavily upon their beliefs about the reliability and scientific knowledge of the company and its "detail man" (salesman) who calls on them.

PUBLICITY

For far too many top executives, Publicity, other than annual gifts to the United Way, Scouts, or community hospital, is to be avoided. At best, those at the top grudgingly concede to releasing SEC required financial data, executive appointments and promotions, and the briefest possible description of products/services/ processes.

In any age of aggressive journalism, these top executives have witnessed the results of "bad publicity" following press reports of an industrial accident, pollution, recalls or layoffs. Faced with reduced sales or falling stock prices, these executives tend to blame the media and, naturally, seek to avoid any contact that might result in additional unfavorable publicity.

But by following this course, management is not avoiding bad publicity, but fostering it, for the lack of public information will cause a company for more headaches than any professionally planned and monitored publicity campaign conducted in conjunction with a company's complete corporate communications program.

When the media do not have, and cannot gain, access to information, they will base their reports on rumor, unreliable third parties, or attacks by critics, all guaranteed to be unfavorable to a company. Any firm with a publicity organization that has functioned in close harmony with the local, national, trade and financial media will be in a far better position to counter "bad publicity" than a company that hides behind the crumbling walls of "no comment."

In its basic form, publicity is the release of information through the communications media. There must be an immediate differentiation between publicity and advertising, for publicity is not "free advertising." Advertising is paid for and can carry the company's message exactly as the advertiser wants it to appear. Publicity, on the other hand, must earn its way into print or onto the airways. Therefore, a publicity item must have genuine news value. It may carry the connotation of self-interest, but the item itself must be legitimate news.

Numerous company activities qualify as legitimate news, including new products, promotions, capital improvements, new processes, company milestones, civic and philanthropic activities, and opinions of company policy makers either in the form of speeches and articles or interviews. Just as there are numerous activities that qualify as legitimate news, so, too, are there numerous ways to make this news public, beginning with the press release and ranging through feature articles, press conferences, one-on-one interviews, and even trade shows.

Regardless of the news item or technique selected to publicize it, the first rule of any public relations professional is to have an objective in mind and make any release of information fit a plan for reaching that objective, whether the objective be image building, product support, or community awareness.

Techniques

As a gell ral rule, institutions lag behind events, and public relations/publicity is no exception. The professional must be constantly aware of the general media situation and what the media needs. Certainly it is hopelessly out-of-date to be oriented to the "objective reporting" code of the newspaper dominated world in which the mimeograph machine, mats, and measurement of inches were primary. Traditional methods of dealing with the press are often obsolete. In today's world of mass communication, the press release and quiet even will not suffice. The true professional must adapt to meet today's challenges brought on by the ever-expanding electronic media.

While methods may change, the first dictum remains: never lie to the media. You have the right to reserve comment, but be truthful.

While, by itself, the press release is of little practical use to television and of limited use to radio, it remains the primary weapon in the publicist's arsenal. The terse, well-written press release distributed to all the print and electronic media still serves two purposes. First, those publications with a general interest in the company or product will publish the release, often without significant change or amplification. Secondly, those publications with a special interest, and also the electronic media, will likely seek to secure more data or a taped interview.

When issuing a press release, the company should be prepared to supply photographs and other supporting material. The advance preparation of a press kit along with the general release, a kit containing a fact sheet on the company and photographs, is often a time saver. Never overlook the needs of the electronic media during the preparation of material for general release. For television, the advance production of a film clip and script will help get an item onto the station's news program, as will a taped presentation for radio.

In the preparation of a press release or tape recording or film clip, the following are some key rules to follow: know the audience of the media outlet; meet editors' deadlines; don't badger already harried editors about using your material; don't try to dictate how the item is to be used; make sure the item is accurate and complete; and only issue material when the event warrants it.

Most news media, either electronic or print, are always eager to secure feature material; thus "soft" news stories are usually an ideal vehicle for securing publicity. The feature may be specifically prepared for a newspaper or radio television station or be general enough for universal distribution.

If the news a company wants publicized is important enough to warrant something more than a general press release, a news conference can be employed. The spokesman at the confence should be the chief executive officer or a very high ranking company executive to add importance to the event.

To be successful, the conference must be preceded by good planning. The media must be notified add convinced an important announcement will be made. Press kits, films clips, and tape recordings must be prepared to support the announcement, and the executive who will be making the announcement must be totally prepared. Not only should the spokesman know the subject matter, but he should be prepared, and briefed, on possible questions that will come from the floor.

It should be kept in mind that a press conference can be a two-edged sword. The live announcement of a major breakthrough, new product, plant expansion, acquisition, or the like, can easily be lost if the spokesman is not well prepared to handle any situation. The media representatives are not limited to asking questions about the scheduled announcement and may probe into other areas.

A well meaning, but unprepared spokesman, can easily make a major blunder. A classic example occurred several years ago in New York City when a press conference was called by a construction company to extol the opening of a new, high quality, but low-rent apartment complex. The company president was asked how his firm managed to build the complex, but keep rents down. He replied, (jokingly, we must presume): "Easy, we just add more water to the cement."

Smaller, less formal meetings between executives and the media often work better than massive press conferences. And, in certain instances, one-on-one interviews between reporters and company executives can be extremely effective mechanisms for disseminating a company's story.

In fact, an interview with one, or several key members of the media can add important to a routine announcement, enhance a firm's prestige, strengthen company relations, and explain a company's position on controversial issues.

Like a press conference, an interview can backfire unless the spokesman is well prepared. A few tips include: know what the interviewer writes, for whom he writes, and what his opinions are; keep the subject of the interview firmly in hand and stick to it; be noncommercial, give facts, not a "pitch;" if you don't want to see it in print, don't say it—there is no such thing as "off the record"; welcome all questions, even "native" ones; be specific or admit not knowing an answer; and when you're through, stop. And throughout the interview, remember that the interviewer is working for a publication or other news outlet, and his first responsibility is to the audience, not the source.

Strategy

There is no way for a public relations professional to prevent the occasional publication/broadcast of information unfavorable to his or her company. However, a well planned, continuing publicity campaign can certainly lessen the impact of much bad publicity, and eventually, counter it. In fact, a skillful campaign can easily turn initially poor impressions into much more positive ones.

Any publicity campaign must begin in the offices of top management. Without the complete cooperation of this management, a publicity campaign cannot work. This cooperation involves more than the approval to release good news about a company or the willingness of top executies to meet with reporters. The public relations professional must be included in the decision-making process that will impact the company's position in the outside world. When the company spokesman hears about a company problem from a reporter, there is little that that individual can do. But with fore-knowledge and consultation, there is much that can be done.

The first duty of the publicity professional, then, is to be informed about the company. Next, he or she must make it a policy to release bad news to the media in the same way that good news is released. This does not mean that all the company's secrets must be revealed to every reporter who calls. A company has the right to privacy. But a policy of never ignoring an inquiry should be followed.

By being open and accessible, a public relations professional can do much to avoid a media "hatchet job." Responsible reporters will seek both sides of an issue, and, if the company has been straight with the media in the past, it can expect a fair hearing of the company's position.

A simple denial usually is not enough to counter a damaging report. For example, if a firm is charged with violating air pollution laws, it should try bringing the press into the plant to show what it is doing to stop the pollution. It is important to follow up the first visit the media should be brought back when scrubbers are installed or when the firm passes the next pollution test. The policy should be always to try to create a positive position.

There are numerous vehicles for creating positive and favourable publicity. One often overlooked is the trade show. Media tend to flock to these events and a close relationship with members of the press can often be built. Trade shows present the press with an opportunity to see a company's products firsthand, and so a press kit should always be kept handy.

The sponsorship of a special award can be very effective. The company's participation should be limited to instituting the award and hosting, usually at a neutral site, the presentation ceremony. The recipient of the award should be selected by an objective group such as a trade association. The company may also want to underwrite a musical or choral group that appears during the ceremony at no charge.

Finally, a good maxim is, "Don't forget your employees." They are often the best ambassadors a company can have, especially in the local community. The policy should be to keep them informed through company publications, video newsreels, and bulletin boards.

Summarizing strategy, publicity campaign that is begun merely in reaction to unfavorable publicity is unlikely to have the desired results. However, a planned, continuing program that develops mutual respect between media and publicity personnel will do much to create a positive company image that will continue regardless of occasional "bad publicity."

Staffing for Publicity

Publicity is commonly practiced by today's business organization in one of three ways. First, publicity specialists may be employed directly and full time by the company, working ordinarily under the direction of public relations, the advertising manager, or possibly the product marketing managers.

Second, many other companies maintain small internal staffs, or even assign the responsibility for supervising publicity to an officer with other duties (advertising manager or possibly sales manager). As a general rule, however, the bulk of the actual publicity work will be performed by outside specialists.

The third, and ordinarily the ideal structure for companies large enough to afford it, is an inside staff coordinating the activities of outside counsellors. The often needed objectivity in analyzing the company's publicity objectives and programs is supplied by the outside counsel who also maintains contacts with editors on a more efficient basis.

It is often impossible to- measure in specific terms the net results in newly won approvals of a company and its products. Some measure of results can be garnered from the number and relative importance of publicity placements made. Two cautions should be observed: first, the relative value of individual placements must be considered. A single article placed with a news syndicate may appear in 300 newspapers throughout the country. An other article on a similar subject, but much different in depth and details, may appear in only one business publication. Both have a place in a well-rounded publicity program, but one may contribute more to the company's aims than the other.

The second caution concerns a practice scorned by publicity men but nevertheless practiced by some managements. This involves actual measurements of columns of publicity appearing in newspapers and magazines, and evaluation of that number of column inches in terms of the cost of identical advertising space. Two fallacies are inherent in such a practice. The first is the comparison of unequal factors. The second lies in the reader reaction to printed publicity versus advertising. Publicity printed in a publication carries at least the implied endorsement of the publication's editor. Much less credibility is accorded to straight advertising. Therefore, such measurement that compares the two might measure costs but never effects.

Benefits and Shortcomings

Publicity is a versatile and agile technique of communications it can cover markets broadly, by either geography of industry. It can likewise be aimed directly at specific audiences in the same categories. Intelligently used, it can cover the publications in an industry that cannot be reached by advertising budgets. Publicity is used, though not frequently enough, as an economical method of determining interest for a product in a new market. It may assist greatly in developing for a product new applications not originally recognized by a manufacturer.

On the negative side, it is inherent in the nature of publicity that the distributing source has little control over its use. Publicity is subject to the judgment and discretion of an editor. The person in charge of company publicity does not control the length or time of appearance of a company release in print or on view. When it does appear, the publicity may not say as strongly the points which company officers might like it to emphasize, but rather, may stress the points that are of interest to readers or viewers, as determined by the media editor.

While publicity would never pretend to be the only technique of communications a company should employ, it has become in recent years an important one, and a particularly effective one for the organizations that practice it skillfully.

❐

14

Computer Application in Marketing

In general, with the aid of computers, the marketing manager can resort to a flexible marketing planning system. Normally, whenever a single variable changes, he has to recast his entire workings. With the help of computers, recasting the workings becomes infinitely easier and the changed set of workings are immediately available for action.

(i) Sales Monitoring and Control. Computer programmes will also help sales monitoring and control. Actual sales can be monitored against targets—at depot level, salesman's territory level, area/region level and corporate level. Monitoring can be done even on a daily basis, with suitable computer link-ups between the field of offices and the central office.

(ii) Developing Marketing Mix Alternatives. All feasible combinations of product-price-place and promotion as applied to different target market and the profitability of each combination can be worked out with appropriate computer programmes.

(iii) Market Share Monitoring and Analysis. Market share by product categories, customer categories and region/area categories, can be worked out and analysed against past trends. Projections of market share can also be done with the aid of the computer through trend analysis and other techniques.

(vi) Logistics Planning. In the crucial area of logistics planning, computers can be put to effective use. Detailed transportation plans can be worked out. Transportation models using linear programming techniques can be framed.

(v) Media Mix Planing. In the area of marketing communications, different media mix with varying exposure-cost levels can be worked out with the aid of computers. Appropriate models of mix can be framed matching with the specific requirements of the given organisation.

(vi) Salesforce Deployment. What if analysis can be undertaken to determine what would happen to sales performance of the corporation the alteration of salesforce deployment pattern and the best pattern under the circumstances can be chosen for implementation.

(vii) Market Surveys and Other Market Research Studies. As regards market surveys and other market research studies, several steps in the tasks can be conveniently, computerised. If the questionnaire is coded for computerisation, enormous volume of data generated by the survey can be, easily tabulated and the required cross tabulations and analysis can also be made in quick time and with precision.

(viii) Product Launch, Planning and Control. The activities involved in a product launch can also be computerised, using network techniques.

(ix) Marketing Cost Analysis. In the chapter on Marketing Control, we had explained how marketing costs have to be analysed under different head... The computer can be of great help in this endeavour.

ORGANISING THE MARKETING OUTFIT FOR COMPUTERISATION

Computerisation in the marketing area calls for considerable preparatory work. If computerisation of the marketing outfit has to be carried out smoothly and if it has to bring in the expected benefits, certain basic requirements will have to be observed at the very beginning. Once the ground is prepared well, introduction and operation of the computerised system become easy.

The complexity of the required hardware and software is directly related to the volume and nature of data processing involved.

A great deal of planning is called for in determining the hardware and software requirements. The unique nature of the marketing function must also be appreciated at the planning stage. Marketing is carried out from a large number of places spread over a large territory. Accordingly, as apart of the preparatory work, a correct assessment of the physical/geographical spread of the marketing organisation and the consequent needs in terms of hardware software, etc. must be made. For example, the networking requirements of the proposed system will largely depend on this dimension. A third requirement is to assess the extent to which other departments of the company are going in for computerisation. It is also essential to analyse the costs of going in for computerisation and the benefits that would accrue from it.

The various factors to be studied as a preparation to computerisation are listed below:

(i) the structure and working of the company, the various divisions and their interdependence in work/information flow/decisions.

(ii) the nature and size of business with special emphasis on the volume and spread of transactions.

(iii) the functions carried out at the various field offices within the marketing outfits area/region etc.

(iv) the organisation structure and working of the marketing department.

{v) functions that are carried out at the marketing head office.

(vi) data volume/data complexity.

(vii) data flow and the event flow at each level.

(viii) human resources presently available.

(ix) training requirements.

The main aim is to have a well-charted and systematic approach to the issue. Haphazard attempt by a few persons in the marketing outfit may not bring in the expected benefits.

(i) Networked Computer Systems will be Particularly Suitable for Marketing Departments. Computers can be connected to one another and a computer system as a whole can be connected to other computer systems. Small systems/ PC's located in the different departments of the marketing division can be connected to a larger central system. Information made available by the departments of the marketing division to the central system can be used by other divisions of the company like production or finance through their systems. The operational a work of the marketing division can be carried out by the small systems/PC's of an on-line basis. The batch processing requirements of the division can be done by the centrally available larger system. All the departments of the marketing as well as other divisions of the company can be connected to the larger system through direct and dedicated links, when the distance involved in short. But, any marketing organisation will usually have a large number of field offices at the area/regional/depot level. The computer systems located at such scattered and distant centres can be connected to the marketing home office through telephone lines (modems). In other words, the large and well distributed public telephone network already available in the country can be used to connect the computer system of the field offices to fuel main system at the home office.

(ii) Establishing Connectivity Standards in the Computer Network Important. For efficient running of the network, there must be consistent, easy to use, interfaces between work stations of different computing power, which may be build around different designs. The right network connectivity and cards must be established throughout the system—standards to which the users adhere, so that the efficiency of the total network does not suffer. Connectivity standards have to be established at three levels—at physical level, systems level and applications level. At the physical level standards relating to installations, telecommunication equipments and services like long distance data transmission, modems, controllers, etc. have to be laid down. At the systems level, connectivity standards will nave to ensure that the network allows the central staff to address any computer on the network, protect sensitive data with any of the computers and distribute new applications to any of the computers in the network, irrespective of locations or the operating system used by the different computers. And at the applications level, the connectivity standards should ensure that the hundreds of applications running on the different computers in the network are freely exchangeable. If such standards in this regard are not established, the marketing outfit may end up with several individual computer systems having their own small isolated data bases which cannot be comprehended and readily used by the other or by the central office.

MARKETING SUB-SYSTEMS

I. Marketing Sub-Systems can be Computerised to Advantage

In any typical large sized marketing outfit, there will be a number of sub-systems within the marketing system. The important ones among them are:

(i) Sales sub-system.

(ii) Stock accounting sub-system.

(iii) Finance sub system (Bank a/c).

(iv) Distribution sub-system.

(v) Marketing services' sub-system.

All these sub-systems, can be computerised. Let us take up a few of these aspects for elaboration.

(a) Sales Sub-system Invoicing and Sales Accounting. In the sales sub-system, with a built-in programme, the computer carries out the invoicing and accounting job in a jiffy. It also simultaneously takes care of the typing work as well. By merely inputting the dealer code, the product code, the depot warehouse code and the quantity issued, the computer prepares the invoice arid prints it out, complete in all respects. It 'calculates' the value at the ruling price the sales tax at the ruling rates, the deal remargins and special discounts as per the prevailing norm and arrives at the net amount payable by the dealer and prepares the invoice.

(b) Stock Accounting Sub-system. In addition to invoice preparation, sales accounting and preparation of statements, the machine can also totally take over the stock accounting and stock reconciliation task. In large marketing outfits, stock reconciliation between the field warehouses and the head office is usually a complex and time-consuming work. The computer can be entrusted with this work.

(c) Finance Sub-system (Bank A/c). The computer can also take care of the accounting and reconciliation of the bank transactions of the marketing outfit. All cheques, drafts and other banking instruments an be captured in the computer; credit advises from the bank on realisation of the amounts can also be captured; and the computer file will serve as a full-fledged record/statement of cheques/ drafts. The statement can be compared with the pass book or statements provided by the bank and the necessary reconciliations can be carried out.

(d) Distribution Sub-system. Let us now take the distribution sub-system and analyse in detail how the use of computers can bring about significant improvements in the management of the distribution function. Since distribution consists of two major parts—physical distribution and management of the channel or dealer network—let us consider the scope of computer applications in each of these areas.

- *(i) Physical Distribution Sub-System.* As far as physical distribution is concerned, one of the traditional problems is that the data required for taking decisions does not become available instantly. For example, the executive in charge of deciding the product shipments to different warehouses/ sales outlets would like to know instantly, the details of the planned sales during the month or fortnight in the concerned territory, the quantity shipped out already against the despatch plan for the period, the quantity in the pipeline and the latest stock position in the concerned warehouse or outlet. Quite often, he does not get all this information on the spot; and by the time he gets all the information pieced together, it only serves the purpose of a post-mortem and not that of decision making. Distribution is one of the areas where an on-line computer system is always appropriate. At the press of a button, it provides all the relevant information and truly serves as a decision support system.

(ii) *Dealer Sub-System.* Now let us turn to management of the distribution channel or dealer network. Computer applications can help the management of the dealer network in several ways. In the first place, the computer will help to maintain a master file on dealer network, where all relevant data relating to the entire dealer network can be stored in a ready-to-use fashion. Data can be organised and instantly retrieved in the specific manner in which it is needed for any given purpose. Names and addresses of all dealers arranged district wise, region wise, state or zone wise is one example of information that will be available in the master file.

(iii) *Computerised Credit Control.* Fourthly, an on-line computer system will be of great help in controlling credit transactions with the dealer network. The credit limits allowed for each dealer will be readily available in the relevant computer file. Since all transactions of sales and payments get entered then and there in the on-line sales accounting system, the amount of credit already availed of by a given dealer and the balance available in his allowed credit limit at any point of time can be had on the spot from the computerised accounts. Subsequent credit sales can be controlled based on this information.

(iv) *Dealer Profile.* In addition to the support provided in the accounting of transactions with the dealers and in credit control, the computer can be of great help to the marketing executive in managing and developing the network of dealers. All relevant information about each dealer can be stored in a computer file. Any changes in any aspect of the profile of the dealer can be inputted as and when such changes take place. And the complete and updated information can be retrieved instantly.

The following are examples of information that can be kept in the file:

(a) Financial position.

(b) Credit limit allowed by the company.

(c) Securities furnished.

(d) Sales performance in the past five years.

(e) Pattern of off take including minimum and maximum levels reached in a week or month.

(f) Payment terms applicable.

(g) Payment behaviour including delays in realisation of cheques.

With the help of this file, any type of analysis that is required can be undertaken. Dealer performance analysis can be one of them. Performance of individual dealers, performance of groups of dealers classified suitably, and performance of the entire network can be analysed. Dealer performance in specific market segments and in specific product categories can also be analysed. Performance of the individual dealer compared to his targets, his past sales and the sales of competing brands in the territory can also be analysed.

ADVANTAGES OF COMPUTERS IN MARKETING MANAGEMENT

The popularity of computers that we see today among business firms and business executives is the direct outcome of the many tangible advantages offered by them. The capabilities of the computer systems are simply astounding. In the first place, the computers help the executive to store and have access to an enonnous quantity of data. As regards off-line storage of data, the capacity is in effect unlimited. Secondly, these machines make computations at an incredible speed, taking millions of instructions per second. Thirdly, they have a tremendous logical capability; they compare data, highlight exceptions or variations and execute instructions based on the results of the comparisons. Fourthly, they are versatile in the sense that they can be used for a variety of applications; they confer the advantage of programmability. In recent years, the machines have become compact, mobile and user friendly. They have also become affordable.

New developments including the advent of personal computers (PC) have enlarged the advantages further

Till recently, computers meant large systems operated by computer experts. These large systems were generally inaccessible to executives in charge of different functions, including marketing. There was a real physical distance between the executives who were the real users of computer outputs and the computer experts who were doing the data processing. The executives were generally diffident about the computer and its relevance to them.

The advent of the new small machine, the personal computer (PC), has radically changed the situation. In India, in recent years, the PC has come in a big way. The PC is one segment that is particularly growing fast. In a comparatively short span of time, business executives, especially marketing executives, in India have become familiar with the PC and have come to appreciate it as a versatile aid in their management tasks.

All the characteristics features of the PC such as compactness, desk top and portable nature, ease of installation and user friendliness have had a great pull effect on the marketing executive . The last mentioned characteristics, *i.e.*, user friendliness, in particular, has made the machine universally acceptable. The user is no longer required to be a computer specialist; many ready to use software packages have become available; and operating systems have become easy and universal. The average executive has started looking at this machine ,as a ready and handy assistant. He uses it for meeting a great variety of needs-data storage, computations, analysis, planning, control and report preparations. And in combination with modern telecom facilities, the computer has vastly expanded his capabilities to handle and utilise information. The 'communication' technology, a synthesis of computer and communication technologies which enables the marketing man of today to get instant information on what is happening in every remote corner of his marketing territory with the least strain on his part.

❐

15

Direct and Online Marketing

Mass marketers have typically sought to reach millions of buyers with a single product and a standard message delivered through the man media. Thus, Procter & Gamble originally launched Crest toothpaste in one version with a single message ("Crest fights cavities"), hoping that 270 million Americans would get the message and buy the brand. Procter & Gamble did not need to know its customers' names or anything else about them, only that they wanted to take good care of their teeth. Most marketing communications consisted of one-way communication directed at consumers, not two-way communication with them.

Direct communications with carefully targeted individual consumers to obtain an immediate response.

In contrast, direct marketing consists of direct communications with carefully targeted individual consumers to obtain an immediate response. Thus, direct marketers communicate directly with customers, often on a one-to-one, interactive basis. They closely match their marketing offers and communications to the needs of narrowly defined segments or even individual buyers. Beyond brand and image building, they usually seek a direct, immediate, and measurable consumer response.

Early direct marketers at a log companies, direct mailers, and tele marketers-gathered customer names and sold their goods mainly through the mail and by telephone. Today, improved database technologies and new media—computers, modems, fax machines, e-mail, the Internet, and online services-permit more sophisticated direct marketing. Their availability and reasonable costs have greatly enlarged direct-marketing opportunities.

Today, most direct marketers see direct marketing as playing an even broader role than simply selling products and services. They see it as an effective tool for interacting with customers to build long-term customer relationships. Thus, catalog companies send birthday cards, information on special events, or small gifts to select members of their customer bases. Airlines, hotels, and other businesses build strong customer relationships through frequency award programs (for example, frequent-flier miles) and club programs. Company Web sites provide ways for customers to "visit" companies, learn about their products and services, interact with company personnel, and participate in entertaining events and activities. In this way, direct marketing becomes direct relationship marketing.

Benefits of Direct Marketing

Direct marketing benefits customers in many ways. Consumers report that home shopping is fun, convenient, and hassle-free. It saves time and introduces them to a larger selection of merchandise. They can do comparative shopping by browsing through mail catalogs and online shopping services, then order products for themselves or others. Industrial customers can learn about available products and services without waiting for and typing up time with sales people.

Sellers also benefit. Direct marketers can buy mailing lists containing names of almost any group: millionaires, new parents, left-handed people, or recent college graduates. They can then personalise and customise their messages. With today's technology, a direct marketers can select small groups or even individual consumers, customise offers to their special needs and wants, and promote these offers through individualised communications.

The direct marketer can build an ongoing relationship with each customer. For example, Nestle's baby food division maintains a database of new parents and mails them six personalised packages of gifts and advice at key stages in the baby's life. Direct marketing can also be timed to reach prospects at just the right moment. Because they reach more interested consumers at the best times, direct-marketing materials receive higher leadership and response. Direct marketing also permits easy testing of alternative media and messages. Finally, direct marketing provides privacy the direct marketer's offer and strategy are less visible to competitors.

FORMS OF DIRECT MARKETING COMMUNICATION

The major forms of direct marketing—include face-to-face selling, direct-mail marketing, catalog marketing, telemarketing, direct-response television marketing, kiosk marketing, and online marketing.

(i) **Face-to-Face Selling.** The original and oldest form of direct marketing is the sales call, which we examined. Today most business-to-business marketers rely heavily on a professional sales force to locate prospects, develop them into customers build lasting relationships, and grow the business.

(ii) **Direct-Mail Marketing.** Direct marketing through single mailings that include letters, ads, samples, foldouts, and other "sales people with wings" sent to prospects on mailing lists, direct-mail marketing involves sending an offer, announcement, reminder, or other item to a person at a particular address. Using highly selective mailing lists, direct marketers enc. out millions of mail pieces each year—letters, ads, samples, fordluts, and other "sales people with wings." Direct mail is well suited to direct, one-to-one communication.

Until recently, all mail was paper based and handled by the U.S. Post Office, telegraphic services, or for-profit mail carriers such as Federal Express, DHL, or Airborne Express. Recently, however, three new forms of mail delivery have become popular:

(a) ***Fax mail.*** Fax machines allow delivery of paper-based messages over telephone lines fax mail has one major advantage over regular mail: The message can be sent and received almost instantaneously. Marketers now routinely send fax mail announcing offers, sales, and other events to prospects and customers with fax machines. Fax numbers of companies and individuals

are now available through published directories. However, some prospects and customers resent receiving unsolicited fax mail, which ties up their machines and consumes their paper.

(b) ***E-mail.*** E-mail (short for electronic mail) allows users to send messages or files directly from one computer to another. Messages arrive almost instantly and are stored until the receiving person retrieves them. Many marketers now send sales announcements, offers, product information, and other messages to e-mail addresses—sometimes to a few individuals, sometimes to large groups. As people begin to receive more e-mail messages, including unimportant ones they may look for an "agent" software program to sort out the more important messages from those than can be ignored or discarded.

(c) ***Voice Mail.*** Voice mail is a system for receiving and storing oral messages at a telephone address. Telephone companies sell this service as a substitute for answering machines. The person with a voice mail account can check messages by dialing into the voice mail system and entering a personal code. Some marketers have set up programs that will dial a large number of telephone numbers and leave the selling messages in the recipients voice mail boxes.

These new forms deliver direct mail at incredible speeds, compared to the post office's-"snail mail" pace. Yet, much like mail delivered through traditional channels, they may be resented as "junk mail" if sent to people who have no interest in them. For this reason, marketers must carefully identify appropriate targets so as not waste their money and recipients' time.

(iii) Catalog Marketing. Direct marketing through catalogs that are mailed to a select list of customers or made available in stores.

Catalog marketing involves selling through catalogs mailed to a select list of customers or made available in stores. Most consumers enjoy receiving catalogs and will sometimes even pay to get them. Many catalog marketers are now even selling their catalogs at bookstores and magazine stands.

Many business-to-business marketers also rely heavily on catalogs. Whether in the form of a simple brochure, three-ring binder, book, or encoded on a video-tape or computer disk, catalogs remain one of today's hardest-working sales tools.

(iv) Telemarketing. Telemarketing—using the telephone to sell directly to consumers—has become the major direct-marketing communication tool. Marketers use outbound telephone marketing to sell directly to consumers and businesses. In bound toll-free 800 numbers are used to receive orders from television and radio ads, direct mail, or catalogs. The average household receives 19 telephone sales calls each year and makes 16 calls to place orders.

Many consumers appreciate many of the offers they receive by telephone. Properly designed and targeted telemarketing provides many benefits, including purchasing convenience and increased product and service information.

(v) Direct-Response Television Marketing. Direct marketing *via* television, including direct-response television advertising or infomercials and home shopping channels.

Direct-response television marketing takes one of two major forms. The first is direct-response advertising. Direct marketers air television spots, often 60 or 120 seconds long, that persuasively describe a product and give customers a toll-free number for ordering. Television viewers often encounter 30 minute advertising programs, or informercials, for a single product. Such direct-response advertising works well for magazines, books, small appliances, tapes and CDs, collectibles, and many other products.

Home shopping channels, another form of direct-response television marketing, are television programs or entire channels dedicated to selling goods and services. Some home shopping channels, such as the Quality Value Channel (QVC) and the Home Shopping Newtork (HSN), broadcast 24 hours a day. On HSN, the program's hosts offer bargain prices on it products ranging from jewellery, lamps, collectible tools, and clothing to power tools and consumer electronics-usually obtained by the home mopping channel at chose out prices. They show is upbeat, with the boosts honking horns, blowing whistles, and praising viewers for their blood taste.

(vi) Kiosk Marketing. Some companies place information and ordering machines—called kiosks (in contrast to vending machines, which dispense actual products)—stores, airports, and other locations. Hallmark and American Greetings kiosks to help customers create personalised cards.

Business marketers also use, kiosks. For example, Down Plastics places kiosks trade shows to collect sales leads and to provide information on its 700 products. The kiosk system reads customer data from encoded registration badges and produces technical data sheets that can be printed fuel kiosk or faxed or mailed to the customer. The system has resulted in a 400 percent increase in qualified sales leads.

ONLINE MARKETING AND ELECTRONIC COMMERCE

Online marketing is conduct through interactive online computer systems, which link consumers with sellers electronically. A modern connects the conswner's computer or television set-top "Web machine" with various services through telephone lines. There are two types of online marketing channels: commercial online services and the Internet.

Marketing conducted through interactive on line computer systems, which link consumers with sellers electronically.

(i) Commercial Online Services. Commercial online services offer online information and marketing services to subscribers who pay a monthly fee. The best-known online services are America Online, Compu Serve, and Prodigy.

Services that offer on line information and marketing services to subscribers who pay a monthly fee, such as America Online, CompuServe, and Prodigy.

After growing rapidly through the mid-1990s, the commercial online services are now being overtaken by the Internet as the primary online marketing channel. In fact, all of the online service firms now offer Internet access as a primary service. The Internet is a vast and burgeoning global web of computer networks.

(ii) World Wide Web. Internet usage has surged with the recent development of the user-friendly World Wide Web and Web browser software such as Netscape Navigator, Microsoft Internet Explorer, and Mosaic. Now, even novices can surf the Net and experience fully integrated test, graphics, images, and sound. Users can send e-mail, exchange views, shop for products, and access news, food recipes, art, and business information. The Internet itself is free, although individual users usually must pay a commercial access provider to be hooked up to it.

(iii) Using E-mail and Webcasting. The automatic down loading of customised information of interest to recipients' PCs, affording an at active channel for delivering Internet advertising or other information content.

A company can encourage prospects and customers to send questions, suggestions, and even complaints to the company via e-mail. Customer service representative can quickly respond to such messages. The company may also develop Internet-based electronic mailing lists of customers or prospects. Such lists provide an excellent opportunity to introduce the company and its offerings to new customers and to build ongoing relationships with current ones.

Using the lists, on-line marketers can send out customer purchasing histories, reminders of service requirements or warranty renewals, or announcements of special events.

Companies can also sign on with any of a number of "Webcasting" services, which automatically download customised information to recipients' PCs. For a monthly fee, subscribers to these services can specify the channels they want—news, company information, entertainment, and others—and the topics they're interested in. Then, rather than spending hours scouring, the Internet, they can sit back while the Webcaster automatically delivers information of interest to their desktops.

Webcasting, also known as "push" programming, affords an attractive channel through which online marketers can deliver their Internet advertising or other information content.

Now, instead of waiting for Web surfers to stumble onto their sites and banner ads, marketers can send animated ads directly to the desktops of target customers. Retailer such as Lands' End and Virtual Vineyards are dabbling with such in-your-face methods to notify subscribers of promotions and even send them order forms. Merchants can approach live sales prospects and not just couch potatoes.

Webcasting service such as Point Cast and Fusion are growing fast and attracting an ever increasing number of advertisers. The major commercial on line services are also beginning to offer Weocasting to their members.

(iv) Integrated Direct Marketing. Direct-marketing campaigns that use multiple vehicles and multiple stages to improve response rates and profits.

Although direct marketing and online marketing have boomed in recent years, many companies still relegate them to minor roles in their marketing and promotion mixes. Too many direct marketers use only a "one-shot" effort to reach and sell a prospect, or a single vehicle in multiple stages to trigger purchases. For example, a magazine publisher might send a series of four direct-mail notices to a household to get a subscriber to renew before giving up. A more powerful approach is integrated direct marketing, which involves using multiple-vehicle, multiplecstage campaigns. Such campaigns can greatly improve response. Whereas a direct-mail piece along might generate a 2 per cent response, adding a toll-free phone number can raise the response rate by 50 per cent. A well-designed outbound telemarketing effort might lift response by an additional 500 per cent. Suddenly, a 2 per cent response has grown to 15 per cent or more by adding interactive marketing channels to a regular mailing.

More elaborate integrated direct marketing campaigns can be used. Consider the multimedia, multistage campaign shown in following figure. Here, the paid ad creates product awareness and stimulates inquiries. The company immediately sends direct mail to those who inquire. Within a few days, the company follows up with a phone call seeking an order. Some prospects will order by phone; others might request a face-to-face sales call. In such a campaign, the marketer seeks to improve response rates and profits by adding media and stages that contribute more to additional sales then to additional costs.

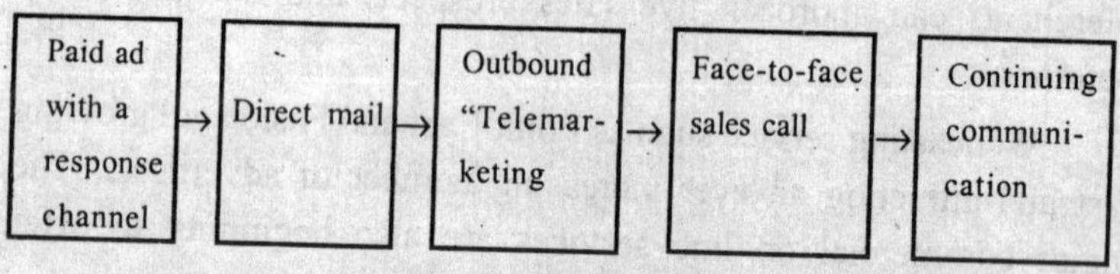

Fig. An Integrated Direct Marketing Campagin

THE BENEFITS OF ONLINE MARKETING

Why have online services become so popular? Online marketing yields benefits to both consumers and marketers.

(i) **Benefits to Consumers.** Online Buying provides the same basic benefits to consumers as other forms of direct marketing. It is convenient: Customers don't have to battle traffic, find a parking space, and walk through seemingly countless stores and aisles to find and examine products. They can compare brands, check out prices, and order merchandise 24 hours a day from any location. Online buying is easy and private: customers face fewer buying hassles and don't have to face salespeople or open themselves up to persuasion and emotional pitches.

Online buying offers consumers some additional advantages. The commercial on line services and the Internet give consumers access to an abundance of comparative information, information about companies, products and competitors. In addition, online buying is interactive and immediate. Consumers often can interact with the seller's site to find exactly the information, products, or services they desire, then order or download them on the spot.

(ii) Benefits to Marketers. Online marketing also yields many benefits to marketers. Because of its one-to one, interactive nature, online marketing is a good tool for customer relationship building. It brings companies and their customers closer together. Companies can interact with customers to team more about specific customer needs and wants and to build customer databases. In turn, online customers can ask questions and volunteer feedback. Based on this ongoing interaction, companies can increase customer value and satisfaction through product and service refinements. They can also tailor their communications and offers to the requirements of specific customers George Fisher, CEO of Eastman Kodak Company, sums it up this way:

> "Online activity gives us a way to meet customer needs and desires that is unparalleled since the days of the door-to-door salesman".

Online marketing can reduce costs and increase efficiency. Online marketers avoid the expense of maintaining a store and the accompanying costs of rent, insurance, and utilities. Because customers deal directly with sellers, online marketing often results in lower costs and improved efficiencies for channel and logistics functions such as order processing, inventory handling, delivery, and trade promotion. Family, communicating electronically often costs less than communicating on paper through the mail. For instance, a company can produce digital catalogs for much less than the cost of printing and mailing paper ones. The relatively low costs of setting up-an on little marketing operation mean that both small and large firms can afford it. For example, it generally costs less to set up an effective Web site than it does to purchase 30 seconds of commercial time on prime-time network television.

Online marketing also offers greater flexibility, allowing the marketer to make ongoing adjustments 10 its offers and programs. For example, once a paper catalog is mailed, the products, prices, and other catalog features are fixed until the next catalog is sent. However, an online catalog can be adjusted daily or even hourly, adapting product assorbnents, prices, and promotions to match changing market conditions.

Finally, the Internet is a truly global medium, which allows buyers and seller to click from one country to another in second. A Web surfer from Paris or Istanbul can access a Lands' End catalog as easily as someone living on 1 Lands' End Lane in Dodgeville, Wisconsin, the direct retailer's home town. Thus, even small online marketers find that they have ready access to global markets.

Despite these many benefits, however, online marketing is not for every company nor for every product. Careful thought has to be given to in, when, and how it should be undertaken.

❑

16

Export Marketing

The basic principles of marketing remain constant whether one is selling goods or services in the home market or overseas. There are, however, additional considerations which apply to exporting, such as an understanding of currency differences and the problems associated with specific tariff structures and quota restrictions, with which the Export Marketing Manager must contend.

Advantages of Exporting

A manufacturing organization which is prepared to enter export markets seriously, gains a number of advantages. Its primary objective, of course, will be to enlarge its profits. This is, however, not the only gain. There are others which, in the long term, can exert an important influence on the company's overall efficiency and commercial competence and which can produce far-reaching benefits. The experience of trading in a number of different markets offers a challenge which can only be met by a constant reappraisal of policies and methods. This in itself creates an invigorating influence throughout the organization. It prevents the somnambulance which is inclined to overtake companies who have achieved their objectives in the narrow confines of a reasonably predictable home market, devoid of strong competition.

If exporting acts as a tonic to Marketing and Sales, it can also be a blessing to the Production and Research Departments. The increased production which the growth of overseas trading will demand can result in the better utilization of under-employed resources of both labour and plant. Furthermore, the multiplicity of markets which exporting can achieve acts as a cushion against fluctuating demand. A recession in one market is frequently offset by boom conditions elsewhere. Thus production problems are eased and plant can be operated more efficiently.

So far as Research and Development is concerned, the existence of export potential tends to reduce the research cost per unit of the product. Perhaps of greater importance, however, is the international feedback of technical information which results when a company operates in foreign markets.

Export Problems

It is one thing to list the advantages of exporting: another to be fully alive to its problems. There was a time, in the early nineteen-fifties, when exporting was regarded as a difficult undertaking by many British businessmen and ever since successive governments have endeavoured to persuade industrialists that there is little to be afraid of in trading overseas, culminating in the famous phrase: 'exporting is fun'. Those experienced in the business know that it is anything but fun! However, the attitude of mind which suggests that overseas trading is not as complex as it is made out to be, creates its own hazards. There are many organizations which, in spite of all the exhortations of government and other agencies to treat exporting as a specialized function, still approach export markets as they would a new segment of their home market.

The problem lies mainly with senior management. At board room level there is still a tendency to think of export markets as convenient dumping grounds for surplus home production. Little thought is given to the suitability of merchandise or the need for consistent supply. The fact that there is no such thing as an all-embracing export market is overlooked. Yet each and every overseas market has different needs and requires a different approach. Too often, there is a marked reluctance to accept modifications to the product to meet these needs or to accept the necessity for a specific marketing approach to individual overseas countries.

SPECIAL FACTORS IN OVERSEAS MARKETING

There is no doubt that an organization which practises a consumer-orientated policy in its home trade will enter the export field better equipped than one in which production calls the tune. The attitude of mind which the modern concept of marketing seeks to invoke—namely, that the product and its presentation should satisfy the market need—is essential to successful exporting. Thus the starting point in the preparation of an export marketing plan, as in the home field, is an under—standing of market requirements followed by a consideration of how these may be met.

Each export market demands an independent study. Among the more important factors which the Marketing Manager should consider are the following:

Stability

Companies whose trading experience has, hitherto, been confined almost wholly to a domestic market, frequently exhibit extreme naivety in their commercial approach to foreign countries. The stability of the local currency needs careful examination before commitments are undertaken. Political stability within the intended market should also be considered. The exporter should be alive to the considerable changes which can occur in a country's external trading policies following a change of government. The relative strength of the opposing political parties and their attitude towards external trade needs to be watched. In selecting suitable export markets for one's merchandise, care must be taken that a considerable marketing investment is not put at risk in a country where a sudden change in the political regime closes the door to future importations.

Indigenous Competition

The technological advance which is currently occurring in most countries of the world and particularly in what are described as the under-developed countries, must tend to encourage protectionist trading policies designed to safeguard their embryo indigenous production. As a result, there are certain markets where the scope for the importer is a short-term one only. This does not mean that the business which is currently available is not worth seeking. The exporter will be wise to recognize the true situation and tailor his marketing investment in such markets to the limited degree of penetration which is likely to be available to him.

Social Conditions

A consumer-orientated marketing policy, as we have seen, examines the social conditions of those to whom the product is directed. In all the various countries of the world there are marked differences in social behaviour. Religious outlook, class structure, the attitude towards women, standards of hygiene and the leisure habits of the population vary, not only from country to country but also from region to region. Climatic conditions play a decisive part in the development of social habits and mental outlook.

Dependability

A British company entering the export field must be alive to the fact that the traditional standards of commercial conduct which appertain to its domestic market do not necessarily apply in all other parts of the world. Whilst it may be assumed that any reasonably astute exporter will establish the financial viability of an overseas customer before trading begins, he will be advised to ensure that the buyer is in a position to pay for the goods he receives promptly. There are certain markets in which business is easier to achieve, such as the under-developed countries, but where very extended credit terms may be required. Alternatively, in highly industrialized markets, such as the United States of America, those of Western Europe and the older Commonwealth countries, in spite of heavier competition for business, the exporter will often have the advantage of obtaining quick payment.

ORGANIZING FOR EXPORTS

Bearing the above factors in mind, we may now consider the type of organization which the Marketing Manager should set up to pursue his exporting objectives.

The Export Manager

To lead the export team he needs an individual possessing a variety of attributes. The ideal Export Manager will be a good mixer, capable of self-discipline, with the ability to make decisions. In addition, he should have a methodical approach because close attention to detail as well as personality and flair play a vital part in successful exporting. He will need to be a reasonably mature person, able to conduct business at all levels within client companies. Preference should be given to a married rather than a single man. The wife of an Export Manager has an important role to play in assisting her husband in the entertaining of visiting overseas customers and there is merit in arranging for her to accompany him on some of his visits abroad where once again she can be of considerable help to him in establishing friendly relationships with clients and their families.

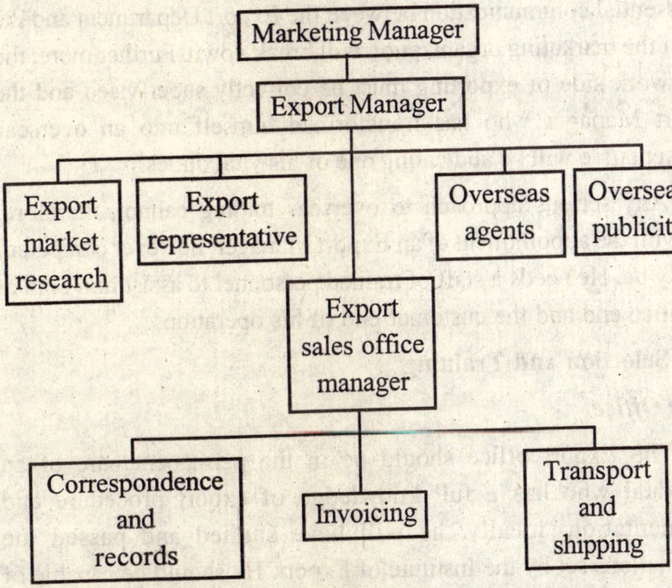

Fig. Organization Chart for an Export Department

An Export Manager should possess not only a complete understanding of export procedure and practice. He must be familiar with the products or services which his company is offering and be able to settle the majority of queries regarding quality or price on the spot and without the necessity to obtain guidance from his Head Office. For this reason it is necessary for him to have the full confidence of the Marketing Manager and the Directors of the company and be fully acquainted with their policies.

The Export Manager will have to spend part of his time in his office managing the Export Department and the remainder overseas, visiting the various markets in which the company is operating, to establish a good personal relationship with individual customers. The amount of time he devotes to overseas travel must depend upon the size of the exporting effort and the number and quality of the staff he has to assist him. It is a cliche to say that one cannot conduct a successful export campaign from behind a desk in Britain. On the other hand, if the man charged with managing exports is nearly always abroad, rarely to be seen or heard at the company headquarters, the essential communication between the Export Department and the rest of the marketing organization will break down. Further more, the paperwork side of exporting must be correctly super-vised and the Export Manager who has transformed himself into an overseas representative will be abdicating one of his vital duties.

Any serious approach to overseas trading cannot, therefore, stop with the appointment of an Export Manager, however competent he may be. He needs a staff of trained personnel to assist him both at the office end and the customer end of his operations.

Staff Selection and Training

In the Office

The Export office should be in the permanent care of an individual who has a full knowledge of export procedure and documentation. Ideally, he will have studied and passed the examinations set by the Institute of Export. He should be capable of handling all correspondence with overseas clients and agents during the absence of the Export Manager, who should be prepared to delegate to him all the routine work involved in export sales, including the placing and progressing of customers' orders with the Production

Department, arranging Letters of Credit, shipping and customs documentation and insurance. The Export Manager, blessed with the assistance of a reliable and experienced office supervisor, is free to devote the major part of his time to other vital aspects of his work, including research into new overseas markets, the scrutiny and appointment of agents and the framing of export policies geared to meet specific market requirements.

In the Field

In selecting salesmen for work in export markets one must look, generally speaking, for individuals with higher qualifications than is usually necessary when filling vacancies in home market territories. This is because the overseas salesman must often assume greater responsibilities than his counterpart at home. He will undoubtedly be responsible for far greater potential business, is likely to be under much less supervision than the home-based salesman and many of his duties, such as the control of local agents, liaison with local distributors or the supervision of local depots, are of a managerial nature.

It is evident that an overseas salesman must have a good education. It is desirable that he should also possess some technical qualifications because; unlike the home-based representative, he will not have the assistance of a technical service department close at hand. An essential qualification, and one that does not appear to be given sufficient weight in many over seas appointments, is the ability to speak fluently the language of the people in the overseas territories concerned.

In arranging a training programme for salesmen who possess all or most of these qualifications, the Export Manager should stress the importance of familiarization with the habits, tastes and general way of life of the people in the specific markets to which a new salesman is to be assigned. So much of the success in selling is dependent upon achieving a good rapport with one's customers, that a man who lacks the ability to understand the motivations of those to whom he is required to sell cannot achieve the best results. (In a companion volume in this series have attempted to examine in depth the need for a careful understanding and appreciation of buyers' motives.)

Secondly, the overseas salesman should receive training in the pattern of the markets in which he will operate. He needs to know the distribution of population, the concentration of industry and the extent and calibre of competitive activity within those markets. He requires instruction in the business practices of the countries concerned and should also have some understanding of the political and economic conditions which exist.

Thirdly, he should be provided with a good grounding in export procedures and practice. These should be coupled with an explanation of the procedures followed by the company in its handling of export business.

Finally, the new export salesman needs to know as much as he can about how the product is produced, its selling features and how these compare with those of both domestic and international competitors, the company's costing policy and how his product is packed, shipped and distributed.

EXPORT RESEARCH

Before he ventures abroad in search of suitable markets for his products, the Export Manager should undertake as much desk research as possible. Overseas travel is expensive and time-consuming. To visit a country without having 'done one's homework' beforehand can be a waste of effort.

The depth of research which can be undertaken will depend very much upon the country concerned. In highly developed Western countries, for instance, there will exist a considerable pool of knowledge in published form upon which the Export Manager can draw. When one is seeking information about less developed regions, however, published data may be scanty or non-existent. Market Research, as we know it in Britain and the United States, is heavily dependent upon the sociological and mathematical sciences. The preparation of statistics requires personnel who have received the necessary training. Indeed, the entire basis of consumer research, as we have seen, lies in response to written or verbal questionnaires. In those areas of the world where literacy among the population is limited or non-existent, the conduct of market research programmes is consequently made more difficult.

Nevertheless, a considerable amount of research can and should be done before visits to prospective markets are undertaken. It may be classified under four headings:

(1) Market Research

(2) Product Research

(3) Distribution Research

(4) Operational Research.

Market Research

Under this heading, one should seek to establish the size, nature and future scope of the market for one's particular product, not forgetting the importance of establishing the strength of both indigenous and international competition. One should bear in mind what has already been said about segmentation in domestic markets. Overseas markets, too, consist of a number of segments and research may disclose the fact that there are certain sectors of what appears to be a generally over-supplied market which have been left unsatisfied by one's competitors. In such circumstances, a visit by the Export Manager to appraise the situation in person, could be a useful next step. On the other hand, where research shows that - a market is fully saturated with supplies of products virtually identical in quality and value to your own, it is unlikely that a personal visit could achieve any worthwhile short-term results.

Product Research

It is important to establish at the outset whether there is likely to be any local desire for one's product as it stands or whether it will require modification. If alterations are necessary, then the likely demand must be sufficient to warrant the inconvenience cost which such modifications may cause one's Production Department. Even a fully consumer-oriented marketing policy does not justify forcing one's factory to run uneconomically.

Apart from the design of the product, one must consider the design of the package. Local customs and taboos must be observed and this could mean special packaging, which again may present costing problems.

The price at which the product can be sold will be dependent, largely, upon the price at which competitive products are sold in the same market. If one cannot affordor wish to afford to make, pack, ship and distribute one's product at this price it may be better to leave this particular market alone until such time as circumstances alter.

Distribution Research

The pattern of distribution is likely to differ from country to country. Before one approaches a specific market it is advisable to establish the existing pattern applicable to one's own type of merchandise and to calculate the effect which this distribution cost will have upon the selling price of your product.

Sometimes it is possible to establish one's own distribution pattern at variance with the traditional methods of the market. This is not without hazard and may bring resistance from customers. Where there is doubt on this matter, a visit of the Export Manager or one of his salesmen, to canvass the views of local customers, can be helpful. Ultimately, one may have to decide upon two conflicting methods: one which the customers prefer and one which will suit the company. From the long-term view, it is probably the former which should be adopted.

Operational Research

The maintenance of customer service is of paramount importance in export marketing. While it is evident that the provision of satisfactory service plays its part in ensuring customer satisfaction and the receipt of repeat business in the home market, when one is competing in foreign markets its effect upon the continuity of the business can be decisive. One's relationship with overseas clients can seldom be as close as with firms at home. Competition for business abroad is international and therefore likely to be extremely fierce. Furthermore, the relative cost of acquiring and re-acquiring business in overseas markets is often considerably higher than in one's domestic market. These factors emphasize the need for a continuing operational research to check that deliveries are made on time, that documentation is correct, that packing is adequate and that aftersales service is maintained satisfactorily.

CUSTOMER VISITS AND REPORTS

Visits to overseas customers should not be regarded as the occasion for a working holiday for directors and other senior management personnel. Exporting is specialized work and a trip abroad undertaken by a senior executive is not necessarily the best means of building export business. It is, of course, desirable that members of the company's top management should meet important overseas buyers. This can often best be done by inviting the buyer to visit the company's headquarters in its home country when a factory tour, accompanied by suitable entertaining, can be provided. When the Top People do go abroad, their objective should be to cement relations with customers, not to establish them. The donkey-work of exporting should be left in the hands of those whose specialized training and experience make them the best people for the job.

An overseas visit, whether it is undertaken by a senior executive, by the Export Manager or an export representative, requires very careful forward planning. A great deal of time and money are to be expended. For the individual undertaking the trip there will also be a considerable expenditure in energy. Travelling is tiring work. If he is to do his job properly, the whole trip needs to be properly organized.

The exporter, approaching a new market for the first time, should know his objectives. These are likely to consist of the following:

(a) To investigate the market potential which has been established by preliminary desk research.

(b) To appoint local distributors and agents following preparatory negotiations conducted by letter.

(c) To visit major customers or potential customers to negotiate new or additional business.

When visiting an overseas customer, the company's representative should possess as much information as possible about the client and the nature of his business. He requires a record of his company's transactions with the firm, as well as of the activity of competitors, where these are known. For this purpose, a card index, set out on the following lines, can be most useful:

Name of Customer:

Address: Telephone No: Cable Address:

Personnel:

Nature of Business:

Types of Outlets Supplied:

Credit Rating: Bankers:

Payment Terms Agreed:

Products Supplied: Date: Quantity Price:

Special Shipping Arrangements:

Competitors' Activities Noted:

Quality Complaints Received:

Service Complaints Received:

Future Prospects:

A record of this kind, which can be updated regularly, provides the visiting exporter with all the essential information he needs for his customer visits.

Having set out his objectives and collected his information, the exporter should prepare a detailed itinerary for each customer visit of his tour. It is desirable that this should be circulated well before he sets off, to the various personnel within the company whose work involves them with the over-seas customers to be visited, as well as to the local agents in the countries concerned. The merit of this arrangement is that the recipients can bring to the attention of the exporter any additional matters which will assist him in his discussions and he can endeavour to obtain for them answers to any specific queries they may have outstanding.

A prototype itinerary of this nature is set out below:

Itinerary for Visit to: Date of Visit:

The following matters will be discussed:

(a) *New Product X.* To quote prices and delivery position.

(b) *Complaint on Product Y.* To investigate complaint and arrange replacement if considered necessary.

(c) *Product Y-Prices.* To negotiate a new price structure to take effect 1st October next.

(d) *Damaged Deliveries.* To investigate complaint of damage to recent deliveries allegedly due to inadequate packing.

(e) *New Competitive Product.* To examine the new competitive product Brand Z and obtain samples, prices, etc., if possible.

DISTRIBUTION ARRANGEMENTS IN EXPORT MARKETS

There are several alternative methods by which the Marketing Manager may distribute his product overseas. In deciding upon the most suitable channel to use, he will need to consider the size of the market he proposes to enter and its characteristics, the nature of his product and the size of his own company organization. It will be obvious that different methods of approach are required according to the above criteria. There are three main types of distribution channel which can be used according to one's circumstances and the policy it is intended to adopt.

(1) The use of domestic distribution organizations.

(2) The use of overseas distributors.

(3) Selling direct to overseas customers.

One can engage in export trading without, as it were, getting one's feet wet. That is to say export business can be conducted solely through domestic channels and there is no necessity for the product manufacturer to involve himself in the problems of foreign currencies or the paraphernalia of export documentation and shipping arrangements.

Distribution *via* Domestic Organizations

The simplest method of all is to supply the product to a wholesaler engaged in export business and let him export it under his own brand name. Alternatively, one may use concessionaires. These are firms which purchase merchandise, usually as principals, on the understanding that the manufacturer gives them the concession to export his products in a particular overseas area. Concessionaires do, in fact, operate very much in the fashion of the manufacturer's export department. However, they pay for the goods they receive in the domestic currency and free the supplier from all exporting cares. They can be useful for limited amounts of overseas business. A point may be reached, however, when the volume of trade involved is such that it can be more profitable for the manufacturer to undertake his own exporting.

Another means of avoiding, or at least minimizing, the possible trials and tribulations of exporting, is to enter into some form of group trading arrangement. This can be useful for a small organization where the amount of export business which is anticipated is considered insufficient to warrant the expense of establishing an export department. Sometimes a small firm will approach a larger company, producing non-competing lines, with the proposal that the major organization should export the small man's product along with their own. This so-called 'pick-a-back' method is often conducted on the basis of the payment of commission or a sharing of costs. The additional lines can assist the economic viability of the larger firm's export operation by reducing its sales and distribution costs.

With a similar aim in view, several small firms, whose interests do not clash, sometimes get together and set up a special export company. This can, however, produce problems for the participants. Jealousies are liable to creep in, especially if it is suspected that the degree of effort being devoted to the sale of one man's lines is less than that given to others.

There are certain categories of overseas business for which it may be impracticable for a single manufacturer to contend on his own. An example is a construction scheme, involving many types of products and skills, which cannot be supplied solely by one firm. In these circumstances, companies enter into a consortium to offer a package deal. The method has been applied with notable success in deals with countries in the Soviet bloc, where all negotiations are conducted with a centralized state purchasing agency.

One of the most widely used methods of exporting without overseas involvement, is to sell to a firm of Export Merchants. Such organizations are generally specialists, dealing primarily in a specific group of products and trading with specific geographical markets. The Export Merchant both buys and sells as principal. He thus relieves the product manufacturer of all the risks involved in overseas trade, he pays promptly for the goods he buys in domestic currency and usually undertakes all packing and shipping arrangements.

The use of an Export house for the distribution of one's product overseas can work very well if one is in a comparatively small way of business and the nature of the product is such that personal communications with the consumer and the creation of goodwill in the overseas market are not considered particularly important. However, by the nature of his business, the Export Merchant usually buys only those goods which he knows he can resell quickly. He purchases the type of merchandise which he is confident will satisfy the immediate demand of his overseas clients and will seldom seek to develop a market for a specific product. Because he is unlikely to have any long-term interest in anyone product his after-sales service may be minimal.

Distribution *via* Overseas Organizations

Where the manufacturer considers it desirable to exercise greater control over the sale of his product in export markets, he will appoint local agents and remunerate them on a commission basis. The situation of a commission agent is not dissimilar to that of a company's representative in the home market except that he is not in the employ of the firm and one does not have the same degree of control over his activities. The agent will canvass for orders among the clientele of the country or countries in which he operates and will undertake all the necessary follow-up duties, including the investigation of any complaints or queries which may arise in respect to quality and service. He will receive a commission on all business which arises from his territory of between 5 and 10 per cent.

The Export Manager must be at pains to ensure that his overseas agents are fully motivated. One of the problems of using an agent is that he will usually represent a number of firms producing non-competing lines. Unless the level of business which he can create and maintain for one's particular product is really worth his while, there is the danger that he will tend to devote the bulk of his activities to the furtherance of his other interests. When an agent, who has established business for a product with a number of accounts, finds that he is not getting adequate support—deliveries are late, correspondence is dealt with tardily, consignments are received damaged—it is inevitable that he will lose interest and fail to develop additional business. The confidence of the agent must, therefore, be maintained by a constant attention to his needs and those of his customers. Regular visits of company personnel to discuss out-standing matters with local agents should also be interspersed with periodic invitations to the agent to visit the company's headquarters to meet the senior management and be kept informed of new product developments and any changes in marketing policies.

A Commission Agent is one who provides a sales service for the exporter. A Distribution Agent, on the other hand, combines the services of a Commission Agent with the carrying of stocks of the product and arranging for their physical distribution to the customers in his territory. There are certain advantages to the product manufacturer in the use of a Distribution Agent. With stocks held locally, a good delivery service can be provided. This may be important where there is an indigenous supply of similar merchandise. A Distribution Agent who is handling several product lines imported from one's own country, is likely to operate a group shipping arrangement through a forwarding agent handling all the various types of merchandise with which he is concerned. Thus group shipment can be provided with a subsequent reduction in costs.

The main problem encountered in the use of Distribution Agents is that some of them become involved in too many types of products and, like the domestic wholesaler in a similar situation, are unable to do justice to anyone of them. Before he appoints a Distribution Agent, the Export Manager should make careful enquiries about his standing in the market in which he operates. He should ensure that the firm concerned possesses sufficient salesmen of the right calibre to sell his product and has adequate facilities in the form of warehouses and transport to provide a satisfactory physical distribution service.

Generally speaking, Commission Agents provide a more suitable means of overseas representation for manufacturers of raw materials and industrial products where local stockholding may not be a necessary factor. For consumer goods, however, where it may be necessary to execute a large number of rather small orders promptly, the Distribution Agent provides a vital service.

A third method of overseas representation is the use of a Franchise Agent. There are certain types of products, such as motor-cars, motor-cycles and various classes of electrical goods, where it may be desirable to ship in the form of components for assembly in the local overseas area. The Franchise Agent is one who is given a franchise by the manufacturer to undertake such assembly. In some instances he may be franchised to actually manufacture the product locally.

Selling Direct to Overseas Customers

There are certain types of overseas business which cannot be conducted suitably through intermediaries. Some large retail outlets, such as departmental or chain stores, prefer to deal direct with the foreign manufacturer. The aggregate size of their orders may be such that the employment of a local Commission Agent or a Distributor becomes unnecessary. Large organizations of this nature often possess fully adequate warehousing facilities to allow them to order merchandise in bulk and to themselves distribute to their own outlets. They will be experienced in the importation of goods and well versed in all the necessary documentation procedure.

A similar situation will arise when one is fulfilling foreign governmental or municipal authority contracts. Here again, there will be a preference for direct dealing with the manufacturer who himself may consider it desirable to maintain close personal control over the transactions.

THE APPOINTMENT OF AGENTS

From the foregoing it will be seen that the appointment of overseas agents is an extremely important function of overseas marketing. Considerable care should be exercised, not only in deciding the type of agent most suitable to handle one's particular product in a particular market, but also to ensure that the specific firm one chooses has adequate knowledge of one's class of merchandise and sufficient experience of the market to achieve the degree of penetration required.

In selecting agents, therefore, there are certain essentials to be considered.

Financial Position

Before negotiations which are intended to lead to the appointment of an agent become too advanced, the Marketing Manager Should satisfy himself about the agent's financial stability. To commence trading in an overseas market through an agent who subsequently fails, due to lack of adequate working capital or inefficient operation, can be a major setback to one's export plans. Some loss of confidence is bound to occur among customers in the territory concerned. All the efforts which the company has already devoted to launching the agency arrangement, are likely to have been wasted. Furthermore, there is the danger that existing business in the area will drain away before a new agent can be found, appointed and set to work on the territory.

Common prudence suggests a careful vetting of proposed agents commencing with a check upon their credentials through one of the finance intelligence houses specializing in such work. The creditworthiness of overseas agents may also be checked, by British firms, with the Export Credits Guarantee Department of the Department of Trade and Industry.

Trading Experience

The majority of agents tend to specialize in both products and markets. In making one's choice, it would be necessary to discover the extent of an agent's knowledge and experience in handling one's particular type of product. If the product is to be sold to industrial users, some considerable technical expertise may be essential. Where the manufacturer has already achieved some trading bridgeheads within the proposed territory, enquiry can sometimes be made among local customers regarding a suitable firm to undertake one's local representation.

The proposed agent's existing contacts in the market is another vital factor. Is his firm well received by local buyers? Does he possess an organization large enough to handle the quantity of business which is envisaged? Above all, what is his trading reputation? Is it for fair-dealing and reliability or has he a past history of sharp practice or of slothfulness in dealing with customers' requirements? The reputation of an agent has a tendency to rub off on to the image of the manufacturer he represents, and the Marketing Manager must be on his guard to ensure that the high standards created by his own company are maintained by those who speak for him in his overseas markets.

Other Lines

Consideration must be given to the other lines which an agent is carrying. Generally speaking, it is desirable that he should not represent manufacturers of competing products. However, there may be advantage to be gained if he has an established agency for certain related types of merchandise, because this will indicate that he has the product knowledge and selling skill needed for a particular class of goods and will possess active contacts for the sale of one's own product. The agency Agreement can specify that competing lines shall not be carried by the agent. One can also stipulate the percentage of time to be devoted to one's product by the agent's sales force. However, the danger of too much effort going to the promotion of other lines to the detriment of one's own can be avoided if the business potential for one's product on the assigned territory is sufficiently attractive, if the product itself has a good selling-proposition and adequate support is given to the agent's efforts.

In drafting an agency Agreement, there are certain important factors to be considered. The product, or group of products, involved, should be exactly specified. Similarly, there should be a precise definition of the territory which is being assigned. The method by which the agent's remuneration is to be calculated and paid must also be stated clearly, together with some definite procedure for the payment of any additional costs which the agent may incur on behalf of the company, such as those of promotion, research and the investigation and settlement of claims resulting from faulty merchandise or other causes. It is most advisable to limit the period of an initial Agreement with an agency to six months or, at the most, one year.

All agency Agreements should, of course, be vetted by the Company Secretary or some other qualified legal adviser.

SALES PROMOTION IN EXPORT MARKETS

The promotion of one's product by means of press and broad casting advertisements, direct mail, cinema advertising, the use of posters and the employment of Public Relations, is just as important in overseas markets as it is at home and is as necessary for industrial products as it is for consumer goods. Indeed, there is a particular aspect to overseas publicity for one's product which might be called a 'commendation value'. Both the industrialist who uses imported materials or components and the man-in-the-street who buys imported consumer products will do so with greater confidence if he sees and hears the merchandise being advertised locally. Advertising lends distinction to the product and commends the user's decision to purchase it.

Having said this, it is important to add the rider that sales promotion in export markets needs an entirely separate approach to similar activity at home.

Both the spoken and the written word can have vastly different connotations from country to country. Apart from the obvious difficulty of language, there are major differences in idiom in the various parts of the globe. Although a common language is spoken in Britain and the United States, it is well known that advertising 'copy' which is most effective in one country can fail completely when transported across the Atlantic.

There are other obstacles, apart from the language difficulty. In certain countries there are very strong religious and social taboos which must be respected. In addition, one must take note of local regulations governing the use of advertisements and promotional material generally. It is advisable, therefore, to use the services of local advertising agencies wherever possible, to avoid the risk of committing 'howlers', or worse.

The media available to the exporter is generally the same as in the home market, but each will require special independent study if it is to be used effectively.

Press Advertising

In most of the developed areas of the world there are newspapers, trade journals and technical publications. In some countries; as, for example, South Africa, newspapers are produced in more than one language for a multilingual population. Some countries have Sunday papers. In others they are not permitted. In some countries the main daily newspaper appears in the morning, as in Britain. In others, it is the evening newspapers which are most widely read.

As is the case in Britain, the majority of newspapers published in overseas countries have a political or a religious bias. Different papers and magazines are produced for different sections of the local community, divided by social class, sex, age, or interests.

When producing illustrated advertisements, care must be taken to ensure that backgrounds conform to the environment of the readership concerned. Considerable 'howlers' can be committed in this respect and vetting by one's local agent before the advert is published is a wise precaution.

Radio and Television

In some of the most promising of export markets, such as Africa and parts of Asia, illiteracy remains a social problem. Here the impact of press advertising will be much less than that of the spoken word. The transistorized radio set has become a powerful medium of consumer product advertising in such areas, but once again local taboos must be watched.

Cinema Advertising

Although in Britain the significance of cinema advertising has tended to decline with diminished audiences in comparison with the nineteen-thirties and forties, in many other countries of the world the cinema enjoys great popular support. The promotion of consumer goods by means of short films which last, like television commercials, for a few minutes only, represents an important advertising medium.

Sales Literature

All sales literature which is designed for use overseas must, of course, be produced in the local language. Although English is widely spoken it is not so frequently read. This is a factor which far too many British publicists fail to appreciate. Technical specifications, also, must be presented in accordance with the systems which are employed locally if these are to be of any practical value to one's overseas clients. Similarly, it is necessary to quote all prices in the local currency.

Public Relations

The importance of good Public Relations in export markets cannot be over-stressed. Once again, however, those whose task it is to prepare 'hand-outs' for the press and other communications media must be fully acquainted with the way of life and the outlook of the local population. More harm than good can result from inept P.R. work in overseas countries.

Announcement regarding the visits of company executives, of new products or services, can do an exceedingly useful back-up job to support the activities of one's local agent and distributors. Publicity of this kind helps to 'personalize' the company for overseas clients and breaks down some of the feeling of remoteness which must attach to a supplier who is based hundreds, and sometimes thousands, of miles away.

❐